Strong Foundations

Evidence informing practice in early childhood education and care

Anna Kilderry
Bridie Raban

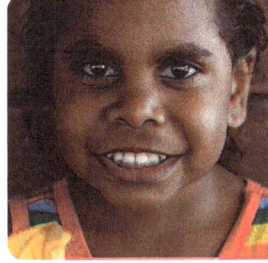

ACER Press

Published in 2025 by Amba Press, Melbourne, Australia
www.ambapress.com.au

First published in 2020 by ACER Press, an imprint of
Australian Council for Educational Research Ltd

© Anna Kilderry & Bridie Raban 2025

This book is copyright. All rights reserved. Except under the conditions described in the Copyright Act 1968 of Australia and subsequent amendments, and any exceptions permitted under the current statutory licence scheme administered by Copyright Agency (www.copyright.com.au), no part of this publication may be reproduced, stored in a retrieval system, transmitted, broadcast or communicated in any form or by any means, optical, digital, electronic, mechanical, photocopying, recording or otherwise, without the written permission of the publisher.

Edited by Michaela Skelly
Cover design, text design and typesetting by Karen Wilson Cover image © ARVD73, Africa Studio, KK Tan, Asada Nami, Mark Nazh, Evgeny Atamanenko, 5 second Studio, AJP and valbar @ shutterstock.com Eva Ozkoidi @ alamay.com

ISBN: 9781923569386 (pbk)
ISBN: 9781923569393 (ebk)

A catalogue record for this book is available from the National Library of Australia.

Foreword by Alison Elliott

Worldwide early childhood education and care (ECEC) faces complex challenges around policy development and implementation generally; as well as ongoing tensions around roles in preparing children for school; ways of engaging families, funding and staffing shortages; and quality, supply, demand and access issues. The research is unequivocal, well-designed early childhood education programs have a host of benefits. They impact positively on children's social-emotional and cognitive development, transition to school and longer term academic achievement. They are especially beneficial for children who are most at risk from living in socially and economically vulnerable circumstances, who might need early intervention and who might otherwise experience problems at school with the attendant consequences. Building a strong foundation early augurs well for smooth transitions to school, reduced later learning problems and associated support costs, and increased school retention.

While children from economically vulnerable families who participate in quality early childhood programs are most likely to benefit socially and academically, too often they can't access quality services. Too many children miss out, most often those in rural and remote locations and in some regional and urban communities. Each community and every child must have access to quality early childhood and health services, yet as successive Australian Early Development Census (AEDC) results demonstrate, there are distinct geographical and community variations in children's developmental outcomes suggesting inequities of provision, access and quality and highlighting scope for improvement (Department of Education, Skills and Employment 2020).

Since Australia's new quality agenda in 2012, early childhood services have embraced a range of governance and operational changes. The agenda's promises of high-quality early learning, more nationally consistent regulatory environments and greater ECEC access for children and their families, were widely welcomed. But transitions to the new regime have not been without challenges. While quality has improved overall as evident in data tracking by the Australian Children's Education and Care Quality Authority (ACECQA 2019, p. 13), some 20% of long day care services still fail to meet standards in one or more National Quality Standard (NQS) domains. But this is a huge improvement on the 40% or so centre-based services[1] not meeting one or more standards in 2013 (ACECQA 2014, p. 13). Despite wide-ranging local and national initiatives to improve early childhood practice, a worrying 15% of services do not meet the NQS, Quality Area 1 – Educational program and practice (ACECQA 2019, p. 15).

---

1   There are some counting discrepancies over time due to different service type inclusions and breakdowns. Data on early childhood services are also not always directly comparable, as enrolments, service types and staff numbers can be measured differently depending on the counting source, the jurisdiction and the time of counting. Some double counting may occur.

Foreword

That many centres struggle to attract and retain a full complement of qualified educators almost certainly contributes to difficulties in meeting core educational standards. It is worth acknowledging at this point that the thousands of early childhood educators and students who commenced work or study since the start of 2012 do not recall a time before the National Quality Framework (NQF). The post-2012 early childhood context is their normal.

The strong growth in ECEC services since the 1990s (15 979 approved services in 2019 and 13 676 in 2013, ACECQA 2019), accommodating around a million children has placed unprecedented demands on recruiting and retaining early childhood educators and supporting and enhancing their professional practice. Ensuring that the nearly 195 000 strong early childhood workforce (Social Research Centre 2017, p. 14) can sustain the quality of these services is no small task. Most challenging for many centres, and especially in some urban, rural and remote areas, is attracting and retaining qualified educators, a problem that is not new (Elliott 2016) or confined to Australia (Akbari & McCuaig 2018).

Overwhelmingly, there is a sense that the quality initiatives of the past few years are having positive outcomes for children and their families, but that quality enhancement and sustainability are largely dependent on a strong professional workforce. Although the early childhood workforce has expanded to meet enrolment growth, staff shortages and turnover are acute in many areas. The reasons for these shortages are complex, and while poor pay, working conditions and limited career opportunities impact negatively on recruitment and retention, the reality of factors such as young women's quest for self-fulfilment, travel and quality family time also drive career decision-making (Elliott 2006; 2016). Unfortunately, shortages of educators tend to be most acute in places where children and families are most vulnerable and at risk; such as in rural and remote communities. In some remote early childhood centres the entire professional staff can turn over in a 12-month period. Clearly, workforce development initiatives are a priority (Elliott 2006; 2016) and it is encouraging to see state, territory and national policy initiatives enhance and strengthen the profession; such as those in the Queensland Department of Education's *Early childhood education and care workforce action plan 2016–19* (and previously 2011–14).

Nationwide, continuous improvements to Initial Teacher Education (ITE) courses and regular reviews of vocational diploma and Certificate III level courses in ECEC are also important in building early childhood workforce capacity. Upskilling initiatives complemented by incentives; such as scholarships to support early childhood study, or upgrade to early childhood from primary teaching, or opportunities for overseas-qualified educators to work in Australia can be especially effective.

Thinking that the challenges experienced by ECEC since the growth spurt of the 1990s are new, is a mistake. They are not. Since the earliest colonial days, public support for and investment in ECEC has been contentious. Contributing to the ebb and flow of momentum for quality early childhood services is varying political and community commitment and uncertain funding. A cohesive, sustainable approach to ECEC has long been elusive. Tensions about whether ECEC should sit in welfare, family, community or education portfolios and how it should be funded continue (Elliott 2016). Even since the NQF reforms, some funding, administrative and regulatory arrangements are jurisdictionally specific with some aspects of early childhood service provision retaining a distinct state or territory focus. Whatever the political and policy debates and uncertainties around early childhood education, children need a quality service with the best possible educators. Effective ECEC programs are dependent on quality inputs; environment, curriculum and pedagogy and especially skilled educators who can plan individualised programs for each child that are informed by contemporary knowledge about learning and development, and developed in partnership with families.

Assuring and strengthening the professional capacity of early childhood educators is at the core of meeting children's development and learning needs in the light of contemporary community expectations. With the quality improvement focus of the NQF, NQS (ACECQA 2020) and EYLF (DEEWR 2009) in mind, together with knowledge of educators' effectiveness in supporting children's development and learning, *Strong foundations* takes a refreshing and visionary approach to strengthening early childhood educator capacity. It draws on a core framework highlighting three key elements central to achieving evidence-informed education systems: awareness, engagement and use.

Each chapter highlights reciprocal relationships between research and practice and journeys through guiding principles around key content to support early childhood educators' learning. Core content knowledge addresses the five EYLF Learning Outcomes (DEEWR 2009) together with the seven NQS Quality Areas (ACECQA 2020).

Highlights in each chapter support clear recognition that children's development is shaped during their first three years, and in utero. All young children and especially babies and toddlers must have rich, positive, nurturing experiences in the early years to grow their language and thinking, and their social-emotional, cognitive and physical development. Cascading evidence about pivotal roles of experiences in these early years signals that babies and toddlers using early childhood settings need especially skilled and nurturing educators (OECD 2018). For children in care for 8–10 hours per day, every day, ensuring rich language and problem-solving activities is critical. While staff–child ratios matter, equally important are the types of adult–child interactions and the richness and foci of language. As a recent Organisation for Economic Co-operation and Development report (OECD 2018, p. 107) stressed: 'in-service training that includes ECEC-specific content relates to better staff–child interactions and child development and learning outcomes for all groups of children, especially in literacy skills' and the value of adult–child interactions is felt most by the youngest children.

Strong foundations is timely and necessary in its focus on strengthening early childhood educators' skills across contexts and pedagogies, and in partnership with families. Bourgeoning early childhood services and strong demand, tempered by ongoing uncertainties around access and funding make it especially important to highlight what is at stake if early childhood educators are not the best they can be. Early childhood education is perhaps our most vital tool for strengthening child and family resilience

Foreword

and for building social justice, community capacity and sustainability. It works to break cycles of hopelessness, vulnerability and poverty in an uncertain world and is both a necessity for working families and an effective way to support and enhance children's development.

Strong foundations highlights that evidence can and does inspire and lead engaged teaching and inform creative practice. A refreshing tone and purposeful intent to view early childhood educators as experts in their own lives makes an ideal base to understand and share ideas to use and adapt the NQF's tools and resources. The book's chapters are not intended to stand alone; ideas overlap and enrich each other with authors drawing on extensive real-world professional experiences.

While primarily designed to assist aspiring and practising early childhood educators in the process of completing formal teaching qualifications, *Strong foundations* also provides more experienced educators with a refresher that enables engagement with relevant evidence across quality dimensions and real-world contexts that shape practice. The pace of change in education means that keeping up-to-date with research and dynamic curriculum and regulatory environments is no easy task. As early childhood educators our role as advocates for children, families and education is critical. Over 100 years ago, the first preschool teachers and other early childhood educators in Australia led reforms in family and child wellbeing. At the cusp of this century's third decade, I'm confident that new generations of educators who are reading this book will be the ones to enhance advocacy for children and families to ensure quality care and education environments that enable a strong voice for the future.

The educational achievement gaps between haves and have-nots, and the high cost of ECEC have become rallying points for families, educators, advocates, unions and policymakers. As a community we must boost social and monetary investment in child and family wellbeing. We must support children's optimal learning and development while also providing quality care so caregivers can work. As educators of the future you hold the key to this quality.

Strong foundations offers timely support to those developing a career in the early childhood sector. It brings research and on-the-ground practice together to support designing and implementing quality early learning experiences. It is not a recipe book for applying the NQS or EYLF. Rather, it intends that you explore policy and practices you see in action or engage with during your professional learning experiences. It acts to inform your practice by highlighting key evidence and explicating strategies and ways to strengthen practice. Provocations, research highlights and case studies are designed to foster your inquiry, supporting you to understand how the reforms of the past decade, now the norm, shape and impact everyday practice. Professional decision-making is informed and enhanced with easy access to evidence that is relevant to everyday practice.

Each chapter in *Strong foundations* will enrich your learning journey and expand your pedagogical boundaries. As you identify learning opportunities and possibilities aligned with the NQS and EYLF you will step through thinking and decision-making processes needed to engage with relevant early childhood discourses, understand the ways in which research underpins good practice and be confident to create environments that enhance babies', toddlers' and young children's development.

References

Australian Children's Education and Care Quality Authority (ACECQA) 2020, *Guide to the national quality framework*, ACECQA, Sydney. Retrieved from https://www.acecqa.gov.au/sites/default/files/2020-01/Guide-to-the-NQF_2.pdf

Australian Children's Education and Care Quality Authority (ACECQA) 2019, *National quality framework snapshot Q4, 2019*, ACECQA, Sydney. Retrieved from https://www.acecqa.gov.au/nqf/snapshots

Australian Children's Education and Care Quality Authority (ACECQA) 2014, *National quality framework snapshot Q4, 2013*, ACECQA, Sydney. Retrieved from https://www.acecqa.gov.au/nqf/snapshots

Akbari, E & McCuaig, K 2018, *Early childhood education report,* Atkinson Centre for Society and Child Development, Ontario Institute for Studies in Education/University of Toronto. Retrieved from http://ecereport.ca/en/

Department of Education, Employment and Workplace Relations (DEEWR) 2009, *Belonging, being & becoming: the early years learning framework for Australia*, Commonwealth of Australia, Canberra. Retrieved from https://docs.education.gov.au/node/2632

Department of Education, Skills and Employment 2020, *Australian early development census,* The Australian Government, Canberra. Retrieved from https://www.education.gov.au/australian-early-development-census

Elliott, A 2006, 'Early childhood education. Pathways to quality and equity', *Australian Education Review*, no. 50. Retrieved from https://research.acer.edu.au/early_childhood_misc/1

Elliott, A 2016, *Looking back: looking forward. Changing contexts for early childhood education.* Australian Museum of Education, Canberra.

Organisation for Economic Co-operation and Development (OECD) 2018, *Engaging young children: lessons from research about quality in early childhood education and care, starting strong*, OEDC, Paris. Retrieved from https://www.oecd.org/education/engaging-young-children-9789264085145-en.htm

Queensland Department of Education and Training 2015, *Early childhood education and care workforce action plan 2016–2019*, Queensland Government, Brisbane. Retrieved from https://earlychildhood.qld.gov.au/careersAndTraining/Documents/workforce-action-plan-16-19.pdf

Social Research Centre 2017, *2016 early childhood and care national workforce census*, Social Research Centre, Melbourne.

Contents

Foreword by Alison Elliott   iii
About the editors and contributors   x
Acknowledgements   xviii

SECTION 1 – The early childhood years: context   1

Chapter 1   Early childhood education and care in challenging times   2
Anna Kilderry and Bridie Raban

Chapter 2   Investigating early childhood practice: insights from a large Australian study   11
Dan Cloney

Chapter 3   The early childhood professional   26
Megan Gibson and Lyn Gunn

Chapter 4   Building inclusive education communities   38
Kathy Cologon

SECTION 2 – Identity, wellbeing and children contributing to their world   50

Chapter 5   Early childhood outdoor environments: places for play, learning and wellbeing   52
Anne-Marie Morrissey, Llewellyn Wishart and Deborah Moore

Chapter 6   Healthy lifestyle behaviours in the first five years of life   76
Rachel Laws, Penny Love, Katherine Downing and Jill Hnatiuk

Chapter 7   Keeping children safe   92
Nicole Downes

Chapter 8   Social and emotional development in early childhood   109
Claire Blewitt, Helen Skouteris, Heidi Bergmeier and Amanda O'Connor

Chapter 9   Facilitating children's agency in early childhood education and care   124
Caroline Scott, Andrea Nolan and Anna Kilderry

SECTION 3 – Children as confident and involved learners — 136

Chapter 10	Play and early childhood pedagogies *Nicole Leggett*	138
Chapter 11	Supporting oral language development in young children *Louise Paatsch and Andrea Nolan*	156
Chapter 12	Early literacy *Bridie Raban*	170
Chapter 13	Learning about STEM *Coral Campbell*	185
Chapter 14	Learning about mathematics *Bob Perry and Sue Dockett*	204
Chapter 15	Learning through the arts *Susan Wright and Jan Deans*	220
Chapter 16	Play and learning in the digital age *Nicola Yelland*	234
Chapter 17	Assessment and documentation for children's learning and development *Bronwyn Reynolds*	250

SECTION 4 – Children and society: building positive futures — 266

Chapter 18	Early years transitions *Sue Dockett and Bob Perry*	268
Chapter 19	Building positive relationships with families and communities *Laura McFarland*	282
Chapter 20	Leading practice in early childhood education *Jo Bird and Angel Mok*	296
Chapter 21	Rethinking research in early childhood: (re)turning the kaleidoscope *Jeanne Marie Iorio and Will Parnell*	310
Chapter 22	Learning to surf: embracing change in the early childhood sector *Jen Jackson*	325

Glossary — 340
Index — 343

About the editors and contributors

About the editors

Anna Kilderry is an Associate Professor of Education (Early Childhood) at Deakin University in Melbourne and has worked as an academic for over 20 years in Australia and England. Researching from a critical perspective, Anna aims to uncover issues of power, disadvantage and privilege in early childhood education. As a former early childhood teacher (ECT), Anna is passionate about early childhood education and the role of teachers and their practice. Leading a range of research projects in both Australia and the UK, Anna has published in the areas of early childhood curriculum, pedagogy, policy and teacher practice, with her work cited internationally.

Bridie Raban is an Honorary Professorial Fellow at Melbourne Graduate School of Education. She has been a professor in England and Hong Kong; a Senior Research Fellow at the Australian Council for Educational Research (ACER) and was seconded to the federal government in Canberra as a research fellow. While in England she was President of the UK Reading Association; recognising her passion and highly recognised work in the field of early literacy development. Bridie has published extensively, most recently with Associate Professor Janet Scull, *Growing up literate: Australian literacy research for practice* (2016). Her major research projects include: the Young Learners' Project; the Preschool Literacy Project; and Children Learning to Read project in the UK.

About the contributors

Heidi Bergmeier is a Research Fellow at the Monash Centre for Health Research and Implementation, Monash University. Her research interests include identifying early modifiable pathways implicated in optimising child development, including caregiver–child relationships and child self-regulation. She has expertise in child attachment security and has worked alongside educators and caregivers to better understand pragmatic adaptations needed to embed approaches for strengthening child development into routine practices and interactions. Heidi works in partnership with researchers, clinicians, organisations and key stakeholders, including families and educators. She recently co-developed a framework to ensure that the voices of people most affected by research, such as service users, are central in all stages of research initiatives.

Jo Bird is a Lecturer and Course Coordinator in Early Childhood Education at the University of New England, Armidale. She successfully completed her PhD which explored children's use of digital technologies in imaginative play and the educators' provision of the various devices, both working and imaginative. Her research interests include children's play, the use of technologies by both children and educators, and early childhood leadership. She loves presenting and both her research and practice aims to inspire others to recognise their leadership worth, and to use technologies in creative ways with children.

Claire Blewitt is a Research Fellow at the Monash Centre for Health Research and Implementation at Monash University. She collaborates with teachers, carers and other professionals across education, health, and social care disciplines to co-design approaches that support educators to foster children's health, learning and wellbeing. Her research interests include social and emotional learning, early childhood mental health, implementation science methodologies, and strengthening the quality of educator–child interactions.

Coral Campbell is an Associate Professor in the School of Education at Deakin University. She has worked in partnership with many early childhood centres and schools locally and has contributed to an enhancement of early childhood science education through the development of early childhood units (science, science and technology, science and the environment, and STEM). She has co-edited *Science in early childhood* (Campbell, Jobling & Howitt 2018) – the first in Australia and now on its fourth revision (in press). Coral is an Early Years Science Special Interest Group (SIG) Coordinator at the European Science Education Research Association (ESERA).

Dan Cloney is a Senior Research Fellow in the Education Policy and Practice (EPP) program and a member of the Centre for Global Education Monitoring (GEM) at ACER. He has expertise in early education, cognitive development, and academic achievement. Dan's research program focuses on the potential for high-quality early childhood education and care (ECEC) programs to support all children to flourish and to reduce development gaps caused by inequality. He is also an Honorary Research Associate at the Murdoch Children's Research Institute (MCRI) and a Research Fellow at the Melbourne Graduate School of Education (MGSE). His recent publications can be found at https://works.bepress.com/dan-cloney/.

Kathy Cologon is a Senior Lecturer in Inclusive Education at the Department of Educational Studies, Macquarie University. With extensive experience in the field prior to commencing her work in academia, followed by a decade of educating teachers for inclusion, and ongoing research engagement with children, families, teachers and allied professionals, Kathy has a depth and breadth of understanding of the many facets of inclusive education. Her book *Inclusive education in the early years: right from the start* (2014), was commissioned by Oxford University Press.

About the editors and contributors

Jan Deans is Associate Director of Early Childhood Education at the University of Melbourne. She is also the Director of the University's Early Learning Centre, which is a research and demonstration preschool that advocates for early childhood pedagogy and acknowledges children as capable and active citizens. Jan is a long-time advocate for teaching and learning through the arts and has worked both locally and internationally in early childhood, primary, tertiary, and special education settings. She has broadly based expertise in relation to early childhood education and service delivery and her recent research interests include learning through dance, music education, social-emotional competence and learning within the natural environment.

Sue Dockett is Emeritus Professor of Early Childhood Education at Charles Sturt University, Australia and Director, Peridot Education Pty Ltd. While recently retired from university life, she remains an active researcher in the field of early childhood education. Sue has been a long-time advocate for the importance of recognising and responding to young children's perspectives. She maintains this position in her current work with children, families and educators in explorations of transitions to school, children's play and learning. Sue has published extensively both nationally and internationally in these areas. She is a co-chair of the SIG on Transitions at the European Early Childhood Education Research Association (EECERA).

Nicole Downes had nine years teaching experience in early childhood education working with children from birth to 5 years, before joining the Early Years team at Deakin University. She is a Lecturer in Education and coordinates early childhood units in her areas of expertise, which include child safety, child wellbeing, behaviour management and guidance, lifespan development and inclusive education. Nicole has been involved in the various research projects in her areas of interest and has presented her research findings at several national and international conferences.

Katherine Downing is an Alfred Deakin Postdoctoral Research Fellow at the Institute for Physical Activity and Nutrition (IPAN) at Deakin University. Her research focuses on physical activity and sedentary behaviour (e.g. screen time) in early childhood (birth to 5 years old). In particular, Katherine is interested in how we can best support educators and caregivers to provide opportunities for young children to increase their physical activity and reduce sedentary behaviour.

Alison Elliot's professional background is in higher education and teacher education with specific research, development and policy experience in early childhood education, literacy learning, teacher professional development and tertiary student (VET and Higher Education) experience. She has held a range of academic and leadership positions in the university sector and has authored many articles and reports. Alison was the long-time editor of the leading professional publication for early childhood educators *Every Child* and a foundation Board member of the Australian Children's Education and Care Quality Authority (2012–15). She is currently Professor of Education at Central Queensland University and an Honorary Professor at the University of Sydney.

Megan Gibson is a Senior Lecturer in the School of Early Childhood and Inclusive Education, Queensland University of Technology (QUT). She has extensive experience as an early childhood educator, including teaching and leadership positions in primary school, kindergarten/preschool and long day care. This work has laid foundations for her program of research on preparing, sustaining and retaining the early childhood workforce. Megan's award-winning doctoral thesis examined early childhood teachers' professional identities.

Lyn Gunn is a Lecturer in the School of Early Childhood and Inclusive Education, QUT, and engaged in a recent secondment as Principal Advisor Curriculum for Childcare & Kindergarten. She has worked across a range of diverse early childhood contexts both in Australia and internationally. Lyn's key areas of teaching and researching include Initial Teacher Education (ITE), pedagogical practice and curriculum. Her acclaimed doctoral thesis was a rhizomatic inquiry into early childhood ITE, with attention to long day care professional experience.

Jill Hnatiuk is a Lecturer in Physical Activity and Health in the Institute for Physical Activity and Nutrition (IPAN), School of Exercise and Nutrition Sciences, Deakin University. Her research interests focus on physical activity promotion in early childhood (birth to 5 years old). She works alongside community organisations and families to understand, promote and incorporate healthy movement behaviours into everyday life. Jill's research has been used to inform public health recommendations, government caregiver websites, VCE curriculum material, early learning centre legislation and professional development workshops for early childhood educators, community leaders and families.

Jeanne Marie Iorio is a Senior Lecturer in Early Childhood Education and Course Coordinator of the Master of Teaching (Early Childhood) at the University of Melbourne. Her research, teaching and writing focuses on disrupting and rethinking accepted educational practices in early childhood and higher education. This work includes rethinking quality as meaning-making; children's relations with place, more-than-human and materials; pedagogical documentation and research methods; and pedagogies originating from the municipal infant-toddler centres and preschools in Reggio Emilia, Italy. Her research project Out and About with Dr Catherine Hamm (La Trobe University) is part of an international research collective (www.commonworlds.net) seeking to understand and document teaching pedagogies.

Jen Jackson is the Education Policy Lead at the Mitchell Institute at Victoria University. She has previously worked in early childhood policy and regulation for the Victorian Government, and in system-wide strategic policy management roles. As a researcher at the University of Melbourne, Victoria University, ACER and the Parliament of Victoria, Jen has conducted a range of research including monitoring education system performance, teacher professional learning and strengthening early learning in economically developing countries. Jen's doctoral research used large-scale survey data to map diversity in the Australian early childhood workforce and examine its implications for practice.

Rachel Laws is Senior Lecturer in Public Health Nutrition at IPAN, Deakin University. She has a background in dietetics and her research focuses on promotion of nutrition in the first 1000 days of life, and translational research. As part of the Early Prevention of Obesity in Childhood (EPOCH) Centre for Research Excellence, Rachel is co-leading a stream of research on translation of evidence in policy and practice. She is passionate about conducting research that makes a difference and translating research into the real world.

Nicole Leggett is a Senior Lecturer in the School of Education at the University of Newcastle. Nicole worked as an ECT and director of early childhood services on the Central Coast of NSW for over 20 years. Her PhD examined the role of the educator as an intentional teacher within Australian early learning environments and investigated the relationship of this role to children's developing creativity, which was awarded the Beth Southwell Research Award for Most Outstanding Education Thesis in 2015. In 2017 Nicole co-led a 12-month research project entitled Research Connections: Practitioner Research Engagement Network for Early Childhood Educators (PRENECE) where participants were guided to develop a centre-based action research project.

Penny Love is an Accredited Practising Dietitian (APD). An early interest into the impacts gained through a population-wide approach of environmental and policy changes led to her PhD research developing food-based dietary guidelines for South Africans. Her public health nutrition career has included a focus on nutrition in the early years, Indigenous nutrition and food security. Penny joined Deakin University in 2013 to deliver a knowledge translation and exchange platform building a community of practice to support obesity prevention efforts across Australia. Her current research focus is on intervention implementation and sustainability for the prevention of childhood obesity.

Laura McFarland is a Senior Lecturer in Early Childhood Education at Charles Sturt University. She earned her doctorate in human development and family sciences, with a focus on early childhood, at the University of Texas at Austin. Laura's teaching interests are research in early childhood, leadership and management, environmental sustainability in early childhood, relationships and pedagogy in early childhood and child development. Her research focuses on educator–family relationships, pedagogy for children birth to 2 years old and supporting mentally healthy communities. Laura formerly worked as an early childhood educator, and as a consultant for Early Childhood Australia (ECA).

Angel Mok is a Lecturer at the University of New England. She is an experienced pre-service teacher (PST) educator who is passionate about supporting students' study in an online learning environment. Prior to her work as a lecturer, Angel worked as a qualified ECT in early childhood settings and an accredited teacher in primary schools in Sydney. She also has experience in working in early childhood settings in Hong Kong. Angel advocates for more support for early career ECTs in their transition to leadership roles, in particular, those in rural and regional areas.

Deborah Moore is a Lecturer in Education (Curriculum and Pedagogy/Early Childhood) at Deakin University. Deb's research interests focus on researching with children and their outdoor environments, especially those places children physically or symbolically construct themselves for their imaginative play. This research interest has extended recently into ECTs' perceptions of these children's outdoor places from a pedagogical and personal perspective. Deb is also interested in teacher engagement with Environmental Education for Sustainability (EEfS) and early childhood professional placement experiences for PSTs and their mentor teachers.

Anne-Marie Morrissey is Associate Professor (Early Childhood Education) at Deakin University. She has extensive experience in the ECEC sector through teaching and research. She has taught in ITE courses for over 20 years and is currently Course Director for the Master of Teaching Early Childhood and Primary/Early Childhood. Prior to working in academia, Anne-Marie had extensive professional experience as an ECT and as coordinator of two large child care centres. Anne-Marie has a particular research interest in outdoor play spaces and natural learning environments and has conducted a number of studies on the influence of design and natural elements on children's play.

Andrea Nolan is Professor of Early Childhood Education, School of Education at Deakin University. She is a member of the university's strategic research centre, Research for Educational Impact. Andrea is founder and Chair of the Victorian Early Childhood Research Consortium, which is a group of 83 cross-disciplinary researchers from Victorian universities who support research capacity building in early childhood. She has worked on a number of state, national and international projects concerning literacy development, program evaluation and professional learning of teachers. Over the past decade she has produced a significant body of research focusing on the capabilities of the early childhood workforce, specifically the professional learning of teachers.

Amanda O'Connor is a Research Fellow at Monash Centre for Health Research and Implementation (MCHRI). Her qualifications include Doctor of Philosophy (psychology), Graduate Diploma of Psychology and Bachelor of Health Science (psychology, health promotion and family studies). She is an expert in implementation science intervention and program development and evaluations. Mandy developed the Educator–Parent Child Relationship (E-PCR) intervention for use by ECEC staff in early childhood settings. Her research interests include parent–child relationships, child development, family violence, and women's health and wellbeing. Mandy works collaboratively with industry partners, intermediary research organisations and multiple academic research centres.

About the editors and contributors

Louise Paatsch is Associate Professor and the Associate Head of School (Research) in the School of Education at Deakin University. Her background is in oral language development, literacy and deaf education in early childhood and primary school settings. Louise's research uses mixed methods approaches; including video methodology, to investigate oral language, play and literacy development; as well as *teacher talk* during intentional oral language teaching; teacher professional learning and teacher as researcher. Louise also researches pragmatic skill development of children and young people with hearing loss who use spoken language, and their hearing peers. Louise has many publications in peer-reviewed journals, book chapters and books, and has presented at both national and international conferences.

Will Parnell is a professor in early childhood education, Chair of the Curriculum and Instruction Department and a pedagogical liaison to the Helen Gordon Child Development Center at Portland State University in the USA. His specialty areas are rethinking readiness; disrupting traditional early childhood research in order to foreground children, teachers and families' voices; creating learning designs and documenting and making young children's learning visible. Will currently serves as president of the National Association of Early Childhood Teacher Educators (NAECTE), a board member for A Renaissance School of Arts and Sciences, committee member of the Reconceptualizing Early Childhood Education program, and President of the Inventing Remida Portland Project.

Bob Perry has recently retired after 45 years of university teaching and research. He is Emeritus Professor at Charles Sturt University and Director, Peridot Education Pty Ltd. In conjunction with Sue Dockett, he continues research, consultancy and publication in early childhood mathematics education; educational transitions, with particular emphasis on transition to primary school; researching with children and evaluation of educational programs. Bob has published extensively both nationally and internationally in these areas. He is a co-chair of the SIG on Mathematics Birth to Eight Years at the European Early Childhood Education Research Association.

Bronwyn Reynolds is a Senior Lecturer in the Faculty of Education at the University of Tasmania where she coordinates several early childhood units in the undergraduate and post-graduate degrees. She has over 30 years of experience in the early childhood sector as an educator, lecturer and researcher. Bronwyn also has extensive experience as a professional learning consultant. Her lecturing and research interests include children's learning, documentation, assessment, curriculum planning and portfolios and leadership in early childhood education.

Caroline Scott recently completed her PhD on children's agency in ECEC at Deakin University. Caroline has been working in higher education for the past decade and holds the qualifications of Bachelor of Arts, Bachelor of Teaching and Master of Education. Working at Deakin University, Victoria University and Swinburne University, Caroline has extensive experience as a both a sessional lecturer and research assistant in the area of early childhood education.

Helen Skouteris is the Monash Warwick Professor of Healthcare Improvement and Implementation Science at Monash University. She has a strong track record in longitudinal multi-factorial research, randomised controlled trials, implementation research and higher degree research supervision. Her research since 2010 has predominantly focused on building agency/capacity in the consumer to make healthy lifestyle choices across preconception, pregnancy, preschool and childhood, including adolescence, to reduce the burden of obesity. Helen's work has also been focused extensively on social service and educational sector improvement that translates to better health outcomes for children, young people, adults and families and is critical to transforming policy across these sectors.

Llewellyn Wishart holds postgraduate qualifications in movement/dance, early childhood and adult education. He is a certified Body-Mind Centering® practitioner and Registered Somatic Movement Educator (ISMETA). He has worked as a teacher in early childhood, adult and ecological education settings and currently lectures in early childhood education at Deakin University. Llewellyn's research interests in early childhood education include nature-based, outdoor and ecological learning; movement and active play outdoors; design of naturalised early childhood outdoor spaces, integral theory and embodied pedagogies.

Susan Wright is Honorary Professor of Arts Education in the Melbourne Graduate School of Education at the University of Melbourne. Her qualifications, teaching and research span music, movement and the visual arts, and she is interested in how people transmediate across modes as they make meaning. She is focused on how the environment influences learning and teaching, and how resources mediate personal agency and community dynamics. Her data centres on semiosis, and the theoretical and practical principles underpinning creativity. Susan advocates for the arts to be the nucleus of the curriculum, and for early learning principles and practices to inform primary, secondary and higher education.

Nicola Yelland is the Professor of Early Childhood Studies in the Melbourne Graduate School of Education at the University of Melbourne. Her teaching and research interests have been related to the use of new technologies in school and community contexts. She has also worked in East Asia and examined the culture and curriculum of early childhood settings. Nicola's work engages with educational issues with regard to varying social, economic and political conditions and thus requires multidisciplinary perspectives. She is the co-editor with Dana Franz-Bentley, of *Found in translation: connecting reconceptualist thinking with contemporary early childhood practices* (2018).

Acknowledgements

There are a number of people we would like to thank. To the publication team at ACER Press, Elisa Webb and Shaneen Goodwin, who have been wonderful to work with, have offered assistance when needed and have been professional throughout, thank you.

To our partners, Adrian (Anna) and Dean (Bridie), for your patience and unwavering support.

We would like to sincerely thank all our reviewers, those who are listed here and others who preferred to remain anonymous, for generously giving their time and expertise. We are very grateful for your considered reviews.

- Dr Anne Keary, Monash University
- Carmel Phillips, Victorian Curriculum and Assessment Authority
- Dr Caroline Cohrssen, Hong Kong University
- Ms Deborah Downes, Department of Health and Human Services
- Professor Donna Pendergast, Griffith University
- Dr Elise Hunkin, RMIT University
- Dr Geraldine Burke, Monash University
- Dr Helen Little, Macquarie University
- Dr Jennifer Cartmel, Griffith University
- Associate Professor Joseph Agbenyega, Monash University
- Dr Karen McLean, Australian Catholic University
- Associate Professor Kym Simoncini, University of Canberra
- Dr Llewellyn Wishart, Deakin University
- Associate Professor Marianne Fenech, University of Sydney
- Dr Mary Hood, Attachment and Relationship Consulting
- Ms Naomi David, Deakin University
- Dr Natalie Robertson, Deakin University
- Mrs Rosemarie Garner, Deakin University
- Associate Professor Susan Hill, University of South Australia
- Tarlee Dowsley, Country Way Early Learning, Mildura

We would also like to thank the following people and organisations for their generous support:

- Adam and Tarlee Dowsley
- Alkira Early Learning Centre
- Allen Family
- C & G Office National, Mildura
- Country Way Early Learning, Mildura
- Dileo Family
- Early Learning Centre, Abbotsford
- Elder St Early Childhood Centre
- Fleming Nurseries, Monbulk
- Hazel Capp
- Jessica Quin
- KU Ourimbah Preschool & Children's Centre
- Mildura West Kindergarten

We would like to thank the following government agencies for providing content:

- Belonging, being and becoming: Early Years Learning Framework for Australia, Department of Education and Training. CC-BY-4.0 International licence.
- National Quality Standard – Australian Children's Education and Care Quality Authority (ACECQA).

Editors' dedication

In memory of Maureen Thorp who sadly passed away in July 2020 after a brave battle with cancer. As a mothercraft nurse, early childhood and TAFE teacher, Maureen is remembered for being a dedicated, creative and passionate early childhood teacher, with a love of young children's learning in the outdoors.

In memory of Cathy Tighe, centre manager, TAFE teacher and early childhood curriculum advisor who passed away suddenly in September 2020. Cathy is remembered for making a positive difference in the ECEC sector over the years, for her enthusiasm of early childhood practice, her generosity and sense of humour.

Publisher's dedication

In memory of Rose Kelly, for her enthusiastic manuscript reviews, her inspirational leadership as Director of Windsor Community Children's Centre and her tireless dedication to the sector. Rose was the heart of our community, the founder of our fire pit, our mentor and our dear friend. Her legacy of courage and inclusion lives on in countless children, families, students and educators.

SECTION 1

The early childhood years: context

Section 1 provides an overview of the Australian early childhood education and care (ECEC) context. It introduces readers to some of the big-picture elements of ECEC including the importance of evidence-informed practice, large-scale research, the changing nature of the ECEC profession and how to build inclusive education communities.

Chapter 1 introduces the book, focusing on how the book came about, and the intention for educators to have an opportunity to revisit and revitalise practice. As the authors have deliberately selected the term 'evidence-informed', instead of 'evidence-based', a rationale is provided for this focus.

Chapter 2 showcases the largest longitudinal ECEC research study to have ever been conducted in Australia, the Effective Early Educational Experiences (E4Kids) study. Readers will better understand the value and limitations of large-scale research with respect to their work with children. The findings from this study indicate that there is still much to embrace if ECEC in Australia is to support all children to achieve their full potential.

Chapter 3 discusses professionalism in ECEC, how it is evolving, and the changing nature of professional identities. Practical applications which draw on evidence-informed insights are included, along with contextually specific expectations, where early childhood educators and teachers potentially work in a range of different settings with diverse curriculum expectations.

Chapter 4 addresses inclusive education, identifying that inclusive education is a fundamental human right for all. This chapter explores inclusion and discusses how educators can build inclusive education communities. This chapter will challenge notions of difference and consider the means of creating pedagogical opportunities for 'belonging, being and becoming' for all Australian children.

CHAPTER 1

Early childhood education and care in challenging times

Anna Kilderry[1] and Bridie Raban[2]

DOI: https://doi.org/10.37517/978-1-74286-555-3_1
[1] Deakin University
[2] University of Melbourne

Introduction

This book has many purposes. First and foremost, it celebrates the progress made by the Australian early childhood education and care (ECEC) profession over the past decade, since the implementation of the Early Years Learning Framework for Australia (EYLF) (DEEWR 2009). Much has happened in ECEC during the last 10 years, with many related policies and initiatives that have substantially changed practice. As part of the policy initiatives set a decade ago, there is now a requirement for all educators to hold a qualification or to be working towards a qualification in ECEC. Each educational setting is regularly assessed and rated against the National Quality Standard (NQS) (ACECQA 2020); educators now share a common professional language and objectives; and there is further recognition of the fundamental importance of education and care in the early years (ACECQA 2020; Pascoe & Brennan 2018).

ECEC is a changing and evolving profession, and has managed considerably well and has embraced quite a lot of change in recent years. As a profession we cannot be too complacent, as the next decade will bring about more changes and challenges. In the Foreword to this book, Professor Alison Elliott has pointed out some of the challenges the ECEC sector needs to confront in the coming years. Many of the challenges identified, namely, maintaining quality education and care across different service types; providing access and equity for all; bridging educational achievement gaps; engaging diverse families in inclusive and respectful ways; understanding and engaging with Indigenous knowledges; addressing workforce development issues, are all issues of critical importance. And, of course, not all these issues can be addressed easily or swiftly, however, by aiming for a more informed and knowledgeable profession, the stronger, more inclusive and resilient the profession will be. Connected to the issue of development of a dynamic and resilient profession, another purpose of the book is to provide evidence-informed information to support educators with their everyday practice. Before we outline what *evidence-informed* practice is, a brief recap about the crossroads and policy achievements the ECEC profession encountered during the last decade.

Sector reform

In 2009, the Council of Australian Governments (COAG) agreed to the National Early Childhood Development Strategy (COAG 2009), a strategy that guided investment in future reforms to support Australian children and their families. Since the 2009 COAG initiative, a more cohesive, inclusive and ambitious national sector reform agenda for ECEC has taken place. Consequently, successive governments have inherited a more robust and accountable system, compared to previous years (Productivity Commission 2020). A significant policy initiative within this sector reform has been the introduction of the National Quality Framework (NQF), commencing in 2012, and recently revised (ACECQA 2020). The ambitious aims of the NQF are to deliver better quality services and promote positive education and development outcomes for all Australian children.

The objectives of the NQF are to:

- ensure the safety, health and wellbeing of children attending education and care services
- improve the educational and developmental outcomes for children attending education and care services
- promote continuous improvement in the provision of quality education services
- establish a system of national integration and shared responsibility between the participating jurisdictions and the Commonwealth in the administration of the NQF
- improve public knowledge, and access to information, about the quality of education and care services
- reduce the regularity and administrative burden for education and care services by enabling information to be shared between participating jurisdictions and the Commonwealth. (ACECQA 2020, p. 9)

As part of the sector reform, the introduction of the EYLF set the benchmark high, offering a vision where all children are to be successful learners, and experience 'belonging, being and becoming' (DEEWR 2009, p. 7). The EYLF is a framework comprising principles and practice with which to build a program leading to five specified Learning Outcomes for all Australian children before starting school (Margetts & Raban 2011; 2020). The aims of the EYLF are to 'extend and enrich children's learning from birth to 5 years and through the transition to school' along with 'recognis[ing] children's right to play and be active participants in all matters affecting their lives'

(DEEWR 2009, p. 5). The development of the EYLF was described by Ortlipp, Arthur and Woodrow (2011, p. 67) as:

> ... a significant symbol of the growing recognition of the importance of the early childhood years within the Australian policy landscape, and has raised hopes and aspirations for what it might achieve for the field ... [and] the EYLF has already generated a kind of authority that is seen to have the potential to raise the status of early childhood work and locate early childhood more powerfully within authorised education discourses, and, in doing so, impact positively on practitioners' view of themselves.

A baseline quantitative evaluation commissioned by the Department of Education, Employment and Workplace Relations (DEEWR) was conducted by Fleer, Shah and Peers (2013) focusing on the effectiveness of the EYLF in raising quality in ECEC. The review found that early childhood educators were generally positive about the EYLF and were becoming familiar with implementation of the national framework's elements, namely the principles, practices and learning outcomes. However, the review noted that levels of awareness about the EYLF varied across different settings; such as long day care, preschool and family day care, and across metropolitan, regional, rural and remote regions.

More recently, White and Fleer (2019) conducted a further study investigating early childhood educator perceptions about the EYLF. The authors maintain that the 2013 baseline evaluation review (Fleer, Shah & Peers 2013) was intended to be an initial review with a follow-up to take place between 2013 and 2019 to see what had changed in the four years. As this had not yet occurred, White and Fleer (2019) conducted their own follow-up study. They found that educators are familiar with the EYLF and said this is 'an achievement' the ECEC profession should be proud of. In addition, they also found that in some areas the practical application of the EYLF requires further extension. They recommend that educators continue to consult educational resources; such as 'government resources, webinars, research in practice booklets and academic literature' with the aim to 'transform professional concepts into practice' (White & Fleer, p. 134). Moreover, according to White and Fleer (2019, pp. 134–5), the areas that educational resources should focus on are 'effective planning, effective assessment, learning activities based on the outcomes of the EYLF for infants, toddlers and pre-school children, and links between the EYLF and the Australian Curriculum'. However, aiming for and maintaining quality in ECEC is not straightforward. Quality in ECEC is a contested and complex issue (Dahlberg, Moss & Pence 2013; Hunkin 2018). Underpinned by various perspectives, assumptions and political aspirations; for example, human capital, social investment and neoliberal agendas, has meant that *quality* is a complicated concept (Hunkin 2018). In her research, Hunkin asks the important question, 'Whose quality?' meaning that definitions of quality can depend on who it concerns and who is doing the assessing. The challenge for the provision of a sustainable quality ECEC system is to accommodate all children and families across the country in accessible, inclusive and equitable ways. We turn to discussing some ways all educators can make a positive difference.

Lifting our game

'Australia can and should do more for its children. Early childhood education offers a great opportunity for Australia to *lift its game*' [emphasis added] (Pascoe & Brennan 2018, p. 7).

As a profession, we are aware that there is room for improvement with regard to access, equity and quality in ECEC. Likewise, the Australian Government acknowledged years ago that there is an amount of work to be done to ensure that children and families experiencing disadvantage and vulnerability can successfully engage in quality ECEC (SCRGSP 2011). In addition, it has been noted that not all policy initiatives will work as planned and effectively address all areas of disadvantage (SCRGSP 2011). Some argue that to address the persistence of inequality in Australian ECEC, the challenge ahead is to 'maintain a balance between social justice goals with the demands of efficiency and productivity' (Molla & Nolan 2019, p. 15).

In an example illustrating the importance of ECEC, Fox and Geddes (2016) discuss evidence showing that two years of preschool has more impact than one, especially for the children most likely to be developmentally vulnerable. Further demonstrating the crucial role the ECEC profession plays, it has been argued that support for children experiencing vulnerability or disadvantage is critical as 'children who start school behind their peers stay behind ... and quality early childhood education can help stop this from happening, and break the cycle of disadvantage' (Pascoe & Brennan 2018, p. 6).

In their report to the Australian Government (including state and territory governments), Pascoe and Brennan (2018) noted a number of specific issues that will need addressing in the near future in order to improve outcomes for Australian children. While they acknowledge the progress made by sector reforms, they stress that Australia's challenge is now to build on these significant positive achievements. They identify the following issues requiring our immediate attention:

- *Funding* – the need for adequate funding, showing that Australia's investment in pre-primary education as a proportion of GDP is 0.2%, leaving Australia as 24th out of 26 Organisation for Economic Co-operation and Development (OECD) countries.
- *Access* – universal access to preschool for 3-year-old children: 3-year-old participation in pre-primary education is 15%, against a 68.6% OECD average, placing Australia 31st out of 35 OECD countries.
- *Support* – greater support for vulnerable families and their children.
- *Engagement* – family and community engagement.

> *Accountability* – transparency and accountability, with respect to data collection and dissemination, clarifying roles and responsibilities between various levels of government.

The most compelling recommendation put forward by Pascoe and Brennan (2018, p. 83) is for enhanced professionalism of the ECEC workforce. The research they cite indicates 'the *single most important element of service quality* is the interaction between child and educator, and training and qualifications improve these interactions [emphasis added]'. Thus, opportunities need to be improved for the recruitment and retention of educators, quality pre-service and in-service education programs, professional learning opportunities, quality leadership capability, workforce diversity, remuneration and conditions of the workforce, engagement with diverse families and importantly, the status of the profession within Australian society. Pascoe and Brennan (2018) urge all Australian governments, through COAG[1], to develop a plan identifying short-, medium- and long-term goals to achieve these recommendations. Recognising that the professionalisation of the ECEC workforce is fundamental to the work educators do, and the outcomes for children and families, this book aims to contribute towards building an 'evidence-informed' profession. An explanation about how that can unfold is now provided.

Evidence-informed practice

Health officials everywhere require *evidence* before taking on certain practices, as people's health, wellbeing and lives are involved. Here we see the demand for *evidenced-based* information which, in the hard sciences such as physics, chemistry, pathology, and so on will give clear solutions. For instance, if a prescribed dose is exceeded, illness will follow. There are clear indications of outcomes related to particular courses of action. However, in education there is no such clear-cut relationship between research outcomes and practical implications. Social science research outcomes give more generalised findings because human experiences are complex and varied, impacted by numerous and different experiences for each person. Because of this, throughout the book we refer to the relationship between research outcomes and practice as evidence-*informed* in contrast to evidence-*based*.

To better understand what evidence-informed practice and ultimately what an evidence-informed profession might look like, we draw on ideas put forward by Coldwell et al. (2017). In their report, they maintain that there are three important elements in achieving evidence-informed education systems, these being, 'awareness, engagement and use'. The three elements are relevant for informing and transforming the Australian ECEC context, with each term explained further:

---

1 COAG was replaced by NFRC in June 2020. https://www.pmc.gov.au/news-centre/government/coag-becomes-national-cabinet

- *Awareness* – defined as 'understanding what research evidence is, knowing how to access research' evidence, 'being able to judge how robust research evidence is, knowing that' research evidence 'can help improve practice, how it does that', and knowing 'how to go about being *evidence informed*'.
- *Engagement* with research – defined as 'thinking that it is important to draw on research evidence to inform and improve practice, and having conversations about the evidence'.
- *Use* – 'any activity where research evidence is actively used to investigate and change practice'. (Coldwell et al. 2017, pp. 50–1)

The three elements, *awareness*, *engagement* and *use*, have guided the chapters in this book, with authors illustrating what evidence-informed practice in ECEC could look like, along with authors providing ideas for practice, provocations to begin conversations about practice, and linking these to the EYLF Learning Outcomes and NQS Quality Areas. We take the view that to achieve a sustainable ECEC system, where equity, high-quality, accessibility, economic viability, affordability and flexibility issues are addressed, is a substantial, complex and ongoing task. Furthermore, the task calls for collective knowledge and collaboration.

Collective knowledge and collaboration

For children to thrive and flourish, all types of people, including family, professionals and community members, need to come together, and work collaboratively to care for, educate and support children. In a professional sense, it takes people from different disciplines and specialist areas to provide the necessary skills, knowledge and support. However, we know that not all disciplinary knowledge is shared by professionals in ECEC, and this can have a detrimental effect on outcomes for children. Shonkoff (2011, p. 983) describes the challenge:

> Neuroscientists who study the impact of adversity on the prefrontal cortex, have limited interaction with psychologists who study effective function in children or adults who live in disorganised environments. Neither group engages regularly with educators who work with children who exhibit problems in emotional stability or self-regulation, nor with policy-makers who make decisions about allocating resources to education, health care, and human services that interact separately with the same children and families. A shared understanding of the common scientific foundations of learning, behaviour, and both physical and mental health offers a compelling strategy for breaking down enduring barriers.

One way of overcoming such barriers is sharing knowledge and evidence across disciplines, thus making information accessible. Another issue to consider when discussing a *shared understanding* across disciplines, is the way information is disseminated. For example, Connell (2019) reminds us that privatisation of knowledge can be dangerous as it can restrict knowledge from society, and that publicly available knowledge is crucial for the wellbeing of communities. Therefore, the main aim of this book is to cross discipline boundaries and bring together interdisciplinary knowledge; insights from research in education, health and social care; child safety; science; mathematics and the arts, all in the one book.

Promoting the rights, needs and aspirations of Aboriginal and Torres Strait Islander children and families

Addressing disadvantage experienced by Aboriginal and Torres Strait Islander children and families is a persistent issue that requires attention in ECEC. Although some of the Australian Government's objectives as part of the Closing the Gap initiative are on track, not all are. What is promising is the focus on collaborative and collective action, and what can be achieved from this positioning. For example, the *Closing the gap report 2020* advocates for a strengthened focus on partnership between governments and Aboriginal and Torres Strait Islander people, and at the heart of this new way of working is 'local action, and a determination to make a difference and to achieve change' (Commonwealth of Australia 2020, p. 5). Picking up on this important agenda, and the type of action required, educators can access information in the Secretariat of National Aboriginal and Islander Child Care (SNAICC 2020a; 2020b) website.

SNAICC is the national peak body representing the interests of Aboriginal and Torres Strait Islander children and families. While all children deserve to thrive and fulfil their potential, SNAICC exists to ensure all Aboriginal and Torres Strait Islander children grow up healthy, happy and safe. Therefore, SNAICC's policy and research work aims to ensure that Aboriginal and Torres Strait Islander children are strong, healthy and grow up connected to family and culture. Through this work there is the aim to provide a strong voice that promotes the rights, needs and aspirations of Aboriginal and Torres Strait Islander children. Resources such as *A place for culture? Early years cultural competency* (SNAICC 2020a), provide cultural competency professional learning for non-Indigenous educators in ECEC. This type of educational resource will assist educators about how to improve service access and service quality for Aboriginal and Torres Strait Islander children and their families (SNAICC 2020a). More information about the cultural competency professional learning program and other resources can be found on the SNAICC (2020b) website (found in the reference list at the end of this chapter).

Navigating the contents of this book

A significant part of the ECEC reform agenda is recognising the role research and evidence plays within professional practice. Addressing this professional practice expectation, this book draws from Australian and international research to showcase current evidence, relevant for educator practice. Each chapter aims to inform the everyday practice of early childhood educators in their work with young children, their families and communities. To this end, this book is intended for all people who work or support the work of those in ECEC, as students, pre-service teachers (PSTs), educators and early childhood teachers (ECTs), early child care professionals, and others who will benefit from reading about evidence to inform their practice. Throughout this book we mostly use the term 'educators', to refer to all those who work in ECEC: teachers, PSTs, students, co-workers and other professionals. However, there are times where these terms need to be distinguished and are used separately.

The contents of this book have been carefully designed and organised to support educators to learn more about a variety of areas of practice, with the aim to revitalise and strengthen practice. The book's content will enable educators to 'closely examine all aspects of events and experiences from different perspectives' (DEEWR 2009, p. 13), creating an *evidence-informed* profession. This book is divided into four sections:

1. The early childhood years: context
2. Identity, wellbeing and children contributing to their world
3. Children as confident and involved learners
4. Children and society: building positive futures.

Each of the sections have a brief introduction, summarising the information contained in each chapter. For convenience for busy educators, the book has been designed to be a *go-to* resource when developing a setting's quality improvement plan (QIP) (ACECQA 2018), where practice is assessed and rated against the Quality Areas. Therefore, each chapter has been written for educators to be able to make clear and strong connections between research evidence, the NQS Quality Areas and EYLF Learning Outcomes.

We are delighted to present to you a book that brings together a comprehensive collection of research findings and insights for the ECEC profession; research work from eminent and emerging researchers from across the country. We invite you to build on the ECEC sector advancements and impressive achievements over the past decade, and to continue to improve and strengthen childrens' and families' outcomes with evidence-informed practice.

References

Australian Children's Education and Care Quality Authority (ACECQA) 2020, *Guide to the national quality framework*, ACECQA, Sydney. Retrieved from https://www.acecqa.gov.au/sites/default/files/2020-01/Guide-to-the-NQF_2.pdf

Australian Children's Education and Care Quality Authority (ACECQA) 2018, *Quality improvement plan template*, ACECQA, Sydney. Retrieved from https://www.acecqa.gov.au/assessment/quality-improvement-plans

Council of Australian Governments (COAG) 2009, *Investing in the early years: a national early childhood development strategy*, Commonwealth of Australia, Canberra.

Commonwealth of Australia 2020, *Closing the gap report 2020*, Department of the Prime Minister and Cabinet, Canberra.

Coldwell, M, Greany, T, Higgins, S, Brown, C, Maxwell, B, Stiell, B, Stoll, L, Willis, B & Burns, H 2017, *Evidence-informed teaching: an evaluation of progress in England*, DFE- RR696a project report, Department for Education, London.

Connell, R 2019, *The good university: what universities actually do and why it's time for radical change*, ZED, London.

Dahlberg, G, Moss, P & Pence, A 2013, *Beyond quality in early childhood education and care: languages of evaluation*, Routledge, Abingdon.

Department of Education, Employment and Workplace Relations (DEEWR) 2009, *Belonging, being and becoming: the early years learning framework for Australia*, Commonwealth of Australia, Canberra. Retrieved from https://docs.education.gov.au/node/2632

Fleer, M, Shah, C & Peers, C 2013, *Quantitative report: baseline evaluation of the early years learning framework*, Department of Education, Employment and Workplace Relations, Canberra.

Fox, S & Geddes, M 2016, *Preschool – two years are better than one: developing a universal preschool program for Australian 3-year-olds – evidence policy and implementation*, policy paper no. 03/2016, Mitchell Institute, Victoria University, Melbourne. Retrieved from http://www.mitchellinstitute.org.au/reports/two-years-preschool/

Hunkin, E 2018, 'Whose quality? The (mis)uses of quality reform in early childhood and education policy', *Journal of Education Policy*, vol. 33, no. 4, pp. 443–56, doi:10.1080/02680939.2017.1352032.

Margetts, K & Raban, B 2011, *The Early Years Learning Framework in practice*, Teaching Solutions, Blairgowrie.

Margetts, K & Raban, B 2020, *The Early Years Learning Framework in practice*, 2nd edn, Essential Resources, Sydney

Molla, T & Nolan, A 2019, 'The "universal access to early childhood education" agenda in Australia: rationales and instruments', *Educational Research for Policy and Practice*, vol. 18, no. 1, pp. 1–16. doi:10.1007/s10671-017-9224-0.

Ortlipp, M, Arthur, L & Woodrow, C 2011, 'Discourses of the early years learning framework: constructing the early childhood professional', *Contemporary Issues in Early Childhood*, vol. 12, no. 1, pp. 56–70, doi:10.2304/ciec.2011.12.1.56.

Pascoe, S & Brennan, D 2018, *Lifting our game: report of the review to achieve educational excellence in Australian schools through early childhood intervention*, The Victorian Government, Melbourne. Retrieved from http://www.education.vic.gov.au/Documents/about/research/LiftingOurGame.PDF

Productivity Commission 2020, *Report on government services 2020*, Part B, 'Section 3 – Early childhood education and care'. Commonwealth of Australia, Canberra. Retrieved from https://www.pc.gov.au/research/ongoing/report-on-government-services/2020/child-care-education-and-training/early-childhood-education-and-care

Shonkoff, JP 2011, 'Protecting brains, not simply stimulating minds', *Science*, vol. 333, no. 6045, pp. 982–83.

Secretariat of National Aboriginal and Islander Child Care (SNAICC) 2020a, *A place for culture? Early years cultural competency*, SNAICC, Melbourne. Retrieved from: www.snaicc.org.au/sector-development/training-programs/place-culture-early-years-cultural-competency

Secretariat of National Aboriginal and Islander Child Care (SNAICC) 2020b, *SNAICC is the national voice for Aboriginal and Torres Strait Islander children*, SNAICC, Melbourne. Retrieved from: https://www.snaicc.org.au/resources

Steering Committee for the Review of Government Service Provision (SCRGSP) 2011, *Overcoming Indigenous disadvantage: key indicators 2011*, Productivity Commission, Melbourne.

White, AD & Fleer, M 2019, 'Early childhood educators' perceptions of the Australian early years learning framework (EYLF): engaged professional learners', *Australasian Journal of Early Childhood*, vol. 44, no. 2, pp. 124–38.

CHAPTER 2

Investigating early childhood practice: insights from a large Australian study

Dan Cloney

DOI: https://doi.org/10.37517/978-1-74286-555-3_2
Australian Council for Educational Research

Introduction

There is a long history of studies that have presented powerful evidence of the effectiveness of high-quality early childhood education and care (ECEC) programs. Importantly, these studies have shown that effective ECEC programs can reduce achievement gaps, including those between children from disadvantaged backgrounds and their more advantaged peers. There is, however, a gap between what these model programs, designed and implemented by educational and developmental experts under non-market conditions, deliver and what everyday ECEC programs deliver. This fact was the motivation for the Effective Early Educational Experiences (E4Kids) study (Tayler, Cloney, Niklas et al. 2016) which aimed to describe the quality of everyday ECEC programs in Australia and how they contributed to the learning and development of Australian children.

E4Kids was implemented around the time of significant national reforms. A focus on quality as a central aspect of ECEC programs of all types – from home-based programs to preschool programs in the year before school – was set out in 2009, in the National Early Childhood Development Strategy (COAG 2009a) and the National Partnership Agreement (COAG 2009b). The E4Kids study recruited its cohort in 2010, and in the years that followed, reforms were implemented including increasing quality standards. In the study, the 2013 version of the National Quality Standard (NQS) (ACECQA 2013) was used, where the provision was 15 hours of programs for all preschool children (COAG 2013). The rollout of universal preschool provision was near a $1 billion Australian-dollar investment over five years. The E4Kids study captured not only the learning and development trajectories of children, but the levels and trajectories in program quality over a rapid period of change for the ECEC sector. Effectiveness was operationalised as being a set of relationships between quality educator practice, structural elements of programs, and issues of equity of availability, along with access and exposure to programs. It was theorised that when these elements were in some optimal state, programs could be described as effective.

When the E4Kids study was being developed, the majority of evidence relied on by the Australian Government came from a handful of US studies that commenced in the 1960s. These studies were purpose-designed with randomised designs, and implemented in disadvantaged communities: the Abecedarian Project (Campbell & Ramey 1994; Ramey & Ramey 1998), High/Scope Perry Preschool study (Schweinhart 2005), and Chicago Longitudinal Study/Child-parent Centre program (Reynolds 2000). These studies demonstrated that children from vulnerable backgrounds benefited in the short and long term (including adult outcomes) from participating in ECEC programs. The High/Scope Perry study, for example, reported effects of approximately 0.90 standard deviations on language and cognitive ability in the short term and in the range of 0.30–0.50 on academic achievement in the long term (Schweinhart 2005). Similarly, the Abecedarian Project reported effect sizes of 1.08 on intelligence at age 4.5 years, and 0.39 at age 15 years (Ramey et al. 2000). Some of the most compelling findings came from economic analysis that reported these programs made a positive return on their investment to the public by reducing negative behavioural outcomes in adulthood (e.g. contact with the criminal justice system), reducing negative health impacts, and through better employment outcomes (Schweinhart 2005). At about this time, economists were also re-analysing much of this data and beginning to extol the benefits of high-quality ECEC programs for children from vulnerable backgrounds. This included the development of the eponymous Heckman Curve – showing that early investments are optimal (particularly for cognitive development) and later remediation is a costlier, and a less efficient investment (Cunha & Heckman 2009; Knudsen et al. 2006).

Other English-speaking countries had run their own large-scale studies during this period. Based on the significant findings of the US model program studies, many countries implemented observational studies – looking at how children and families benefited from simply participating in the ECEC programs provided in the everyday sector. These studies tended to show much more marginal findings, and sometimes even negative findings. Studies in Canada, for example, showed negative effects (Baker, Gruber & Milligan 2008), although later reanalysis was less pessimistic (Kottelenberg & Lehrer 2013). Observational studies in the US showed small to moderate effects (NICHD Early Child Care Research Network 2006), and analysis of programs, including Early Head Start (Love et al. 2005) and Head Start (Puma et al. 2010), specifically for vulnerable children, showed effect sizes for short-term effects of less than 0.3 for cognitive outcomes. In the UK, the impact of attending more effective, compared to less effective ECEC programs was 0.15 (Sammons et al. 2007). For context, an effect size of zero would indicate no relationship between attending ECEC and learning outcomes, and some researchers have attempted to describe the magnitude of effect sizes; for example, 0.2 would be considered a small effect and greater than 0.6 a large effect in education (Hattie 2009).

It is clear, from the results presented, there is a gap between the promise of high-quality ECEC programs provided under study conditions and everyday ECEC programs. The gap between these two sets of programs is related to access and exposure (did children access ECEC programs, and for how many hours), and quality. Evidence on the access, usage and quality of ECEC programs did not exist for Australia at the level that could be generalised to make comments about the effectiveness of the system. This chapter describes the major findings of the E4Kids study and places them in a context of a need for large-scale and representative data in Australia. The chapter concludes by discussing where to next for research on ECEC programs in Australia.

Methods

Study sample

The E4Kids study was conducted over five years, from 2010, and included three years of direct observation of children and ECEC programs. The sample was drawn by taking a representative sample of (formal, or licenced) ECEC programs in Australia, and then sampling intact rooms of children within sampled settings. A cluster randomised sample of 2494 children who attended ECEC programs at 3–4 years of age were recruited from programs delivered in Victoria and Queensland in 2010 (Tayler, Cloney, Adams et al. 2016). In addition, 157 children who did not access such programs in 2010 were identified through Commonwealth Government sources and were recruited as a control group to the study. The program and control groups did not differ significantly in terms of gender, community and family socio-economic status (SES) or the primary language spoken at home.

Key measures

The focus of the E4Kids study was most acutely interested in the way that ECEC programs contribute to children's learning and development, particularly cognitive development. The reader can refer to the study protocol for details about the full set of measures (including structural quality, social and emotional skills, and contextual features like household factors and educator learning and development) (Tayler, Cloney, Adams et al. 2016).

ECEC program quality

In the E4Kids study, the main aspect of program quality measured was pedagogical, or *interaction* quality. That is, not structural elements such as adult–child ratios or the physical environment, but the interactions between adults and children, and children and children that occur during the program. This is because interactions are the aspect of ECEC practice and quality that are continually found to be correlated with learning and development gains (Burchinal, Kainz & Cai 2011; Hamre et al. 2013) while structural aspects (e.g. adult–child ratios, staff qualifications) are considered necessary preconditions for the provision of high-quality interactions (Chien et al. 2010). The instrument chosen in the E4Kids study to measure interaction quality was the Classroom Assessment Scoring System (CLASS) (Pianta, La Paro & Hamre 2008). The CLASS measures three domains of interaction quality:

- *Emotional support* – positive and negative climate, teacher sensitivity and regard for children's perspectives
- *Classroom organisation* – behaviour management, productivity and the use of instructional learning formats or multiple modalities
- *Instructional support* – concept development, quality of feedback and language modelling.

Each domain is continuous with a range of one (low-quality) to seven (high-quality). Scores from three to five are considered moderate quality.

Two important assumptions were made in the E4Kids study in relation to quality. The first is that the 10 indicators and three domains of the CLASS are appropriate for all types of ECEC programs and are not dependant on the implementation of a specific curriculum, or pedagogical approach (Pianta, La Paro & Hamre 2008). High-quality observations could be expected to be seen in all settings. The second was that certain aspects of quality would be more strongly linked to particular outcomes than other aspects. For example, aspects of 'instructional support' (which includes classical teaching strategies like quality of feedback) should be more strongly related to cognitive and academic outcomes than to social and emotional outcomes (Pianta & Hamre 2009).

Children's learning and development

The main learning and development measure in the study was the Woodcock Johnson III (WJIII) (McGrew & Woodcock 2001). The WJIII had been previously used in several US studies (Burchinal et al. 2008; Gormley et al. 2005; NICHD Early Child Care Research Network & Duncan 2003). It captures key aspects of both domain-general cognitive skills (problem-solving and executive functioning) as well as early academic skills (vocabulary and simple mathematical operations) (Kaufman et al. 2012). The main domains used in the study were 'brief intellectual ability', 'verbal ability' and 'applied problems'.

The *brief intellectual* ability scale is a cognitive performance cluster made up of the subscales:

- *Verbal comprehension* – CHC[1] broad ability of comprehension knowledge
- *Concept formation* – CHC broad ability of fluid reasoning
- *Visual matching* – CHC broad ability of processing speed.

---

1 Cattell–Horn–Carroll Theory (CHC) is a theory of the structure of cognitive abilities (McGrew 1997).

The *verbal ability* cluster is made up of the four subscales of verbal comprehension:

- picture vocabulary
- synonyms
- antonyms
- verbal analogies.

Verbal ability captures both spoken and receptive language and is predictive of oral language ability as well as academic performance (Mather & Woodcock 2001a).

Applied problems measures quantitative knowledge and assesses mathematical operations (Mather & Woodcock 2001a). The WJIII assessments are appropriate, and norm-referenced for individuals from age 2 years old to more than 90 years old. Importantly the assessments are appropriate for measuring growth (McGrew & Woodcock 2001b).

The study's theoretical and analytical approach

The E4Kids study is a longitudinal and observational study. This means that children were recruited to the study, and their developmental progress and ECEC program exposure tracked over several years. The programs that children attended were selected as a product of their families' preferences and the availability in their local community. In order to relate ECEC program participation to learning and development in the context of an observational study it is also important to build an understanding (and to model) other important factors in children's lives: factors that influence the likelihood that they go to any one program, as well as factors that influence their learning and development. It is important to recognise that these factors are often related. For instance, the same factors that influence a family's choice of ECEC program also influence learning and development. The E4Kids study followed best practice from other large-scale studies of ECEC (Duncan & Gibson-Davis 2006; NICHD Early Child Care Research Network & Duncan 2003) as well as the sampling and weighting strategies of large-scale assessments in international studies (Adams & Wu 2002). A full description of the technical design of the study can be found in the study protocol (Tayler, Cloney, Adams et al. 2016).

In order to capture all of the key inputs into family decision-making around ECEC programs, and the learning and development of children, the E4Kids study designed a conceptual framework which is summarised in **Figure 2.1** (Cloney 2016). Importantly, the causal process is strongly aligned with traditional theorisations about how educators influence children's learning and development. In the shaded sections, the particular context of the local community and indeed country play a role, while the circles represent the influence of the home learning environment (HLE) and quality interactions on children's developmental outcomes (noting that individual traits of the child may moderate that relationship). Such a model is consistent with the bio-ecological model that posits many levels of influence (Bronfenbrenner & Ceci 1994) as well as classical educational theories that describe learning as an innately social process (Vygotsky 1978).

In addition to this mapping, there is a simultaneous selection process (selection is a statistical term and does not imply an active selection by families, and instead may be interpreted as families acting under a set of constraints), whereby families are able to select from the set of ECEC programs provided in their jurisdiction, and available in their local neighbourhood (they may not exist, or there may be other barriers; such as capacity constraints). Families are also constrained by socio-economic factors, as well as other factors including the needs of other children in the household. These selection factors not only influence the kind of ECEC programs the child is exposed to, but also influence the home learning environment. For example, families of higher SES tend to provide more stimulating home environments (Niklas et al. 2016). The longitudinal aspect of the study could be thought about in terms of the core elements of this conceptual framework being observed repeatedly over time: there are many measures of children's outcomes, ECEC quality, and other contextual factors over the years the study is conducted.

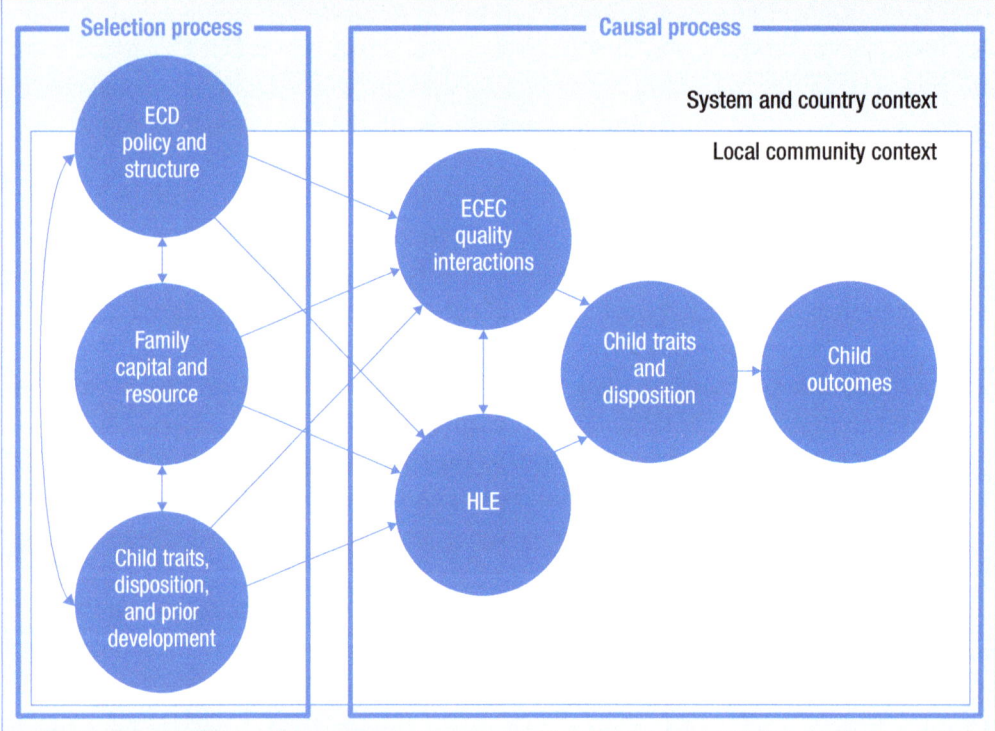

Figure 2.1 Theoretical framework of the E4Kids study
Note: ECD is early childhood development.

Major findings

The key findings of the E4Kids study relate to the level of *quality* in Australian ECEC programs, the use of ECEC programs before school (*access* and *exposure*), the impact of

ECEC programs on *learning* and development outcomes, and perhaps most significantly, *equity* issues deeply embedded in the Australian ECEC system. Together these findings provide insights about the effectiveness of everyday ECEC programs in Australia.

Quality

Overall, the level of *instructional support* is the aspect of quality most likely to impact cognitive development, but in Australian ECEC programs in the study, this is low (Pianta, La Paro & Hamre 2008). This is true in nearly all ECEC services in the study, with fewer than 1% of children attending ECEC programs rated as *high* on instructional support (Cloney, Cleveland, Tayler et al. 2016; Tayler et al. 2013). Other aspects of quality are relatively higher, showing that instructional support is the key area where there is significant scope for improvement (*see* **Figure 2.2**). In this figure, the boxplot shows that the midpoint of the box (the median) for 'emotional support' is above the dotted line at 5 on the CLASS scale. More than 50% of ECEC programs are considered high quality on this domain. Conversely, the midpoint of the 'instructional support' domain is below the dotted line at 3 on the CLASS scale. More than 50% of ECEC programs are considered low quality on this domain. This is similar to findings in the US on the CLASS, and in the UK on other similar measures of quality (Tayler et al. 2013).

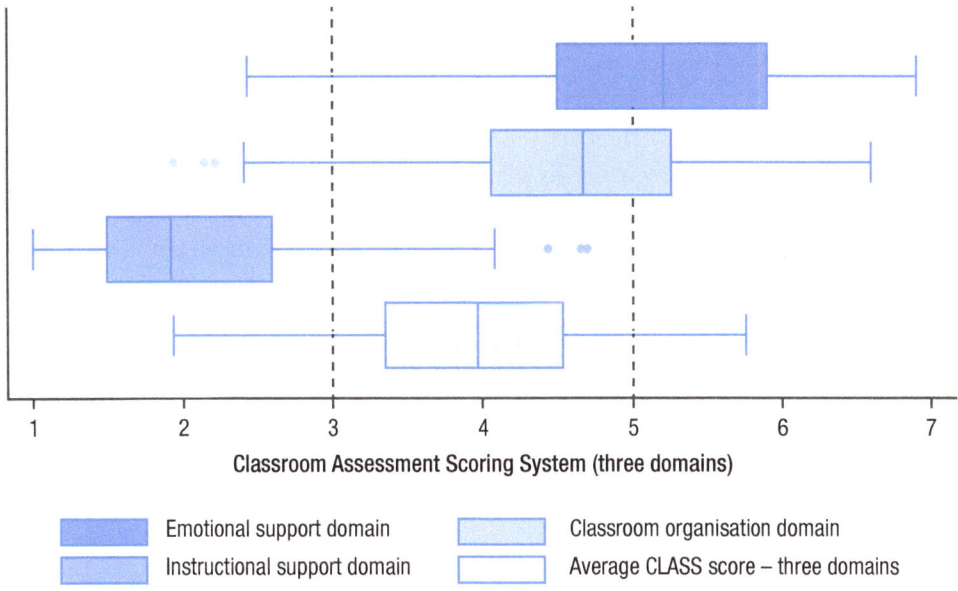

Figure 2.2 Observed quality of Australian ECEC programs on the CLASS
Adapted from Tayler et al. (2013).

Between different service provision types, there were important differences in quality. Taking the average of the three CLASS scales (a measure of global educator–child interactions), long day care (LDC) settings scored significantly lower than preschool settings. On average the difference was 0.55 on the scale that ranges from 1 to 7 (or nearly 75% of a standard deviation on this measure). This finding reinforced earlier studies, using alternate measures (e.g. the Infant/Toddler Environmental Rating Scale ITERS), that showed preschools (typically stand-alone, sessional programs for children in the year or two before school led by degree-qualified teachers) typically scored higher than child care settings (typically full-day programs for children 0–6 years old led by vocationally trained educators.[2] (Bowes et al. 2009; Fenech, Sweller & Harrison 2010). This finding was interpreted to be related to a mix of factors, including that at the time of the study preschool rooms were required to be led by educators with at least a bachelor's degree, while the majority of educators in LDC settings held a certificate or diploma (or equivalent on-the-job training) (Tayler et al. 2013).

This analysis was extended to look explicitly at the role of qualifications with respect to quality, and it was found that the qualification of leaders was particularly important. Settings with university-qualified directors had scored more highly on all CLASS domains than those without these qualifications. Directors with post-graduate qualifications scored more highly again. Importantly, degree-qualified educators were shown to score more highly on instructional support (Tayler, Cloney, Niklas et al. 2016).

Access

A significant consideration about the effectiveness of ECEC settings is whether children access them (at all) and when they do, whether they get exposed to enough practice to have a lasting effect. When thinking about access to ECEC programs, it is important to consider the age of children when they first come to ECEC programs (age of entry) and the amount of time children are in attendance (this may be measured across a single year or aggregated across many). In some studies, the relationship between access, usage, learning and development is described as a 'dose-response'. A positive dose-response implies that as the number of hours increases the developmental benefit also increases (Cloney 2016).

Children are more likely to use ECEC programs as they get older, and as they get older, they use them for longer hours. In E4Kids, 34% of children attended ECEC programs for more than 30 hours per week in the year before school, while only 11% of the children in E4Kids were attending for more than 30 hours three years earlier. Children from more advantaged families; for example, those where parents were employed and where the SES was higher, typically attended for more hours. Conversely, children with developmental delays or a disability were likely to attend for fewer hours (Gilley et al. 2015).

---

[2] Note that the author recognises that contemporary Australian LDC settings are likely to offer preschool programs and have a degree-qualified pedagogical leader).

Learning

At entry to the study (generally between 3 to 4 years of age) there were already visible differences between children in the levels of their learning. For example, for *verbal ability* the average score in the first year of the study was 441, with a variance of 161 (or a standard deviation = 12.7), meaning that we could expect that approximately 60% of children will have verbal ability scores between 428 and 453. As children grew over the three years, the individual differences between children grew. Children who were initially low achieving, were even further behind than their peers three years later. The children in the lowest developing group entered the study with outcomes below the expected level of ability for their age, and they remained the lowest developing group at the end of the study. This trajectory means this particular group of children were not only behind their peers, they were continuing to fall behind. This was true on all three major outcomes *verbal ability*, *applied problems* and *brief intellectual ability* (Tayler, Cloney & Niklas 2015).

The children most likely to be in the lowest developing group were children from the most disadvantaged backgrounds. For example, between 30 and 40% of children in the lowest developing group lived in the least advantaged areas in Australia (*see* Pink 2008), while fewer than 10% of these children lived in the most advantaged areas. When considering family home practices, children who were read to less frequently (not every day), and who did not speak English at home, had the poorest developmental outcomes (Tayler, Cloney & Niklas 2015).

Equity

In aggregate, the E4Kids study findings about quality, access and learning present a challenging set of results and strongly imply that there are equity gaps in the ECEC sector. To address these issues, these three aspects of the study were combined into a set of analyses investigating how ECEC programs were supporting children's learning and development and how contextual factors relating to advantage and disadvantage may be playing a role.

One key finding was that quality programs are not found in all neighbourhoods in Australia. In fact, the likelihood of finding a high-quality setting is related to the relative advantage of the neighbourhood. This was because there were more programs and greater capacity in the most advantaged neighbourhoods, and they tended to be higher quality. Furthermore, children from more advantaged SES backgrounds were more likely to attend higher quality programs (Cloney, Cleveland, Tayler et al. 2016) in part because families tend to choose ECEC settings in their own neighbourhoods or close to home (Cloney, Cleveland, Hattie et al. 2016). On instructional support, programs in the least advantaged areas (lowest quintile) were 0.23 to 0.26 CLASS scale scores lower than those in the most advantaged areas (5th and 4th quintiles respectively), a significant effect given the average instructional support score in the least advantaged areas was 1.51 (Cloney, Cleveland, Hattie et al. 2016).

This pattern of children from less advantaged areas being less likely to access the highest quality programs meant that there were two major influences on children's learning and development. These major influences are ECEC exposure and socio-economic factors. For example, each additional hour of ECEC exposure of children at age 4 contributed to children's *verbal ability*, as did exposure to higher *instructional support*. As instructional support improved by 1 standard deviation, children gained an extra month of learning on verbal ability. These findings were similar for *applied problems* and *brief intellectual ability*. These gains were, however, largely overtaken by socio-economic factors. Children from high socio-economic families entered the study at 3–4 years of age, already 1.5 months ahead of their peers in verbal ability. Children who lived in well-resourced, highly advantaged areas were a further 3 months ahead again. These children also tended to develop at a faster rate, being the equivalent of another 3 months ahead of their less-advantaged peers at the end of the study. These findings were similar for applied problems and brief intellectual ability (Cloney 2016).

Implications of the findings

The organisation of the ECEC sector presents substantial equity barriers for children from the most vulnerable backgrounds. These children are least likely to access the highest quality programs and because of this they gain the least from the sector. This means that we are unlikely to deliver outcomes that narrow achievement gaps (that emerge early and persist, or grow wider across the life course), and are attributable to relative disadvantage, rather than the latent ability or aptitude of children. There are pathways that can lead to improvements in the effectiveness of the sector, and they relate to improving the quality of all programs (acknowledging that instructional quality is low in many settings) (*see* **Figure 2.2**), and putting a particular focus on resourcing programs in the most disadvantaged areas to provide the highest quality programs. To achieve this, there are implications at several levels, namely, research, policy and most importantly, practice.

Conclusion

Future research

International research, along with Australian studies, such as E4Kids, have informed ECEC program effectiveness. High-quality program studies mentioned early in this chapter have been shown to be effective and reduce inequalities related to disadvantage. ECEC programs generally, however, can have difficulty delivering similar impact due to structural barriers limiting quality and equity for all children. A new generation of research is required at two levels, for instance, ongoing large-scale studies that drive improvement and accountability, and focused smaller scale research that demonstrates effective intervention on ECEC quality and children's learning.

At the large scale, ongoing work is needed to show how to measure the full breadth of quality ECEC practice and, for example, how these measures relate to the newly revised NQS (ACECQA 2020). Similarly, there is only limited understanding of how specific elements of quality practice (e.g. instructional support) influence specific learning and development outcomes for all children. Recent work has shown that there are relatively few measures of learning and development that are suited to assessing individual children's growth and the impact of specific practice on that growth (Cloney, Jackson & Mitchell 2019). This is especially true of children's social and emotional skills, that have been criticised as being measured poorly (Zaslow et al. 2006) taking the previous review by Vandell and Wolfe (2000).

At the smaller scale there are some studies emerging that focus on quantifying different intervention models. The Victorian Advancing Early Learning (VAEL) study for example, assessed the effectiveness of in-service training on improving quality, using the CLASS measure as an outcome (Pilsworth et al. 2017).

Translating research into practice

Translating research into practice is a way to ensure that what professionals do to engage in continual quality improvement, and what they do to support children's learning and development, is most likely to be successful. For example, thinking about how research should inform assessment practices can support the collection of rigorous evidence about local impact. Recent work has shown that this does not need to resemble formative assessment in school settings, but, instead might be informed by valid and reliable assessments. These assessments can foster a more informed understanding of children's acquisition of knowledge, skills and abilities. Current examples of this include the Victorian Curriculum and Assessment Authority's (VCAA) *Learning practice guide* (Jackson et al. 2019). Alternatively, translating research into practice could involve using better techniques to target areas of quality improvement. For example, if educators and services have evidence-informed understandings about where they are succeeding and where they require improvement, then they can work on aspects of their current practice to help set achievable and explicit targets (Cloney 2018; Cloney & Hollingsworth 2018).

At the policy level, there is clear need to support all ECEC settings to engage in quality improvement. In addition, ECEC settings in the most vulnerable areas need to be resourced to provide high-quality programs. Such high-quality programs are more likely to lead to the reduction of learning and development gaps that are related to structural inequality and disadvantage.

Large-scale studies can influence policy by producing not only evidence of success, but by illustrating where there are opportunities to improve. At the time of the E4Kids study, the first universal access to ECEC programs was in the preschool year, at age 4. This policy gave children access to 15 hours a week, or approximately 600 hours per year. Evidence of learning gaps emerging earlier than this have led to rapid policy change, including new proposals by state governments to implement two years of universally available preschool, starting at age 3. For example, see the 3-year-old preschool initiative by the Department of Education and Training Victoria (DET 2020). This could potentially double children's exposure to ECEC programs. The policy case for this change includes other international evidence and the results of the E4Kids study (Fox & Geddes 2016). Similarly, calls to improve quality for all children have been supported by the results of research (Fox & Geddes 2016; Torii, Fox & Cloney 2017). Ongoing evidence is needed to ensure we can track success and address gaps to ensure all children get the best start in life.

RESEARCH INTO PRACTICE

Educators collect evidence about their impact for many reasons:
- To describe their impact and the progression of each child's knowledge, skills and abilities. This can be used to communicate with families, communities and other professionals.
- To learn about what learning and development looks like across many related but distinct outcome domains. By engaging in cycles of professional reading and learning, as well as collecting evidence about what children can do, educators are making visible what learning looks like – in areas like cognition and executive function, early literacy and numeracy, and social and emotional skills.
- To improve their practice by thinking critically and implementing in planning better alignment between their explicit pedagogy and use of materials and the specific learning and development needs of the children in their program.
- To support learning in this area, there are numerous documents to consume, but educators should choose carefully and select sources informed by evidence. This might include, for example, practice guides and literature reviews prepared by the VCAA (e.g. Jackson et al. 2019).

Acknowledgement

The E4Kids study was led by Chief Investigator, Emeritus Professor Collette Tayler. Collette sadly passed away on 1 December 2017. Her career was dedicated to improving the lives of all young children and ensuring that all children had the best start in life. Her vision to bring together perspectives from education, educational measurement, psychology, policy and economics to generate and respond to questions about how ECEC programs could contribute to optimal life course development, reduce disadvantage and produce public benefits for society, was realised in the E4Kids study.

Endnote

E4Kids is a project of the Melbourne Graduate School of Education at the University of Melbourne and was conducted in partnership with Queensland University of Technology.

E4Kids was funded by the Australian Research Council Linkage Projects Scheme (Grant LP0990200), the Victorian Government Department of Education and Early Childhood Development, and the Queensland Government Department of Education, Training and Employment.

E4Kids was conducted with academic collaboration with the University of Toronto at Scarborough; the Institute of Education, The University of London; and the Royal Children's Hospital, Melbourne.

The final report of the E4Kids study can be downloaded here: https://doi.org/10.4225/49/58f99f47a2ab4

References

Adams, RJ & Wu, M (eds) 2002, *PISA 2000 technical report*, Organisation for Economic Co-operation and Development, Paris. Retrieved from https://www.oecd-ilibrary.org/education/programme-for-international-student-assessment-pisa_9789264199521-en

Australian Children's Education and Care Quality Authority (ACECQA) 2013, *Guide to assessment and rating for regulatory authorities*, ACECQA, Sydney. Retrieved from http://files.acecqa.gov.au/files/Assessment%20and%20Rating/Guide%20to%20Assessment%20and%20Rating%20for%20Regulatory%20Authorities_130109.pdf

Baker, M, Gruber, J & Milligan, K 2008, 'Universal child care, maternal labor supply, and family well-being', *Journal of Political Economy*, vol. 116, no. 4, pp. 709–45.

Bowes, J, Harrison, L, Sweller, N, Taylor, A & Neilsen-Hewett, C 2009, *From child care to school: influences on children's adjustment and achievement in the year before school and the first year of school*, NSW Department of Community Services, Sydney.

Bronfenbrenner, U & Ceci, S J 1994, 'Nature-nuture reconceptualized in developmental perspective: a bioecological model', *Psychological Review*, vol. 101, no. 4, pp. 568–86, doi:10.1037/0033-295x.101.4.568

Burchinal, M, Howes, C, Pianta, R, Bryant, D, Early, D, Clifford, R & Barbarin, O 2008, 'Predicting child outcomes at the end of kindergarten from the quality of pre-kindergarten teacher–child interactions and instruction', *Applied Developmental Science*, vol. 12, no. 3, pp. 140–53, doi:10.1080/10888690802199418.

Burchinal, M, Kainz, K & Cai, Y 2011, 'How well do our measures of quality predict child outcomes? A meta-analysis and coordinated analysis of data from large-scale studies of early childhood settings', in MJ Zaslow, I Martinez-Beck, K Tout & T Halle (eds), *Quality measurement in early childhood settings*, Paul H Brookes, Baltimore.

Campbell, FA & Ramey, CT 1994, 'Effects of early intervention on intellectual and academic achievement: a follow-up study of children from low-income families', special issue, *Child Development*, vol. 65, no. 2, pp. 684–98.

Chien, NC, Howes, C, Burchinal, M, Pianta, RC, Ritchie, S, Bryant, DM, Clifford, RM, Early, D M & Barbarin, OA 2010, 'Children's classroom engagement and school readiness gains in prekindergarten', *Child Development*, vol. 81, no. 5, pp. 1534–49.

Cloney, D 2016, *Accessibility and effectiveness of early childhood education and care for families from low socioeconomic status backgrounds in Australia*, University of Melbourne. Retrieved from http://hdl.handle.net/11343/112371

Cloney, D 2018, 'Breaking the link between disadvantage and development in early childhood settings in Australia', *Teaching practices that make a difference: insights from research*, ACER Research Conference, Sydney. Retrieved from: https://research.acer.edu.au/cgi/viewcontent.cgi?article=1328&context=research_conference

Cloney, D, Cleveland, G, Hattie, J & Tayler, C 2016a, 'Variations in the availability and quality of early childhood education and care by socioeconomic status of neighbourhood', *Early Education and Development*, vol. 27, no. 3, pp. 384–401, doi:10.1080/10409289.2015.1076674.

Cloney, D, Cleveland, G, Tayler, C, Hattie, J & Adams, R 2016, 'The selection of ECEC programs by Australian families: quality, availability, usage and family demographics', *Australasian Journal of Early Childhood*, vol. 41, no. 4, pp. 16–35.

Cloney, D & Hollingsworth, H 2018, 'Using measures of pedagogical quality to provide feedback and improve practice', in J Lodge, J Cooney Horvath & L Corrin (eds), *Learning analytics in the classroom: translating learning analytics research for teachers* (chapter 14), Routledge, London.

Cloney, D, Jackson, J & Mitchell, P 2019, *Assessment of children as confident and involved learners in early childhood education and care*, Victorian Curriculum and Assessment Authority, Melbourne. Retrieved from https://www.vcaa.vic.edu.au/Documents/earlyyears/EYLitReviewLearning.pdf

Council of Australian Governments (COAG) 2009a, *Investing in the early years: a national early childhood development strategy*, Commonwealth of Australia, Canberra.

Council of Australian Governments (COAG) 2009b, *National partnership agreement on early childhood education*, Commonwealth of Australia, Canberra.

Council of Australian Governments (COAG) 2013, *National partnership agreement on universal access to early childhood education*, Commonwealth of Australia, Canberra.

Cunha, F & Heckman, JJ 2009, 'The economics and psychology of inequality and human development', *Journal of the European Economic Association*, vol. 7, no. 2–3, pp. 320–64, doi:10.1162/JEEA.2009.7.2-3.320.

Department of Education and Training Victoria (DET) 2020, *Three-year-old kindergarten*, DET, Melbourne. Retrieved from https://www.education.vic.gov.au/about/programs/Pages/three-year-old-kinder.aspx

Duncan, GJ & Gibson-Davis, CM 2006, 'Connecting child care quality to child outcomes: drawing policy lessons from nonexperimental data', *Evaluation Review*, vol. 30, no. 5, pp. 611–30, doi:10.1177/0193841X06291530.

Fenech, M, Sweller, N & Harrison, L 2010, 'Identifying high-quality centre-based childcare using quantitative data-sets: what the numbers do and don't tell us', *International Journal of Early Years Education*, vol. 18, no. 4, pp. 283–96.

Fox, S & Geddes, M 2016, *Preschool – two years are better than one: developing a universal preschool program for Australian 3 year olds – evidence, policy and implementation*, policy paper no. 03/2016, The Mitchell Institute, Melbourne. Retrieved from www.mitchellinstitute.org.au

Gilley, T, Tayler, C, Niklas, F & Cloney, D 2015, 'Too late and not enough for some children: early childhood education and care (ECEC) program usage patterns in the years before school in Australia', *International Journal of Child Care and Education Policy*, vol. 9, no. 1, pp. 1–15, doi:10.1186/s40723-015-0012-0 l.

Gormley, WT, Gayer, T, Phillips, D & Dawson, B 2005, 'The effects of universal pre-K on cognitive development', *Developmental Psychology*, vol. 41, no. 6, pp. 872–84, doi:10.1037/0012-1649.41.6.872.

Hamre, B, Pianta, RC, Jason, TD, DeCoster, J, Mashburn, AJ, Jones, SM, Brown, JL, Cappella, E, Atkins, M, Rivers, SE, Brackett, MA & Hamagami, A 2013, 'Teaching through interactions: testing a developmental framework of teacher effectiveness in over 4000 classrooms', *The Elementary School Journal*, vol. 113, no. 4, pp. 461–87, doi:10.1086/669616.

Hattie, J 2009, *Visible learning: a synthesis of over 800 meta-analyses relating to achievement*, Routledge, Oxford.

Jackson, J, Noble, K, Iorio, JM, Cloney, D & Mitchell, P 2019, *Learning practice guide: children are confident and involved learners*, Victorian Curriculum and Assessment Authority, Melbourne. Retrieved from https://www.vcaa.vic.edu.au/Documents/earlyyears/LearningPGweb24102019.pdf

Kaufman, SB, Reynolds, MR, Liu, X, Kaufman, AS & McGrew, KS 2012, 'Are cognitive *g* and academic achievement *g* one and the same *g*? An exploration on the Woodcock–Johnson and Kaufman tests', *Intelligence*, vol. 40, pp. 123–38, doi:10.1016/j.intell.2012.01.009.

Knudsen, EI, Heckman, JJ, Cameron, JL & Shonkoff, JP 2006, 'Economic, neurobiological, and behavioral perspectives on building America's future workforce', *Proceedings of the National Academy of Sciences*, vol. 103, no. 27, pp. 10155–62, doi:10.1073/pnas.0600888103.

Kottelenberg, MJ & Lehrer, SF 2013, 'New evidence on the impacts of access to and attending universal child-care in Canada', *Canadian Public Policy*, vol. 39, no. 2, pp. 263–85.

Love, JM, Eliason, KE, Ross, C, Raikes, H, Constantine, J, Boller, K, Brooks-Gunn, J, Chazan-Cohen, R, Tarullo, LB, Brady-Smith, C, Fuligni, AS, Schochet, PZ, Paulsell, D & Vogel, C 2005, 'The effectiveness of early head start for 3-year-old children and their parents: lessons for policy and programs. *Developmental Psychology*, vol. 41, no. 6, pp. 885–901, doi:10.1037/0012-1649.41.6.885.

Mather, N & Woodcock, RW 2001a, *Woodcock-Johnson III tests of achievement examiner's manual*, Riverside Publishing, Rolling Meadows, IL.

Mather, N & Woodcock, RW 2001b, *Woodcock-Johnson III tests of cognitive abilities examiner's manual*, Riverside Publishing, Rolling Meadows, IL.

McGrew, KS 1997, 'Analysis of the major intelligence batteries according to a proposed comprehensive Gf-Gc framework, in DP Flanagan, JL Genshaf & PL Harrison (eds), *Contemporary intellectual assessment: theories, tests and issues*, Guilford, New York.

McGrew, KS & Woodcock, RW 2001, *Woodcock-Johnson III technical manual*, Riverside Publishing, Rolling Meadows, IL.

National Institute of Child Health & Human Development (NICHD), Early Child Care Research Network & Duncan, G J 2003, 'Modeling the impacts of child care quality on children's preschool cognitive development', *Child Development*, vol. 74, no. 5, pp. 1454–75.

National Institute of Child Health & Human Development (NICHD) & Early Child Care Research Network 2006, 'Child-care effect sizes for the NICHD study of early child care and youth development', *American Psychologist*, vol. 61, no. 2, pp. 99–116, doi:10.1037/0003-066x.61.2.99.

Niklas, F, Nguyen, C, Cloney, D, Tayler, C & Adams, R 2016, 'Self-report measures of the home learning environment in large scale research: measurement properties and associations with key developmental outcomes', *Learning Environments Research*, vol. 19, no. 2, pp. 181–202, doi:10.1007/s10984-016-9206-9.

Pianta, RC & Hamre, B 2009, 'Conceptualization, measurement, and improvement of classroom processes: standardized observation can leverage capacity', *Educational Researcher*, vol. 38, no. 2, pp. 109–19, doi:10.3102/0013189x09332374.

Pianta, RC, La Paro, KM & Hamre, B 2008, *Classroom assessment scoring system manual: preschool (pre-k) version*, Brookes, Baltimore.

Pilsworth, N, MacBean, C, Tayler, C, Page, J, Eadie, P & Niklas, F 2017, *Victorian advancing early learning study*, final report, University of Melbourne.

Pink, B 2008, *Socio-economic indexes for areas (SEIFA): technical paper*, ABS catalogue no. 2039.0.55.001, Australian Bureau of Statistics, Canberra.

Puma, M, Bell, S, Cook, R, Heid, C, Shapiro, G, Broene, P, Jenkins, F, Fletcher, P, Quinn, L, Friedman, J, Ciarico, J, Rohacek, M, Adams, G & Spier, E 2010, *Head start impact study. Technical report*, Administration for Children & Families, Washington DC.

Ramey, CT, Campbell, FA, Burchinal, M, Skinner, ML, Gardner, DM & Ramey, SL 2000, 'Persistent effects of early childhood education on high-risk children and their mothers', *Applied Developmental Science*, vol. 4, no. 2, pp. 2–14, doi:10.1207/S1532480XADS0401_1.

Ramey, CT & Ramey, SL 1998, 'Prevention of intellectual disabilities: Eearly interventions to improve cognitive development', *Preventive Medicine*, vol. 27, no. 2, pp. 224–32, doi: 10.1006/pmed.1998.0279.

Reynolds, AJ 2000, *Success in early intervention: the Chicago child-parent centers*, University of Nebraska Press, Lincoln.

Sammons, P, Sylva, K, Melhuish, E, Siraj-Blatchford, I, Taggart, B, Grabbe, Y & Barreau, S 2007, *Effective pre-school and primary education 3–11 project (EPPE 3–11): summary report – influences on children's attainment and progress in key stage 2: cognitive outcomes in Year 5*, University of Wollongong Press. Retrieved from https://ro.uow.edu.au/cgi/viewcontent.cgi?article=2684&context=sspapers

Schweinhart, LJ 2005, *Lifetime effects: the High/Scope Perry Preschool study through age 40*, High/Scope Press, Ypsilanti.

Tayler, C, Cloney, D, Adams, R.J, Ishimine, K, Thorpe, K & Nguyen, C 2016, 'Assessing the effectiveness of Australian early childhood education and care experiences: study protocol', *BMC Public Health*, vol. 16, no. 1, pp. 1–12, doi:10.1186/s12889-016-2985-1.

Tayler, C, Cloney, D & Niklas, F 2015, 'A bird in the hand: understanding the trajectories of development of young children and the need for action to improve outcomes', *Australasian Journal of Early Childhood*, vol. 40, no. 3, pp. 51–60.

Tayler, C, Cloney, D, Niklas, F, Cohrssen, C, Thorpe, K, Page, J & D'Aprano, A 2016, *Final report to the partner organisations for the effective early education experiences (E4Kids) study*, Melbourne Graduate School of Education, doi:10.4225/49/58f99f47a2ab4.

Tayler, C, Ishimine, K, Cloney, D, Cleveland, G & Thorpe, K 2013, 'The quality of early childhood education and care services in Australia', *Australasian Journal of Early Childhood*, vol. 38, no. 2, pp. 13–21.

Torii, K, Fox, S & Cloney, D 2017, *Quality is key in early childhood education in Australia*, Mitchell Institute, Victoria University, Melbourne. Retrieved from http://www.mitchellinstitute.org.au/wp-content/uploads/2017/10/Quality-is-key-in-early-childhood-education-in-Australia.pdf

Vygotsky, LS 1978, 'Interaction between learning and development, in M Cole (ed), *Mind in society: the development of higher psychological processes*, Harvard University Press, Cambridge, MA.

Zaslow, M, Halle, T, Martin, L, Cabrera, N, Calkins, J, Pitzer, L & Margie, NG 2006, 'Child outcome measures in the study of child care quality', *Evaluation Review*, vol. 30, no. 5, pp. 577–610, doi:10.1177/0193841X06291529.

CHAPTER 3

The early childhood professional

Megan Gibson and Lyn Gunn

DOI: https://doi.org/10.37517/978-1-74286-555-3_3
Queensland University of Technology

LINKS TO NATIONAL QUALITY STANDARD

Quality Area 4: Staffing arrangements
- Standard 4.2: Professionalism – management, educators and staff are collaborative, respectful and ethical.
- Element 4.2.1: Professional collaboration – management, educators and staff work with mutual respect and collaboratively, and challenge and learn from each other, recognising each other's strengths and skills.
- Element 4.2.2: Professional standards – professional standards guide practice, interactions and relationships.

Quality Area 7: Governance and leadership
- Standard 7.2: Leadership – effective leadership builds and promotes a positive organisational culture and professional learning community.
- Element 7.2.3: Development of professionals – educators, coordinators and staff members' performance is regularly evaluated and individual plans are in place to support learning and development.

Introduction

The language of profession and professionalism emerged from occupations in the early 18th century, thereby distinguishing an initially small number of occupations, including religion, law and medicine (Rodd 2013). Features such as training, professional development and policies point to professionalism, along with technical skills, specialist knowledge and qualifications, and meeting high standards and regulations (Moss 2006;

Oberhuemer 2005; Osgood 2006). Arguably, though not uncontested (Grieshaber & Graham 2017), such a focus enhances working conditions and the status of the professional worker (Mooney et al. 2003).

An examination of professionalism, and its infiltration into many fields, provides a landscape on which to consider the permeation of professionalism into early childhood education. A middle-class notion of professionalism positions an occupation as a central marker of modern identity (Cowman & Jackson 2005). Many occupations that have, in the recent past, been identified and constructed in terms of technical attributes, are now referred to as professions. To become a profession and/or the making of a profession is referred to as 'professionalisation'. Increasingly, professionalisation has gained momentum across traditionally female-dominated, attribute-based occupations (Rabe-Kleberg 2006). Likewise, professionalisation has entered the early childhood lexicon. In a study conducted by Bretherton (2010, p. 34) an examination of workforce development strategies with employers and employees makes a compelling link between professionalism and quality: 'higher level specialisation and professionalism among staff would permit greater workforce autonomy and the ability to exercise professional judgment and therefore produce higher quality care environments'.

Discourses of professionalism

There are multiple ideas in educational literature about what constitutes a professional, with Timperley and Alton-Lee (2008) outlining three:

1. A professional must possess a large degree of talent and skill.
2. A professional must use a body of knowledge that supports their work.
3. A professional must have the autonomy to make decisions that marry skills with knowledge to solve complex problems.

Proponents of this third conception of a professional, argue that educators need to engage in complex thinking to be effective in their jobs. These arguments are based on the idea that working with children is far more complex than any list of predetermined categories could hope to capture (Webb 2009).

Two distinct discourses, 'managerial professionalism' and 'democratic professionalism', dominate Australian education policy documents at both Commonwealth and state and territory levels (Sachs 2001; 2003). These discourses shape the work of teachers and teaching, for instance, setting 'the limits of what can be said, thought and done with respect to debates and initiatives designed to enhance the political project of teacher professionalism' (Sachs 2001, p. 151). Sachs examines *managerial professionalism*, which highlights accountability, devolution and decentralisation, and professionalism 'that gains its legitimacy through the promulgation of policies and the allocation of funds associated with those policies' (2001, p. 152). Sachs links this discussion with schools, teachers, principals, regional and central offices, not early childhood settings.

However, there is resonance with the early childhood policy landscape in Australia, which in recent years has moved towards a centralised, consistent approach to quality standards. Sachs describes *democratic professionalism*, which demystifies professional work and strengthens relationships between teachers and other people associated with the education community. A key focus is on participative decision-making, collaboration and cooperative action. This is consistent with the focus in not-for-profit, community-based early childhood settings on developing a sense of community with democracy and shared decision-making (Wannan 2005). Oberhuemer (2005) takes up the concept of democratic professionalism specifically within early childhood, noting the focus on interactions with children, working with families, centre management and leadership styles, and the underlying knowledge base. A collaborative approach where different voices within the community are listened to opens possibilities for considering professionalism and the professional early childhood educator (Rinaldi 2006).

Regulating the early childhood professional

Over the past decade, early childhood education and care (ECEC) in Australia has undergone a period of rapid regulatory and legislative change. Since 2007, new regulatory frameworks have emerged as part of an early years' reform agenda, under the umbrella of the 'education revolution' (ALP 2007). This reform agenda precipitated significant changes (including curriculum, quality standards and national law), requiring new ways for early childhood professionals to work within these different legislative and regulatory frameworks. While early childhood professionals had been required to work within legislative and regulatory frameworks for many decades prior to 2007, the shift post-2007 – with curriculum and regulatory consistency across jurisdictions – significantly shifted expectations for early childhood educators (Fenech, Sumsion & Shepherd 2010; Grieshaber & Graham 2017). This has not been an easy or comfortable transition, with Fenech, Sumsion and Shepherd (2010) promoting 'resistance-based professionalism'. Such an approach acknowledges early childhood educators as key to the provision of high-quality services, and contests 'the power of regulatory frameworks to tightly prescribe what early childhood teachers do and what quality centres should look like', while at the same time upholding ECEC as a 'specialist, complex field' (Fenech, Sumsion & Shepherd 2010, p. 101). Thus, the 'regulated early childhood professional' is required to enact agency, making decisions about how to engage with the regulatory landscape.

Increased policy demand for four-year degree qualified early childhood educators to work in prior-to-school settings has implications for the preparation of the early childhood professional. Workforce analyses suggest that for some time now policy demand for early childhood educators outstrips supply (Elliott 2016; Jackson 2020; Press, Wong & Gibson 2015; Productivity Commission 2011). A key contributor to this workforce issue is that, when consulted, pre-service teachers (PSTs), at least in Bachelor of Education (Early Childhood – birth to 8 years old) courses, report they plan *not* to work with very young children in ECEC (Thorpe et al. 2011). Moreover, empirical and anecdotal evidence suggests the majority of PSTs in the early childhood – birth to 8-year old degree, disregard working in long day care in particular (Gibson 2013;

Thorpe, Millear & Petriwskyj 2012), which is problematic because this site is where there are requirements of workforce policy.

Regulations are seen as both supporting and constraining professional work in early childhood education (Fenech 2006; Fenech, Sumsion & Goodfellow 2006; Grieshaber 2000; Novinger & Brien 2003). Research into the work of early childhood professionals in Sydney (Fenech, Sumsion & Goodfellow 2006) established links between the regulatory environment and professional practice. The study identified benefits of accreditation of ECEC settings and regulations, though at the same time, noted shortcomings, including unfulfilled intentions and unintended outcomes. The researchers raised 'the possibility that early childhood professionals may be acquiescing to the demand of regulatory bodies at the expense of their practical wisdom' (Fenech, Sumsion & Goodfellow 2006, p. 56). An early childhood professional who focuses on practical considerations and 'wise practice' (Goodfellow 2001, p. 4) works within the regulatory frameworks that are in place, though does not let them drive practice, thus identifying that regulatory frameworks can both enable and constrain the professional role.

Gendering the early childhood professional

The early childhood workforce is made up, predominantly, of women (Ailwood 2008; Jackson 2020; Moss 2006; Osgood 2012; Osgood, Francis & Archer 2006; Press 2017). This gendered nature of the workforce in early childhood is defined through both the high percentage of women who constitute the workforce and the feminised nature of the work (Osgood 2012). In sectors with a high proportion of women in the workforce, there is consistently lower pay, lower conditions and lower recognition (Whitehouse 2011). In Australia, the majority (91.1%) of the early childhood workforce are female (Department of Education and Training 2017, p. 16). Early childhood educators continue to be haunted by notions that their jobs are *women's work* that comes naturally and that any woman can do it (Ailwood 2008; Osgood 2012).

The nature of the work in early childhood is described as *feminised work*, requiring the *soft skills* (Hatcher 2000, p. 153) of care, nurturance (Ailwood 2008) and love (Page 2011). The maternalism discourse dominates the career trajectories and professional identities of people working in feminised occupations, such as early childhood (Ailwood, 2008; Bown, Sumsion & Press 2010; Rabe-Kleberg 2006). Moss (2006, p. 6) draws on the maternalism discourse to describe a category of the early childhood educator as a 'substitute mother'. This construction positions early childhood education within care and domestic labour paradigms. Elsewhere in the literature, there are calls to distinguish *professional* from *mother* (Dalli 2002). Ailwood (2008, p. 159) suggests that the discourses of 'motherhood and teacher hood' are intertwined, 'thus enabling and legitimising the place of women in the education of young children'. Rabe-Kleberg (2006, p. 2) highlights the interdependency of professionalism and maternalism and explains the complexities of these 'two social phenomena'. Her contention is that 'motherliness (and female qualities in general) can contribute to the formation of a profession' (Rabe-Kleberg 2006, p. 2). It is argued that these qualities contribute to 'the lack of symbolic value attached to the work that they [early childhood educators] undertake, and hence their public image and status' (Osgood 2010, p. 16).

Professional identities

Early childhood educators' professional identities are produced through any number of discourses. Existing studies have looked closely at some of the ways in which discourses produce early childhood educators' professional identities (*see* for example, Gibson 2013; 2015; Moss 2006; Krieg 2010; Osgood 2006; 2012; Langford 2006; Thomas 2009; Whitebook & Ryan 2011). Studies such as that by Warren (2013) link the discursive production of identities with the complexities of the nature of work in early childhood. Elsewhere, attention has also been given to discourses of gender, maternalism, care and developmentalism (Langford 2006; Moss 2006; Osgood 2012). Others, such as Colley (2006) and Page (2011), pay particular attention to discourses around care and maternalism. Other studies have focused on the ways in which pay, conditions, qualification requirements and educator preparation play some part in producing early childhood educators' professional identities (Irvine et al. 2016; Krieg 2010; Langford 2006; Whitebook & Ryan 2011).

The 'good' early childhood educator

One prominent early childhood educator identity is that of the 'good' early childhood educator. The identity of a *good* early childhood educator has been shaped in part by practices that are located in childhood texts and construct a particular way of being an early childhood educator (Langford 2006). A key part of being a good early childhood educator is the specialised knowledge of children's development (Arthur et al. 2018; Dalli et al. 2011; Follari 2015; McArdle, Gibson & Zollo 2015). At the same time, a critical part of being an early childhood educator is to engage with diversity (Langford 2006) and to actively question dominant ways or one way of thinking. This is not to say that particular knowledge is not important, though also of importance is the capacity for an early childhood educator to think critically and to think about the place of diversity in being a *good* early childhood educator. Langford (2006, p. 116) explains that underlying assumptions, in particular curriculum and pedagogy approaches, construct a particular early childhood educator as *good* and that this in turn contributes to the identity of a particular kind of educator.

The 'advocate-activist' early childhood educator

Another possible identity available to early childhood educators, which is featured in the literature is the 'advocate-activist'. This identity is a shift from the *good* early childhood educator identity and enables other possibilities of being an early childhood educator. This advocacy discourse calls for educators to 'speak on behalf of others' (Sumsion 2006, p. 3) and become active in bringing about change in the field. These changes are often about rights and may focus on children, families or educators themselves. An advocate focuses on a goal of what needs fixing and sets about making this happen. In comparison to the good educator, an activist requires educators to resist and challenge frames of reference and 'underpinning assumptions' (Sumsion 2006, p. 3). For example, an advocate for quality in early childhood settings may focus on the National Quality Standard (NQS) and the associated measures to ensure quality. An activist for quality in ECEC may look further at issues of equity, access and ethics, and in doing so, may focus on the power that shapes the quality measurement tools.

Within the *advocacy–activism* discourse, early childhood educators are positioned as *risk-takers*, willing to engage in conflict and critique. Sumsion (2006) draws on this discourse as she encourages early childhood educators to become ethically and politically aware and to take up the baton of activism. The activist identity opens different possibilities for the future and, in doing so, paves the way to challenge power that resides with some individual groups (Sachs 2003).

The 'entrepreneurial' early childhood educator

Another professional identity that appears in the literature, and is available to early childhood educators, is the 'entrepreneurial' identity (Sachs 2003). This identity positions educators within a framework of accountability and practices derived from the corporate world. The notion of 'corporatising' the educator (McWilliam 1999, p. 7) is underpinned by 'marketisation' and provides the *corporate professional* with all the regalia of an organisation that is predominantly shaped through entrepreneurship and enterprise. An *entrepreneurial identity* positions an educator as efficient, responsible and accountable (Sachs 2003). This works to produce compliance, underpinned by working in a technocratic way (MacNaughton 2005).

Social entrepreneurship with a focus on change and transformation has entered the early childhood leadership lexicon, with a call for organisations to be more socially responsive (Waniganayake et al. 2017). An early childhood professional, as a social entrepreneur, leads within frameworks of social change and social justice.

Being and becoming an early childhood professional

What early childhood professionals should 'know, do and understand'

Over the past decade, discussions about quality have been heavily framed around 'what educators should know, do and understand' (Bransford Darling-Hammond & Le Page 2005; OECD 2006). This construction of *quality* draws on two pivotal understandings of effective education. Firstly, effective educators have deep knowledge and understanding of the content, curriculum and learners that they work with; what educators should know and understand. Secondly, effective educators have refined pedagogical and professional skills; what educators should be able to do, and how they do it (Bransford Darling-Hammond & Le Page 2005). Contemporary understandings of quality have been informed by a portfolio of studies that have examined *expert* and *effective* educators and their practices (e.g. Hattie 2009; Sylva et al. 2003).

RESEARCH HIGHLIGHT

Research being undertaken by Harrison et al. (2016–20) is investigating what exemplary early childhood educators do. In the Exemplary Educators study, new technologies combined with a new approach will, for the first time, make visible the nature and complexity of educators' work (Press 2017).

It pays particular attention to the personal, professional and organisational resources that support the work of exemplary educators. The networks of professional relationships and communication in the day-to-day work of educators is key. The research uses three phases of data – time use, diary (with data collected via a smartphone app), focus groups/case studies – to generate portraits to capture the complexity of exemplary early childhood educators (Press, Wong & Harrison 2017). The three levels of data collection enable breadth and depth, capturing the individual, professional and organisational dimensions of exemplary educators' work.

By investigating the complexity of early childhood educators' work, the research is informing strategies to better attract, prepare, recognise, support and retain a professional, high-quality workforce. It is lifting educators' professional status, improving employment practices and providing evidence-informed content for pre-service education and in-service professional support.

Despite research into dimensions of effective practices for preschool-aged children, when it comes to working with very young children, what educators *should know, understand, and be able to do* is hotly debated. In Australia, the US and UK, the pendulum of policy debate swings between affirmations that very young children need highly skilled educators (ACECQA 2020a) and recommendations that substitute *motherly care* is sufficient (Productivity Commission 2014). These debates are informed by multiple political, historical, social, ethical and economic agendas (Dahlberg & Moss 2005) and involve advocates from numerous disciplinary domains who promote the need for very young children to have highly skilled educators.

A comprehensive literature review conducted by Dalli et al. (2011) highlights particular skills needed by educators for effectively working with children from birth to 3 years old. In summary, these include deep knowledge and critical understanding of: child development; creating appropriate curriculum; specialised infant and toddler pedagogies that focus on relationships and responsiveness; affective interpersonal skills for engaging with very young children, families and interdisciplinary professionals; and, skills to engage in deep critical reflection (Dalli et al. 2011). This skill set has also been reiterated by Recchia (2015) and Recchia and Shin (2016) in the US.

In Australia, the Australian Professional Standards for Teachers (APST) (Australian Institute for Teaching and School Leadership [AITSL] 2011) and Qualification assessment guidelines for organisation applicants (ECEC Qualification Guidelines) (ACECQA 2020b) are relevant for consideration. Briefly, the APST comprise seven standards:

1. Know students and how they learn
2. Know the content and how to teach it
3. Plan for and implement effective teaching and learning
4. Create and maintain supportive and safe environments
5. Assess, provide feedback and report on student learning
6. Engage in professional learning
7. Engage professionally with colleagues, parents/carers and the community. (AITSL 2011)

Critiques of the APST have drawn attention to the school-centric language, and its marginalisation of educators who work with very young children (McArdle, Gibson & Zollo 2015; The SiMERR National Research Centre 2012). The Australian Children's Education and Care Quality Authority (ACECQA, 2014) says that the ECEC Qualification Guidelines differ in intent from the APST in that they focus on program content, or input, rather than graduate performance standards, or output. Briefly, the ECEC Qualification Guidelines articulate six curriculum specifications for early childhood education training program inclusion:

1. Child development and care
2. Teaching pedagogies
3. Education and curriculum studies
4. Family and community contexts
5. History and philosophy of early childhood
6. Early childhood professional practice. (ACECQA 2020b)

Significantly, there is also explicit attention directed towards play-based pedagogies, guiding young learners, advocacy and professional identity. Early childhood training programs cannot be accredited if they do not demonstrate that they meet these curriculum specifications. The complexity of articulating quality and being an early childhood professional, in terms of the *what* and *how* of their work with young children, remains ever evolving and challenging (Ingvarson & Rowe 2007). Moreover, there are current gaps in research about what educators should know, do and understand, particularly when it comes to working with very young children (Ryan & Gibson 2016; White & Dalli 2016). These gaps require focused research attention to enable deeper understandings about how to best prepare educators for their work.

Contextually specific expectations for early childhood professionals

Work in the early childhood field, as defined by the Organisation for Economic Co-operation and Development (OECD 2006), focuses on children from birth to 8 years old. Working with this age-span requires specialised knowledge, understandings, dispositions and pedagogical skills that take into account contextually specific expectations for working with young children. Unlike primary school teachers who predominantly teach in a primary school, early childhood educators potentially work in a range of different settings with diverse curriculum expectations. Noteworthy, there are a number of degree models in Australia that qualify early childhood educators. While the origins of early childhood educator preparation focused on the OECD definition of early childhood, with early childhood birth to 8 years of age degree qualifications, models include a number of variations; with four-year undergraduate and two-year postgraduate degree programs providing the majority of course offerings.

Several contextually specific factors particular to early childhood are discussed in the literature: setting diversity, curriculum expectations, working with families, and working with very young learners. These factors are significant to consider because they contribute to understanding the expectations of early childhood professionals. Working with very young children requires early childhood educators to have deep understandings of the 'multiple languages' (Vecchi 2010, p. 160) that children use to articulate their thinking. Early childhood educators are expected to understand children's diverse ways of communicating their developing theories and ideas (DEEWR 2009).

Conclusion

The teaching workforce is Australia's largest professional body (Mitchell Institute for Health and Education Policy 2015). For early childhood professionals, gaining recognition as members of this group is imperative but difficult. Dissonance and tension among regulatory entanglements, economic agendas, historical constructions of school-based teachers and marginalisation of very young children and those who work with them, means that the membership and recognition that early childhood professionals require is fraught with barriers. Every early childhood educator emerges from a range of qualification types (e.g. birth to 5 years, 5 to 8 years, birth to 12 years). There is growing critique of early childhood educator preparation with a birth to 12 focus, with these courses preparing primary school teachers, not early childhood educators (Boyd & Newman 2019). Nonetheless in recent years, partly through the early years reform agenda, early childhood educators in Australia have been undergoing a professional metamorphosis.

The significance of research for sustaining and moving a profession forward is highlighted in the influential international report *Teachers matter: attracting, developing and retaining effective teachers* (OECD 2005). The imperative to continue developing a rich portfolio of rigorous and authentic evidence-informed research is deemed to be critical for advancing professionalism (Cochran-Smith & Zeichner 2005). The current body of research on professionalism contributes important understandings concerning the early childhood professional and serves as foregrounding for further inquiry, understandings and applications of what it means to be an early childhood professional.

RESEARCH INTO PRACTICE

While considering the following questions, make notes about how you would both enact and re-consider professionalism in early childhood.

How can you:
- promote professionalism, confidentiality and ethical conduct?
- use critical reflection to challenge beliefs?
- promote the personal and collective strengths of an early childhood team?
- share the successes of an early childhood team with families?
- provide opportunities for educators, coordinators and other staff to have conversation and discussions to further develop their skills, or to improve professional practice and relationships?

References

Ailwood, J 2008, 'Mothers, teachers, maternalism and early childhood education and care: some historical connections', *Contemporary Issues in Early Childhood*, vol. 8, no. 2, pp. 157–65.

Arthur, L, Beecher, B, Death, E, Dockett, S & Farmer, S 2018, *Programming and planning in early childhood settings*, 6th edn, Cengage, Melbourne.

Australian Children's Education & Care Quality Authority (ACECQA) 2020a, *Qualification assessment information and guidelines for organisation applicants*, ACECQA, Sydney. Retrieved from https://www.acecqa.gov.au/qualifications/assessment/approval/early-childhood

Australian Children's Education & Care Quality Authority (ACECQA) 2020b, *Qualification assessment guidelines for organisation applicants*, Attachment 1: Early childhood teacher or equivalent, ACECQA, Sydney. Retrieved from https://www.acecqa.gov.au

Australian Labor Party (ALP) 2007, *The Australian economy needs an education revolution: new directions on the critical link between long term prosperity, productivity growth and human capital investment*, ALP, Canberra.

Bown, K, Sumsion, J & Press, F 2009, 'Influence on politicians' decision making for early childhood education care policy: what do we know? What don't we know?', *Contemporary Issues in Early Childhood*, vol. 10, no. 3, pp. 194–217, doi:10.2304/ciec.2009.10.3.194.

Boyd, W & Newman, L 2019, 'Primary + Early Childhood = chalk and cheese? Tensions in undertaking an early childhood/primary education degree', *Australasian Journal of Early Childhood*, vol. 44, no. 1, pp. 19–31, doi:10.1177/1836939119841456.

Bransford, J, Darling-Hammond, L & Le Page, P 2005, 'Introduction', in L Darling-Hammond & J Bransford (eds), *Preparing teachers for a changing world: what teachers should learn and be able to do*, Jossey-Bass, San Francisco, pp. 1–39.

Bretherton, T 2010, *Developing the childcare workforce: understanding 'fight' or 'flight' amongst workers*, Workplace Research Centre, University of Sydney. Retrieved from https://www.ncver.edu.au/__data/assets/file/0019/2872/2261.pdf

Cochran-Smith, M & Zeichner, K 2005, 'Executive summary: the report of the AERA panel on research and teacher education', in M Cochran-Smith & K Zeichner (eds), *Studying teacher education: the report of the AERA panel on research and teacher education*, Lawrence Erlbaum Associates, Mahwah, NJ, pp. 1–36.

Colley, H 2006, 'Learning to labour with feeling: class, gender and emotion in child care education and training', *Contemporary Issues in Early Childhood*, vol. 7, no. 1, pp. 15–29.

Cowman, K & Jackson, LA 2005, 'Middle-class women and professional identity', *Women's History Review*, vol. 14, no. 2, pp. 165–80.

Dahlberg, G & Moss, P 2005, *Ethics and politics in early childhood education*, Routledge Falmer, Oxon.

Dalli, C 2002, 'Constructing identities: being a "mother" and being a "teacher" during the experience of starting childcare', *European Early Childhood Education Research Journal*, vol. 10, no. 2, pp. 85–101.

Dalli, C, White, EJ, Rockel, J, Duhn, I, Buchanan, E, Ganly, S & Wang, B 2011, *Quality early childhood education for under-two-year-olds: what should it look like? A literature review*, Ministry of Education, Auckland.

Department of Education, Employment and Workplace Relations (DEEWR) 2009, *Belonging, being and becoming: the early years learning framework for Australia*, Commonwealth of Australia, Canberra. Retrieved from https://docs.education.gov.au/node/2632

Department of Education and Training 2017, *2016 early childhood education and care national workforce census*, The Social Research Centre, Melbourne.

Education Services Australia 2011, *Australian professional standards for teachers*. Retrieved from http://www.aitsl.edu.au/docs/default-source/apst-resources/australian_professional_standard_for_teachers_final.pdf

Elliott, A 2016, 'Looking back: looking forward: changing contexts for early childhood education', *Historical Perspectives on Education*, monograph no. 10, Australian National Museum of Education, Canberra.

Fenech, M 2006, 'The impact of regulatory environments on early childhood professional practice and job satisfaction: a review of conflicting discourses', *Australian Journal of Early Childhood*, vol. 31, no. 2, pp. 49–57.

Fenech, M, Sumsion, J & Goodfellow, J 2006, 'The regulatory environment in long day care: a "double edged sword" for early childhood professional practice', *Australian Journal of Early Childhood*, vol. 31, no. 3, pp. 49–58.

Fenech, M, Sumsion, J & Shepherd, W 2010, 'Promoting early childhood teacher professionalism in the Australian context: the place of resistance', *Contemporary Issues in Early Childhood*, vol. 11, no. 1, pp. 89–105.

Follari, L 2015, *Foundations and best practices in early childhood education: history, theories, and approaches to learning*, 3rd edn, Pearson, New Jersey.

Gibson, M 2013, '"I want to educate school age children": producing early childhood teacher professional identities', *Contemporary Issues in Early Childhood*, vol. 14, no. 2, pp. 127–37.

Gibson, M 2015, '"Heroic victims": discursive constructions of early childhood teacher professional identities', *Journal of Early Childhood Teacher Education*, special issue: The future of early childhood teacher education in a time of changing policy, standards and programming, vol. 26, no. 2, pp. 42–155.

Goodfellow, J 2001, 'Wise practice: the need to move beyond best practice in early childhood education', *Australian Journal of Early Childhood*, vol. 26, no. 3, pp. 1–6.

Grieshaber, S 2000, 'Regulating the early childhood field', *Australian Journal of Early Childhood*, vol. 25, no. 2, pp. 1–6.

Grieshaber, S & Graham, LJ 2017, 'Equity and educators enacting the Australian early years learning framework', *Critical Studies in Education*, vol. 58, no. 1, 89–103, doi:10.1080/17508487.2015.1126328.

Harrison, LJ, Wong, S, Gibson, M, Cumming, T, Press, F & Ryan, S 2016–20, *Exemplary early childhood educators at work: a multi-level investigation*, Australian Research Council, linkage grant LP160100532.

Hatcher, C 2000, 'Practices of the heart: the art of being a good listener', in C O'Farrell, D Meadmore, E McWilliam & C Symns (eds), *Taught bodies*, Peter Lang, New York, pp. 121–35.

Hattie, J 2009, *Visible learning: a synthesis of over 800 meta-analyses relating to achievement*, Routledge, Oxon.

Ingvarson, L & Rowe, K 2007, *Conceptualising and evaluating teacher quality: substantive and methodological issues*. Retrieved from http://research.acer.edu.au/learning_processes/8

Irvine, S, Thorpe, K, McDonald, P, Lunn, J & Sumsion, J 2016, *Money, love and identity: initial findings from the National ECEC workforce study. Summary report from the national ECEC workforce development policy workshop*, Queensland University of Technology, Brisbane.

Jackson, J 2020, 'Every educator matters: evidence for a new early childhood workforce strategy for Australia', paper presented at the Mitchell Institute Early Childhood Workforce Development Research-to-Policy Roundtable, Macquarie University, Sydney.

Krieg, S 2010, 'The professional knowledge that counts in Australian contemporary early childhood teacher education', *Contemporary Issues in Early Childhood*, vol. 11. No. 2, pp. 144–55, doi:10.2304/ciec.2010.11.2.144.

Langford, R 2006, 'Discourses of the good early childhood educator in professional training: reproducing marginality or working toward social change', *International Journal of Educational Policy, Research & Practice: Reconceptualizing Childhood Studies*, vol. 7, pp. 115–25.

MacNaughton, G 2005, *Doing Foucault in early childhood studies: applying poststructural ideas*, Routledge, Oxon.

McArdle, F, Gibson, M & Zollo, L 2015, *Being an early childhood educator: bringing theory and practice together*, Allen & Unwin, Sydney.

McWilliam, E 1999, *Pedagogical pleasures*, Peter Lang, New York.

Mitchell Institute for Health and Education Policy 2015, '*A blueprint for initial teacher education and teacher workforce data*, Victoria University, Melbourne.

Moss, P 2006, 'Structures, understandings and discourses: possibilities for re-visioning the early childhood worker', *Contemporary Issues in Early Childhood*, vol. 7, no. 1, pp. 30–41.

Mooney, A, Moss, P, Cameron, C, Candappa, M, McQuail, S & Petrie, P 2003, *Early years and childcare international evidence project*, Thomas Coram Research Unit, Institute of Education, University of London.

Novinger, S & Brien, L 2003, 'Beyond "boring, meaningless shit" in the academy: early childhood teacher educators under the regulatory gaze', *Contemporary Issues in Early Childhood*, vol. 4, no. 1, pp. 3–31.

Oberhuemer, P 2005, 'Conceptualising the early childhood pedagogue: policy approaches and issues of professionalism', *European Early Childhood Education Research Journal*, vol. 13, no. 1, pp. 5–16.

Organisation for Economic Co-operation and Development (OECD) 2005, *Teachers matter: attracting, developing and retaining effective teachers*, OECD, Paris. Retrieved from https://www.oecd.org/edu/school/34990905.pdf

Organisation for Economic Co-operation and Development (OECD) 2006, *Starting strong II: early childhood education and care policy*, OECD, Paris.

Osgood, J 2006, 'Deconstructing professionalism in early childhood education: resisting the regulatory gaze', *Contemporary Issues in Early Childhood*, vol. 7, no. 1, pp. 5–14.

Osgood, J 2010, 'Narrative methods in the nursery: (re)- considering claims to give voice through processes of decision making', *Reconceptualizing Educational Research Methodology*, vol. 1, no. 1, pp. 14–28.

Osgood, J 2012, *Narratives from the nursery: negotiating professional identities in early childhood*, Routledge, Oxon.

Osgood, J, Francis, B & Archer, L 2006, 'Gendered identities and work placement: why don't boys care', *Journal of Education Policy*, vol. 21, no. 3, pp. 305–21.

Page, J 2011, 'Do mothers want professional carers to love their babies?', *Journal of Early Childhood Research*, vol. 9, no. 3, pp. 310–23.

Press, F 2017, 'Understanding and valuing the work of early childhood educators', *Bedrock*, vol. 22, no. 1, pp. 8–9.

Press, F, Wong, S & Gibson, M 2015, 'What can qualitative research contribute to work and family policy?', *Journal of Family Studies*, special issue: What can qualitative research contribute to work and family policy?, vol. 21, no. 1, pp. 87–100.

Press, F, Wong, S, Harrison, L & Gibson, M 2017, 'Understanding what great early childhood educators do: new Australian research', *Cascades*, research edition, pp. 15–16.

Productivity Commission 2011, *Early childhood development workforce: productivity Commission research report*, Australian Government, Canberra.

Productivity Commission 2014, *Childcare and early childhood learning*, Productivity Commission inquiry report, vol. 73, Australian Government, Canberra.

Rabe-Kleberg, U 2006, 'Beyond the limits of female practice: rethinking professionalisation processes in traditionally female occupations', paper presented at the Early Years Seminar Series, Queensland University of Technology, Brisbane.

Recchia, S 2015, 'Preparing teachers for infant care and education, in L Couse & S Recchia (eds), *Handbook of early childhood teacher education*, pp. 89–103, Routledge, New York.

Recchia, S & Shin, M 2016, 'From the guest editors: preparing early childhood teachers for infant care and education', *Journal of Early Childhood Teacher Education*, vol. 37, no. 4, pp. 261–63, doi:10.1080/10901027.2016.1242051.

Rinaldi, C 2006, *In dialogue with Reggio Emilia: listening, researching and learning*, Routledge Falmer, Oxon.

Rodd, J 2013, *Leadership in early childhood: the pathway to professionalism*, 4th edn, Allen & Unwin, Crows Nest.

Ryan, S & Gibson, M 2016, 'Preservice early childhood teacher education', in L Couse & S Recchia (eds), *Handbook of early childhood teacher education*, pp. 195–208, Routledge New York.

Sachs, J 2001, 'Teacher professional identity: competing discourses, competing outcomes', *Journal of Educational Policy*, vol. 16, no. 2, pp. 149–61.

Sachs, J 2003, *The activist teaching profession*, Open University Press, Buckingham.

Sumsion, J 2006, 'From Whitlam to economic rationalism and beyond: a conceptual framework for political activism in children's services', *Australian Journal of Early Childhood*, vol. 31, no. 1, pp. 1–9.

Sylva, K, Melhuish, E, Sammons, P, Siraj-Blatchford, I & Taggart, B 2003, *The effective provision of pre-school education (EPPE) project: findings from the pre-school period*, research brief no. RBX 15-03, Department for Education and Skills, London.

The SiMERR National Research Centre 2012, *Consultation on the application of the Australian professional standards for teachers (APST) to teachers working in early childhood education and care services: report to AITSL/ACECQA*, SiMERR, Armidale. Retrieved from http://www.aitsl.edu.au

Thorpe, K, Boyd, W, Ailwood, J & Brownlee, J 2011, 'Who wants to work in child care? Preservice early childhood teachers' consideration of work in the childcare sector', *Australasian Journal of Early Childhood*, vol. 36, no. 1, pp. 85–94.

Thorpe, K, Millear, P & Petriwskyj, A 2012, 'Can a childcare practicum encourage degree qualified staff to enter the childcare workforce?', *Contemporary Issues in Early Childhood*, vol. 13, no. 4, pp. 317–27, doi:10.2304/ciec.2012.13.4.317.

Timperley, H & Alton-Lee, A 2008, 'Reframing teacher professional learning: an alternative policy approach to strengthening valued outcomes for diverse learners', *Review of Research in Education*, vol. 32, no. 1, pp. 328–69, doi:10.3102/0091732X07308968.

Vecchi, V 2010, *Art and creativity in Reggio Emilia: exploring the role and potential of ateliers in early childhood education*, Routledge, Oxon.

Waniganayake, M, Cheeseman, S, Fenech, M, Hadley, F & Shepherd, W 2017, *Leadership: contexts and complexities in early childhood education*, 2nd edn, Oxford University Press, Melbourne.

Wannan, L 2005, 'A cautionary tale from Australia', *Canadian Council of Social Development*, briefing session note. Retrieved from http://www.ccsd.ca

Webb, T 2009, *Teacher assemblage*, Sense Publishers, Rotterdam.

White, E & Dalli, C 2016, 'Policy and pedagogy for birth-to-three year olds', in E J White & C Dalli (eds), *Policy and pedagogy for under three-year-olds: cross-disciplinary insights and innovations*, Springer, Singapore, pp. 1–14.

Whitebook, M & Ryan, S 2011, *Degrees in context: asking the right questions about preparing skilled and effective teachers of young children*, preschool policy brief, no. 22, National Institute for Early Education Research with the Center for the Study of Child Care Employment, Berkeley, pp. 1–16. Retrieved from https://cscce.berkeley.edu/files/2011/DegreesinContext_2011.pdf

Whitehouse, G 2011, 'Recent trends in pay equity: beyond the aggregate statistics', *Journal of Industrial Relations*, vol. 43, no. 1, pp. 66–78.

CHAPTER 4

Building inclusive education communities

Kathy Cologon

DOI: https://doi.org/10.37517/978-1-74286-555-3_4
Macquarie University

LINKS TO NATIONAL QUALITY STANDARD

Quality Area 6: Collaborative partnerships with families and communities
- Standard 6.2: Collaborative partnerships – collaborative partnerships enhance children's inclusion, learning and wellbeing.
- Element 6.2.2: Access and participation – effective partnerships support children's access, inclusion and participation in the program.

LINKS TO EARLY YEARS LEARNING FRAMEWORK

Learning Outcome 1: Children have a strong sense of identity
- Children develop knowledgeable and confident self-identities.

Learning Outcome 2: Children are connected with and contribute to their world
- Children develop a sense of belonging to groups and communities and an understanding of the reciprocal rights and responsibilities necessary for active community participation.
- Children respond to diversity with respect.
- Children become aware of fairness.

Introduction

A key goal identified within the Early Years Learning Framework for Australia (EYLF) is that through early childhood education and care (ECEC) 'all young Australians become successful learners; confident and creative individuals; and active and informed citizens' (DEEWR 2009, p. 5). The notion of 'all young Australians' can easily slip past unnoticed but is actually a fundamental focus. Of course, 'all young Australians' includes children across the full breadth of human diversity. Meeting this goal therefore requires a clear and urgent focus on genuine inclusion. Consequently, a primary focus of ECEC is a necessarily conscious, open and warm embracing of all aspects of human diversity and working towards building inclusive communities. That is, communities within which we all belong – in all our diversities – as equally valued members, drawing together diverse experiences, beliefs and 'ways of knowing' (DEEWR 2009, p. 14). At the core of this are essential considerations of belonging, respect and dignity; including confident and positive self and community identities.

Civil rights activist, Audre Lorde (1994), famously wrote, 'It is not our differences that divide us. It is our inability to recognise, accept and celebrate those differences'. In keeping with Lorde's wisdom, from the outset one important issue to address in this chapter is the problem of misunderstanding inclusion as being about assimilation, rather than recognising that inclusion is about diversity. By this I mean that building an inclusive community does not mean pretending that everyone is, can be, or should be, *the same*. Nor is it about pretending that children *don't notice difference*. Despite the common tendency for adults to suggest otherwise, children *do* notice difference. However, children do not necessarily think that there is anything negative about difference.

Noticing human diversity is natural. Sometimes children may surprise us with which particular differences they notice between people, but the fact that children do notice difference should be expected and supported. Problems arise only when negative connotations become attached to difference. Indeed, children are not born prejudiced, but from a very young age they are enculturated into the prejudices of the communities in which they live (Connolly, Smith & Kelly 2002; Mevawalla 2020; Atkinson & Srinivasan 2014; Watson 2018). In fact, research shows that as humans our understandings of diversity develop at a very young age (Keenan, Connolly & Stevenson 2015; Watson 2018). Young children's dialogue and behaviours demonstrate the internalisation of enculturated understandings as they identify some of us as tragic or lesser *others* (Connolly, Smith & Kelly 2002; Smith, Alexander & D'Souza Juma 2014; Watson 2018). Additionally, as Rietveld (2010, p. 27) notes, children who are excluded are:

> … likely to internalise the messages that they are inferior, incompetent and undesirable peer group members, which in turn is likely to negatively impact on their motivation to seek inclusion, thus interfering with their learning of culturally valued skills.

While this reveals the negative potential of prejudiced enculturation for children's dignity and perceptions of themselves and others, it also demonstrates the importance of and possibilities for creating opportunities for young children to recognise and appreciate diversity (Lalvani & Bacon 2019). Importantly, research shows that when provided with such opportunities, young children can both understand and seek to challenge and change social oppression (Silva & Langhout 2011; Souto-Manning 2009). This highlights the considerable importance of critically reflecting on the many evident and hidden ways in which we intentionally and, more often, unintentionally teach children what is valuable and what is *lesser* in who and how we are as people. This also underlines the importance of building inclusive communities from the earliest childhood years onwards.

In working towards inclusion, rather than mistakenly thinking that difference is the problem, we need to actively recognise and embrace all aspects of human diversity. We need to celebrate these diversities as a wonderful aspect of our education communities, and plan from the outset for the reality of this diversity within the groups of people who can and should co-exist, on an equal basis, within every education community.

What is an inclusive education community?

'Inclusive education' is about everyone learning, growing and flourishing – together – in all our diversities. 'Inclusive education' involves creating pedagogical opportunities and environments that intentionally set out to ensure genuine and valued full participation of all of us. To create a community, everyone needs to have the opportunity to belong. Inclusive education involves embracing human diversity and welcoming everyone as equally valued members of the education community. This requires engaging respectfully, recognising human dignity and promoting what Jacobson (2009) refers to as social dignity. Inclusive education is also one key part of working towards an inclusive society for everyone. However, there are a lot of things that are called inclusion and inclusive education that are not at all inclusive – instead they are actually examples of exclusion. Consequently, in order to address the question of what inclusive education is, we also need to understand what inclusive education is *not*.

There are many practices of segregation, exclusion and integration that are often presented as 'inclusion'. This misappropriation of the term forms a serious barrier to inclusion (Allan 2010; Baglieri et al. 2011; Lalvani 2013). To be clear, segregation, exclusion, and integration are *never* inclusion (UN General Assembly 2016). This is easiest to understand in relation to 'segregation'. Segregation occurs when a group of children are separated on the basis of one particular aspect of human diversity. For example, when children who experience disability are segregated into a *special* group, class, centre or school (UN General Assembly 2016).

Exclusion from education occurs most obviously when a child is prevented from attending a particular education setting for some or all of the time. This is what is referred to as 'macro-exclusion'. Another form of exclusion that is not necessarily always as obvious and is therefore much less often recognised is 'micro-exclusion' (D'Alessio 2011). Micro-exclusion occurs when a child is enrolled within a mainstream setting, that claims to be inclusive, but where the child is actually excluded some or all of the time through the environment, pedagogy and attitudes in practice. Micro-exclusion often occurs when what is intended as support for inclusion inadvertently excludes a child (Cologon 2014). Placement in a separate part of the classroom for some or all of the time, only permitting partial attendance, inauthentic or absent opportunities to genuinely participate, and viewing a child as a burden are all examples of micro-exclusion. Micro-exclusion occurs:

> ... when children are given separate activities (often with different staff) that are not connected with what the rest of the group is doing, or when they are removed from the class for particular lessons. Micro-exclusion also occurs when someone is not fully included as a valued member of the classroom community (often as a consequence of other forms of micro-exclusion) ... micro-exclusion commonly occurs when integration is misunderstood as inclusion. (Cologon & D'Alessio 2015, p. 185)

'Integration' is where children may be physically located in the same place for some or all of the time, but not actually included (UN General Assembly 2016). Integration is generally a practice of assimilation where the child is expected to change to fit into the setting or else be excluded (Cologon 2019). Assimilation being the idea that, rather than embracing diversity, people can only be *included* if they can be *the same enough*, or learn to fit within existing structures, systems and practices. Such approaches violate dignity and are never inclusive. If our efforts are working towards assimilation, then we are working counter to inclusion. So, we can see this as a red flag – if we are trying to change the child we need to start asking some important questions about what we are doing, why and for whom.

While segregation and macro-exclusion are sometimes confused for or misappropriated as inclusion, micro-exclusion and integration are very commonly misunderstood as inclusion (Cologon 2014; 2019). To unpack this common misunderstanding a little further, while the collocation of children – across all forms of diversity – in the same ECEC settings is one of the essential first steps towards inclusion, inclusion requires more than collocation. Inclusion involves genuine valuing and full participation of every child. It is about transforming the education setting to be inclusive, rather than about changing the child to fit into exclusionary settings and systems (Slee 2018). It involves *all* children – across the full breadth of diversity – belonging and engaging in education and all aspects of life *together*. Inclusion involves acknowledging and embracing the fact that we are all unique individuals and working to make our pedagogy and environments fit to the diversity of all of us as humans (Cologon 2019).

Importantly, inclusive education is not charity or a privilege, it is not optional or an additional extra, but rather inclusion is an essential component of a functioning society and a fundamental human right for *all* (D'Alessio 2011; Degener 2016; Kliewer 1998). Inclusion is not about granting special favours, nor about changing someone to fit the elusive norm in order to be granted access to the community. Rather, it is about recognising our shared humanity and moving beyond false notions of entitlement towards building communities that are inclusive of all of us – communities within which we can all genuinely belong.

Inclusive education involves genuine valuing and full participation of all of us. There is no *them* and *us* in inclusion, only an *us* to which we all belong (Cologon 2019). Inclusion involves all of us engaging in education and all aspects of life *together* – in all our diversities.

For many, the term 'inclusion' brings to mind minority groups and people who experience disability in particular, but, really, inclusion is about all of us. In an education setting this means that inclusive education is about every person in that community – every child and every adult, including the students, teachers and other staff, families and community members (Cologon 2014). However, it is also the case that some of us are more likely to be *excluded* than others of us. This means that while always clearly recognising that inclusion is about everyone, we also need to pay very close attention to making sure that there are no individuals or groups of people who are excluded, being forced to the margins, or at risk of being excluded.

Arenas of exclusion change over time and across contexts. However, it is the case that people who experience disability are the largest minority group in the world (WHO 2011) and the most likely to be excluded in Australia (Hobson 2010) and internationally (UNESCO Institute for Statistics & UNICEF 2015). Even within explicit efforts towards anti-bias education, people who experience disability are often seemingly forgotten or ignored (Lalvani & Bacon 2019). While considerable efforts continue to be made to address these issues, ableist discrimination, racism, classism and heteronormativity continue to be pressing and present issues, alongside a myriad of intersectional realities of oppression for so many people (Karmiris 2019). Bringing about inclusion requires addressing all aspects of the prejudice, bias and exclusion that form this oppression.

From time to time, arguments crop up that inclusion 'doesn't work for some people' – and often this is in relation to people who have been ascribed particular labels, or people who communicate through behaviours that others find challenging. However, this is a misunderstanding based on notions of assimilation, integration and exclusion. By contrast, 'there is no "type" of student "eligible" (nor "ineligible") for inclusion – inclusion is about and for *all of us*' (Cologon 2019, p. 17) and when it is actually inclusion, not integration or assimilation misrepresented as inclusion, it really does benefit everyone. In fact, this is so much the case that it has become a common saying that 'if inclusion isn't working, it isn't inclusion'. Indeed, it is more than a decade now since Dempsey (2008 p. 59) concluded that '(t)he argument over whether inclusion works is ended. Inclusion does work', noting that the key is to ensure that the pedagogical and environmental conditions are in place to facilitate such inclusion.

Why is inclusive education important?

Having considered what inclusive education is – and is not – I would like to return now to the earlier consideration in this chapter of why inclusion is important. There are both practical and philosophical reasons for the importance of inclusive education.

As Loreman (2014, p. 460) writes: 'Inclusive education can now be justified as an approach supported philosophically, in international declarations, and empirically through research on its efficacy'.

We now know from more than six decades of research evidence that inclusive education has benefits for everyone (Cologon 2019; Hehir et al. 2016). The research evidence demonstrates that inclusive education involves higher quality education for all children with associated academic and social benefits.

In a systematic review of the research evidence in 2016, Harvard academic Thomas Hehir and his colleagues concluded 'there is clear and consistent evidence that inclusive educational settings can confer substantial short- and long-term benefits' (Hehir et al. 2016, p. 2). Research provides evidence that inclusive education enhances learning opportunities, creates pedagogical experiences that are more responsive to the diversity of children, supports positive communication and behaviour development, facilitates greater valuing of and responsiveness to human diversity, enables a sense of belonging and a positive sense of self and self-worth and supports the development of increased flexibility and adaptability (e.g. Ainscow & Cesar 2006; Dessemontet & Bless 2013; Farrell et al. 2007; Finke, McNaughton & Drager 2009; Hehir et al. 2016; Purdue, Ballard & MacArthur 2001; Rouse & Florian 2006; Szumski, Smogorzewska & Karwowski 2017).

Research also provides evidence that although teachers may have concerns or fears about inclusive education, once they begin to engage with inclusion and gain some experience as inclusive educators they not only feel positive about inclusive education, they also become better teachers for all children, including engaging with their students more frequently, more deeply and at higher levels (Cologon 2012; Hehir & Katzman 2012; Jordan & Stanovich 2001; Jordan, Glenn & McGhie-Richmond 2010). Teachers have been found to develop positive attitudes towards inclusive education and build confidence in their ability to be inclusive through experience and support (e.g. Chiner & Cardona 2013; Cologon 2012; Giangreco et al. 1993; Jordan & Stanovich 2001; Jordan, Glenn & McGhie-Richmond 2010; Purdue, Ballard & MacArthur 2001). Teachers report increased personal satisfaction and professional growth through the experience of inclusive education (Finke, McNaughton & Drager 2009; Giangreco et al. 1993).

Unsurprisingly then, inclusive education has also been explicitly recognised as a fundamental human right for every person, from early childhood onwards (UN General Assembly 2016). This has important and widespread implications, including the fact that Australia (among many nation states) is obliged under international law to enact policy and legislation to ensure that every Australian does have genuine access to a fully inclusive education, from early childhood onwards. This involves putting into place 'appropriate legislative, administrative, budgetary, judicial, promotional, and other measures toward the full realization of the right' (Jonsson 2007, p. 118).

Inclusion is also a matter of dignity. In theorising dignity, Jacobson (2009) identifies two different aspects of dignity, human dignity and social dignity. Both of these conceptualisations of dignity are important in relation to inclusive education.

Jacobson (2009) identifies human dignity as a universal, undeniable, irrevocable and fundamental aspect of what it is to be human. It follows, therefore, that to seek to deny human dignity is in fact to dehumanise – to deny a person's humanity. In recognising that we are all human we are also recognising human dignity and human rights of every person.

So, while human dignity is an essential part of what it is to be human, and at the core of the upholding of all human rights, Jacobson (2009) identifies social dignity as being produced through interactions and relationships between individuals, groups and societies. This means that social dignity can be supported and promoted, or it can be denied or violated (Jacobson 2009). Social dignity involves both 'dignity-of-self' (i.e. a sense of self-respect and self-worth) and 'dignity-in-relation' (perceived value by others as demonstrated through individual and collective behaviours). Therefore, what it is to have social dignity is wrapped up in what it is to be a valued person within a particular context (Jacobson 2009). Social dignity encompasses what it is to belong, to be included, or what it is to be excluded within any given community. Consequently, genuine inclusion becomes essential to a person's dignity.

To unpack this a little further, let's consider the matter of participation. What it is to participate is relational and participation occurs through endeavours towards, and realisations of, belonging (Vandenbussche & De Schauwer 2018). As stated in the EYLF, 'Experiencing belonging – knowing where and with whom you belong – is integral to human existence' (DEEWR 2009, p. 7). Belonging and inclusion are inseparable. Belonging gives us identity and upholds social dignity. This leads us to important considerations regarding the implications for belonging or not belonging within ECEC communities.

Building inclusive education communities

'Inclusive education is everybody's business and is a process where we consider the complex ways in which barriers prevent students accessing, authentically participating and succeeding in education' (Slee 2011, p. 84).

Australian educators have identified that respecting diversity, taking a collaborative approach, appreciating families and communities, and recognising every child as a valuable and rightful participant in every education setting are essential underpinnings to building an inclusive education community (Cologon 2010; Mackenzie, Cologon & Fenech 2016; Wright 2017). However, enacting these values requires identifying and addressing the many barriers to inclusion that exist within and beyond ECEC settings.

There are a number of key issues that early childhood educators need to consider in working towards inclusive education in ECEC. First, it is essential to carefully consider and develop a clear understanding of what inclusion actually is and to recognise and debunk misappropriations of inclusion. As addressed earlier in this chapter, inclusion involves more than just presence. Inclusion is not about assimilation and we need to be open to asking ourselves the hard questions about the purposes of what we are doing to make sure that we are never accidentally working towards assimilation instead of inclusion. Inclusion requires ongoing commitment and engagement in critical reflection and action. Some important considerations include making sure that:

- all children are welcome, valued and the contribution they make is recognised
- all experiences are set up in order to facilitate the participation, dignity and belonging of every child
- all necessary supports for inclusion are provided and embedded within everyday practices
- if additional staff are employed to facilitate inclusion then they work inclusively
- there are no segregated (separate) groups, units, classes, curriculums or settings
- all children are involved in all aspects of learning
- all children are supported to flourish.

In provisioning the spaces within which we engage with children and families, we also need to ensure that there are positive representations of human diversity present within the environments and the materials we use. For example, within the books, images and other media, and all play and other materials that include representation of people (Cologon 2013; Ellis 2015; Favazza et al. 2017; Martinez-Bello & Martinez-Bello 2016; Salvador 2017).

Children's participation is essential to belonging, dignity and inclusion. However, there are also many other layers that we need to engage with that promote and support, or deny and violate, dignity, belonging and inclusion. Returning to the considerations of noticing *difference* from earlier in this chapter, when we silence children when they notice and want to discuss difference we need to consider what we are actually doing. As adults we may feel uncomfortable, but we need to stop and ask ourselves why we feel this way. We need to address this dysconsciousness about diversity (Broderick & Lalvani 2017). We also need to recognise what we might be unintentionally teaching children through our dysconsciousness. If we do not provide opportunities for children to openly engage with matters of diversity, then we are teaching children that diversity is taboo. From this, we (probably unintentionally) contribute to enculturating children into existing prejudices and oppressions (Watson 2018). Instead we need to welcome difference, openly engage with discussions around all our differences, and create spaces for children to critique and challenge the oppressions that are present in the world around us.

Sometimes engaging in these processes of transformation results in considerable conflict. It is important to think carefully about how we might reconcile any tensions in our own understandings and practices, as well as how we might work collaboratively with colleagues, children and families to address any misunderstandings, tensions or disagreements that may arise about inclusion. It is also important to think about what we might be able to do immediately within an ECEC setting and what we might need to work on gradually over time.

RESEARCH HIGHLIGHT

Elizabeth Jackson-Barrett and Libby Lee-Hammond (2018) conducted a research project in which they engaged young Aboriginal and non-Aboriginal children and their teachers in On Country Learning, a project about the 'Canning River Kids', building on the idea of the forest schools from which *bush kindy* developed.

A respected Elder from the local Aboriginal community led the project. The On Country Learning project offered transformational possibilities for facilitating inclusion in the ways in which education settings 'engage with Aboriginal perspectives while facilitating deep learning through ... culturally responsive pedagogies' (Jackson-Barrett & Lee-Hammond 2018, p. 86).

Taking a child-centred approach, the project involved active, collaborative and experimental hands-on learning and co-construction.

> The guiding principle of this work is that local Aboriginal cultural knowledge is the source of children's identity, belonging and wellbeing ... The children learn to connect with their culture, language and history, through stories, songs, dances and using materials, being shown by their cultural teachers, the Elders that exemplify the continuous connection to the land, language and culture on which the project takes place (Jackson-Barrett & Lee-Hammond 2018, pp. 92–3).

In this project the researchers used the Aboriginal methodology of Yarning and recorded these Yarning sessions as interviews. The major themes emerging from the interviews were:

- Social and emotional benefits of On Country Learning, particularly increased confidence and engagement on the part of the children
- Cultural knowledge and understanding as a result of participating in On Country Learning
- Curriculum and pedagogy outcomes arising from On Country Learning.

The teachers involved in the study expressed important benefits of this inclusive approach for developing cultural knowledge:

> I've worked with Aboriginal children pretty much my whole career but I've never brought it into the classroom as much, you know, the understanding because I didn't know. I wasn't going to teach it (culture) specifically – it would have just been very superficial, whereas through the Bush school (On Country Learning) I am deeper in the history and everything ... it's definitely building my own understanding, absolutely. [Teacher interview] (Jackson-Barrett & Lee-Hammond 2018, p. 97)

Conclusion

As explored within this chapter, inclusive education is a fundamental human right for all children. We know from the research evidence that inclusive education is better for everyone – children, teachers, educators and families. Inclusion has benefits for the academic, social and communication development of all children. Inclusive education supports positive behaviour and reduces negative ECEC experiences. Inclusive education is an approach that promotes dignity and belonging, and enables every child to flourish holistically. Inclusion in the early years is also the foundation for an inclusive society. Building inclusive communities is not always easy, but it is always possible and always important. Inclusive education is an ongoing process involving a commitment to always increasing inclusivity and decreasing exclusion – it needs to be worked at consistently over time – one step at a time. In working towards building inclusive communities, we will not always be at the ideal of where we hope to be, but we can always move forward from where we are to being one step more inclusive. There are many barriers that children and families face and so often teachers and educators are the key to removing these barriers and making inclusive education possible. Fundamentally, building inclusive communities – with all of the benefits that it brings for everyone – requires changing from an option to exclude to a presumption of inclusion.

RESEARCH INTO PRACTICE

Inclusive education is an evidence-informed and philosophically important approach to ECEC. Inclusive education is also a fundamental human right for all people from early childhood onwards. Building inclusive education communities is not without challenges, but is worthwhile.

In getting started, it may be helpful to:
- document a clear vision and shared set of values for working towards inclusion
- create a space to work together to build a shared understanding and collaborative starting point, and provide resources and support to enable this
- identify current strengths and enablers (practical and attitudinal)
- identify current barriers (practical and attitudinal)
- document what change is needed:
  - what will this change look like when it has happened?
  - will this change be consistent with inclusive values?
- build on current strengths and acknowledge current barriers, identify the steps that might enable the process of transformation from *where we are* to *where we are going*
- determine what support, knowledge and skills are needed to enable these steps
- identify where this support and learning can come from
- choose a starting point (small and bigger) and begin
- take action, document, observe, reflect, review and continue this cycle. (Cologon 2019, p. 44)

References

Ainscow, M & Cesar, M 2006, 'Inclusive education ten years after Salamanca: setting the agenda', *European Journal of Psychology of Education*, vol. 21, no. 3, pp. 231–38, doi: 10.1007/BF03173412.

Allan, J 2010, 'The inclusive teacher educator: spaces for civic engagement', *Discourse*, vol. 31, no. 4, pp. 411–22, doi:10.1080/01596306.2010.504359.

Atkinson S & Srinivasan P 2014, 'The possum hunt: a ghost story for pre-schoolers? Death, continuity and the revival of aboriginality in Melbourne', in K Cologon (ed.), *Inclusive education in the early years: right from the start*, University Press, Melbourne, pp. 152–168.

Baglieri, S, Bejoian, LM, Broderick, AA, Connor, DJ & Valle, J 2011, '[Re]claiming "inclusive education" toward cohesion in educational reform: disability studies unravels the myth of the normal child', *Teachers College Record*, vol. 113, no. 10, pp. 2122–54. Retrieved from https://www.tcrecord.org

Broderick, A & Lalvani, P 2017, 'Dysconscious ableism: toward a liberatory praxis in teacher education', *International Journal of Inclusive Education*, vol. 21, no. 9, pp. 894–905, doi:10.1080/13603116.2017.1296034.

Chiner, E & Cardona, MC 2013 'Inclusive education in Spain: how do skills, resources, and supports affect regular education teachers' perceptions of inclusion?', *International Journal of Inclusive Education*, vol. 17, no. 5, pp. 526-41, doi: 10.1080/13603116.2012.689864.

Cologon, K 2010, 'Inclusion is really what teaching is', *ARNEC Connections*, vol. 3, pp. 45–48.

Cologon, K 2012, 'Confidence in their own ability: postgraduate early childhood students examining their attitudes towards inclusive education', *International Journal of Inclusive Education*, vol. 16, no. 11, pp. 1155–73, doi:10.1080/13603116.2010.548106.

Cologon, K 2013, 'Growing up with "difference": Inclusive education and the portrayal of characters who experience disability in children's literature', *Write4Children: The International Journal for the Practice and Theories of Writing for Children and Children's Literature*, vol. 4, no. 2, pp. 100–20.

Cologon, K 2014, 'Better together: inclusive education in the early years', in K Cologon (ed.), *Inclusive education in the early years: right from the start,* Oxford University Press, Melbourne, pp. 3–26.

Cologon, K 2019, *Towards inclusive education: a necessary process of transformation*, Children and Young People with Disability Australia (CYDA), Melbourne. Retrieved from https://www.cyda.org.au/LiteratureRetrieve.aspx?ID=217220

Cologon, K & D'Alessio, S 2015, 'Dall'ideologia alla pratica scolastica. Facilitatori per losviluppo dell'educazione inclusiva nei contesti scolastici italiani', in R Vianello & S Di Nuovo (eds), *Quale scuola inclusiva in Italia? Oltre le posizioni ideologiche: risultati della ricercar*, Erickson, Trento, pp. 181–208.

Connolly, P, Smith, A & Kelly B 2002, 'Too young to notice?', *The cultural and political awareness of 3–6 year olds in Northern Ireland*, Community Relations Council, Belfast. Retrieved from http://www.paulconnolly.net/publications/too_young_to_notice.pdf

D'Alessio, S 2011, *Inclusive education in Italy: a critical analysis of the policy of integrazione scolastica,* Sense, Rotterdam.

Degener, T 2016, 'Disability in a human rights context', *Laws*, vol. 5, no. 3, pp. 35–59, doi:10.3390/laws5030035.

Dempsey, I 2008, 'Legislation, policies and inclusive practices', in P Foreman (ed.), *Inclusion in action,* 2nd edn, Cengage Learning, Melbourne, pp. 37–62.

Department of Education, Employment and Workplace Relations (DEEWR) 2009, *Belonging, being and becoming: the early years learning framework for Australia*, Commonwealth of Australia, Canberra. Retrieved from https://docs.education.gov.au/node/2632

Dessemontet, RS & Bless, G 2013, 'The impact of including children with intellectual disability in general education classrooms on the academic achievement of their low-, average-, and high-achieving peers', *Journal of Intellectual & Developmental Disability*, vol. 38, no. 1, pp. 23–30, doi:10.3109/13668250.2012.757589.

Ellis, K 2015, *Disability and popular culture: focusing passion, creating community and expressing defiance*, Ashgate, Surrey.

Farrell, P, Dyson, A, Polat, F, Hutcheson, G & Gallannaugh, F 2007, 'SEN inclusion and pupil achievement in English schools', *Journal of Research in Special Education Needs*, vol. 7, no. 3, pp. 172–78, doi: 10.1111/j.1471-3802.2007.00094.x.

Favazza, PC, Ostrosky, MM, Meyer, LE, Yu, S & Mouzourou, C 2017, 'Limited representation of individuals with disabilities in early childhood classes: alarming or status quo?', *International Journal of Inclusive Education*, vol. 21, no. 6, pp. 650–66, doi:10.1080/13603116.2016.1243738.

Finke, EH, McNaughton, DB & Drager, KDR 2009, 'All children can and should have the opportunity to learn: general education teachers' perspectives on including children with autism spectrum disorder who require AAC', *Augmentative and Alternative Communication*, vol. 25, no. 2, pp. 110–22, doi:10.1080/07434610902886206.

Giangreco, MF, Dennis, R, Cloninger, C, Edelman, S & Schattman, R 1993, 'I've counted Jon: transformational experiences of teachers educating students with disabilities', *Exceptional Children*, vol. 59, no. 4, pp. 359–72, doi:10.1177/001440299305900408.

Hehir, T & Katzman, LI 2012, *Effective inclusive schools designing successful schoolwide programs*, Jossey-Bass, San Francisco.

Hehir, T, Grindal, T, Freeman, B, Lamoreau, R, Borquaye, Y & Burke, S 2016, *A summary of the evidence on inclusive education*, Alana & ABT Associates, San Paulo. Retrieved from https://alana.org.br/wp-content/uploads/2016/12/A_Summary_of_the_evidence_on_inclusive_education.pdf

Hobson, L 2010, *How is Australia faring?: social inclusion and people with disability*, Australian Federation of Disability Organisations, Melbourne.

Jackson-Barrett, E & Lee-Hammond, L 2018, Strengthening identities and involvement of Aboriginal children through learning on country', *Australian Journal of Teacher Education*, vol. 43, no. 6, pp. 86–104, doi: 10.14221/ajte.2018v43n6.6.

Jacobson, N 2009, 'A taxonomy of dignity: a grounded theory study', *BMC International Health and Human Rights*, vol. 9, no. 3, doi:10.1186/1472-698X-9-3.

Jonsson, U 2007, 'Millennium development goals and other good intentions' in P Pinstrup-Andersen & P Sandøe (eds), *Ethics, hunger and globalization: in search of appropriate policies*, Springer, Singapore, pp. 111–29.

Jordan, A & Stanovich, P 2001, 'Patterns of teacher–student interaction in inclusive elementary classrooms and correlates with student self-concept', *International Journal of Disability, Development and Education*, vol. 4, no. 1, pp. 33–52, doi:10.1080/10349120120036297.

Jordan, A, Glenn, C & McGhie-Richmond, D 2010, The Supporting Effective Teaching (SET) project: the relationship of inclusive teaching practices to teachers' beliefs about disability and ability, and about their roles as teachers', *Teaching & Teacher Education*, vol. 26, no. 2, pp. 259–66, doi: 10.1016/j.tate.2009.03.005.

Karmiris, M 2019, 'No place like home? Care and disability in the inclusive elementary classroom – a consideration of the ethical conundrums amidst disorienting intersubjective encounters', *International Journal of Inclusive Education*, online first, doi:10.1080/13603116.2019.1651412.

Keenan, C, Connolly, P & Stevenson C 2015, *The effects of universal preschool- and school-based education programmes in reducing ethnic prejudice and promoting respect for diversity among children aged 3–11: a systematic review,* Campbell Library, Queens University Belfast.

Kliewer, C 1998, 'The meaning of inclusion', *Mental Retardation*, vol. 36, no. 4, pp. 317–22, doi:10.1352/0047-6765(1998)036<0317:TMOI>2.0.CO;2.

Lalvani, P 2013, 'Privilege, compromise, or social justice: teachers' conceptualizations of inclusive education' *Disability & Society*, vol. 28, no. 1, pp. 14–27, doi:10.1080/09687599.2012.692028.

Lalvani, P & Bacon, JK 2019, 'Rethinking "we are all special": anti-ableism curricula in early childhood classrooms', *Young Exceptional Children*, vol. 22, no. 2, pp. 87–100, doi:1096250618810706.

Lorde, A 1994, *Our dead behind us*, Norton Publishers, New York.

Loreman, T 2014, 'Measuring inclusive education outcomes in Alberta, Canada', *International Journal of Inclusive Education*, vol. 18, no. 5, pp. 459–83, doi:10.1080/13603116.2013.788223.

Mackenzie, M, Cologon, K & Fenech, M 2016, 'Embracing everybody: approaching the inclusive early childhood education of a child labelled with autism from a social relational understating of disability', *Australasian Journal of Early Childhood*, vol. 41, no. 2, pp. 4–12, doi:10.1177%2F183693911604100202.

Martinez-Bello, VE & Martinez-Bello, JT 2016, 'Bodies displayed on walls: are children's bodies represented in an inclusive way in the pictures on the walls in their early childhood educational environments?', *Early Years*, vol. 37, no. 2, doi:10.1080/09575146.2016.1165186.

Mevawalla Z 2020, *Critical consciousness, social justice and resistance: the experiences of young children living on the streets in India*, Peter Lang, New York.

Purdue, K, Ballard, K & MacArthur, J 2001, 'Exclusion and inclusion in New Zealand early childhood education: disability, discourses and contexts', *International Journal of Early Years Education*, vol. 9, no. 1, pp. 37–49, doi:10.1080/0966976012004417 8.

Rietveld, C 2010, 'Early childhood inclusion: the hidden curriculum of peer relationships', *New Zealand Journal of Educational Studies*, vol. 45, no. 1, pp. 17–32. Retrieved from http://hdl.handle.net/10092/5223

Rouse, M & Florian, L 2006, 'Inclusion and achievement: student achievement in secondary schools with higher and lower proportions of pupils designated as having special educational needs', *International Journal of Inclusive Education*, vol. 10, pp. 481–93, doi:10.1080/13603110600683206.

Salvador, A 2017, *More than just toys: toys that represent impairment, their online accessibility and diversity in Australia, and early childhood educators' perspectives towards them*, unpublished master's thesis, Macquarie University, Sydney.

Silva, JM & Langhout, RD 2011, 'Cultivating agents of change in children', *Theory & Research in Social Education*, vol. 39, no. 1, pp. 61–91, doi:10.1080/00933104.2011.10473447.

Slee, R 2011, *The irregular school: exclusion, schooling and inclusive education*, Routledge, Abingdon.

Slee, R 2018, *Inclusive education isn't dead, it just smells funny*, Routledge, London.

Smith, K, Alexander, K & D'Souza Juma, A 2014, 'Gender *matters* in the early years classroom', in K Cologon (ed.), *Inclusive education in the early years: right from the start*, Oxford University Press, Melbourne, pp. 133–51.

Souto-Manning, M 2009, 'Negotiating culturally responsive pedagogy through multicultural children's literature: towards critical democratic literacy practices in a first grade classroom', *Journal of Early Childhood Literacy*, vol. 9, no., 1, pp. 50–74, doi:10.1177/1468798408101105.

Szumski, G, Smogorzewska, J & Karwowski, M 2017, 'Academic achievement of students without special educational needs in inclusive classrooms: a meta-analysis', *Educational Research Review*, vol. 21, pp. 33–54, doi:10.1016/j.edurev.2017.02.004.

United Nations General Assembly 2016, *Convention on the rights of a person with a disability; general comment number 4 on the right to inclusive education (CPRPD)*, United Nations, New York. Retrieved from http://tbinternet.ohchr.org/_layouts/treatybodyexternal/Download.aspx?symbolno=CRPD/C/GC/4&Lang=en

United Nations Educational, Scientific and Cultural Organization (UNESCO) & Institute for Statistics & United Nations International Children's Emergency Fund (UNICEF) 2015, *Fixing the broken promise of education for all: findings from the global initiative on out-of-school children*, UIS, Montreal. Retrieved from http://dx.doi.org/10.15220/978-92-9189-161-0-en

Vandenbussche, H & De Schauwer, E 2018, 'The pursuit of belonging in inclusive education – insider perspectives on the meshwork of participation', *International Journal of Inclusive Education*, vol. 22, no. 9, pp. 969–82, doi:10.1080/13603116.2017.1413686.

Watson, K 2018, 'Unspeakable: the discursive production of a "tragic subject" among children in the early childhood classroom', *International Journal of Inclusive Education*, online first, doi:10.1080/13603116.2018.1532535.

World Health Organization (WHO) 2011, *World report on disability*, WHO, Geneva. Retrieved from https://www.who.int/disabilities/world_report/2011/accessible_en.pdf

Wright, KTW 2017, *Investigating the practical application of the social relational model of disability: examining early childhood educator's inclusive education*, unpublished master's thesis, Macquarie University, Sydney.

SECTION 2

Identity, wellbeing and children contributing to their world

Section 2 explores evidence relating to the Early Years Learning Framework for Australia (EYLF) Learning Outcomes 1, 2 and 3 about children's identity, their contribution to their world and their wellbeing.

Chapter 5 provides evidence-informed guidance for early childhood professionals on creating quality outdoor spaces for young children that enhance their play, learning and wellbeing. Based on concepts of affordances and biophilic design, different 'lenses' and 'mapping' tools provide resources for the effective evaluation and creation/re-creation of spaces through understanding how both children and educators use and feel about their outdoor spaces. Practical tips are included to guide both the design of new spaces and the enhancement of existing ones.

Chapter 6 outlines the critical importance of the first five years of life and the types of strategies educators can put into place during this sensitive period. It provides current research evidence about healthy lifestyle behaviours including early childhood nutrition, physical activity and sedentary behaviour; all crucial to optimal child development.

Chapter 7 presents information and evidence about how we can keep children safe. The chapter focuses on child protection, legislation and policy, including the *National principles for child safe organisations* (AHRC 2018) and the Victorian *Child Safe Standards* (CCYP 2015) in relation to practice and what it means to be a child safe organisation. In reading this chapter, educators will understand some of the circumstances that can put young children at risk and how to keep children safe.

Chapter 8 discusses evidence about children's social and emotional development from health and psychology research in relation to early childhood practice. The authors maintain that early childhood is a critical window for children's social and emotional development and a time where children learn about social cues and use prosocial behaviours to develop positive relationships with peers and adults. Risk and protective factors for children's social and emotional development are presented along with an argument about the importance of the educator's role.

Chapter 9 acknowledges children as capable agentic citizens in their own right, with the chapter describing what children's agency looks like and how educators can facilitate it. The authors discuss research findings that have implications for practice, showing how educators can identify and support children's agency. An expanded theorisation of children's agency is shared to enable educators to instil courage in children to enact their agency in ECEC settings.

CHAPTER 5

Early childhood outdoor environments: places for play, learning and wellbeing

Anne-Marie Morrissey, Llewellyn Wishart and Deborah Moore

DOI: https://doi.org/10.37517/978-1-74286-555-3_5
Deakin University

LINKS TO NATIONAL QUALITY STANDARD

Quality Area 2: Children's health and safety
- Element 2.1.3: Healthy lifestyle – healthy eating and physical activity are promoted and appropriate for each child.
- Element 2.2.1: Supervision – at all times reasonable precautions and adequate supervision ensure children are protected from harm and hazard.

Quality Area 3: Physical environment
- Element 3.1.1: Fit for purpose – outdoor and indoor spaces, buildings, fixtures and fittings are suitable for their purpose, including the access of every child.
- Standard 3.2: Use – the service environment is inclusive, promotes competence and supports exploration and play-based learning.
- Element 3.2.1: Inclusive environment – the outdoor and indoor spaces are organised and adapted to support every child's participation and to engage every child in quality experiences in both built and natural environments.

LINKS TO THE EARLY YEARS LEARNING FRAMEWORK

Learning Outcome 1: Children have a strong sense of identity
- Children feel safe, secure and supported.

> **Learning Outcome 2: Children are connected with and contribute to their world**
> - Children become socially responsible and show respect for the environment.
>
> **Learning Outcome 3: Children have a strong sense of wellbeing**
> - Children take increasing responsibility for their own health and physical wellbeing.
>
> **Learning Outcome 4: Children are confident and involved learners**
> - Children resource their own learning through connecting with people, place, technologies and natural and processed materials.

Introduction

It is a legal requirement under the National Quality Standard (NQS) for early childhood settings to provide quality outdoor play spaces, and for educators to effectively plan for their outdoor spaces as important sites for children's play, learning and wellbeing (ACECQA 2020). To do this requires three things:

- the design, creation and maintenance of quality physical spaces
- educators' informed understanding of their own outdoor spaces and how they can be used
- planning for outdoor spaces that is evidence-informed and accounts for multiple perspectives including those of children.

In practice, outdoor spaces in early childhood settings can vary in quality from barely meeting minimum requirements to outstanding natural environments that are supportive of play and learning, and the wellbeing of children and educators (Herrington, Brunelle & Brussoni 2017). The following anecdotal observation from one of the author's personal experiences while visiting an early childhood setting illustrates how low the quality can be:

> A group of 15 4-year-old children were crowded into a small, narrow space for their outdoor play time. Apart from a swing hovering over a spongy, wet and clearly mouldy rubber-rock surface, the only other play area for the children was a thin sprinkle of dirty sand positioned under the building, with a few broken buckets and a spade or two. Generally, the behaviour of the children was agitated and angry, with little settled nor imaginative play evident. The educators commented that they could not understand why the children were not able to *play properly* when they were outside and were considering dramatically reducing the time the children spent outside as a result.

The quality of an outdoor play space is influenced by a number of factors including: the basic physical facilities and resources; the professional knowledge, practice and advocacy of educators; and, decisions by management. Whatever the character of the given physical space, educators can significantly enhance its quality through their practice, and integrate it as an essential element in their planning for teaching and learning.

What do quality early childhood outdoor spaces look like?

Over the past few decades, place-based researchers have shown that outdoor play, and play places, are extremely important to young children (Hart 1979; Moore 1986; Rasmussen 2004). Studies also confirm the importance of natural environments. Outdoor spaces strong in natural elements, along with an appropriate selection of manufactured and built features, provide the best environments for play, learning and wellbeing. Recent studies (Little 2017; Little, Elliott & Wyver 2017; Waller et al. 2017) provide compelling evidence that play in natural environments enables young children to be successful, agentive and active learners in ways that poorly designed, manufactured and highly artificial outdoor environments do not do (Campbell & Speldewinde 2019; Robertson, Morrissey & Moore 2019).

Artificial environments that are not well-designed and are dominated by generic fixtures, risk exhibiting a sense of *placelessness* and disconnection from what Kellert (2013, p. 13) describes as the 'culture and ecology of place'. Participatory research with children, which included child photography, mapmaking and storytelling, emphasises a connection to place as an important source of wellbeing (Moore, Morrisey & Robertson 2019). For example, in a comparative study of two outdoor settings, 4-year-old Harry described how he liked 'playing in the grass' in this photo of a grassed area in his outdoor play space (*see* **Figure 5.1**).

Research has shown the following characteristics and features of outdoor play spaces to be important to children; supportive of their physical and dramatic play and sense of wellbeing: tall trees, bushes and plants (Hart 1979; Rasmussen 2004); grassy patches (Moore, Morrissey & Robertson 2019); swings, seats and boats (Robertson, Morrissey & Moore 2019); hidden places in clumps of bamboo, bushes and grasses (Moore, 2017; Roe, 2007); mounds, slopes and balancing logs (Wishart, Cabezas-Benalcázar, Morrissey & Versace 2018); plentiful loose parts (Morrissey, Scott & Rahimi 2017); gravel pathways, rocks and tracks (Rasmussen 2004; Wishart, Cabezas-Benalcázar, Morrissey & Versace 2018). By contrast, children have mentioned they do not like 'concrete paths', 'dirty sand' and 'taking away the trees' (Moore, Morrissey & Robertson 2019).

Seen and measured

An important step in planning for the outdoors is understanding your space and how it is used. Traditionally, the assessment of children's outdoor play spaces has focused on physical characteristics, such as spatial dimensions, and the presence of conventional

Figure 5.1 Harry says, 'I can play anything I want … and make footprints anywhere … I like cooling-down and playing in the grass' (Moore, Morrissey & Robertson 2019, p. 12).

equipment like climbing frames, trestles, balance beams, built cubby houses, sandpits and bike paths. Other resources such as bikes, buckets and spades, balls and outdoor blocks are also traditionally seen as important in supporting children's play and physical activity outside.

There are, however, other ways of looking at outdoor play spaces that can provide a more in-depth and focused perspective, alternative *lenses* for looking at an outdoor space and understanding how it can work for children and educators. As with a camera lens, these different ways of looking can be focused to provide a *picture* of what is 'seen and measured' (Heikkinen 2010, p. 274) as needed, to inform planning for achieving desired outcomes.

Affordances

The concept of 'affordances' can be understood as a way of looking at an environment, to understand the opportunities for meaningful activity or experiences it provides (Gibson 1979; Heft 1988). It is about the relationship between people and their environment, and the opportunities afforded by a particular environment that depends on the characteristics of the individuals interacting with it. The affordances offered by an early childhood outdoor space will vary according to children's age, development and experiences, as well as contextual factors, such as whether an affordance is promoted by educators. For example, the same outdoor feature or area can provide different affordances for toddlers compared to preschool children as illustrated in **Figure 5.2**.

An affordance lens can enable educators to see opportunities for action or experience from a child's viewpoint, and in relation to all elements in an environment, including natural elements as well as manufactured and built resources. For example, while a balance beam between two trestles provides opportunities for practising balance skills, children may also see opportunities or affordances for balancing in a collection of rocks, a garden border or a low wall (Morrissey, Scott & Wishart 2015). Children may see climbing affordances in a climbing frame, but also in the branches of a tree or a bin placed against a wall. Adopting the child's view through an affordance lens, assists in creating engaging and challenging outdoor spaces, and can also help in identifying potential hazards and how to avoid them.

Drawing on the work of leading researchers, **Table 5.1** provides examples of types of affordances that may be found in outdoor play spaces along with potential benefits, and risk management considerations in regard to health and safety.

Early childhood outdoor environments: places for play, learning and wellbeing

Figure 5.2 For a 2-year-old this log provides a challenging affordance for balancing activity; while a 4-year-old may perceive affordances for imaginative, hidden play around the log and its grassy surrounds.

Table 5.1 Outdoor play space affordances

Affordance	Examples	Potential benefits	Health and safety *NQS 2.2.1, 3.3.1*
Climbable feature	Climbing frame, ladder, wall, raised edging/border, gate/fence/railing, trees, stacked objects, rocks	Climbing activity leading to agility, fitness, coordination; challenge *NQS 2.1.3, 2.2.1, 3.2* *EYLF LO 1, 3*	Avoid unintended climbing affordances, e.g. over fences/gates, inappropriate heights
Jumping off feature	A-frame, climbing frame, beam, wall, raised edging/border, steps, tree, rocks	Physical activity leading to agility, fitness, coordination; challenge *NQS 2.1.3, 3.2* *EYLF LO 1, 3*	Consider jump heights, fall surfaces, collisions with reference to relevant regulations and standards, individual contexts, and individual child and cohort capacities and interests
Places for seclusion/hiding	Built structure; vegetation, e.g. bushes, grass; constructions, e.g. child-built cubbies; the illusion of seclusion with low bushes in a maze shape for children to crawl through	Experiences of seclusion, refuge, privacy; uninterrupted play for individuals, small groups; sense of place, ownership, secret places *NQS 3.2.1* *EYLF LO 1, 3*	Necessary supervision while enabling a sense of privacy
Mouldable/manipulative	Sand; dirt; clay; loose parts, e.g. leaves, twigs, stones, tanbark	Fine-motor activity: grasping, holding, throwing, moving, creating; imaginatively transforming *NQS 3.2, 3.2.1* *EYLF LO 2, 3, 4*	Avoid choking hazards for babies and toddlers; poisonous plants
Places offering views/perspectives	Elevated places; hidden places to look out from; framings and looking through, e.g. fences, slats, branches, leaves and grass into community	New perspectives; sense of place and space; exploration; connections *NQS 3.2, 3.2.1* *EYLF LO 2, 4*	Avoid inappropriate heights

Early childhood outdoor environments: places for play, learning and wellbeing

Table 5.1 (continued)

Affordance	Examples	Potential benefits	Health and safety NQS 2.2.1, 3.3.1
Nature and wildlife	Vegetation including trees, bushes, flowers, grass; wildlife, e.g. insects, birds, possums; access to views of sky and large trees; opportunities to experience the seasons, weather, sun and shade	Connections to the natural world; environmental understanding; empathy; sense of place; appreciation of natural beauty NQS 3.1.1, 3.2.1 EYLF LO 2, 4, 5	Avoid: poisonous plants, bee stings, spider bites etc; awareness of allergies; teach children safe and respectful interactions with wildlife; protection from over exposure to sun, electrical storms, wild winds

Note: Adapted from Heft (1988); Lerstrup and Konijnendijk van den Bosch (2016); Refshauge, Stigsdotter, Lamm and Thorleifsdottir (2015).

As well as identifying affordance features in their outdoor spaces, educators can use an affordance lens to assess whether their space provides affordances to support their planning goals. For example, are there affordances that support different types of physical activity? Are there opportunities for children to be challenged and to engage with manageable risk? Are there resources and space available for children to create their own cubbies or secluded places where they can engage in uninterrupted, private play? Are there places for children to *hide away* to enable time away from the rest of the group, as a restorative measure for self-regulation as in the example in **Figure 5.3**.

In **Figure 5.3**, 6-year-old Laura's photo of her *bushy place* offers affordances for seclusion and hiding, as well as a unique perspective of looking through the branches (Moore 2015). **Figure 5.4** illustrates a small tree with low branches, which provided several affordances for children in a regional preschool and was a popular play feature. Children would climb into the branches from where they could view their play space from a higher level. The tree offered a site for imaginative play, and children often pretended they were birds sitting in the tree, demonstrating an imaginative connection with wildlife. The tree also provided loose parts for play; such as bark, leaves and pods. Unfortunately, these affordances were not recognised by management, and the tree was cut down.

Figure 5.3 Bushy place

Figure 5.4 A small tree

Mapping

Mapping is a strategy that can be used to observe and measure children's activity and use of spaces, places and resources within the outdoor environment (Robertson, Morrissey & Moore 2019; Wishart, Cabezas-Benalcázar, Morrissey & Versace 2018). A basic template or map of the outdoor space can be used as a base on which to plot or document data from observations of children's activity in the space. In seeking to understand the data collected, and why things happen where they do, educators have a basis for planning and quality improvement. Mapping can include:

- usage, for example, numbers and intensity of children using an area or resource
- who uses the space or resources, for example, gender, age, solitary, groups, presence of educators
- children's own mapping, for example, favourite spaces/places or features, what they do where
- educator mapping, for example, what they do where, favourite places/resources, challenging or problem areas, issues of supervision
- where different things happen, for example, sociodramatic play, vigorous physical activity, solitary or group play, quiet, secluded play.

Figure 5.5 provides an example of how a template may be used by educators for mapping of children's sociodramatic play in an outdoor space over two morning sessions in a preschool, with each episode indicated by a dot. Here, the mapping indicates that the sandpit and bushes nearby, along with the mud patch and A-frames, were where most episodes of sociodramatic play occurred. The educators also noted that natural materials such as sand, mud and loose parts, were intensively used and imaginatively transformed in the play. The purpose-built cubby, where educators assumed much of the sociodramatic play would be happening, only hosted one brief episode. The mapping process assisted the educators to understand how and where children used space and resources for sociodramatic play and provided information to enable them to plan their outdoor space to further support it. It also informed a proposed redevelopment of the outdoor space. A map like the one in **Figure 5.5** could be created by inserting shapes and images in a platform such as Microsoft PowerPoint; alternatively, a hand-drawn version would suffice.

Felt and experienced

Adopting a holistic approach to planning for outdoors involves looking through multiple lenses and understanding the importance of children's and adults' subjective experience in the space (Jørgensen 2014; Moore, Morrissey & Robertson 2019; Ward, Goldingay & Parson 2019; Wishart 2018; Wishart & Rouse 2019). Evidence can be gathered about what is 'felt and experienced' (Heikkinen 2010, p. 274) by children and educators through various strategies including: documentation of conversations, artefacts, photographs, stories, emotion mapping, and memory boxes of collected found materials (Clandinin & Connelly 2000).

Early childhood outdoor environments: places for play, learning and wellbeing

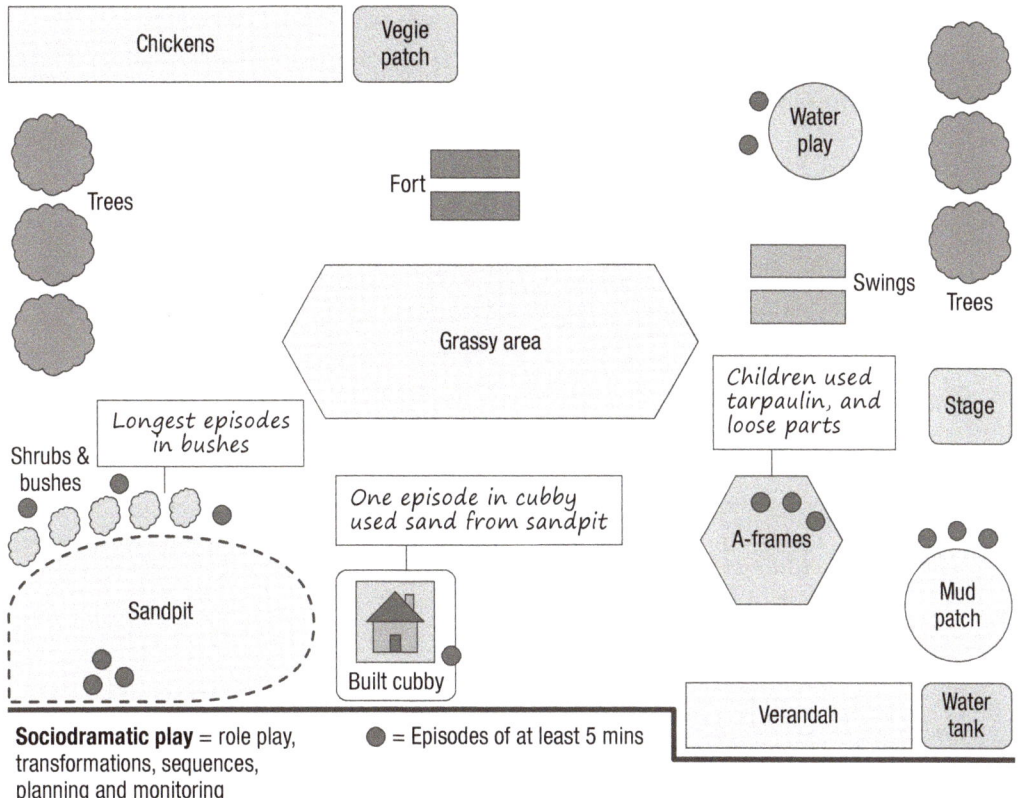

Figure 5.5 Educators' mapping of children's sociodramatic play in an outdoor play space

Using emotion mapping to understand educators' experience of outdoor spaces

Educators' feelings about their outdoor play spaces is an important factor in their responses and actions in those spaces, and how those spaces are used within their program (Copeland et al. 2012; Dyment & Coleman 2012; McClintic & Petty 2015). Mapping can be a useful tool for educators to explore their own experiences of outdoor spaces, identifying what is working well and where there may be challenges or tensions. For example, if there are areas of an outdoor play space where educators feel calm, active and frequently experience a sense of professional satisfaction, it suggests that those areas are working well as learning spaces. Alternatively, spaces where educators consistently feel stressed, frustrated or experience overwhelming demands, suggests those areas may not be working well and that changes may be needed, either in practice or the spaces themselves.

Extending on the mapping strategy described earlier, educators can use emotion mapping (Schenetti & Guerra 2018) as a strategy to reflect on their feelings about areas within their outdoor play space. Educators can select what emotions they would

Strong Foundations

like to map in their outdoor space, to help them understand how different areas are supporting or impeding their practice and point towards areas for change.

Figure 5.6 draws on research (Schenetti & Guerra 2018; Wishart & Rouse 2019) to provide a hypothetical example of educators' emotion mapping at a preschool setting. It shows educators responding to natural features; such as trees, shrubs, a sandpit and a herb/sensory garden, with a sense of calm that also reflected the children's greater calm in those areas. Understanding their own sense of calm in these areas can help educators understand children's perspectives on these spaces and assist in planning. Other areas create feelings of stress for educators about children's safety around a log hut climbing feature, and continual demands to settle disputes around the bike track, built cubby and swings. Possible responses to this data could include educators exploring their perspectives on challenge and risk, and developing approaches to support children in developing strategies to independently resolve disputes.

Figure 5.6 shows where and what they feel in particular areas of the outdoor play space. Gaining a better understanding of the sense of wellbeing experienced by children, educators and families in the outdoor play space can enable desirable programming

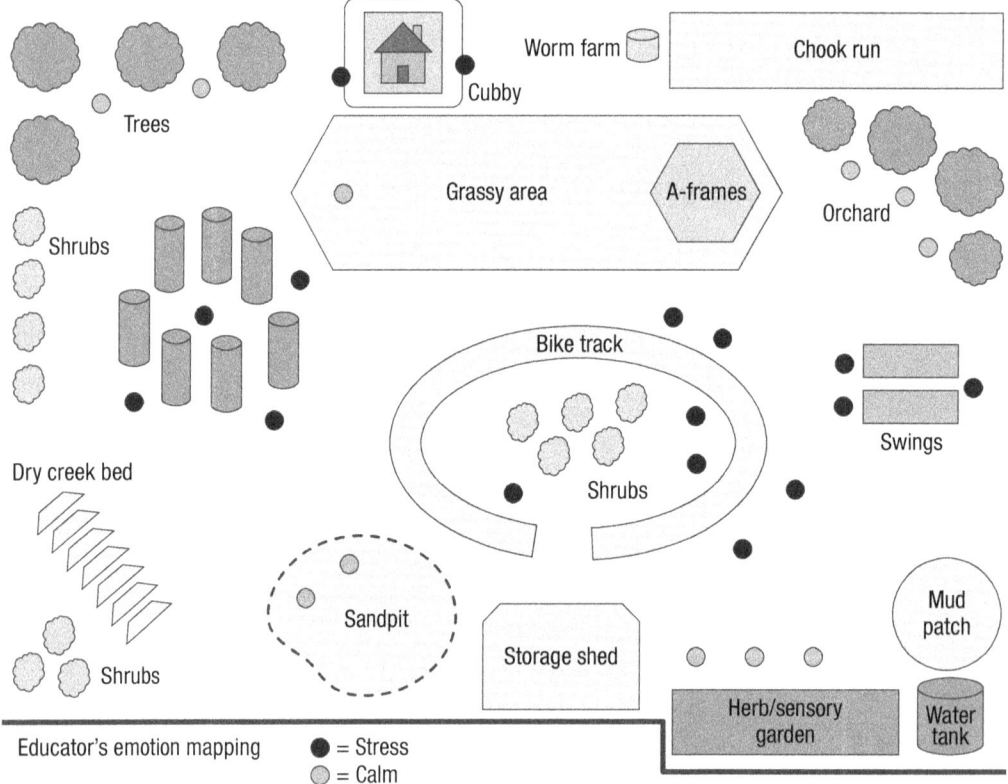

Figure 5.6 Educators' emotion mapping

goals and design outcomes to be identified. It can also be used to have educators critically reflect on their organisation and design of their outdoor area. We explore these considerations in greater depth in the section that follows on design and practice.

Design and practice: how design principles can inform early childhood outdoor pedagogy

Biophilic design principles (Kellert, Heerwagen & Mador 2013) and other evidence-informed design approaches such as the *Seven Cs* (Herrington, Lesmeister, Nicholls & Stefiuk 2007), are worthy of follow-up by readers. They can inform the creation of rich and engaging outdoor play spaces that support play, learning and wellbeing. Herrington et al. identified the seven key physical characteristics of outdoor environments that contribute to early childhood development, the Seven Cs, which include: Designing for Character; Context; Connectivity; Clarity; Chance; Change; and Challenge. These approaches can inform the creation of rich and engaging outdoor play spaces that support play, learning and wellbeing. 'Biophilic design' seeks to enrich all aspects of wellbeing through positive contact between people and nature (Kellert, Heerwagen & Mador 2013; Heerwagen 2018). Outdoor play spaces that support contact with nature (Kellert, Heerwagen & Mador 2013) enhance children's positive *affective* experience of these play spaces. These principles can inform design ranging from the creation of new spaces through to renovation and modification of existing spaces facing practical constraints. The following example details two key biophilic design principles, *prospect* and *refuge* in conjunction with desirable design outcomes.

RESEARCH HIGHLIGHT

In biophilic design, the convergence of prospect (access to views) and refuge (sense of enclosure) is described as the capacity 'to see without being seen' (Appleton as cited by Heerwagen & Gregory 2013, p. 234). Appealing outdoor places may simultaneously provide spaces of prospect and refuge that children can retreat to and look out from without being seen (*see* **Figure 5.3**, **5.11** and **5.13**). Prospect may also relate to views at child height into the distance or from a point of elevation. Researchers have found that children have a preference for views from a height (Merewether & Fleet 2014; Morrissey, Scott & Rahimi 2017; Wishart, Cabezas-Benalcázar, Morrissey & Versace 2018; Wishart & Rouse 2019). In one project, a researcher's notes illustrated children's preferences for climbing up to the highest vantage point of a vertical log structure (*see* **Figure 5.7** and **5.8**).

continued…

Figure 5.7 'Xander then walked up through the tunnel to the circular logs and climbed up them like steps. He said "I like to climb this. My friends have never done it."'

Figure 5.8 'Oscar took me over to the vertical logs and said he likes them because he gets to climb and says, when up the top he likes to "pretend I'm an eagle" and then made some eagle sounds. He took a photo of where he first climbed up and then the top of the logs where he sat to pretend to be an eagle.' [Educator record] (C Scott, personal communication, January 2015)

It should be noted that biophilic designers and researchers (Browning, Ryan & Clancy 2014; Moore & Copper Marcus 2013) have identified positive associations between wellbeing, cognitive functioning and views of nature from points of elevation (i.e. from windows in houses).

Desirable design outcomes

Drawing on biophilic design principles, this section identifies desirable design outcomes with illustrated examples and practical tips for incorporating them into outdoor play spaces. **Table 5.2** can be used as a 'Research into practice' tool (located at the end of this chapter) to analyse your outdoor space according to biophilic design principles.

Extensive and meaningful experiences of the natural world

Research has confirmed that children have an inherent inclination towards natural environments, where they can develop connection with their local place, a sense of belonging, and form lasting sensory memories of play (Lester & Maudsley 2006). Natural environments also enable calming responses in children facing emotional stresses (Berto 2014). Outdoor spaces rich in biodiversity enhance children's experiences of nature (*see* **Figure 5.9**) as well as providing for the biophilic design principle connected with the pedagogy of the natural world.

Figure 5.9 Child collecting natural materials

Tip: You can create a set of 'explorer back packs' for young children that includes: binoculars; magnifying glasses or magnifying cube; a pastry brush (to help children remember to not handle insects); a bird identification book; an insect identification laminated sheet; a clipboard with note paper and textas to visually record any discoveries.

The importance of trees to children

Research has shown that trees, especially large old trees, hold a particularly special place for children and their outdoor play (Hart 1979; Moore 1986). In terms of affordances, trees can provide a space at their roots or lower branches for constructing cubbies, while also providing natural materials for pretend play including bark, twigs and seedpods. Children have been seen to positively respond to the presence of old trees, seemingly because of their age, structure and impressive appearance. For example, one child in Moore's (2015, p. 136) study, 6-year-old Sonya, said, 'We pretend to talk to that big [Peppercorn] tree because it's my favourite … It's very old, I'm sure it was here when a castle was here'. The biophilic design principle of *prospect* fits well here.

Figure 5.10 Alice's secret place

Figure 5.10 illustrates Alice's photo of her *secret place*; hidden in a bush that was clearly visible to others even though they (other children and educators) did not know what it meant to Alice (Moore 2010).

Tip: If there is a lack of space or suitable soil to plant a tree or trees in the environment you are working in, small trees are a good option. Varieties such as citrus trees, dwarf apple trees and/or dwarf flowering silver princess eucalyptus with beautiful silver gumnuts, can be added in clumps of large pots, half wine barrels and/or planter boxes with wheels.

Places of refuge and calm

Hidden spaces for uninterrupted, private imaginative play are important for children's identity, feelings of security and emotional restoration (Moore 2017). While there is a perception that children must be visible at all times to educators, the NQS requires educators to know where the children are, while providing spaces for exploration and imaginative play, rather than requiring children to be in plain sight all of the time. This design outcome aligns with the biophilic design principle of 'refuge', where children are enabled to construct their own enclosures, sometimes just for the 'illusion of seclusion' (Heerwagen & Gregory 2013). In this way, adults know where children are without having to interrupt or intrude into their hidden spaces and imaginative play.

Figure 5.11 Clumping bamboo

Figure 5.11 illustrates a hidden, private place among clumping bamboo where children constructed a place for refuge and emotional restoration (Moore 2010). In **Figure 5.12**, light floaty material tied between two trees provides a canopy for children to feel enclosed in their own constructed place. *Tip:* To replicate these spaces, you can provide large pieces of light material for children to drape over trees, shrubs or climbing equipment to enable a sense of enclosure and refuge. Provide bushy areas with child-friendly plants; such as clumping bamboo, *Lomandra* grasses or golden *Diosma* for children to construct their own private play places. Climbing plants growing over structures can also provide a sense of enclosure and refuge.

A sense of place

Participatory research with children describes how children consistently desire to make their own places outdoors, marking out where particular play experiences and emotions are felt, and creating a sense of belonging to those places (Hart 1979; Rasmussen 2004). This sense of place links well with the biophilic design principles of *refuge* and *playfulness*.

Figure 5.12 Light floaty material

In relation to **Figure 5.13**, 4-year-old Frank said, 'That's my secret place, in the bush up there' pointing to the thin bush beside the fence line of his early childhood setting as he took this photo (Moore 2015).

Tip: You can provide areas of bushes and shrubs in naturalised clumps and/or large pots of plants throughout the outdoor play space, particularly along the fence line (not so close to the fence to provide possible climbing footholds) where children tend to prefer to create places than in open, busy and exposed areas.

Places that support sociodramatic play

Sociodramatic play involves the coordination of higher order thinking in children's play with others and provides a crucial context for children to practise language, thinking and social skills (Bergen 2002; Whitebread 2010). There is some evidence that the quality of outdoor spaces can impact on the frequency and quality of children's sociodramatic play, either positively or negatively. Sociodramatic play is at its richest and most frequent when children have the opportunity to play in outdoor spaces with a combination of appropriate manufactured and built resources and equipment, and a rich natural environment providing plentiful loose parts and secluded spaces (Cloward Drown & Christensen 2014; Morrissey, Scott & Rahimi 2017; Robertson, Morrissey & Moore 2019). Biophilic design principles based on *playfulness* show a close connection with this design outcome, demonstrating the need for pedagogical planning for outdoor play (McClintic & Petty 2015).

Early childhood outdoor environments: places for play, learning and wellbeing

Figure 5.13 Frank's photograph of his secret place

In **Figure 5.14**, 4-year-old Georgia makes use of readily available natural resources for her imaginative play (Moore 2015). *Tip:* Identifying the local tree arborist will facilitate a plentiful supply of freshly cut branches and logs for children to use in their play. Branches can be used by the children to make their own cubbies, bird hides (a shelter to watch birds from) and flexible constructions with twigs, gumnuts and leaves.

Places for varied and challenging affordances for physical activity

Tim Gill's (2007) work on risk aversion in our modern society has called for adults to manage potential outdoor play space risk through a risk-benefit analysis rather than removing anything that may appear even a little risky from an adult perspective. Children's ability to see short and long distances and move accordingly is promoted through the use of varied surfaces, balancing and climbing opportunities in outdoor play spaces (Little 2017). In contrast, children who are only presented with hard, flat surfaces or only evenly spaced climbing equipment will have less opportunity to identify, assess and negotiate changing and challenging physical experiences. In terms of biophilic design, this design outcome fits well with the notion of *sensory variability*, which refers to changes in terrain and topography to challenge and engage children's physical activity outdoors.

In **Figure 5.15**, children are using uneven logs in a playground to balance and negotiate their bodies in space. Logs of varied shape and texture can provide balance challenges for children practising concentrating on where they are walking. If children are only presented with flat walking surfaces, they are less likely to learn how to negotiate and to take responsibility for where and how they move.

Figure 5.15 Girls climbing on logs
Source: Flemings Nurseries Pty Ltd. Used with permission.

Places for outdoor pedagogy and learning about the natural world

Outdoor spaces rich in natural elements offer opportunities for children to learn about the natural world and simply experience the joy and wonder of being outdoors, in line with the *biodiversity* principle under biophilic design. Spaces with multiple forms of vegetation that also provide havens for wildlife, facilitate rich pedagogical opportunities for children's ecological and scientific understanding. Outdoor spaces also provide a context for children and educators to engage in sustainability practices (ACECQA 2020).

Early childhood outdoor environments: places for play, learning and wellbeing

Figure 5.14 Georgia and imaginary play using natural materials

Figure 5.16 shows an example of an early childhood setting successfully creating habitats for wildlife so to support scientific exploration of the natural world and biodiversity. *Tip:* Habitats for wildlife can be created through the introduction and protection of indigenous plants and fauna within the fences of an early childhood environment. For example, butterflies can be encouraged to visit by providing colourful, butterfly-attracting flat flowering plants, shallow bowls of water for butterflies to drink and long, leafy indigenous grasses for caterpillars to thrive in. The absence of chemical poisons in early childhood gardens make them a perfect habitat for butterflies.

Figure 5.16   Creating habitats for wildlife
Source: Llewellyn Wishart.

Places of sensory experience and a sense of aesthetics

The opening vignette for this chapter is an example of how artificial, 'plastic fantastic' playgrounds do not enable settled, engaged nor highly imaginative play for young children, despite the brochures marketing brightly coloured plastic equipment as 'safe and fun'. These artificial play spaces are devoid of the sensory richness, variety and the sheer beauty provided by nature. As Carson (1998) proposed, children have an innate sense of beauty that is fostered in natural environments. Researchers have found that sensory-rich natural environments are especially valuable for children's language, imaginative and cognitive development (Kellert et al. 2013). Educators also respond to the beauty and calm provided by natural surrounds (Schenetti & Guerra 2018), which aligns well with the biophilic design principle of *sensory variability* (Kellert, Heerwagen & Mador 2013).

Tip: As well as being beautiful, this weeping mulberry tree in **Figure 5.17** can be pruned to enable an upper canopy for a shady place, or left to hang to the ground to enable a sense of refuge. Deciduous fruit trees such as this, provide a wonderful form of enticement and sensory variability across the seasons with shade, flowers, fruiting, changes in leaf colour and the dropping of leaves in winter. Weeping mulberry trees

Figure 5.17   Weeping mulberry
Source: Llewellyn Wishart.

provide berries for ground foraging and leaves enabling the possibility of interest and engagement with silkworms.

Conclusion

Informed by research evidence and understanding of their own outdoor spaces, educators can plan to support play, learning and wellbeing outdoors. The strategic use of frameworks and lenses to analyse their outdoor space, provides educators with insights into design aspects and the diverse perspectives of those using the space. This can enhance reflective practice, promote EYLF Learning Outcomes and strengthen settings' quality improvement plans (QIP) to meet the NQS relating to outdoor environments.

RESEARCH INTO PRACTICE

Biophilic design

Apply some design principles and create a 'space analysis table', such as in the example below, to design or redesign an outdoor play space or area with children and your team.

Table 5.2 Biophilic design outdoor play space analysis

Biophilic design principles	Is the design principle already evident? (yes/no)	Describe and comment	Where and how could the biophilic principle be applied or improved upon in your early childhood service's outdoor spaces?	What do children value in relation to the biophilic principle? What are their views on how their outdoor space works or could be changed in relation to the principle? What do their well-trod pathways show you?
Biodiversity (rich, varied vegetation, varied terrain and topographic features, presence of animals)				
Prospect (ability to see into the distance, views)				
Refuge (sense of enclosure or shelter, canopy effects, private and secret spaces)				

continued...

Table 5.2 (continued)

Biophilic design principles	Is the design principle already evident? (yes/no)	Describe and comment	Where and how could the biophilic principle be applied or improved upon in your early childhood service's outdoor spaces?	What do children value in relation to the biophilic principle? What are their views on how their outdoor space works or could be changed in relation to the principle? What do their well-trod pathways show you?
Sensory variability (changes in colour, light, texture, temperature over time and in spaces, natural patterns and rhythms, changes in terrain and topography leading to multi-sensory enrichment)				
Sense of playfulness (natural and loose objects and materials, spaces designed to surprise, amuse and heighten playful behaviour)				

Note: Based on the design principles of Kellert, Heerwagen and Mador (2013).

References

Australian Children's Education and Care Quality Authority (ACECQA) 2020, *Guide to the national quality framework*, ACECQA, Sydney. Retrieved from https://www.acecqa.gov.au/sites/default/files/2020-01/Guide-to-the-NQF_2.pdf

Berto, R 2014, 'The role of nature in coping with psycho-physiological stress: a literature review on restorativeness', *Behavioural Sciences*, vol. 4, no. 4, pp. 394–409, oi:10.3390/bs4040394.

Bergen, D 2002, 'The role of pretend play in children's cognitive development', *Early Childhood Research and Practice*, vol. 4, no. 1, pp. 1–13.

Browning, WD, Ryan, CO & Clancy, JO 2014, *14 patterns of biophilic design*, Terrapin Bright Green llc, New York.

Campbell, C & Speldewinde, C 2019, 'Bush kinder in Australia: a new learning "place" and its effect on local policy', *Policy Futures in Education*, vol. 17, no. 4, pp. 541–59, doi:10.1177/1478210317753028.

Carson, R 1998, *The sense of wonder*, Harper & Row, New York.

Clandinin, DJ & Connelly, FM 2000, *Narrative inquiry: experience and story in qualitative research*, Jossey-Bass, San Francisco.

Cloward Drown, KK & Christensen, KM 2014, 'Dramatic play affordances of natural and manufactured outdoor settings for preschool-aged children', *Children, Youth and Environment*, vol. 24, no. 2, pp. 53–77, doi:10.7721/chilyoutenvi.24.2.0053.

Copeland, KA, Kendeigh, CA, Saelens, BE, Kalkwarf, HJ & Sherman, SN 2012, 'Physical activity in child-care centers: do teachers hold the key to the playground?', *Health Education Research*, vol. 27, no. 1, pp. 81–100.

Dyment, J & Coleman, B 2012, 'The intersection of physical activity opportunities and the role of early childhood educators during outdoor play: perceptions and reality', *Australasian Journal of Early Childhood*, vol. 37, no. 1, pp. 90–98.

Gibson, JJ 1979, *The ecological approach to visual perception,* Houghton Mifflin, Boston.

Gill, T 2007, *No fear: growing up in a risk-averse society*, Calouste Gulbenkian Foundation, London.

Hart, R 1979, *Children's experience of place*, Irvington, New York.

Heft, H 1988, 'Affordances of children's environments: a functional approach to environmental design', *Children's Environmental Quarterly*, vol. 15, pp. 29–37.

Heikkinen, K 2010, 'Integral mind, brain and education', in S Esbjoèrn-Hargens, J Reams & O Gunnlaugson (eds), *Integral education: new directions for higher learning*, Suny, Albany, NY, pp. 271–88.

Heerwagen, JH 2018, 'Can nature be a health intervention', in T Beatley, C Jones & R Rainey (eds), *Healthy environments, healing spaces: practices and directions in health, planning and design*, University of Virginia Press, Charlottesville.

Heerwagen, JH & Gregory, B 2013, Biophilia and sensory aesthetics', in SR Kellert, JH Heerwagen & M Mador (eds), *Biophilic design: the theory, science and practice of bringing buildings to life*, Wiley, Hoboken, NJ.

Herrington, S, Brunelle, S & Brussoni, M 2017, 'Outdoor play spaces in Canada: as if children mattered', in T Waller, E Arlemalm-Hagser, EBH Sandseter, L Lee-Hammond, K Lekies & S Wyver (eds), *The sage handbook of outdoor play and learning,* Chapter 9, Sage, London.

Herrington, S, Lesmeister, C, Nicholls, J & Stefiuk, K 2007, *7Cs: an informational guide to children's outdoor play spaces,* Consortium for Health, Intervention, Learning and Development. Retrieved from https://sala.ubc.ca/sites/sala.ubc.ca/files/documents/7Cs.pdf

Jørgensen, KA 2014, *What is going on out there? What does it mean for children's experiences when the kindergarten is moving their everyday activities into the nature – landscapes and its places,* unpublished doctoral dissertation, Department of Pedagogical, Curricular and Professional Studies, Faculty of Education, University of Gothenburg, Sweden.

Kellert, SR 2013, 'Dimensions, elements and attributes of biophilic design', in SR Kellert, JH Heerwagen & M Mador (eds), *Biophilic design: the theory, science and practice of bringing buildings to life,* John Wiley & Sons, Hoboken, NJ.

Kellert, SR, Heerwagen, JH & Mador, M (eds) 2013, *Biophilic design: the theory, science and practice of bringing buildings to life.* John Wiley & Sons, Hoboken, NJ.

Lerstrup, I & Konijnendijk van den Bosch, C 2016, 'Affordances of outdoor settings for children in preschool: revisiting Heft's functional taxonomy', *Landscape Research*, vol. 42, no. 1, pp. 47–62, doi:10.1080/01426397.2016.1252039.

Lester, S & Maudsley, M 2006, *Play, naturally: a review of children's natural play,* commission for Playday, Children's Play Council, London. Retrieved from www.playday.org.uk

Little, H 2017, 'Promoting risk-taking and physically challenging play in Australian early childhood settings in a changing regulatory environment', *Journal of Early Childhood Research*, vol. 15, no. 1, pp. 83–98.

Little, H, Elliott, S & Wyver, S (eds) 2017, *Outdoor learning environments: spaces for exploration, discovery and risk-taking in the early years,* Allen & Unwin, Sydney.

McClintic, S & Petty, K 2015, 'Exploring early childhood teachers' beliefs and practices about preschool outdoor play: a qualitative study', *Journal owf Early Childhood Teacher Education*, vol. 36, no. 1, pp. 24–43, doi:10.1080/10901027.2014.997844.

Merewether, J & Fleet, A 2014, 'Seeking children's perspectives: a respectful layered research approach', *Early Child Development and Care*, vol. 184, no. 6, pp. 897–914.

Moore, D 2010, *Only children can make secret places: children's secret business of place,* unpublished master's thesis, Monash University, Melbourne.

Moore, D 2015, *A place within a place: toward new understandings on the enactment of contemporary imaginative play practices and place,* unpublished doctoral dissertation, Australian Catholic University, Melbourne.

Moore, D 2017, 'The private play places of children', in H Little, S Elliott & S Wyver (eds), *Outdoor learning environments: spaces for exploration, discovery and risk-taking in the early years,* Chapter 9, Allen & Unwin, Sydney.

Moore, D, Morrissey, AM & Robertson, N 2019, 'I feel like I'm getting sad there: early childhood outdoor playspaces as places for children's wellbeing', *Early Child Development and Care*, doi:10.1080/03004430.2019.1651306.

Moore, RC 1986, *Childhood's domain: play and place in child development,* Croom Helm, London.

Morrissey, AM, Scott, C & Rahimi, M 2017, 'A comparison of sociodramatic play processes of preschoolers in a naturalised and a traditional outdoor space', *International Journal of Play*, vol. 6, no. 2, pp. 177–97.

Morrissey, AM, Scott, C & Wishart, L 2015, 'Infant and toddler responses to a redesign of their outdoor space' *Children, Youth and Environments*, vol. 25, no. 1, pp. 29–56.

Nedovic, S & Morrissey, A 2013, 'Calm, active and focused: children's responses to an organic outdoor learning environment', *Learning Environments Research*, vol. 16, no. 2, pp. 281–95.

Rasmussen, K 2004, 'Places for children–children's places', *Childhood*, vol. 11, no. 2, pp. 155–73, doi:10.1177/0907568204043053.

Refshauge, AD, Stigsdotter, UK, Lamm, B & Thorleifsdottir, K 2015, 'Evidence-based playground design: lessons learned from theory to practice', *Landscape Research*, vol. 40, no. 2, pp. 226–46, doi:10.1080/01426397.2013.824073.

Robertson, N, Morrissey, AM & Moore, D 2019, 'From boats to bushes: environmental elements supportive of children's sociodramatic play outdoors', *Children's Geographies*, doi:10.1080/14733285.2019.1630714.

Roe, M 2007, 'Feeling "secrety": children's views on involvement in landscape decisions' *Environmental Education Research*, vol. 13, no. 4, pp. 467–85.

Schenetti, M & Guerra, E 2018, 'Emotion map making: discovering teacher's relationships with nature', *Asia-Pacific Journal of Research in Early Childhood Education*, vol. 12, no. 2, pp. 31–56.

Waller, T, Arlemalm-Hagser, E, Sandseter, EBH, Lee-Hammond, L, Lekies, K & Wyver, S (eds) 2017, *The Sage handbook of outdoor play and learning,* Sage, London.

Ward, T, Goldingay, S & Parson, J 2019, 'Evaluating a supported nature play programme, parents' perspectives', *Early Child Development and Care*, vol. 189, no. 2, pp. 270–83, doi:10.1080/03004430.2017.1317764.

Whitebread, D 2010, 'Play, metacognition and self-regulation', in P Broadhead, J Howard & E Wood (eds), *Play and learning in the early years,* Sage, London, pp. 161–76.

Wishart, LE 2018, 'Early childhood educator perceptions of children's physical activity and the outdoors', *New Zealand International Research in Early Childhood Education*, vol. 21, no. 1, pp. 1–16.

Wishart, L, Cabezas-Benalcázar, C, Morrissey, AM & Versace, VL 2018, 'Traditional vs naturalised design: a comparison of affordances and physical activity in two preschool playscapes', *Landscape Research*, vol. 44, no. 8, pp. 1031–49, doi:10.1080/01426397.2018.1551524.

Wishart, L & Rouse, E 2019, 'Pedagogies of outdoor spaces: an early childhood educator professional learning journey' *Early Child Development and Care*, vol. 189, no. 14, pp. 2284–98.

CHAPTER 6

Healthy lifestyle behaviours in the first five years of life

Rachel Laws, Penny Love, Katherine Downing and Jill Hnatiuk

DOI: https://doi.org/10.37517/978-1-74286-555-3_6
Deakin University

LINKS TO NATIONAL QUALITY STANDARD

Quality Area 2: Children's health and safety
- Standard 2.1: Health – each child's health and physical activity is supported and promoted.
- Element 2.1.3: Healthy lifestyle – healthy eating and physical activity are promoted and appropriate for each child.

LINKS TO EARLY YEARS LEARNING FRAMEWORK

Learning Outcome 1: Children have a strong sense of identity
- Children develop knowledgeable and confident self-identities.

Learning Outcome 3: Children have a strong sense of wellbeing
- Children take increasing responsibility for their own health and physical wellbeing.

Introduction

This chapter explores the current evidence on early childhood nutrition, physical activity and sedentary behaviour. In the first five years of life, these health behaviours are crucial to optimal child development. They are also particularly malleable; therefore, creating environments that help children to shape and develop these health behaviours sets them up for a healthy start with lifelong benefits.

Infants

Children are at their most vulnerable in the first two years of life, especially during infancy (birth to 1 year) when growth and development peak. This is also the time that many parents/caregivers return to work and children use early childhood settings. Early childhood educators and the care environment thus have a critical role to play in promoting optimal nutrition and physical development opportunities for healthy growth and development.

Physical activity

A physically active infant is able to freely explore their environment. This means lots of 'floor-based' play, in a variety of positions, spread throughout the day. It is important that the space available for infants is safe and supervised. Infants who are in a room with other children who are mobile may benefit from having a separate area that is specifically dedicated to them.

For infants who are not yet mobile, at least 30 minutes of 'tummy time' is recommended throughout the day (Department of Health [DoH] 2017). Tummy time is important because it gives infants the opportunity to strengthen their neck and back muscles, which is essential for later movement. Evidence suggests that infants who play on their tummy have better gross motor performance compared to those who play on their back (De Kegel et al. 2013). It can be beneficial to position toys slightly out of children's reach, to encourage them to reach or move to get them. Using reflective devices (e.g. mirrors) or positioning yourself in front of children's view can encourage them to lift their head.

As some infants do not immediately enjoy tummy time on the floor, alternatives like having tummy time on an educator's lap may help the infant to become more comfortable with the position. Even short periods of tummy time; for example, a couple of minutes at a time regularly during the day, are beneficial and educators should be encouraged to continue to practise tummy time with children each day, gradually trying to increase the duration.

As children become mobile, providing environments that promote movement is advised. The National Quality Standard (NQS) (ACECQA 2020, p. 152) suggests that educators should provide safe areas and encourage babies to practise rolling over, sitting, crawling, standing, walking and climbing. A large (i.e. big enough for a few infants and educators to move around at one time), open and safe floor area is recommended, away from cribs or sleeping areas (Isbell & Isbell 2007). Providing a variety of materials to crawl over, and items that children can use to safely pull themselves up to standing, is also recommended. Choose only a few appropriate toys or objects for infants to play with at any one time. Too many choices may overwhelm infants and discourage focused attention. Alternating toys and materials that are offered to infants will help avoid them becoming disinterested, which may make them less likely to move around (Isbell & Isbell 2007).

Sedentary behaviours

Screen time; for example, TV viewing, electronic games and tablet/phone use, is not recommended for children under 2 years of age (DoH 2017). There are no known developmental benefits of screen time in this age group, but it has been associated with negative impacts on brain and motor development, emotional health and wellbeing, and weight status (Poitras et al. 2017). Further, screen time at age 6 months is unfavourably associated with cognitive development, language development and auditory comprehension (Tomopoulos et al. 2010). Conversely, there are favourable associations between storytelling and reading to infants and language development in the toddler and preschool years (McKean et al. 2015), suggesting that these activities have much greater benefits than screen time.

Although infancy is a period where children may be content to remain in bouncers, highchairs or stationary play centres for extended periods, it is not recommended that children be restrained for more than one hour at a time (this includes moving from one restraint device to another, e.g. from a bouncer to a high chair) (DoH 2017). Minimising situations that restrict movement is important for their ability to learn to move. Infants who often have play time in a bouncer or an infant seat have significantly lower motor performance (De Kegel et al. 2013) and increased risk of overweight and obesity (Sijtsma, Sauer, Stolk & Corpeleijn 2013) compared to infants who have less play time in these devices.

Nutrition and healthy eating

Optimum nutrition in early life is critical for a child's health and development, laying the foundations for healthy eating habits for life. Infant feeding guidelines from around the world (National Health and Medical Research Council 2012; WHO 2002) advise that breastmilk is the only food and fluid babies need to meet their nutritional requirements from birth to around 6 months of age. If breastfeeding is not possible, infant formula is the only suitable alternative to breastmilk until the baby is 12 months of age. At around 6 months of age, a baby's iron stores become depleted and as breastmilk and formula are not good sources of iron, the introduction of iron-rich solid foods is required. From 6 to 12 months the amount of breast or formula milk that a baby consumes therefore reduces, while the volume of solid food increases until baby transitions to family foods.

Responsive feeding

Feeding in a way that responds to babies' hunger and fullness signs is termed *responsive feeding* (Black & Aboud 2011). Non-responsive feeding; such as pressuring the baby to finish the bottle or their food, may override their innate ability to self-regulate their intake. This has been shown to be associated with a high risk of unhealthy weight gain in infancy (Mihrshahi, Battistutta, Magarey & Daniels 2011) and overweight and obesity in childhood (Hurley, Cross & Hughes 2011).

It is recommended that all babies should be fed on demand in response to showing signs of hunger (e.g. being alert, rooting or sucking, mouth opening) (Hetherington 2017) rather than by the clock. Crying can be a late sign of hunger, but babies cry for many reasons. It is important to identify other possible reasons for crying (e.g. tiredness, over stimulation, dirty nappy, too hot or cold, unwell) rather than always using a bottle or food to soothe. Educators should also be alert to signs of fullness; such as turning away and closing the mouth, which are signals to stop feeding. Babies will vary in how often and how much they feed from day to day in response to growth spurts and thirst; this is completely normal.

Supporting breastfeeding in early childhood settings

Breastfeeding is well recognised for providing short- and long-term health benefits for both mother and baby (Victora et al. 2016). Returning to work is a common reason women stop breastfeeding (Steurer 2017). Practical support that the setting can provide to support mothers to continue breastfeeding includes:

- being positive and supportive of breastfeeding and using expressed breastmilk to feed
- having a comfortable, private place for mothers to breastfeed or express
- providing safe storage of breastmilk.

Fresh breastmilk can be stored:

- at room temperature (26 °C or lower) for 6–8 hours (however, storing in the fridge is preferable)
- in the coldest spot in the fridge for 3 days
- in the freezer – compartment inside a fridge (–15 °C) for 2 weeks; separate door to fridge (–18 °C) for 3 months; deep freezer (–20 °C) for 6–12 months.

Frozen breastmilk should be thawed in the fridge only. Gently shake to mix together any milk that has separated. Warm the milk in a bowl of hot (but not boiling) water and test the temperature on the inside of your wrist before giving it to the baby – it should feel warm or cool, not hot.

Optimal infant formula feeding

A recent summary of evidence (Appleton et al. 2018) has found that the type of formula offered as well as the way it is prepared and fed to babies can influence growth.

RESEARCH HIGHLIGHT

For optimal growth, the Australian *Infant feeding guidelines* (National Health and Medical Research Council 2012) recommend that carers:

- *Choose a formula with a lower amount of protein.* A large randomised controlled trial (Koletzko et al. 2009) found that a higher protein content of infant formula is associated with unhealthy weight gain. Breastmilk contains about 1–1.1 g of protein per 100 ml. Infant formulas available in Australia have a protein content within the range of 1.3–2 g per 100 ml, so choosing a formula at the lower end of this range is preferable. No studies have shown any advantages in using follow-on formulas (those labelled for 6 months plus), which tend to have more protein than infants need.
- *Follow preparation instructions carefully to ensure formula isn't under or over concentrated.*
  1. Only use the scoop provided with the tin.
  2. Use level, lightly packed scoops.
  3. Add water first, then the powder.
  4. Do not add anything else to the bottle.
- *Introduce a sippy cup at 6 months, phase out bottles by 12 months.* Encourage families to provide a sippy cup and start offering small amounts of water in the cup with meals. Only water, breast or formula milk should be offered in the cup.

Optimal bottle feeding

Whether you are feeding a baby a bottle of expressed breastmilk or formula, it is important that you hold the baby when doing so. This might seem obvious, but it can be tempting to let older babies feed themselves or put them into a cot with a bottle to go to sleep. This is not recommended as it can increase the risk of choking, tooth decay, ear infections, unhealthy weight gain and disturbed sleep. Holding a baby close to feed while maintaining eye contact is also important for bonding; it also enables you to recognise the signs the baby provides to let you know they are full. Remember that the information on the formula tin about how much and how often to feed is a rough guide only and educators should not worry if the baby does not drink as much or as often as suggested, as long as they are having plenty of wet nappies (five or more wet disposable nappies, or at least six to eight pale wet cloth/reusable nappies over 24 hours) and are growing and developing normally. Any unused breast or formula milk should be discarded at the end of a feed.

Introduction of solids – from mush to family foods

The Australian *Infant feeding guidelines* (National Health and Medical Research Council 2012) recommend introducing solids to babies at around 6 months of age or when they show signs of readiness including:

- holding their head up and sitting with some support

- reaching out, opening their mouth and/or putting hands in their mouth
- still showing hungry signs (e.g. mouth opening, sucking fists) after a breast/formula feed
- no longer sticking their tongue out when food is put in their mouth ('extrusion reflex')
- making chewing and biting movements.

At around 5–6 months of age, educators should watch for these signs which will happen at different times for different babies. Solid foods are not recommended before 4 months of age.

Due to declining iron stores at around 6 months of age, first foods should be high in iron; such as iron fortified baby cereals, meat, fish, chicken, legumes (i.e. baked beans or lentils) and leafy green vegetables (National Health and Medical Research Council 2012). There is good evidence (Barends et al. 2019) that offering vegetables (particularly vegetables low in sugar; such as broccoli, spinach, cauliflower) before fruit can enhance vegetable acceptance. It is also recommend to include allergenic foods; such as peanut butter, cooked egg, small amount of dairy foods such as cheese or yoghurt or small amounts of cow's milk in cooking (but not as a main drink) and wheat products, even if the baby has a family history of allergies (National Health and Medical Research Council 2012). Exposure to allergenic foods in the first 6–12 months of life is thought to be important in preventing food allergies later in life. Educators should watch for any reactions (i.e. a rash or upset tummy) and if you do notice any, stop that food and encourage families to see their general practitioner (GP) for further advice.

Foods to avoid until baby is at least 12 months of age include:

- any foods that might be a choking hazard (e.g. nuts and any hard foods)
- honey, which can cause botulism (a serious bacterial infection)
- cow's and goat's milks (except in small quantities in cooking)
- foods high in salt or sugar (biscuits, juice, soft drinks, chips, chocolate, cake, lollies, ice cream etc) which can replace more nutritious foods
- tea (including herbal teas) and coffee
- the addition of sugar, salt (including stocks), fats and oils to foods.

Babies starting solid foods at 6 months of age can quickly move from pureed to mashed and finger foods, with the aim of transitioning to family foods by 12 months. It is important to introduce lumpy food before 10 months to avoid feeding difficulties later; such as only accepting smooth or soft foods. Textured foods (including finger foods) are important in helping babies learn how to chew their food (no teeth required) which then helps them to speak. Finger foods such as cooked vegetables, soft fruit and bread also encourage babies to explore foods and feed themselves.

RESEARCH HIGHLIGHT

What is baby-led weaning?

'Baby-led weaning', where infants are encouraged to feed themselves instead of traditional spoon feeding, has become popular. Evidence suggests that compared to spoon feeding, this approach to complementary feeding can result in less food fussiness and greater enjoyment of food at 12 months without any detrimental effects on infant nutrient intake, child growth or choking risk (Taylor et al. 2017; Williams Erickson et al. 2018).

Finally, remember it takes time for babies and young children to learn to accept new tastes and textures. Evidence suggests (Barends et al. 2019) that it can take up to 10–15 tries of a new food before a child learns to accept it, so it's important to continue to offer a previously rejected food, even if a caregiver tells you that it's refused at home. Avoid using coercion, pressure or rewards during feeding as this can override an infant's natural ability to self-regulate their intake and lead to fussy eating. Simply remove any uneaten food after a given period of time (20 minutes is usually plenty) without comment.

For more information, join the free massive open online course 'Infant nutrition: from breastfeeding to baby's first solids' available from Future Learn.

Toddlers and preschool children

The toddler and preschool years are marked by increasing autonomy and independence. Educators are in an ideal position to role model and provide young children with opportunities to learn and develop healthy lifestyle behaviours through active play and positive eating habits.

Physical activity

Once children are walking, their physical activity levels will increase and take the form of locomotor activities (e.g. running), balance skills (e.g. hopping, jumping) and ball skills (e.g. throwing, catching). For children 2–5 years of age, the current guidelines recommend at least 3 hours of physical activity spread throughout the day; more is better (DoH 2017). From 3 years of age, the guidelines also recommend that at least 1 hour of this physical activity involves high-energy play.

Although children tend to move more frequently than adults, it is important to recognise that much of the activity that they undertake is of light intensity (i.e. slow walking or standing with minimal movement) and undertaken in short bursts (Hnatiuk et al. 2012). It is a common misconception that young children are naturally active; preschool-aged children have been shown to spend around 16% of their time being physically active, and only around 5% of their time in physical activity that is highly energetic (Hinkley et al. 2012). It is important that toddlers and preschool children have the opportunity to participate in high-energy play (fast running, jumping) as this is important for children's heart health and motor skill development (Carson et al. 2017). Additionally, incorporating weight-bearing (e.g. running, jumping) and muscle-strengthening activities (e.g. climbing) are important for optimising bone health (Carson et al. 2017).

Educator perceptions of physical activity have been shown to limit or enable physical activity opportunities for children (Coleman & Dyment 2013). When planning learning experiences, educators should consider how they can offer opportunities for children to be active. For example, where can they offer opportunities for children to stand rather than sit, move rather than stand, or move fast rather than slow? It is important to remember that physical activity can be incorporated into most everyday learning activities (e.g. dancing or acting out poems or songs). Movement does not just have to occur during a specific structured 'physical activity' session. That being said, structured physical activity sessions have been shown to elicit higher intensity physical activity (Van Cauwenberghe et al. 2013) and develop fundamental movement skills. Thus, offering a balance between structured and unstructured (active free play) movement opportunities within programming is critical as highlighted in NQS Quality Area 2 – Children's health and safety.

Time outdoors and risky play

Spending time outdoors elicits higher physical activity among young children (Bingham et al. 2016). For this reason, structuring lots of outdoor time for children each day is important. Access to pathways and open areas (Sando 2019), and the incorporation of natural features (Fjørtoft 2001) appear to be particularly important for facilitating energetic play.

Educators might also consider the frequency of outdoor play. Children tend to be most active during the first 15 minutes of going outdoors (Pate et al. 2013). Thus, by structuring several shorter periods of outdoor play across the entire day, children may engage in more physical activity than if the same total time was provided in one allotment.

As part of the NQS Quality Area 2, it is suggested that early childhood settings encourage children to identify and manage risks in their play, including providing opportunities for children to problem-solve. *Risky play* involves uncertainty; for example, play at height, play at high speed, and 'rough-and-tumble' play (Sandseter 2007). Risky outdoor play has positive effects on physical activity levels, social health, risk management, self-confidence, mental health and independence (Brussoni et al. 2015; Hüttenmoser 1995; Lavrysen et al. 2017; Sandseter & Kennair 2011), with benefits outweighing potential harms (Brussoni et al. 2015). Educators can encourage risky play by:

- ensuring that adult/child ratios provide adequate levels of supervision
- providing opportunities for challenge so that children experience the perception of risk without being placed at risk of injury

- verbally encouraging children to take risks to extend their skill level and providing physical support (i.e. hand-holding) when necessary. (Adapted from Little 2010)

Physical literacy

Physical literacy is a term that refers to building the skills, knowledge and behaviours that give children the confidence and motivation to be active throughout life (Australian Sports Commission 2019). Physical literacy is not just about developing physical skills, but also the psychological (e.g. enjoyment, confidence), social (e.g. cooperation, fair play) and cognitive (e.g. knowledge, understanding of rules) skills to participate in physical activity and sport.

Educators can support children's development of physical literacy by providing regular opportunities to engage in key fundamental movement skills including locomotor activities (i.e. running, jumping, hopping, skipping), ball skills (i.e. throwing, catching, kicking, striking) and stationary and dynamic (while moving) balance activities. Importantly, unlike milestones, such as crawling and walking, children's fundamental movement skills need instruction and feedback to develop (Barnett et al. 2016).

Additionally, educators can help develop children's psychological, social and cognitive physical literacy by deliberately targeting these skills in their programming. Such as:

- providing a range of activities for children to participate in, and delivering them in an age-appropriate, relaxed, fun manner
- providing games and activities that are progressively more challenging, but achievable to foster confidence
- incorporating activities into their programming that engage children in physical activities as a group and require that they work together to achieve a goal to foster cooperation.

Sedentary behaviours

Between the ages of 2–5 years, it is recommended that children have no more than 1 hour of screen time per day; less is better (DoH 2017). Many children will use screens at home, so limiting their exposure to screens in early childhood settings is desirable to help them meet recommendations. Screen time has detrimental associations with cognitive and motor development, emotional health and wellbeing, and weight status (Poitras et al. 2017). Additionally, the interactivity of screens is limited compared with learning from an educator (Radesky & Christakis 2016). Any time spent on screens can also take away time and opportunities for other activities, including reading, quiet play and physical activity.

It is also important to minimise the amount of time that children spend sitting continuously for long periods. Preschool children sit, on average, for around 80% of their waking hours (Hnatiuk et al. 2014), so reducing this time while in early childhood settings is crucial. Educators can try implementing active movement breaks during the day (De Decker et al. 2013). Activities that children would usually do sitting down can easily be adapted to be done standing up (Downing et al. 2018); for example, removing chairs from tables to encourage children to stand for arts and crafts, and introducing movement into story time.

RESEARCH HIGHLIGHT

Physical activity and sedentary behaviour recommendations for young children

Physical activity:
Toddlers (1–2 years old) should spend ≥180 minutes per day doing a variety of physical activities, including energetic play; such as running, jumping and twirling, spread throughout the day – more is better.
Preschool children (3–5 years old) should spend ≥180 minutes per day in a variety of physical activities, of which 60 minutes is energetic play; such as running, jumping and kicking and throwing, spread throughout the day – more is better.

Sedentary behaviour:
Toddlers should not be restrained for more than 1 hour at a time (e.g. in a stroller, car seat or highchair) or sit for extended periods. For toddlers younger than 2 years old, screen time is not recommended during sedentary periods. For those aged 2 years old, screen time should be no more than 1 hour in total throughout the 24-hour period – less is better. When toddlers are sedentary, educators are encouraged to engage with them through activities; such as reading, singing, puzzles and storytelling.
Preschool children should not be restrained for more than 1 hour at a time (e.g. in a stroller or car seat) or sit for extended periods. Sedentary screen time should be no more than 1 hour in total throughout the 24-hour period – less is better. When preschool children are sedentary, educators are encouraged to engage with them through activities; such as reading, singing, puzzles and storytelling. (Based on DoH 2017)

Nutrition and healthy eating

Young children are impressionable, which provides a perfect opportunity to help them form positive attitudes to food. Eating a variety of foods, in adequate amounts, and being exposed to healthy feeding practices is key to establishing lifelong healthy habits.

As part of the NQS Quality Area 2, early childhood settings are encouraged to promote or provide healthy foods, drinks and snacks that are:

- nutritious and adequate in quantity
- appropriate to meet each child's growth needs

- appropriate for any specific cultural, religious or health requirements
- not high in fat, salt or sugar
- available throughout the day as a midday meal with a morning and afternoon snack.

What should young children be eating while in an early childhood setting?

As with infants, an important component of healthy eating is the division of mealtime responsibility. The educator is responsible for *what* foods are offered, *when* and *where* they are eaten; and the young child decides *which* foods and *how* much to eat. A good way to remember this is *adult provides: child decides*.

Educators can role model and encourage healthy eating regardless of whether children are provided meals in their setting or food from home. A variety of foods comprising the core food groups (vegetables, fruit, wholegrains, legumes/lean meats and dairy) should be offered each day to provide the essential nutrients for growth and development. Discretionary items; such as cakes, biscuits, lollies, chocolates, chips, soft drinks, cordials etc do not contain essential nutrients and can displace healthier foods. Discretionary items should therefore not be offered and should be discouraged if provided from home. In particular, celebrations should include a non-food focus; such as wearing a birthday hat, with healthy food being provided in a creative way (e.g. watermelon with candles).

Water is the only drink that young children require while in an early childhood setting, and they should have access to drinking water at all times. Unflavoured milk can also be offered as a drink, but only in small amounts and after eating so it does not replace food intake.

The amount of food offered to children will depend on the length of time they spend in the setting. Most commonly, children will have breakfast and dinner at home. Young children should therefore be offered food around mid-morning (e.g. platter of cut fruit or a small apple); midday/lunch (e.g. wholegrain sandwich with lettuce, grated carrot, shredded chicken); and mid-afternoon (e.g. rice cakes with cottage cheese and tomato and cucumber slices). If food is provided by the early childhood setting, an accurate weekly menu should be displayed in the setting and available to families.

The types and amounts of foods to offer young children per day are described in the *Australian dietary guidelines* and illustrated in the *Australian guide to healthy eating* (National Health and Medical Research Council 2013).

How should young children be eating while in care?

The encouragement and modelling of responsive feeding practices that enable young children to determine which foods and how much to eat have shown positive effects on stimulating healthy eating habits (Larsen 2015). Commonly referred to as 'child feeding practices', research has shown that children's food preferences are directly related to the feeding practices they experience (Musher-Eizenman 2007). Given the early childhood setting serves as a proxy home environment, positive child feeding practices should be modelled by both caregivers and educators.

- *Child control* – is the child's ability to self-regulate their food intake. Young children only need to eat until they feel satisfied. Self-regulation and listening to their hunger cues can be encouraged by enabling children to serve themselves or serving smaller amounts of food and letting children ask for more; using child-sized cutlery and crockery; and removing the food if they start to play with it or start to get restless at the table.
- *Pressure to eat* – such as encouragement or coercion to have one more bite or finish everything on the plate can promote overeating or fussy eating. Appetites differ between children and can fluctuate on a daily basis. Children also have small stomachs. If a child picks at one meal, they will probably make up for it at the next. Healthy snacks and meals should therefore be offered at regular times each day, with children left to decide if and how much they will eat in a relaxed environment.
- *Food restrictions and rewards* – such as withholding food as punishment or providing a food as reward can promote unhealthy attitudes about foods. Behaviour should be guided using appropriate non-food related activities.
- *Monitoring and regulating* – of foods eaten by a child may be useful to provide feedback to families, but it should not be used to pressure children to eat more or less. If a food is commonly rejected, such as vegetables, continue to offer it using different preparation methods, such as raw carrot sticks instead of cooked; or alternate varieties within the same food group, such as pumpkin instead of carrots.
- *Modelling, involvement and teaching* – are important ways of demonstrating appropriate mealtime behaviour to children, such as table manners, social interaction and mindful eating. Eating with children, especially eating the same foods as them, and showing enthusiasm for eating healthy foods in front of children can encourage them to try new foods (Matwiejczyk et al. 2018; Scaglion 2018). Children also learn from being involved in mealtime activities such as table setting, serving themselves (i.e. pouring water from a jug into their cup or making their own sandwiches), and talking about the foods being eaten (taste, colour, smell, how they are grown). Learning about food can also happen away from mealtimes, such as baking or cooking activities, growing and harvesting vegetables and reading books about food. Providing a healthy food environment within the setting is another important form of modelling, such as having a centre-based 'healthy eating policy' regarding foods/drinks brought from home, special occasions and fundraising.

RESEARCH HIGHLIGHT

How to feed fussy eaters?

- Provide a variety of healthy foods and encourage children to decide how much of each to eat.
- Continue to offer foods that are refused and encourage children to taste.
- Make mealtimes enjoyable and model healthy eating behaviours when feeding children.
- Discretionary items should not be offered before meals.
- Establish a regular mealtime routine, including a time limit (20–30 minutes) after which uneaten food is removed without alternative food being offered until the next planned meal.
- If a child eats a very limited range of foods for an extended period of time, seek a referral to an Accredited Practising Dietitian (APD). (Based on DoH 2015)

Working in partnership with families

Providing feedback to families about how their child has participated in mealtimes is as important as the type and quantity of food eaten during the day. Communication with families about foods or drinks that cannot be eaten due to allergy, cultural or religious reasons is vital. Some families may be vegans, vegetarians or follow cultural or religious eating patterns where certain foods are avoided. These values need to be respected and discussed with the family to identify what alternatives can be offered on the menu.

Educators have opportunities to communicate physical activity and screen time guidelines to families, along with strategies and tips for optimising these behaviours at home. If a child enjoys a particular game or activity, instructions for this game or activity can be shared with families. This might also occur if educators notice that a child needs additional help to develop a particular movement skill. Educators can also share ideas for active play in small spaces, using low-cost equipment, as these are often barriers cited by families to children being active.

Conclusion

Early childhood settings provide an ideal opportunity for the establishing of lifelong healthy lifestyle behaviours in early infancy and childhood. In Australia, the National Quality Framework (NQF) (ACECQA 2020) supports this aim by promoting healthy eating and physical activity appropriate for each child while in an early childhood setting. National evidence-informed resources are available to assist in implementing these guidelines, such as *Get up & grow: healthy eating and physical activity for early childhood*, *Australian dietary guidelines*, *Infant feeding guidelines*, and *Australian guidelines for physical activity*. Educators play an essential role in the implementation of these guidelines influencing the health behaviours of future generations.

RESEARCH INTO PRACTICE
Reflect on your practices to enhance healthy eating and physical activity opportunities.
How can you:
- arrange the outdoor and indoor physical environments and the curriculum in a way that supports movement?
- create opportunities for children to engage in risky play that are safe and appropriate?
- achieve learning outcomes without the use of screens?
- engage with families (teachable moments) to support them in establishing healthy behaviors within the home and the early childhood environment?
- ensure that the mealtime environment supports the principles of *adult provides: child decides*?

References

Australian Children's Education and Care Quality Authority (ACECQA) 2020, *Guide to the national quality framework*, ACECQA, Sydney. Retrieved from https://www.acecqa.gov.au/sites/default/files/2020-01/Guide-to-the-NQF_2.pdf

Appleton, J, Russell, CG, Laws, R, Fowler, C, Campbell, K & Denney-Wilson, E 2018, 'Infant formula feeding practices associated with rapid weight gain: a systematic review', *Maternal & Child Nutrition*, vol. 14, no. 3, p. e12602, doi:10.1111/mcn.12602.

Australian Sports Commission 2019, *Physical literacy framework*. Retrieved from https://www.sportaus.gov.au/physical_literacy

Barends, C, Weenen, H, Warren, J, Hetherington, MM, de Graaf, C & de Vries, JHM 2019, 'A systematic review of practices to promote vegetable acceptance in the first three years of life', *Appetite*, vol. 137, pp. 174–97, doi:10.1016/j.appet.2019.02.003.

Barnett, LM, Stodden, D, Cohen, KE, Smith, JJ, Lubans, DR, Lenoir, M, Iivonen, S, Miller, AD, Laukkanen, A, Dudley, D, Lander, NJ, Brown, H & Morgan, PJ 2016, 'Fundamental movement skills: an important focus', *Journal of Teaching in Physical Education*, vol. 35, no. 3, pp. 219–25.

Bingham, DD, Costa, S, Hinkley, T, Shire, KA, Clemes, SA & Barber, SE 2016, 'Physical activity during the early years: a systematic review of correlates and determinants', *American Journal of Preventive Medicine*, vol. 51, no. 3, pp. 384–402, doi:10.1016/j.amepre.2016.04.022.

Black, MM & Aboud, FE 2011, 'Responsive feeding is embedded in a theoretical framework of responsive parenting', *The Journal of Nutrition*, vol. 141, no. 3, pp. 490–94, doi:10.3945/jn.110.129973.

Brussoni, M, Gibbons, R, Gray, C, Ishikawa, T, Sandseter, EB, Bienenstock, A, Chabot, G, Fuselli, P, Herrington, S, Janssen, I, Pickett, W, Power, M, Stranger, N, Sampson, M & Tremblay, MS 2015, 'What is the relationship between risky outdoor play and health in children? A systematic review', *International Journal of Environmental Research and Public Health*, vol. 12, no. 6, pp. 6423–54, doi:10.3390/ijerph120606423.

Carson, V, Lee, EY, Hewitt, L, Jennings, C, Hunter, S, Kuzik, N, Stearns, JA, Unrau, SP, Poitras, VJ, Gray, C, Adamo, KB, Janssen, L, Okely, AD, Spence, JC, Timmons, BW & Sampson, M & Tremblay, MS 2017, 'Systematic review of the relationships between physical activity and health indicators in the early years (0–4 years)', *BMC Public Health*, vol. 17, supp. 5, p. 854, doi:10.1186/s12889-017-4860-0.

Coleman, B & Dyment, JE 2013, 'Factors that limit and enable preschool-aged children's physical activity on child care centre playgrounds', *Journal of Early Childhood Research*, vol. 11, no. 3, pp. 203–21, doi:10.1177/1476718x12456250.

De Decker, E, De Craemer, M, De Bourdeaudhuij, I, Wijndaele, K, Duvinage, K, Androutsos, O, Iotova, V, Lateva, M, Alvira, JMF, Zych, K, Manios, Y & Cardon, G 2013, 'Influencing factors of sedentary behavior in European preschool settings: an exploration through focus groups with teachers', *Journal of School Health*, vol. 83, no. 9, pp. 654–61, doi:10.1111/josh.12078.

De Kegel, A, Peersman, W, Onderbeke, K, Baetens, T, Dhooge, I & Van Waelvelde, H 2013, 'New reference values must be established for the Alberta infant motor scales for accurate identification of infants at risk for motor developmental delay in Flanders', *Child: Care, Health and Development*, vol. 39, no. 2, pp. 260–67, doi:10.1111/j.1365-2214.2012.01384.x.

Department of Health (DoH) 2015, *Get up & grow: healthy eating and physical activity for early childhood resource,* DoH, Canberra. Retrieved from https://www1.health.gov.au/internet/main/publishing.nsf/Content/phd-early-childhood-nutrition-resources

Department of Health (DoH) 2017, *Australian 24-hour movement guidelines for the early years (birth to 5 years): an integration of physical activity, sedentary behaviour and sleep,* Commonwealth of Australia, Canberra.

Downing, KL, Salmon, J, Hinkley, T, Hnatiuk, JA & Hesketh, KD 2018, 'Feasibility and efficacy of a parent-focused, text message-delivered intervention to reduce sedentary behavior in 2- to 4-year-old children (mini movers): pilot randomized controlled trial', *JMIR mHealth and uHealth,* vol. 6, no. 2, p. e39, doi:10.2196/mhealth.8573.

Fjørtoft, I 2001, 'The natural environment as a playground for children: the impact of outdoor play activities in pre-primary school children', *Early Childhood Education Journal,* vol. 29, no. 2, pp. 111–17, doi:10.1023/A:1012576913074.

Future Learn n.d, *Infant nutrition: from breastfeeding to baby's first solids.* Retrieved from https://www.futurelearn.com/courses/infant-nutrition

Hetherington, MM 2017, 'Understanding infant eating behaviour – lessons learned from observation', *Physiology and Behavior,* vol. 176, pp. 117–24, oi:10.1016/j.physbeh.2017.01.022.

Hinkley, T, Salmon, J, Okely, AD, Crawford, D & Hesketh, K 2012, 'Preschoolers' physical activity, screen time, and compliance with recommendations', *Medicine & Science in Sports & Exercise,* vol. 44, no. 3, pp. 458–65, doi:10.1249/MSS.0b013e318233763b.

Hnatiuk, J, Ridgers, ND, Salmon, J, Campbell, K, McCallum, Z & Hesketh, K 2012, 'Physical activity levels and patterns of 19-month-old children', *Medicine & Science in Sports & Exercise,* vol. 44, no. 9. pp. 1715–20, doi:10.1249/MSS.0b013e31825825c4.

Hnatiuk, JA, Salmon, J, Hinkley, T, Okely, AD & Trost, S 2014, 'A review of preschool children's physical activity and sedentary time using objective measures', *American Journal of Preventive Medicine,* vol. 47, no. 4, pp. 487–97, doi:10.1016/j.amepre.2014.05.042.

Hurley, KM, Cross, MB & Hughes, SO 2011, 'A systematic review of responsive feeding and child obesity in high-income countries', *The Journal of Nutrition,* vol. 141, no. 3, pp. 49–501, doi:10.3945/jn.110.130047.

Hüttenmoser, M 1995, 'Children and their living surroundings: empirical investigations into the significance of living surroundings for the everyday life and development of children', *Children's Environments,* vol. 12, no. 4, pp. 403–13. Retrieved from http://www.jstor.org/stable/41514991

Isbell, C & Isbell, RT 2007, 'On the move: environments that stimulate motor and cognitive development in infants, *Dimensions of Early Childhood,* vol. 35, no. 3, pp. 30–35.

Koletzko, B, von Kries, R, Closa, R, Escribano, J, Scaglioni, S, Giovannini, M, Beyer, J, Demmelmair, H, Gruszfeld, D, Dobrzanska, A, Sengier, A, Langhendries, JP, Rolland Cachera, MF & Grote, V 2009, 'Lower protein in infant formula is associated with lower weight up to age 2 y: a randomized clinical trial', *The American Journal of Clinical Nutrition,* vol. 89, no. 6, pp. 1836–45, doi:10.3945/ajcn.2008.27091.

Larsen, JK, Hermans, HR, Sleddens, EF, Engels, RC, Fisher, JO & Kremers, SP 2015, 'How parental dietary behavior and food parenting practices affect children's dietary behavior. Interacting sources of influence?', *Appetite,* vol. 89, pp. 246–57, doi: 10.1016/j.appet.2015.02.012.

Lavrysen, A, Bertrands, E, Leyssen, L, Smets, L, Vanderspikken, A & De Graef, P 2017, 'Risky-play at school. Facilitating risk perception and competence in young children', *European Early Childhood Education Research Journal,* vol. 25, no. 1, pp. 89–105, doi:10.1080/1350293X.2015.1102412

Little, H 2010, *Finding the balance: early childhood practitioners' views on risk, challenge and safety in outdoor play settings,* paper presented at the Australian Association for Research in Education, Melbourne.

Matwiejczyk, L, Mehta, K, Scott, J, Tonkin, E & Coveney, J 2018, 'Characteristics of effective interventions promoting healthy eating for pre-schoolers in childcare settings: an umbrella review', *Nutrients,* vol. 10, no. 3, doi:10.3390/nu10030293.

McKean, C, Mensah, FK, Eadie, P, Bavin, EL, Bretherton, L, Cini, E & Reilly, S 2015, 'Levers for language growth: characteristics and predictors of language trajectories between 4 and 7 years', *PLOS ONE,* vol. 10, no. 8, p. e0134251, doi:10.1371/journal.pone.0134251.

Mihrshahi, S, Battistutta, D, Magarey, A & Daniels, LA 2011, 'Determinants of rapid weight gain during infancy: baseline results from the NOURISH randomised controlled trial', *BMC Pediatrics,* vol. 11, no. 99. Retrieved from http://www.scopus.com/inward/record.url?eid=2-s2.0-80355131528&partnerID=40&md5=648a93cb2584dd92f593ce07c7f14a84

Musher-Eizenman DHS 2007, 'Comprehensive feeding practices questionnaire: validation of a new measure of parental feeding practices', *Journal of Pediatric Psychology,* vol. 32, no. 8, pp. 960–72.

National Health and Medical Research Council 2012, *Infant feeding guidelines,* Commonwealth of Australia, Canberra.

National Health and Medical Research Council 2013, *Australian dietary guidelines* Commonwealth of Australia, Canberra.

Pate, RR, Dowda, M, Brown, WH, Mitchell, J & Addy, C 2013, 'Physical activity in preschool children with the transition to outdoors', *Journal of Physical Activity and Health,* vol. 10, no. 2, pp. 170–75.

Poitras, VJ, Gray, CE, Janssen, X, Aubert, S, Carson, V, Faulkner, G, Goldfield, GS, Reilly, JJ, Sampson, M & Tremblay, MS 2017, 'Systematic review of the relationships between sedentary behaviour and health indicators in the early years (0–4 years)', *BMC Public Health,* vol. 17, no. 5, p. 868, doi:10.1186/s12889-017-4849-8.

Radesky, JS & Christakis, DA 2016, 'Increased screen time: implications for early childhood development and behavior', *Pediatric Clinics,* vol. 63, no. 5, pp. 827–39, doi:10.1016/j.pcl.2016.06.006.

Sando, OJ 2019, 'The outdoor environment and children's health: a multilevel approach', *International Journal of Play,* vol. 8, no. 1, pp. 39–52, doi:10.1080/21594937.2019.1580336.

Sandseter, EBH 2007, 'Categorising risky play – how can we identify risk-taking in children's play?', *European Early Childhood Education Research Journal,* vol. 15, no. 2, pp. 237–52, doi:10.1080/13502930701321733.

Sandseter, EBH & Kennair, LEO 2011, 'Children's risky play from an evolutionary perspective: The anti-phobic effects of thrilling experiences', *Evolutionary Psychology*, vol. 9, no. 2, doi:10.1177/147470491100900212.

Scaglioni, S, De Cosmi, V, Ciappolino, V, Parazzini, F, Brambilla, P & Agostoni, C 2018, 'Factors influencing children's eating behaviours', *Nutrients*, vol. 10, no. 6, doi: 10.3390/nu10060706.

Sijtsma, A, Sauer, PJ, Stolk, RP & Corpeleijn, E, 2013, 'Infant movement opportunities are related to early growth – GECKO Drenthe cohort', *Early Human Development*, vol. 89, no. 7, pp. 457–61, doi:10.1016/j.earlhumdev.2013.04.002.

Steurer, LM 2017, 'Maternity leave length and workplace policies' impact on the sustainment of breastfeeding: global perspectives', *Public Health Nursing*, vol. 34, no. 3, pp. 286–94, doi:10.1111/phn.12321.

Taylor, RW, Williams, SM, Fangupo, LJ, Wheeler, BJ, Taylor, BJ, Daniels, L, Fleming, EA, McArthur, J, Morison, B, Erickson, LW, Davies, RS, Bacchus, S, Cameron, SL & Heath, AM 2017, 'Effect of a baby-led approach to complementary feeding on infant growth and overweight: a randomized clinical trial', *JAMA Pediatrics*, vol. 171, no. 9, pp. 838–46, doi:10.1001/jamapediatrics.2017.1284.

Tomopoulos, S, Dreyer, BP, Berkule, S, Fierman, AH, Brockmeyer, C & Mendelsohn, AL 2010, 'Infant media exposure and toddler development', *Archives of Pediatrics & Adolescent Medicine*, vol. 164, no. 12, p. 1105–11, doi:10.1001/archpediatrics.2010.235.

Van Cauwenberghe, E, De Craemer, M, De Decker, E, De Bourdeaudhuij, I & Cardon, G 2013, 'The impact of a teacher-led structured physical activity session on preschoolers' sedentary and physical activity levels', *Journal of Science and Medicine in Sport*, vol. 16, no. 5, pp. 422–26, doi:10.1016/j.jsams.2012.11.883.

Victora, CG, Bahl, R, Barros, AJ, Franca, GV, Horton, S, Krasevec, J, Murch, S, Sankar, MJ, Walker, N & Rollins, NC 2016, 'Breastfeeding in the 21st century: epidemiology, mechanisms, and lifelong effect', *Lancet*, vol. 387, no. 10017, pp. 475–90, doi:10.1016/s0140-6736(15)01024-7.

Williams Erickson, L, Taylor, RW, Haszard, JJ, Fleming, EA, Daniels, L, Morison, BJ, Leong, C, Fangupo, LJ, Wheeler, BJ, Taylor BJ, Te Morenga, L, McLean, RM & Heath, AM 2018, 'Impact of a modified version of baby-led weaning on infant food and nutrient intakes: the BLISS randomized controlled trial', *Nutrients*, vol. 10, no. 6, doi:10.3390/nu10060740.

World Health Organization (WHO) 2002, *Infant and young child nutrition: global strategy on infant and young child feeding*, WHO, Geneva.

CHAPTER 7

Keeping children safe

Nicole Downes

DOI: https://doi.org/10.37517/978-1-74286-555-3_7
Deakin University

LINKS TO THE NATIONAL QUALITY STANDARD

Quality Area 2: Children's health and safety
- Standard 2.2: Safety – each child is protected.
- Element 2.2.1: Supervision – at all times, reasonable precautions and adequate supervision ensure children are protected from harm and hazard.
- Element 2.2.2: Incident and emergency management – plans to effectively manage incidents and emergencies are developed in consultation with relevant authorities, practised and implemented.
- Element 2.2.3: Child protection – management, educators and staff are aware of their roles and responsibilities to identify and respond to every child at risk of abuse or neglect.

LINK TO EARLY YEARS LEARNING FRAMEWORK

Learning Outcome 1: Children have a strong sense of identity
- Children feel safe, secure and supported.

Note of warning: distressing content included in this chapter

This chapter contains explicit information and details about all forms of child abuse which may cause some readers distress. It is advised that readers practice self-care by being aware of levels of discomfort and seek support when needed. Call Lifeline on 13 11 14 or visit the website at lifeline.org.au, if needed.

Introduction

Over the past two decades, high-impact research has provided insurmountable evidence to support the long-held belief that the most critical periods of development occur in the early years (NSCDS 2007; Shonkoff & Phillips 2000). During the early years of life children are particularly vulnerable, as they rely solely on their caregivers to meet their physical and emotional needs for survival and positive life outcomes (Bowlby 1969). Studies have demonstrated that high levels of emotional responsiveness and positive interactions support healthy development, wellbeing and learning outcomes (Shonkoff 2006). Whereas exposure to neglect and child abuse in the early years has been found to have harmful effects on brain development (Mustard 2006; Shonkoff, Boyce & McEwen 2009) and is strongly associated with delays in development and poor life outcomes (WHO 2018). Furthermore, the prevalence of child abuse in society affects the growth and economic prosperity of nations (OECD 2001; Heckman 2000; WHO 2018).

The United Nations Convention on the Rights of the Child (UNCRC) stipulates that all children have the right to be free from harm in mind, body and soul (UN 1989). Society's role in keeping children safe is a universal challenge and the responsibility of every citizen (WHO 2006). Though it is difficult to discuss the horrific reality of child abuse, this is exactly what needs to happen in order to bring the issue to the attention of communities and have it in the forefront of our minds. For too long, silence has favoured the perpetrators of child abuse and failed to protect children; however, this is changing. The devastating impact of child abuse is now well evidenced and understood, and a nascent global movement aims to eradicate child abuse in the 21st century (UNICEF 2018). This requires a whole-systems approach, where pathways are forged and the problems targeted collectively using diverse strategies, across all relevant sectors, with all key stakeholders involved (WHO 2006). Promisingly, more research is being undertaken to enhance our understandings and make effective recommendations. Moreover, social media provides a platform for child rights advocates to share information and provoke meaningful discussion. Public campaigns and events have raised awareness of child safety issues that can empower children and strengthen families so that they are vigilant.

Early childhood educators and professionals are important advocates, implementing new child safe principles to embrace a child safety culture within their settings. Educators play an instrumental role in keeping children safe in their settings, online, at home and in the wider community (DET 2016). As such, it is important for educators to reflect on their commitment to end child abuse. This requires enhanced levels of knowledge and skills in child protection and child safety issues so that they are capable of responding appropriately to suspected cases of child abuse, and create educational environments that promote child safety, prevent child abuse and effectively support children who have experienced abuse. This chapter aims to enhance understanding of child safety issues and explain how educators can embed this knowledge into their practice to keep children safe.

Keeping children safe in the 21st century

Societies have a special duty of care to ensure all children have the opportunity to achieve their full potential, particularly those who are vulnerable and at risk of abuse and neglect (DEECD 2014).

Child safety in Australia

Data from the Australian Institute of Health and Welfare (AIHW 2020) reports 170 200 (1 in 33) children received child protection services in 2018–19. Emotional abuse was the most substantiated (54%), followed by neglect (21%), physical abuse (15%) and sexual abuse (10%). The 2020 AIHW report identified trends based on the past five years, showing an increase in notifications, investigations and substantiations of all forms of child abuse compared to the 2013–14 data. Not surprisingly, the national spending has also increased, with the most recent figure reported at $5.5 billion spent in providing protection and out-of-home care for Australia's children (AIHW 2020). The Australian Government has responded to recommendations from the recent *Child rights report* (National Children's Commissioner 2019) and committed to end child abuse through the implementation of new legislation, policies, initiatives and funding to various support services that serve to protect the nation's children from harm (COAG 2009). For instance, the Victorian Government has a dedicated website addressing all aspects of child abuse (*see* DET 2016).

Evidenced by the alarming statistics of child abuse presented here, it is known that young children are frequent victims of neglect and abuse, including physical and mental violence (AIHW 2020). It is suggested that over 90% of child abuse is perpetrated by someone the child knows and often trusts (AIFS 2014), which is especially traumatic and destructive (Briggs 2012). There are many reasons why children are highly vulnerable to abuse, as their age and lack of experience means they have a reduced capacity to comprehend what is happening to them, limited physical ability to avoid or resist an abuser, and are less able to seek the protection of others (Briggs 2012). Children are also less capable of assessing the motives of others, are taught to obey adults, and may not know their rights and so have little ability to seek protection when someone hurts them (DET 2016). Some children are even more vulnerable to abuse than others, based on various factors including age, gender, ethnicity, disability and prior abuse or neglect (WHO 2018).

Circumstances that put children at risk of abuse

Knowledge of family circumstances that put children at risk of abuse enables educators to formulate a better understanding of the whole picture. There are many family circumstances that put children at risk of abuse; for example, divorce/separation, substance abuse/addiction, financial stress, mental illness, lack of social support, lack of education, limited understanding of child development, homelessness, caregiver childhood history of abuse, isolation and parental intellectual disability. Being able to draw on knowledge of families, in conjunction with identification of indicators of abuse, supports educators' ability to identify abuse and make a report to the appropriate organisation (ARACY 2017). Though it is difficult to think about or discuss the details of child abuse, this is what needs to be done in order to bring these issues to light for the purpose of professional practice and influencing social discourse surrounding child safety. Equipped with in-depth knowledge and understandings about child safety, communities can protect children.

Child sexual abuse

Article 34 of the UNCRC states that children have the right to be free from sexual abuse and Article 39 states children have the right to be free of any kind of exploitation (UN 1989). 'Child sexual abuse' is when a person uses power or authority over a child to involve them in sexual activity, which can include a wide range of sexual acts including fondling the child's genitals, oral sex, vaginal or anal penetration by a penis, finger or other object or exposure of the child to pornography (DET 2016, p. 15). It is important to remember that sexual abuse does not always involve physical contact or force. Perpetrators use tricks, threats, bribes, guilt and/or physical force to make children take part in sexual activities and to prevent them from telling anyone about the abuse (Briggs 2012).

Responding to child sexual abuse

The AIHW (2020) data revealed that there were 4714 substantiated cases of child sexual abuse in Australia in 2018–19. The vast majority of sexual abuse occurs in the home, at the hands of someone known to the child (AIFS 2014). All adults in Australia are mandated to report suspected child sex abuse to the police. Indicators of child sexual abuse can be found at https://www.education.vic.gov.au/childhood/professionals/health/childprotection/Pages/ecidentifying.aspx (DET 2016).

Impact of child sexual abuse

Short-term effects of child sexual abuse can include inappropriate sexual behaviour, withdrawn behaviours, acting out, depression, low self-esteem, sexually aggressive behaviour and developmental regression (including baby talk and bed wetting). Long-term effects of sexual abuse can include sexual dysfunction, anxiety, depression, higher suicide risk, re-victimisation, drug and alcohol dependency and an increase in mental illness (Briggs 2012). Sexual abuse is perhaps the most confronting form of child maltreatment and the most difficult to comprehend. Despite this, it is essential to overcome the traditional barrier of silence that has let perpetrators continue to abuse countless children and left victims feeling unable to seek help. Only by speaking openly and sharing information can society reduce the occurrence of sexual abuse and be prepared to effectively respond to instances of sexual abuse.

Child physical abuse

Article 37 of the UNCRC (UN 1989) states that no child is to be punished in a cruel and harmful way. 'Child physical abuse' is when a physical injury is inflicted on a child purposefully (non-accidentally) through the use of physical force, resulting in harm to the child. 'This includes hitting, beating, kicking, shaking, biting, strangling, scalding, burning, poisoning and suffocating. Much physical violence against children in the home is inflicted with the object of punishing' (WHO 2006, p. 10).

It should be noted at this point that although there is a clear global initiative to end all corporal punishment of children, domestic corporal punishment remains legal in many countries around the world, including Australia (Global Initiative to End All Corporate Punishment 2020). In order to effectively identify and appropriately respond to physical abuse, educators need to know the difference between domestic corporal punishment and physical abuse. Fundamentally, this distinction comes down to using physical force in either a *reasonable* or *unreasonable* way. The *Crimes Amendment (Child Protection-Physical Mistreatment) Act 2001* (NSW) (*see* NSW Department of Education 2019) states that force applied to any part of the head or neck of a child or to any other part of the body that results in bruising, marking or other injury lasting longer than a short period is *unreasonable*.

Responding to child physical abuse

The AIHW (2020) data revealed that there were 6986 substantiated cases of physical abuse in Australia in 2018–19. Educators are mandated and/or have a duty of care to make a report if a belief is formed on reasonable grounds that a child is suffering or is likely to suffer significant physical harm. In most states and territories, physical abuse must be reported to both the police and child protection services (if abuse is occurring in the home) as soon as it is possible to do so. Indicators of child physical abuse can be found at https://www.education.vic.gov.au/childhood/professionals/health/childprotection/Pages/ecidentifying.aspx (DET 2016).

Impact of child physical abuse

Effects of physical abuse include external and internal injuries, deafness, brain damage, aggressive behaviours, drug and alcohol abuse, low self-esteem, mental health problems, self-harm, increased risk of suicide, re-victimisation, delinquency and adult criminality (Briggs 2012). Porter (2016) adds that, although legal in some jurisdictions, domestic corporal punishment is a controlling form of behaviour management that impairs the healthy development of autonomy, empathy, self-esteem and social relationships throughout the lifespan.

Child emotional abuse

Article 19 of the UNCRC (UN 1989) states that children have the right to not be harmed in mind or body. 'Child emotional abuse' is when a child is rejected, isolated, ignored, discriminated against, humiliated and ridiculed (DET 2016).

Responding to child emotional abuse

The AIHW (2020) data revealed that emotional abuse is the most common, with 25 736 substantiated cases in Australia in 2018–19. Educators have either a duty of care or are mandated to make a report if a belief is formed on reasonable grounds that a child is suffering from neglect. Depending on the state legislation and with consideration to the severity of the emotional abuse suspected, reports should be made to referral agencies that can offer families support, and/or police and child protection services. Indicators of child emotional abuse can be found at https://www.education.vic.gov.au/childhood/professionals/health/childprotection/Pages/ecidentifying.aspx (DET 2016).

Impact of child emotional abuse

Emotional abuse in one form or another is said to be a component of all other types of abuse, and can consist of both acts of commission (e.g. verbal abuse) or omission (e.g. withholding affection and/or attention) and is considered to be the most damaging form of abuse (Briggs 2012). Behaviours that constitute emotional abuse in educational settings include:

- overly limiting the use of the toilet
- threatening to tell caregivers of unsatisfactory work
- rejecting children or their behaviour
- using verbal put-downs
- harassing and letting others belittle or harass children
- labelling children as clumsy, stupid, and so on.
- screaming until children cry
- using fear, for example, throwing things across the room
- providing continuous experiences of failure. (Briggs 2012)

Educators have a duty of care to every child to treat them with respect and uphold the practices outlined in the Early Childhood Australia Code of Ethics (ECA 2016). Practices that constitute emotional abuse need to be reported.

Child neglect

Article 24 of the UNCRC states that children have the right to safe water to drink and to nutritious food and Article 27 states that children have the right to a clean and safe environment to live and to have all basic needs met (UN 1989). 'Child neglect' is a failure to provide a child with an adequate standard of living, including a safe place to live, nutrition, clean water, appropriate clothing, supervision, access to medical care and education (resulting in harm to the child's physical wellbeing and development) (DET 2016). There are many types of neglect including physical, psychological, emotional, medical, educational and supervisory neglect.

Responding to child neglect

The AIHW (2020) data revealed that there were 9883 substantiated cases of neglect in Australia in 2018–19. Educators have either a duty of care or are mandated to make a report if a belief is formed on reasonable grounds that a child is suffering from neglect. Depending on the state legislation and with consideration to the severity of the suspected neglect, reports should be made to referral agencies that can offer families support, and/or police and child protection services. Indicators of child neglect can be found at https://www.education.vic.gov.au/childhood/professionals/health/childprotection/Pages/ecidentifying.aspx (DET 2016).

Impact of child neglect

The National Scientific Council on the Developing Child (NSCDC 2007) has provided extensive evidence from decades of research that shows the devastating impact of neglect on children's overall development and life outcomes. Brain architecture is firmly established in the first three years of life, paving the way for all future learning and relationship quality (Shonkoff 2006). Neglect impacts on neurological pathways in the brain and wires children for stress responses to stimuli, rather than normal, healthy responses, thereby impacting on learning potential and life outcomes. In addition, neglect has been found to set a disorganised attachment style and internal working model that impacts on future social functioning and the quality of relationships (Bowlby 1969). It is important to note that neglect can be severe enough to result in death, for example, in cases of medical neglect (untreated illness or injury) and supervisory neglect (children left alone unsupervised). In cases of neglect, establishing positive relationships with families enables educators to provide advice and referrals to support services that can assist to protect the child from neglect by improving living conditions.

Family violence

'Family violence' is a pattern of behaviour through which a person seeks to control and dominate another person (DVRCV n.d.). Family violence occurs at the hands of family members in the home, and can involve emotional, physical and sexual abuse as well as psychological harm, threats and social and financial abuse (DET 2016). Children can be either direct victims of family violence (e.g. being emotionally, physically or sexually abused) or passive victims (e.g. witnessing the abuse of a parent or sibling).

Responding to family violence

In 2016–17, 288 children were hospitalised with injuries inflicted by a parent or family member (AIHW 2019). Educators have either a duty of care or are mandated to make a report if a belief is formed on reasonable grounds that a child is suffering from neglect. Depending on the state legislation and with consideration to the severity of the family violence, reports should be made to referral agencies that can offer families support, and/or police and child protection services. Indicators of family violence can be found at https://www.education.vic.gov.au/childhood/professionals/health/childprotection/Pages/ecidentifying.aspx (DET 2016).

Impact of family violence

Family violence is a major health and welfare issue in Australia (AIHW 2019). The impact of family violence on children includes mental health issues; such as depression and anxiety, increased aggression, low self-esteem, the presence of pervasive fear, loneliness, school difficulties, peer conflict, impaired cognitive functioning, increased likelihood of substance abuse and homelessness (AIHW 2019; DET 2016). Media coverage of the deaths of young children as a result of family violence have been a driving force in the *Third action plan 2016–19 of the national plan to reduce violence against women and their children 2010–22* (Commonwealth of Australia 2016) to reduce violence through prevention and early intervention, greater support services and effective response to children living in family violence.

Child safe legislation and policy

The Council of Australian Governments (COAG 2009) endorsed a framework that has a long-term vision to reduce child abuse and neglect of Australian children and promote wellbeing. The framework is underpinned by the UNCRC (UN 1989), with a focus on the following six supportive outcomes:

- Children live in safe and supportive families and communities.
- Children and families access adequate support to promote safety and intervene early.
- Risk factors for child abuse and neglect are addressed.
- Children who have been abused or neglected receive the support and care they need for their safety and wellbeing.
- Indigenous children are supported and safe in their families and communities.
- Child sexual abuse and exploitation is prevented and survivors receive adequate support. (COAG 2009, p. 11)

Legislation and policy frameworks addressing child safety vary across Australia. Each state and territory have their own mandatory reporting schemes and are informed by legislation and Acts that stipulate the specificities (AIFS 2017).

Reporting pathways

A report is to be made to child protection, police, or referral and support agencies, depending on the type of abuse and the circumstances surrounding the abuse. Typically, when it is suspected that children are at immediate risk of significant harm, a report would be made to the police and/or child protection (AISF 2017). For cases of child abuse and neglect where the risk of significant harm is low, reports would be made to referral agencies that can offer families support with finances, parenting skills, counselling and other assistance.

It is essential that educators document all observations/discussions/information that support their concerns – the more details that can be provided, the stronger the report will be. When making a notification, the agency will expect educators to provide important details, including the child's name, date of birth, gender, home address, family structure and any other relevant information that can support their assessment and response to the report.

National principles for child safe organisations

The *National principles for child safe organisations* (AHRC 2018) (National Principles) provide a consistent approach to keeping children safe for all organisations that work with children in Australia. In line with the Victorian Child Safe Standards (regulated by the Commission for Children and Young People [CCYP] 2015), the National Principles were prompted by recommendations from the Royal Commission (FCDC 2013a; 2013b) *Betrayal of trust* inquiry which looked into institutional responses to child sexual abuse. The 10 principles aim to promote child safety.

> National Principles:
> - Child safety and wellbeing is embedded in organisational leadership, governance and culture.
> - Children and young people are informed about their rights, participate in decisions affecting them and are taken seriously.
> - Families and communities are informed and involved in promoting child safety and wellbeing.
> - Equity is upheld and diverse needs respected in policy and practice.
> - People working with children and young people are suitable and supported to reflect child safety and wellbeing values in practice.
> - Processes for complaints and concerns are child-focused.
> - Staff and volunteers are equipped with the knowledge, skills and awareness to keep children and young people safe through ongoing education and training.
> - Physical and online environments promote safety and wellbeing while minimising the opportunity for children and young people to be harmed.

- Implementation of the national child safe principles is regularly reviewed and improved.
- Policies and procedures document how the organisation deals with abuse. (AHRC, 2018)

The implementation of the Child Safe Standards (CCYP 2015) and National Principles work together to support the national framework for protecting Australia's children. Early childhood education settings must reflect on their setting's current child safe policies, pedagogies and practices, and make the required changes needed to improve the culture of child safety for young children. It is critical that educators have a comprehensive understanding of their obligations to keep children safe under a duty of care and as a mandated reporter, including the educational components discussed in this chapter.

Early Childhood Australia Code of Ethics

The Code of Ethics (ECA 2016) is underpinned by the UNCRC (UN 1989) and provides educators across the country with guidance in providing safe and nurturing environments and interactions for young children. The Code of Ethics provides a basis for critical reflection, a guide for professional behaviour, principles to inform individual and collective decision-making and a framework for reflection about the ethical responsibilities. It also makes explicit the ethical responsibilities to act in the face of injustice and when unethical practice occurs.

Duty of care

In states and territories where some types of child abuse do not fall under mandatory reporting, and for those who are not mandated reporters, educators and professionals are guided by their duty of care to keep children safe. Educators have a duty of care to take reasonable steps to protect children from harm (DEECD 2014; DET 2016).

CASE STUDY

There have been many cases of child abuse and neglect in Australia that have gained public attention and contributed to current legislation and child safe practices. In particular the case of 2-year-old Daniel Valerio has made a significant impact. Mandatory reporting was introduced in Victoria in 1992 following the heavily publicised case of Daniel, who died from internal abdominal injuries sustained from ongoing child abuse at the hands of his stepfather. The media reported Daniel's extensive injuries to include over 100 bruises and two broken collarbones, and though it was later discovered that Daniel had been seen by 21 professionals, including several doctors and a teacher, only one anonymous call

continued...

was made to child protection. The media coverage surrounding Daniel's death highlighted the flaws of a voluntary reporting system, as Daniel had presented with many physical and behavioural indicators of significant child abuse, yet duty of care did not compel professionals to make a notification.

Reflective questions

- What type/s of abuse are evident?
- What behavioural and/or physical indicators of abuse are identifiable?
- What risk factors are present?
- What are the reporting obligations for an early childhood educator in this scenario? (Note: refer to state and territory mandatory reporting legislation.)

Child safety in practice

As the second highest reporter of child abuse in Australia (AIHW 2020), educators play a crucial role in keeping children safe at home, in educational settings, online and in the community. Educators' practice is guided by child safe frameworks, standards, legislation and policy, which work together to keep children safe. It is critical that educators have a comprehensive understanding of their obligations and are vigilant in embedding these in their professional practice. Informed by an in-depth knowledge of child safety issues and a clear understanding of child safe frameworks, standards and legislation, educators are able to effectively practice child safety to support young children. Practice that serves to keep children safe from harm is multifaceted and aimed at preventing child abuse from occurring in the first place, promoting child safety in educational settings, home and communities, and responding appropriately to suspected cases of abuse to protect children from harm. This section covers key areas for educators to enhance their knowledge and practice in keeping children safe.

Training in child safety

Child safety training is one of the most important components in keeping children safe from harm (Briggs 2012; DET 2016). When educators are highly knowledgeable in all areas of child safety, they are better able to identify abuse, to respond appropriately and to provide support for traumatised children.

The AIHW report (2020) again identified educators as the second highest notifiers of child abuse in Australia (20%), highlighting the critical role educators play in keeping children safe. The responsibility of educators as agents in protecting young children means that attention needs to be paid to ensure they are equipped with the knowledge and skills required to keep children safe, and as such the importance of having educators who are highly trained in matters of child safety cannot be overstated. However, there are challenges faced by early childhood educators when it comes to reporting and responding effectively to suspected cases of child abuse, which often result in delays in notifications and therefore children who are at further risk of harm. After forming a belief that a child is being abused, notifiers typically wait one month before making a report.

Research has shown that professionals working with children have had difficulties in their notification experiences, leading to feelings of confusion and dissatisfaction with the system (Blaskett & Taylor 2003). Educators in particular are said to be reluctant and indecisive in the notification process (Goddard, Saunders, Stanley & Tucci 2002; Walsh, Farrell & Schweitzer 2005). There have been several reasons suggested for this, including fear of being wrong, fear of reprisal, unawareness of reporting obligations, uncertainty of reporting pathways and a general lack of knowledge about child safety issues. Professional development and training in child safety are ways to address these issues that impact on educators' ability to responding effectively to suspected child abuse.

Training in child safety is known to be a critical component in keeping children safe (Briggs 2012). Educators with enhanced child safety knowledge and skills are able to identify and respond appropriately to suspected child abuse, as well as understand how to create child safe environments that support traumatised children. Briggs (2012, pp. 71–2) suggests several areas that should be a focus of training in child safety; such as:

- in-depth knowledge of the different forms of child abuse
- how to identify physical and behavioural indicators of all forms of child abuse
- understanding circumstances that put children at risk of abuse
- how to respond appropriately to a child's disclosure of abuse
- knowledge of legislation, regulations and policies for reporting child abuse and neglect
- knowing how to report suspected child abuse using reporting pathways
- the ability to uphold and teach children about their rights in the room
- the knowledge and skill set to deliver protective education information to young children
- an in-depth understanding of trauma and how to modify the environment and pedagogy to support children to recover from child abuse through trauma-informed practice.

Responding to a disclosure

There are many different ways in which child maltreatment can be identified. For example, observation of physical and behavioural indicators of abuse, reports by others who know the child, drawings, hints and questions, or a direct disclosure by the child. The term 'disclosure' is used to describe information provided by a child in relation to child abuse. A 'purposeful disclosure' is when a child deliberately tells you they are experiencing abuse. An 'accidental disclosure' is when the child reveals information that indicates they are experiencing abuse, or they may discuss the abuse their 'friend' is experiencing, or someone who knows the child may tell you about the abuse.

Many people assume that children will just tell other people if they are being abused, however this is often *not* the case. More commonly children will give clues or hints that suggest maltreatment, sometimes to test the waters before disclosing more information, and sometimes with the belief that they have made a clear disclosure of abuse.

As Briggs (2012, p. 54) states:

> A knowledgeable professional can identify and handle signs of abuse in psychologically helpful ways. An uninformed professional can cause additional harm by dismissing, ignoring, misreading or punishing disclosure of sexual abuse in particular.

It is therefore essential that educators have the knowledge and skills needed to appropriately respond to a disclosure of abuse. **Table 7.1** outlines some key points to remember when responding to a disclosure of abuse.

Trauma informed practice

'Understanding the experience of the abused and neglected child assists us to develop compassion, patience and empathy. It is a key intervention in itself' (CSC 2007, p. ii). Early childhood trauma, as a result of abuse and neglect, has negative impacts on development and brain maturation (Shonkoff 2006). Given the prevalence of abuse and neglect in early childhood, every step should be taken to safeguard children who are at risk and to support the recovery of those who have experienced abuse through trauma-informed practice (McMahon & Keenan 2008; WHO 2006).

'Trauma' occurs when an event or situation is so frightening that the survival response is activated in the brain, which releases copious amounts of adrenaline and other chemicals, causing the heart to beat faster and pupils to dilate – this is an important function to enable a person to respond to the threat (ACF 2018). The prefrontal cortex (responsible for complex cognitive behaviour, attention, decision-making and impulse control) is impaired when the survival response is activated, as the brain requires all its energy and attention for survival. Once the threat subsides, cortisol (the stress hormone) is released in the brain to support the return to normal brain and body function. There are two types of trauma: 'acute trauma', which is a once off, intense frightening experience (e.g. a car accident); and 'complex/ongoing trauma', which is repeated experiences of threat and stress (e.g. child abuse and neglect). With complex/ongoing trauma, the survival response (freeze, flight or fight) is activated in the brain for extended periods of time. Experiences of complex/ongoing trauma derail healthy brain development, with damaging effects on learning, memory, social functioning, impulse control and emotional regulation across the lifespan (ACF 2018).

Table 7.1 Responding appropriately to a disclosure

Educators should …	Educators should not …
• maintain a calm appearance and manage feelings of sadness, anger, shock • give the child their full attention • listen without interrupting • consider body language and non-verbal communication, and active listening techniques (where appropriate) • provide statements to reassure the child (e.g. 'You have done the right thing by telling me', 'You have been very brave', 'It is not your fault', 'I am sorry this has happened to you', 'I will do everything I can to help') • tell the child that they believe them • accept their disclosure (as much or little as they want to tell) and their use of terminology/slang; enable them to take their time • ask open-ended questions • answer questions as simply and honestly as possible • make a plan with the child • tell them what will happen next.	• make promises that cannot be kept (e.g. 'I promise not to tell anyone', 'I promise this will never happen to you again') • keep the abuse a secret • answer questions to which they do not have the answers • interrogate, investigate, or ask more questions than necessary • confront the perpetrator • ask leading questions (e.g. 'Did Dad hit you?') • discuss the child with others not directly involved in helping • touch the child or remove clothing to view injuries • notify the family • question the child's story or ask 'why' questions (which implies blame) • try to change the child's mind if they recant • interrupt or fill silences • show or display shock, anger or disapproval • assume the abuse was a terrible experience (child can feel shame if they experienced pleasure) • correct the child's use of slang.

Note: Adapted from Arthur-Kelly, Lyons, Butterfield and Cordon (2010); DET (2016); Goldsworthy (2015); Hunter, Kennedy, Partridge and Rime (2002); WHO (2006).

Children who have experienced trauma can present as either hypervigilant (hyper-aroused) or dissociative (hypo-aroused) (Briggs 2012). Hypervigilance stems from the child's need for control as a way to protect themselves from abuse, meaning they are on constant lookout for danger and are primed to respond quickly. Hypervigilant children can appear agitated, are easily distracted by noises and people, often interrupt others and have difficulty regulating their emotions (ACF 2018; CSC 2007). Dissociation is a way for the child to escape harmful situations and experiences by shutting down, as they have learned that no amount of hypervigilance can protect them from abuse. Dissociated children can appear quiet, distant, withdrawn, disengaged and are often described as daydreamers (ACF 2018; CSC 2007). Either of the aforementioned coping mechanisms in response to trauma impairs the child's ability to actively engage in learning and socialising.

Children with histories of abuse are developmentally much younger than their chronological age. Impacts on learning include reduced cognitive capacity, sleep disturbance causing poor concentration, difficulties with memory making learning harder, language delays including reduced capacity for listening, understanding and expressing, and disorganised thought patterns which can make them seem thoughtless and uncaring (CSC 2007).

Impacts on social-emotional development include a need for control (causing conflict with educators and other children), attachment difficulties (making attachment to the setting problematic), poor peer relationships (may include inability to read body language/facial expression/others' intentions/rules of relationships and play, i.e. turn-taking and sharing), unstable living situation (reducing learning and capacity to engage with a new setting), and affect dysregulation (hyperarousal or dissociation which can lead to oppositional, aggressive behaviour, emotional outbursts, or disconnected, disengaged behaviour) (CSC 2007).

In educational settings, the indicators of trauma are often overlooked and misunderstood, resulting in children being labelled as disruptive, naughty, daydreamers or even at times misdiagnosed with attention deficit disorders (ADHD), due to the similarity in indicators (Szymanski, Sapanski & Conway 2011). It is imperative that educators are able to identify signs of trauma and work effectively to support traumatised children through trauma-informed practice. 'Trauma-informed practice' requires educators to understand the impact of trauma on learning, development and behaviour. There are several basic practices that educators can embed to support traumatised children, including understanding the child, establishing and maintaining trusting relationships, creating structure/routine and managing their own emotions (CSC 2007). There are examples of how these work in practice, as well as many other practice suggestions in the *Calmer classrooms* (CSC 2007) document and the *Making space for learning: trauma informed practice in schools* (ACF 2018).

Conclusion

This chapter has presented some of the key aspects of child safety and has highlighted the important role educators have to play. As well as meeting their legal and ethical obligations, educators contribute to the global movement to end all violence against children by promoting, practising and teaching child rights in educational settings. Educators also have a responsibility to stay informed with contemporary research, policies, practices and procedures relating to child safety.

Keeping children safe

CASE STUDY

One of the children in your setting, Sarah (4 years), has been arriving late to preschool over the past few weeks. She sometimes forgets to bring lunch and you've noticed her clothes often appear unwashed. You were surprised to find Sarah sleeping in the home corner twice last week. You discuss this with her mother, who tells you that she recently lost her regular job and has had to take on some shift work which has caused disruptions to their routine. Sarah's mum seems exhausted and said she is finding it hard to stay on top of everything.

Reflective questions

- What type/s of abuse are evident?
- What behavioural and/or physical indicators of abuse are identifiable?
- What risk factors are present?
- What are the reporting obligations for an early childhood educator in this scenario? (Note: refer to state and territory mandatory reporting legislation.)

References

Arthur-Kelly, M, Lyons, G, Butterfield, N & Cordon, C 2010, 'Building positive relationships through effective communication', in M Arthur-Kelly, G Lyons & M Ford (eds), *Classroom management: creating positive learning environments*, 3rd edn, Cengage Learning, Melbourne.

Australian Childhood Foundation (ACF) 2018, *Making space for learning: trauma informed practice in schools*, Australian Government Department of Families, Housing, Community Services and Indigenous Affairs, Melbourne. Retrieved from https://professionals.childhood.org.au/app/uploads/2018/08/ACF325-Making-Space-For-Learning-Book-v4.pdf

Australian Human Rights Commission (AHRC) 2018, *National principles for child safe organisations*, AHRC. Retrieved from https://childsafe.humanrights.gov.au/sites/default/files/2019-02/National_Principles_for_Child_Safe_Organisations2019.pdf

Australian Institute of Family Studies (AIFS) 2014, *Who abuses children?*, Child Family Community Australia, Australian Government, Melbourne. Retrieved from https://aifs.gov.au/cfca/publications/who-abuses-children

Australian Institute of Family Studies (AIFS) 2017, *Mandatory reporting of child abuse and neglect*, Australian Government, Melbourne. Retrieved from https://aifs.gov.au/cfca/publications/mandatory-reporting-child-abuse-and-neglect

Australian Institute of Health and Welfare (AIHW) 2019, *Family, domestic and sexual violence in Australia: continuing the national story*, Australian Government, Canberra. Retrieved from https://www.aihw.gov.au/getmedia/b180312b-27de-4cd9-b43e-16109e52f3d4/aihw-fdv4-FDSV-in-Australia-2019_in-brief.pdf.aspx?inline=true

Australian Institute of Health and Welfare (AIHW) 2020, *Child protection Australia 2018–19*, Australian Government, Canberra. Retrieved from https://www.aihw.gov.au/getmedia/3a25c195-e30a-4f10-a052-adbfd56d6d45/aihw-cws-74.pdf.aspx?inline=true

Australian Research Alliance for Children and Youth (ARACY) 2017, *ARACY annual report*, ARACY, Canberra. Retrieved from https://www.aracy.org.au/publications-resources/command/download_file/id/372/filename/ARACY_Annual_Report_2017.pdf

Blaskett, B & Taylor, S. C 2003, *Facilitators and inhibitors of mandatory reporting of suspected child abuse: a research report*, The Criminology Research Council, Australian Government Canberra. Retrieved from https://crg.aic.gov.au/reports/200102-09.pdf

Bowlby, J 1969, *Attachment and loss: attachment vol. 1*, Penguin, London.

Briggs, F 2012, *Child protection: the essential guide for teachers and other professionals whose work involves children*, JoJo Publishing, Melbourne.

Child Safety Commissioner (CSC) 2007, *Calmer classrooms: a guide to working with traumatised children*, CSC, Melbourne. Retrieved from https://www.acesconnection.com/g/aces-in-education/clip/calmer-classrooms-a-guide-to-working-with-traumatised-children-pdf

Commission for Children and Young People (CCYP) 2015, *Child Safe Standards – managing the risk of child abuse in schools*, ministerial order no. 870. Retrieved from https://ccyp.vic.gov.au/child-safety/being-a-child-safe-organisation/

Commonwealth of Australia (2016), *Third action plan 2016–19 of the national plan to reduce violence against women and their children 2010–22*, Australian Government, Melbourne. Retrieved from https://plan4womenssafety.dss.gov.au/the-national-plan/third-action-plan/

Council of Australian Governments (COAG) 2009, *Protecting children is everyone's responsibility: national framework for protecting Australia's children 2009–2020,* Commonwealth of Australia, Melbourne.

Department of Education and Early Childhood Development (DEECD) 2014, *Vulnerable children action plan: the departments plan to implement Victoria's vulnerable children strategy 2013–2022*, Early Childhood Strategy Division, Department of Education and Early Childhood Development and Victorian Curriculum and Assessment Authority, Melbourne.

Department of Education and Training (DET) 2016, *Identifying signs of child abuse,* Victoria State Government, Melbourne. Retrieved from https://www.education.vic.gov.au/childhood/professionals/health/childprotection/Pages/ecidentifying.aspx

Domestic Violence Resource Centre Victoria (DVRCV) n.d., *What is domestic violence?*, Victorian State Government, Melbourne. Retrieved from https://www.dvrcv.org.au/about/what-domestic-violence.

Early Childhood Australia (ECA) 2016, *Early childhood of Australia code of ethics*, ECA, Canberra.

Family and Community Development Committee (FCDC) 2013a, *Betrayal of trust inquiry. Inquiry into the handling of child abuse by religious and other non-government organisations,* vol. 1, FCDC. Retrieved from https://www.parliament.vic.gov.au/images/stories/committees/fcdc/inquiries/57th/Child_Abuse_Inquiry/Report/Preliminaries.pdf

Family and Community Development Committee (FCDC) 2013b, *Betrayal of trust inquiry. Inquiry into the handling of child abuse by religious and other non-government organisations,* vol. 2, FCDC. Retrieved from https://www.parliament.vic.gov.au/file_uploads/Inquiry_into_Handling_of_Abuse_Volume_2_FINAL_web_y78t3Wpb.pdf

Global Initiative to End All Corporal Punishment of Children 2020, *Global report: 2019. Progress towards ending corporal punishment of children*, Global Initiative to End All Corporal Punishment of Children, London. Retrieved from http://endcorporalpunishment.org/wp-content/uploads/global/Global-report-2019.pdf

Goddard, CR, Saunders, BJ, Stanley, JR & Tucci, J 2002, *A study in confusion: factors which affect the decisions of professionals when reporting child abuse and neglect*, Australian Childhood Foundation, Melbourne.

Goldsworthy, K 2015, *Responding to children and young people's disclosures of abuse,* practitioner resource, Australian Institute of Family Studies, Child Family Community Australia, Australian Government, Melbourne. Retrieved from https://aifs.gov.au/cfca/publications/responding-children-and-young-people-s-disclosures-abu

Heckman, JJ 2000, 'Policies to foster human capital', *Research in Economics*, vol. 54, no. 1, pp. 3-56. Retrieved from https://ideas.repec.org/a/eee/reecon/v54y2000i1p3-56.html

Hunter, S, Kennedy, K, Partridge, S & Rimer, P 2002, *'Responding effectively to disclosure' I'm a great kid: a program for the primary prevention of child abuse*, teacher's guide, rev. edn, Toronto Child Abuse Centre, Toronto, pp. 20–23.

McMahon, L & Keenan, P 2008, *NICCY rights review 2008*. Retrieved from https://dera.ioe.ac.uk/9123/1/NICCY%20Rights%20Review%202008%20.pdf

Mustard, MD 2006, 'Experience-based brain development: scientific underpinnings of the importance of early child development in a global world', *Paediatric Child Health*, vol. 11, no. 9, pp. 571–72, doi:10.1093/pch/11.9.571.

National Scientific Council on the Developing Child (NSCDC) 2007, *How early child care affects later development*, Harvard University, Cambridge, MA. Retrieved from http://www.developingchild.net

National Children's Commissioner 2019, *In their own right: children's rights in Australia. Children's rights report*, Australian Human Rights Commission, Sydney. Retrieved from https://www.humanrights.gov.au/our-work/childrens-rights/publications/childrens-rights-report-2019

NSW Department of Education 2019, *Child protection and respectful relationships education*, New South Wales Education, Sydney. Retrieved from https://education.nsw.gov.au/teaching-and-learning/curriculum/key-learning-areas/pdhpe/child-protection-and-respectful-relationships-education

Organisation for Economic Co-operation and Development (OECD) 2001, *Starting strong: early childhood education and care*, OECD, Paris.

Porter, L 2016, *Young children's behaviour: guidance approaches for early childhood educators*, Allen and Unwin, Sydney.

Shonkoff, JP 2006, 'A promising opportunity for developmental and behavioural paediatrics at the interface of neuroscience, psychology, and social policy: remarks on receiving the 2005 C Anderson Aldrich Award', *Paediatrics*, vol. 118, no. 5, pp. 2187–91.

Shonkoff, JP & Phillips, D 2000, *From neurons to neighborhoods: the science of early childhood development*, National Academies Press, Washington.

Shonkoff, JP, Boyce, WT & McEwen, BS 2009, 'Neuroscience, molecular biology, and the childhood roots of health disparities: building a new framework for health promotion and disease prevention', *The Journal of the American Medical Association*, vol. 301, no. 21, pp. 2252-59.

Steering Committee for the Review of Government Service Provision (SCRGSP) 2019, *Report on government services 2019,* Productivity Commission, Melbourne.

Szymanski, K, Sapanski, L & Conway, F 2011, 'Trauma and ADHD – Association or diagnostic confusion? A clinical perspective', *Journal of Infant, Child and Adolescent Psychotherapy*, vol. 10, no. 1, pp. 51–59.

United Nations (UN) 1989, *Convention on the rights of the child*, United Nations, Geneva. Retrieved from www.refworld.org/docid/3ae6b38f0.html

United Nations International Children's Emergency Fund (UNICEF) 2018, *INSPIRE – indicator guidance and results framework – ending violence against children: how to define and measure change*, UNICEF, New York.

Walsh, K, Farrell, A & Schweitzer, R 2005, *Critical factors in teachers' detecting and reporting child abuse and neglect: implications for practice*, Abused Child Trust, Brisbane.

World Health Organisation (WHO) 2006, *Preventing child maltreatment: a guide to taking action and generating evidence*, WHO, Geneva. Retrieved from www.who.int/violence_injury_prevention/publications/violence/child_maltreatment/en/

World Health Organisation (WHO) 2018, *INSPIRE handbook. Action for implementing the seven strategies*, WHO, Geneva.

CHAPTER 8

Social and emotional development in early childhood

Claire Blewitt, Helen Skouteris, Heidi Bergmeier and Amanda O'Connor

DOI: https://doi.org/10.37517/978-1-74286-555-3_8
Monash Centre for Health Research Implementation, School of Public Health and Preventive Medicine, Monash University

LINKS TO NATIONAL QUALITY STANDARD

Quality Area 5: Relationships with children
- Standard 5.1: Relationships between educators and children – respectful and equitable relationships are maintained with each child.
- Element 5.1.1: Positive educator to child interactions – responsive and meaningful interactions build trusting relationships which engage and support each child to feel secure, confident and included.

LINKS TO EARLY YEARS LEARNING FRAMEWORK

Learning Outcome 1: Children have a strong sense of identity
- Children learn to interact in relation to others with care, empathy and respect.

Learning Outcome 3: Children have a strong sense of wellbeing
- Children become strong in their social and emotional wellbeing.

Introduction

The social and emotional competencies that emerge in early childhood are crucial for children's ongoing health, development and wellbeing. Through responsive and nurturing relationships, interactions and experiences, young children learn to understand

and regulate their emotions, attention and behaviour, equipping them to form prosocial relationships and engage in learning before they commence school. Conversely, difficulty navigating early social-emotional milestones can hinder a child's emotional regulation and social behaviour. High-quality early childhood education and care (ECEC) programs can strengthen the social, emotional and cognitive skills that are crucial for future learning and wellbeing, especially for children experiencing economic disadvantage or early social-emotional difficulties. The Early Years Learning Framework for Australia (EYLF) (DEEWR 2009) recognises the important role that early childhood programs play in fostering children's self-awareness, identity, wellbeing, confidence and connection to their world through holistic, responsive and intentional pedagogical practices.

Early childhood: a critical window for social and emotional development

Social-emotional milestones in early childhood

Social and emotional development refers to a broad and interrelated set of skills. In a review of the social-emotional domains most often captured in theoretical models, Halle and Darling-Churchill (2016) suggest 'social competence', 'emotional competence', 'self-regulation' and 'behaviour problems' are important to understanding, assessing and supporting children's development. *Social competence* refers to appropriate social interactions, and the ability to form and maintain positive interpersonal relationships (Denham et al. 2009). During early childhood, children typically begin to understand social cues and use prosocial behaviours to develop positive relationships with peers and close adults. *Emotional competence* describes children's capacity to recognise, describe and express their emotions, understand the feelings of others, and regulate their emotional responses (Denham et al. 2016). Children often begin to show empathy in the preschool years, with increasing ability to reflect on how their own words and actions might impact others. *Self-regulation* describes children's capacity to control their thoughts, feelings and behaviour in a socially appropriate way. Calming down, paying attention during a group activity or persisting with a challenging task showcase self-regulation skills. Finally, *behaviour problems* capture inappropriate behaviours or those that hinder a child's ability to adapt and function within family, early learning or social settings. They include internalising emotions or behaviours (e.g. worry, anxiety, withdrawal, sadness) and externalising behaviours (e.g. aggression, noncompliance, impulsivity, hostility) (Halle & Darling-Churchill, 2016).

Problematic behaviours in early childhood

For some young children, difficulties in early social-emotional functioning can predict oppositional behaviours, poor attention and emotional problems, increased risk of poor academic performance, antisocial behaviour, and longer term adverse outcomes including depression, obesity, diabetes and heart disease, higher rates of unemployment, substance abuse, family violence, and suicide in adolescence and adulthood (Aviles, Anderson & Davila 2006; Bor, McGee & Fagan 2004; IOM & NRC 2015; OECD 2015; Smart et al. 2005). Globally, it has been estimated that between 9.5 and 14.2% of children aged 5 and under experience serious emotional and behavioural challenges that have a significant impact on their day-to-day activities and require high levels of support (Brauner & Stephens 2006).

Risk and protective factors for children's social-emotional development

There are many factors that can shape young children's mental health. The social ecological framework (Bronfenbrenner 1977; 1979) provides a means to consider the social, environmental, community, political and economic factors that may influence children's development and behaviour. Acknowledging family as the first and foremost influence, the model in **Figure 8.1** illustrates that other individuals; such as early childhood educators, can support a child's health and wellbeing.

Socio-economic disadvantage is an important predictor of social-emotional difficulties and behavioural problems (Kiernan & Huerta 2008; Shonkoff & Phillips 2000; West, Denton & Reaney 2001; Yoshikawa, Aber & Beardslee 2012). In a review of 30 studies examining the prevalence of challenging behaviour in young children from low-income families, Huaqing Qi and Kaiser (2003) found almost 30% of disadvantaged children exhibited problems compared to an expected 3–6% in the general population. Other familial factors including parental mental health, low self-efficacy and stress, certain parenting styles, exposure to family violence, and insecure caregiver–child attachment histories, in addition to individual factors; such as genetics, temperament, physical health and cognitive functioning, can contribute to difficulties in a child's social-emotional development (Anthony et al. 2005; Bayer et al. 2011; Goldfeld et al. 2014; Groh et al. 2017; Kitzmann, Gaylord, Holt & Kenny 2003).

Strengthening children's social and emotional development in early childhood settings

Participation in high-quality ECEC can improve the social, emotional and cognitive skills that support children's future learning and wellbeing (Barnett 2011; Camilli, Vargas, Ryan & Barnett 2010; Oberklaid et al. 2013). Of all the activities and practices that occur in the early years classroom, the quality of interactions between educators and children are a crucial driver of children's learning and development (Early, Pan, Maxwell & Ponder 2017; Mashburn et al. 2008). This is especially evident for children experiencing economic disadvantage (Duncan & Sojourner 2013).

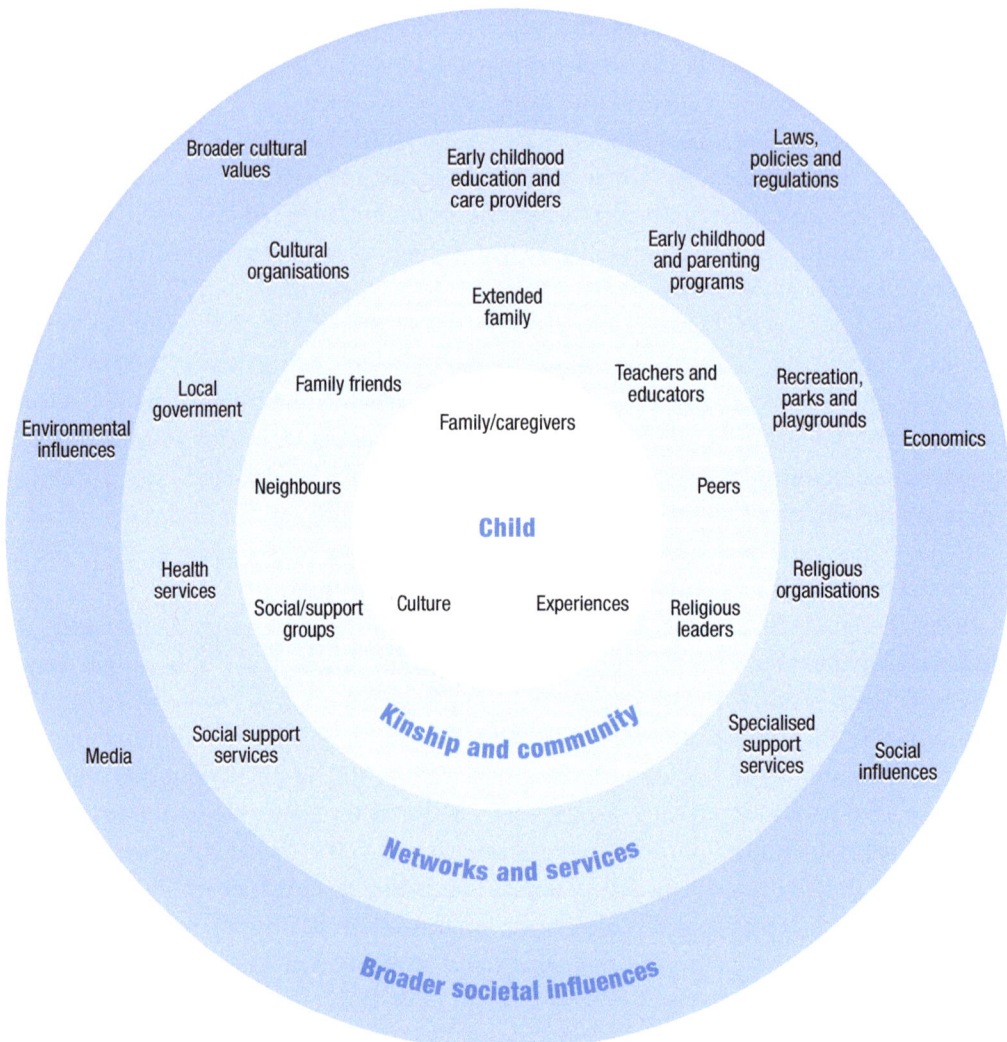

Figure 8.1 Social ecological framework
Adapted from the VEYLDF (DET, 2016).

Importance of educator–child relationships in early years settings

Early childhood educators play a vital role, as caregivers, in supporting the social and emotional development of children in their care. Strong connections within this dyadic relationship have been found to improve children's health, emotional wellbeing, problem behaviours, social and academic skills (Forry, Moodie, Simkin & Rothenberg 2011; Mortensen and Barnett 2015). 'Attachment theory' is a useful framework to describe and explore the enduring connections that develop between children and their caregivers; it recognises that a deep emotional bond between caregiver and child is crucial for a child's development (Bowlby 1969).

Attachment is the significant psychological connection a child has with a caregiver and is characterised by specific behaviours expressed by the caregiver and child through their interactions (Bowlby 1969). In order to feel safe and secure, children engage in proximity seeking behaviours (calling, smiling, crying and seeking close physical contact) with caregivers, especially when feeling threatened or upset; they also use their caregivers as a secure base from which to explore (Ainsworth 1990). Caregivers' engagement with and responsiveness to the child significantly influences the attachment process. Caregiver retrieving behaviours (nurturance and care) are activated by the child's proximity seeking behaviours, serving as a protective function and building the attachment bond between the caregiver and the child. Responding sensitively, appropriately and caring for the child's needs enables the child to be confident the caregiver is available for protection and emotional support, and promotes feelings of safety and security (Ainsworth 1990; Bowlby 1969).

High-quality relationships are recognised as those exhibiting sensitivity and closeness through caring, warm, affectionate and emotionally positive interactions and bi-directional exchanges (Heatly & Votruba-Drzal 2017; Pianta 1999). Quality relationships are vital in supporting children's developmental achievements, such as trust in others, sense of self and effectance (ability to explore and influence the environment) (Bornstein, Suwalsky & Breakstone 2012). O'Brien and Mosco (2012) suggest core principles underpinning positive caregiver–child relationships include understanding, mutual respect and open communication; these factors contribute to children's social and emotional learning (SEL) through exposure to empathy, prosocial behaviours and interpersonal and intrapersonal skills. Caregivers and educators are uniquely placed to establish high-quality relationships that support children's social and emotional development.

Due to the nature of the educator–child relationship, attachment theory frameworks have been utilised to examine the influence of the relationship on children's development (Rolfe 2004). Key relationship elements (closeness, conflict and dependency) have been found to be critical in the caregiving relationship for the developing child in early years settings (Pianta & Steinberg 1992; Pianta, Steinberg & Rollins 1995). Educator–child relationship quality has been found to mediate children's internalising and externalising behaviours, and elevated levels of educator–child conflict has been associated with externalising behaviour in late childhood (O'Connor, Collins & Supplee 2012). Educators who provide safe and secure environments encourage children to demonstrate empathy and care towards others, manage their emotional responses, and initiate social interactions (Denham & Burton 1996).

Everyday interactions shape children's social, emotional and cognitive learning

Educator–child interactions are defined as the daily back and forth instructional and emotional exchanges between the educator and child throughout the day (Hamre et al. 2012). These daily interactions between an educator and child build and strengthen the educator–child relationship, and strongly contribute to children's learning and development (Bronfenbrenner & Morris 1998). Research indicates that high-quality sensitive interactions are associated with increased positive and decreased negative behaviour, especially for children with below average social skills (Garbacz et al. 2014), and enhanced language, pre-academic and social skills (Burchinal et al. 2008).

The Teaching Through Interactions (TTI) framework has been used in early childhood settings to explore three broad domains of educator–child interactions, identified through theory and research, that support children's development (Hamre & Pianta 2007). 'Emotional support' focuses on positive, consistent and sensitive interactions that foster children's prosocial and self-regulatory skills, and may reduce the impact of behavioural challenges on learning. The 'classroom organisation' domain examines how educators facilitate classroom interactions which contribute to children's behaviours and attention, and encourage self-regulation, executive control and cognitive development. It encompasses effective behaviour management, management of instructional time and routines, the provision of instructional learning formats that maximise engagement, and the degree to which ineffective classroom management leads to disruption. Finally, 'instructional support' considers children's learning based on how facts are interconnected, organised and scaffolded. Instructional interactions to promote children's cognitive and language development serve to control frustration, increase interest, motivation and effort. A general domain of 'responsivity' crossing all domain-specific interactions is characterised by recognising and responding to children's cues in a timely manner, and individualising teaching style to the child's need and engagement.

The TTI framework has been applied within professional learning programs for educators that seek to improve educator–child interactions. Evaluations of these programs report that participating educators displayed greater knowledge of, and skills in: identifying effective interactions; more effective emotional and instructional interactions (Hamre et al. 2012); improved emotional and instructional supports (Early, Pan, Maxwell & Ponder 2017); strategies to facilitate children's higher order thinking skills (Pianta et al. 2014); and improvements in children's language and literacy (Mashburn et al. 2010). Overall, the TTI framework suggests that high-quality, responsive relationships, founded in emotional, organisational and instructional support are associated with improved outcomes for children. Supporting educators to intentionally foster children's SEL through the TTI framework domains may be an effective approach to improve relationships and interactions between educators and children, and children's subsequent social-emotional wellbeing (Blewitt, Morris et al. 2018).

Social and emotional learning

Social and emotional learning relies heavily on high-quality educator–child interactions to strengthen children's social and emotional competencies through teaching, modelling and practice. SEL is defined by the Collaborative for Academic, Social and

Emotional Learning (CASEL) as the acquisition and application of knowledge and skills across five domains of social-emotional competence: self-awareness, social awareness, self-management, relationship skills, and responsible decision-making (Weissberg, Durlak, Domitrovich & Gullotta 2015). Approaches to SEL in early childhood settings include explicit lesson-based skill instruction, embedding intentional practices, techniques and strategies into everyday interactions and activities, and integrating SEL into other areas of learning (CASEL 2013; Weissberg et al. 2015). The application of SEL approaches in ECEC settings requires careful consideration of the unique developmental characteristics of young children; such as their emerging cognitive abilities that underpin social and self-awareness, and their limited ability to regulate behaviour compared to older peers (Bierman & Motamedi 2015). It is also important to recognise the influence of the physical learning environment on children's social and emotional skills. The layout, furniture, equipment, toys and visuals in the room, use of consistent and predictable routines and cues, and structuring the space to encourage engagement with peers and educators support SEL and can be particularly beneficial for children experiencing specific behavioural or emotional challenges.

Increasingly, SEL programs are delivered within a response-to-intervention (RTI) framework (Greenberg, Domitrovich, Weissberg & Durlak 2017; Shepley & Grisham-Brown 2019). RTI typically includes a three-tiered approach to assess, identify and support children's needs through evidence-informed intervention. As shown in **Figure 8.2**, the first tier of RTI includes universal programming offered to all children in the group. For SEL, these Tier 1 programs are delivered to all children, offering a preventative approach to promote social-emotional capabilities at the whole group scale. Tier 2 SEL programs are targeted, hence they are delivered to select children at risk of, or already experiencing, social, emotional or behavioural challenges, who may

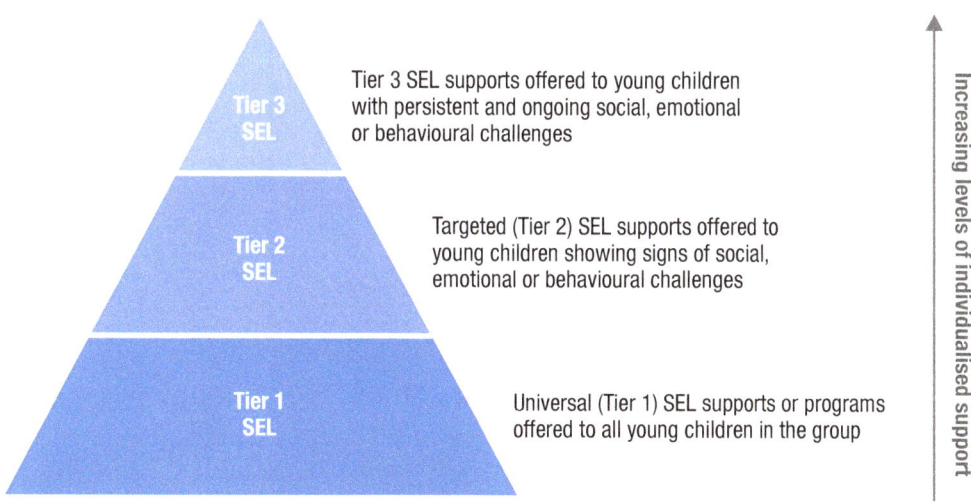

Figure 8.2 Multi-tiered approach to SEL

not have responded to universal supports. Finally, Tier 3 interventions are delivered to children requiring intensive and individualised support (Macklem 2011).

Universal SEL

Universal preventative SEL approaches are conceptualised as delivering curriculum components and teaching practices intentionally designed for fostering optimal child development by supporting children's social-emotional skills, which in turn, enhance their wellbeing, learning outcomes and may prevent future mental health issues (Weissberg et al. 2015). Universal SEL approaches are largely designed to be incorporated into typical classroom routines and activities; such as storytelling, role play and singing, and may involve explicit and active instruction, modelling, opportunity for practice, and reinforcement (Blewitt, Fuller-Tyszkiewicz et al. 2018). Programs tend to draw on overlapping *social-cognitive*, *emotional* and *self-regulation* theoretical perspectives that recognise the interplay between the development of cognitive structures (including those involved in promoting long-term self-regulation) and foundational social-emotional competencies (Bierman & Motamedi 2015; McClelland, Tominey, Schmitt & Duncan 2017):

- *Social-cognitive learning* frameworks propose that social behaviour is learned through cognitive processes that take place in a social context, in which children learn to interpret social cues and scenarios by observing and imitating others, problem-solving, and through direct instructions and feedback (Bandura & Walters 1963; Bierman & Motamedi 2015; McClelland, Tominey, Schmitt & Duncan 2017).
- *Emotional learning* frameworks emphasise the interrelationships between emotional arousal (e.g. stress), emotional reactivity and ability to regulate emotions in fostering social-emotional development. In the context of SEL interventions, curricula may include a focus on building children's ability to recognise differing emotions, develop language to help label and express emotions and implement strategies (often play-based) for regulating responses (Greenberg 2006; Izard 2002).
- *Self-regulation learning* frameworks acknowledge the role that executive function skills (e.g. brain structures involved in controlling impulses, such as those needed for sitting still and listening in a group and dealing with frustration) play in building children's capacity to engage in goal-directed behaviour and regulate emotions, which in turn decreases aggressive behaviours and promotes social and learning competence (Bierman & Motamedi 2015).

Universal SEL programs can address a broad and interrelated set of cognitive, behavioural, and affective skills or target focal skills that encourage specific competencies; such as mindfulness, coping and resilience, social problem-solving and conversational strategies. Not surprisingly then, a number of research reviews (McCabe & Altamura 2011; McClelland et al. 2017; Schindler et al. 2015) have been conducted over the past decade to contrast and compare SEL interventions to uncover which approaches might be most effective for improving SEL in the preschool years. Building this evidence base has not been an easy task due the challenges of comparing differing theoretical perspectives, approaches and outcome measures. However, collective evidence indicates that SEL programs can lead to significant improvements in a broad range of children's social and emotional competencies as well as learning and behavioural self-regulation skills.

RESEARCH HIGHLIGHT

Blewitt, Fuller-Tyszkiewicz et al. (2018), including authors in this chapter, recently expanded this body of work by conducting an in-depth assessment of early childhood curriculum based SEL intervention trials published between 1995 and 2017. Fifty-one SEL programs were examined across 79 studies; while the quality of evidence for these studies varied, it showed the largest effects for measures of *emotional competence*, which encompasses a sense of awareness and skills that are pivotal for navigating friendships and developing prosocial relationships.

Findings also highlighted the importance of supporting educators through in-depth training to introduce and maintain approaches, and engaging families in interventions, as research shows early learning models that include families lead to stronger outcomes (Neville et al. 2013). Greatest improvements in outcomes were found for older children, however, this is likely to represent marked increases in self-regulation, language and knowledge that occur during preschool years (Blair 2002; Greenberg 2006; Riggs et al. 2006).

RESEARCH HIGHLIGHT

The Promoting Alternative Thinking Strategies (PATHS) has been identified as an SEL preschool curriculum program that is supported by a robust evidence base (e.g. Bierman et al. 2014; Bierman et al. 2008; Domitrovich, Cortes & Greenberg 2007). Its curriculum aims to increase children's social and emotional skills by targeting four domains: prosocial friendship skills, emotional understanding and emotional expression, self-control, and problem-solving skills, including interpersonal negotiation and conflict resolution.

It is delivered by educators across 33 sessions as part of circle time, through modelling stories and discussions, and using puppet characters, photographs and educator role-play demonstrations. Children are provided opportunities to practise the target skills with educator support after each session. The program also involves families through communication and support materials, including home resources and learning activities. Children are given stickers and information to take home to prompt families to engage them in conversations about their days in the early childhood setting and support their learning at home.

Early intervention approach

Certain behavioural challenges emerge in infancy as part of normative developmental changes and tend to decrease from the age of 4 years old, in line with gains in cognitive, language and social-emotional skills. However, this trajectory is not universal for all children; particularly for those whose development has already been impacted by early experiences of social and economic disadvantage (Cree et al. 2018; Huaqing Qi & Kaiser 2003). Targeted SEL interventions are designed to provide levels of SEL support beyond what is offered through universal programs. The majority of targeted intervention programs that have been evaluated have focused on reducing externalising behaviour problems (Carpenter & Nangle 2002; Vancraeyveldt et al. 2015), exhibited through a cluster of aggressive and disruptive behaviours – and to a much lesser extent, have addressed withdrawal/extreme shyness (e.g. Anderson et al. 2018; Li et al. 2016). The predominant focus on externalising behaviours is not surprising given their potential to disrupt classroom routines and the fact they can track into adolescence and adulthood, increasing the risk for future antisocial (Aviles, Anderson & Davila 2006) and criminal behavior (Moffitt et al. 2011). In the absence of effective targeted interventions, early experiences of social and behavioural problems are likely to impact longer term academic, relationship and mental health outcomes (Schindler et al. 2015; Tremblay 2010).

Targeted SEL interventions tend to adopt three main approaches:

- *One-on-one interventions* between the early childhood teacher (ECT) or other early years professional and child, aimed at promoting prosocial behaviours through instructional practices, discussion, role-playing social skills, and follow-up with support to apply new skills into play with peers (Conroy et al. 2015).
- *Instructional-based approaches* delivered in small groups of children at risk of behavioural problems to strengthen their social and emotional skills. These approaches focus on self-awareness, self-management, social awareness, relationship-management and responsible decision-making, and can combine SEL with early literacy, through storytelling, discussions and activities (Daunic et al. 2013).
- *Relationship-based dyadic interventions* targeting peer-to-peer dyadic friendship quality and educator–child relationship for strengthening SEL outcomes. A dyadic peer-focused approach can involve pairing a child exhibiting the target behavior (i.e. aggression) with a friend without the target behaviour with dyads participating in social skills training and partnering in a project providing opportunities to practice conflict resolution with support from a facilitator (Salvas, Vitaro, Brendgen & Cantin 2016). Educator–child relationship approaches largely focus on improving the quality of affective and behavioural interactions that underpin teaching strategies used for building prosocial skills, emotional competence and ongoing learning (Vancraeyveldt et al. 2015).

Research evaluating targeted SEL interventions is still emerging, however, preliminary evidence produced by our author team and others (Blewitt, O'Connor, Morris et al. 2019; Blewitt, O'Connor, May et al. 2019; Schindler et al. 2015) suggests that programs targeting children experiencing social, emotional or behavioural challenges are promising. Despite differing approaches, programs generally include overlapping components; such as a focus on behaviour modification and either explicitly targeting or indirectly emphasising the importance of high-quality educator–child relationships for supporting strategies that build children's prosocial skills. Regardless, of the varying quality of evidence available, collective findings support the efficacy of educator-led targeted SEL programs for increasing social competence and behavioural regulation and decreasing challenging behavior in preschool-aged children at risk of escalating maladaptive behavior (Conroy et al. 2015; Daunic et al. 2003; Drogan & Kern 2014; Stanton-Champan, Walker & Jamison 2014; Sutherland et al. 2018).

BEST in CLASS is a targeted training and coaching intervention that aims to support educators to enhance positive educator–child interactions and promote social and emotional competence in young children at risk for emotional and behavioural disorders (Conroy et al. 2019). The program encourages educators to intentionally embed BEST in CLASS practices into reciprocal interactions they may have with target children during everyday routines. The program, delivered through a workshop and practice-based coaching, focuses on building effective teaching skills; such as reminding the target child of rules when being disruptive, providing opportunities for the child to respond and providing behaviour-specific praise when the child demonstrates appropriate behaviour (Conroy et al. 2019). BEST in CLASS has been evaluated in two large cluster randomised controlled trials (Conroy et al. 2019; Sutherland et al. 2018), showing significant improvements in educator–child interaction quality and children's social skills, engagement, and reduction in problem behaviours.

Conclusion

Early childhood educators can play a vital role in fostering children's social and emotional development. Through nurturing relationships and interactions, explicitly teaching SEL using universal or targeted programming, or intentionally supporting SEL through everyday interactions and practices, high-quality early childhood programs can have an enduring impact on children's health, relationships and wellbeing. There are several reasons why encouraging SEL in the early years may be particularly beneficial. Importantly, it may play a role as an early intervention or prevention approach for children experiencing behavioural difficulties, economic vulnerability or other risk factors. In addition, research suggests SEL may have unique leverage for children aged 3–6 years when their language and executive functions are rapidly developing. Furthermore, SEL in the early years targets an age when children are especially receptive to external guidance and support (Bierman & Motamedi 2015).

RESEARCH INTO PRACTICE

The following questions may help you to reflect on how your relationships, interactions and everyday practices in the early childhood environment can foster children's social and emotional development.

- How might you recognise a child's social and emotional strengths? How might you recognise a child who is having difficulty with their social and emotional skills?
- How can your relationships with children support their social, emotional and cognitive development?
- Think about all the interactions and conversations you have with children throughout the day (Hint: consider arrivals, transitions, mealtimes, rest times and farewells too). How can you encourage children's social and emotional development through your everyday interactions and practice?
- How would you describe SEL? How can you encourage children's SEL through integrated teaching and learning approaches, including child-led play and learning, guided play and learning, and adult-led learning?
- How can you work collaboratively with families to share information about children's social and emotional development and implement SEL strategies across home and early childhood settings?

References

Ainsworth, M 1990, 'Some considerations regarding theory and assessment relevant to attachments beyond infancy', in MT Greenberg, D Cicchetti & EM Cummings (eds), *Attachment in the pre-school years*, University of Chicago Press, pp. 463–88.

Anderson, D, Trinh, SM, Caldarella, P, Hansen, BD & Richardson, MJ 2018, 'Increasing positive playground interaction for kindergarten students at risk for emotional and behavioral disorders', *Early Childhood Education Journal*, vol. 46, no. 5, pp. 487–96.

Anthony, LG, Anthony, BJ, Glanville, DN, Naiman, DQ, Waanders, C & Shaffer, S 2005, 'The relationships between parenting stress, parenting behaviour and preschoolers' social competence and behaviour problems in the classroom', *Infant and Child Development: An International Journal of Research and Practice*, vol. 14, no. 2, pp. 133–54.

Aviles, AM, Anderson, TR & Davila, ER 2006, 'Child and adolescent social-emotional development within the context of school', *Child and Adolescent Mental Health*, vol. 11, no. 1, pp. 32–39.

Bandura, A & Walters, RH 1963, *Social learning and personality development*, Holt Rinehart and Winston, New York.

Barnett, WS 2011, 'Effectiveness of early educational intervention', *Science*, vol. 333, pp. 975–78.

Bayer, JK, Ukoumunne, OC, Lucas, N, Wake, M, Scalzo, K & Nicholson, JM 2011, 'Risk factors for childhood mental health symptoms: national longitudinal study of Australian children', *Pediatrics*, vol. 128, no. 4, pp. e865–79.

Bierman, KL, Domitrovich, CE. Nix, RL, Gest, SD, Welsh, JA, Greenberg, MT, Blair, C, Nelson KE & Gill, S 2008, 'Promoting academic and social-emotional school readiness: the head start REDI program', *Child Development*, vol. 79, no. 6, pp. 1802–17.

Bierman, KL & Motamedi, M 2015, 'Social-emotional learning programs for preschool children', in JA Durlak, CE Domitrovich, RP Weissberg & TP Gullotta (eds), *Handbook for social and emotional learning: research and practice*, Guilford, New York, pp. 3–19.

Bierman, KL, Nix, RL, Heinrichs, BS, Domitrovich, CE, Gest, SD, Welsh, JA & Gill, S 2014, 'Effects of head start REDI on children's outcomes 1 year later in different kindergarten contexts', *Child Development*, vol. 85, no. 1, pp. 140–59.

Blair, C 2002, 'School readiness: integrating cognition and emotion in a neurobiological conceptualization of children's functioning at school entry', *American Psychologist*, vol. 57, no. 2, pp. 111–27.

Blewitt, C, Fuller-Tyszkiewicz, M, Nolan, A, Bergmeier, H, Vicary, D, Huang, T, McCabe, P, McKay, T & Skouteris, H 2018, 'Social and emotional learning associated with universal curriculum-based interventions in early childhood education and care centers: a systematic review and meta-analysis', *JAMA Network Open*, vol. 1, no. 8.

Blewitt, C, Morris, H, Nolan, A, Jackson, K, Barrett, H & Skouteris, H 2018, 'Strengthening the quality of educator-child interactions in early childhood education and care settings: a conceptual model to improve mental health outcomes for preschoolers', *Early Child Development and Care*, doi.org/10.1080/03004430.2018.1507028.

Blewitt, C, O'Connor, A, May, T, Morris, H, Mousa, A, Bergmeier, H, Jackson, K, Barrett, H & Skouteris, H 2019, 'Strengthening the social and emotional skills of pre-schoolers with mental health and developmental challenges in inclusive early childhood education and care settings: a narrative review of educator-led interventions', *Early Child Development and Care*, doi.org/10.1080/03004430.2019.1704283.

Blewitt, C, O'Connor, A, Morris, H, May, T, Mousa, A, Bergmeier, H, Nolan, A, Jackson, K, Barrett, H & Skouteris, H 2019, 'A systematic review of targeted social and emotional learning interventions in early childhood education and care settings', *Early Child Development and Care*, doi.org/10.1080/03004430.2019.1702037.

Bor, W, McGee, TR & Fagan, AA 2004, 'Early risk factors for adolescent antisocial behaviour: an Australian longitudinal study', *Australian and New Zealand Journal of Psychiatry*, vol. 38, no. 5, pp. 365–72.

Bornstein, MH, Suwalsky, JTD & Breakstone, DA 2012, 'Emotional relationships between mothers and infants: knowns, unknowns, and unknown unknowns', *Development & Psychopathology*, vol. 24, no. 1, pp. 113–23.

Bowlby, J 1969, *Attachment and loss: volume 1 attachment*, Basic Books, New York.

Brauner, CB & Stephens, CB 2006, 'Estimating the prevalence of early childhood serious emotional/behavioral disorders: challenges and recommendations', *Public Health Reports*, vol. 121, no. 3, pp. 303–10.

Bronfenbrenner, U 1977, 'Toward an experimental ecology of human development', *American Psychologist*, vol. 32, no. 7, pp. 513–31.

Bronfenbrenner, U 1979, *The ecology of human development*, Harvard University Press, Cambridge, MA.

Bronfenbrenner, U & Morris, PA 1998, 'The ecology of developmental processes', in W Damon & RM Lerner (eds), *Handbook of child psychology: theoretical models of human development*, John Wiley & Sons, Hoboken, NJ, pp. 993–1028.

Burchinal, M, Howes, C, Pianta, R, Bryant, D, Early, D, Clifford, R & Barbarin, O 2008, 'Predicting child outcomes at the end of kindergarten from the quality of pre-kindergarten teacher–child interactions and instruction', *Applied Developmental Science*, vol. 12, no. 3, pp. 140–53.

Camilli, G, Vargas, S, Ryan, S & Barnett, WS 2010, 'Meta-analysis of the effects of early education interventions on cognitive and social development', *Teachers College Record*, vol. 112, no. 3, pp. 579–620.

Carpenter, EM & Nangle, DW 2002, 'Effects of brief verbal instructions on aggression: a replication in a head sart setting', *Child & Family Behavior Therapy*, vol. 24, no. 4, pp. 21–38.

Collaborative for Academic, Social and Emotional Learning (CASEL) 2013, *2013 CASEL guide: effective social and emotional learning programs: preschool and elementary school edition*, CASEL, Chicago.

Conroy, MA, Sutherland, KS, Algina, J, Ladwig, C, Werch, B, Martinez, J, Jessee, G & Gyure, M 2019, 'Outcomes of the BEST in CLASS intervention on teachers' use of effective practices, self-efficacy and classroom quality', *School Psychology Review*, vol. 48, no. 1, pp. 31–45.

Conroy, MA, Sutherland, KS, Algina, JJ, Wilson, RE, Martinez, JR & Whalon, KJ 2015, 'Measuring teacher implementation of the "BEST in CLASS" intervention program and corollary child outcomes', *Journal of Emotional and Behavioral Disorders*, vol. 23, no. 3, pp. 144–55.

Cree, RA, Bitsko, RH, Robinson, LR, Holbrook, JR, Danielson, ML, Smith, C, Kaminski, JW, Kenney, MK & Peacock, G 2018, 'Health care, family, and community factors associated with mental, behavioral, and developmental disorders and poverty among children aged 2–8 years – United States, 2016', *Morbidity and Mortality Weekly Report*, vol. 67, no. 50, pp. 1377–83, doi: 10.15585/mmwr.mm6750a1.

Daunic, A, Corbett, N, Smith, S, Barnes, T, Santiago-Poventud, L, Chalfant, P & Gleaton, J 2013, 'Brief report: integrating social-emotional learning with literacy instruction: an intervention for children at risk for emotional and behavioral disorders', *Behavioral Disorders*, vol. 39, no. 1, pp. 43–51.

Denham, SA & Burton, R 1996, 'A social-emotional intervention for at-risk 4-year-olds', *Journal of School Psychology*, vol. 34, no. 3, pp. 225–45.

Denham, SA, Ferrier, DE, Howarth, GZ, Herndon, KJ & Bassett, HH 2016, 'Key considerations in assessing young children's emotional competence', *Cambridge Journal of Education*, vol. 46, no. 3, pp. 299–317.

Denham, SA, Wyatt, TM, Bassett, HH, Echeverria, D & Knox, SS 2009, 'Assessing social-emotional development in children from a longitudinal perspective', *Journal of Epidemiology and Community Health*, vol. 63, pp. l37–52.

Department of Education, Employment and Workplace Relations (DEEWR) 2009, *Belonging, being and becoming: the early years learning framework for Australia*, Commonwealth of Australia, Canberra. Retrieved from https://docs.education.gov.au/node/2632

Department of Education and Training (DET), 2016, *Victorian early years learning and development framework*, DET, Melbourne.

Domitrovich, CE, Cortes, RC & Greenberg, MT 2007, 'Improving young children's social and emotional competence: a randomized trial of the preschool "PATHS" curriculum', *The Journal of Primary Prevention*, vol. 28, no. 2, pp. 67–91.

Drogan, RR & Kern, L 2014, Examination of the mechanisms underlying effectiveness of the turtle technique. *Topics in Early Childhood Special Education*, vol. 33, no. 4, pp. 237-48.

Duncan, GJ & Sojourner, AJ 2013, 'Can intensive early childhood intervention programs eliminate income-based cognitive and achievement gaps?', *Journal of Human Resources*, vol. 48, no. 4, pp. 945–68.

Early, DM, Pan, Y, Maxwell, KL & Ponder, BB 2017, 'Improving teacher–child interactions: a randomized control trial of making the most of classroom interactions and my teaching partner professional development models', *Early Childhood Research Quarterly*, vol. 38, pp. 57–70.

Forry, ND, Moodie, S, Simkin, S & Rothenberg, L 2011, *Family–provider relationships: a multidisciplinary review of high quality practices and associations with family, child, and provider outcomes*, US Department of Health and Human Services (HHS), Administration for Children and Families (ACF) & Office of Planning, Research and Evaluation (OPRE), Washington.

Garbacz, LL, Zychinski, KE, Feuer, RM, Carter, JS & Budd, KS 2014, 'Effects of teacher–child interaction training (TCIT) on teacher ratings of behavior change', *Psychology in the Schools*, vol. 51, no. 8, pp. 850–65.

Goldfeld, S, Kvalsvig, A, Incledon, E, O'Connor, M & Mensah, F 2014, 'Predictors of mental health competence in a population cohort of Australian children', *Journal of Epidemiology and Community Health*, vol. 68, no. 5, pp. 431–37.

Greenberg, MT 2006, 'Promoting resilience in children and youth: preventive interventions and their interface with neuroscience', *Annals of the New York Academy of Sciences*, vol. 1094, no. 1, pp. 139–50.

Greenberg, MT, Domitrovich, CE, Weissberg, RP & Durlak, JA 2017, 'Social and emotional learning as a public health approach to education', *Future of Children*, vol. 27, no. 1, pp. 13–32.

Groh, AM, Fearon, RP, van IJzendoorn, MH, Bakermans-Kranenburg, MJ & Roisman, GI 2017, 'Attachment in the early life course: meta-analytic evidence for its role in socioemotional development', *Child Development Perspectives*, vol. 11, no. 1, pp. 70–76.

Halle, TG & Darling-Churchill, KE 2016, 'Review of measures of social and emotional development', *Journal of Applied Developmental Psychology*, vol. 45, no. 1, pp. 8–18.

Hamre, BK & Pianta, RC 2007, 'Learning opportunities in preschool and early elementary classrooms', in RC Pianta, MJ Cox & KL Snow (eds), *School readiness and the transition to kindergarten in the era of accountability*, Paul H Brookes, Baltimore, pp. 49–83.

Hamre, BK, Pianta, RC, Burchinal, M, Field, S, LoCasale-Crouch, JL, Downer, JT & Scott-Little, C 2012, 'A course on effective teacher–child interactions: effects on teacher beliefs, knowledge, and observed practice', *American Education Research Journal*, vol. 49, no. 1, pp. 88–123.

Heatly, MC & Votruba-Drzal, E 2017, 'Parent– and teacher–child relationships and engagement at school entry: mediating, interactive, and transactional associations across contexts', *Developmental Psychology*, vol. 53, no. 6, pp. 1042–62.

Huaqing Qi, C & Kaiser, AP 2003, 'Behavior problems of preschool children from low-income families: review of the literature', *Topics in Early Childhood Special Education*, vol. 23, no. 4, pp. 188–216.

Institute of Medicine (IOM) & National Research Council (NRC) 2015, *Transforming the workforce for children birth through age 8: a unifying foundation*, The National Academies Press, Washington.

Izard, CE 2002, 'Translating emotion theory and research into preventive interventions', *Psychological Bulletin*, vol. 128, no. 5, pp. 796–824.

Kiernan, KE & Huerta, MC 2008, 'Economic deprivation, maternal depression, parenting and children's cognitive and emotional development in early childhood', *The British Journal of Sociology*, vol. 59, no. 4, pp. 783–806.

Kitzmann, KM, Gaylord, NK, Holt, AR & Kenny, ED 2003, 'Child witnesses to domestic violence: a meta-analytic review', *Journal of Consulting and Clinical Psychology*, vol. 42, no. 2, pp. 339–52.

Li, Y, Coplan, RJ, Wang, Y, Yin, J, Zhu, J, Gao, Z & Li, L 2016, 'Preliminary evaluation of a social skills training and facilitated play early intervention programme for extremely shy young children in China', *Infant & Child Development*, vol. 25, no. 6, pp. 565–74.

Macklem, GL 2011, 'Evidence-based Tier 1, Tier 2, and Tier 3 mental health interventions in schools', in GL Macklem (ed.), *Evidence-based school mental health services*, Springer, New York, pp. 19–37.

Mashburn, AJ, Downer, JT, Hamre, BK, Justice, LM & Pianta, RC 2010, 'Consultation for teachers and children's language and literacy development during pre-kindergarten', *Applied Developmental Science*, vol. 14, no. 4, pp. 179–96.

Mashburn, AJ, Pianta, RC, Hamre, BK, Downer, JT, Barbarin, OA, Bryant, D & Howes, C 2008, 'Measures of classroom quality in prekindergarten and children's development of academic, language, and social skills', *Child Development*, vol. 79, no. 3, pp. 732–49.

McCabe, PC & Altamura, M 2011, 'Empirically valid strategies to improve social and emotional competence of preschool children', *Psychology in the Schools*, vol. 48, no. 5, pp. 513–40.

McClelland, MM, Tominey, SL, Schmitt, SA & Duncan, R 2017, 'SEL interventions in early childhood', *The Future of Children*, vol. 27, no. 1, pp. 33–47.

Moffitt, TE, Arseneault, L, Belsky, D, Dickson, N, Hancox, RJ, Harrington, H, Houts, R, Poulton, R, Roberts, BW, Ross, S, Sears, MR, Thomson, M & Caspi A 2011, 'A gradient of childhood self-control predicts health, wealth, and public safety', *Proceedings of the National Academy of Sciences*, vol. 108, no. 7, pp. 2693–98.

Mortensen, JA & Barnett, MA 2015, 'Teacher–child interactions in infant/toddler child care and socioemotional development', *Early Education and Development*, vol. 26, no. 2, pp. 209–29.

Neville, HJ, Stevens, C, Pakulak, E, Bell, TA, Fanning, J, Klein, S & Isbell, E 2013, 'Family-based training program improves brain function, cognition, and behavior in lower socioeconomic status preschoolers', *Proceedings of the National Academy of Sciences of the United States*, vol. 110, no. 29, pp. 12138–43.

O'Brien, K & Mosco, J 2012, 'Positive parent–child relationships', in S Roffey (ed.), *Positive relationships: evidence based practice across the world*, Springer, Dordrecht, pp. 91–107.

O'Connor, EE, Collins, BA & Supplee, L 2012, 'Behaviour problems in late childhood: the roles of early maternal attachment and teacher–child relationship trajectories', *Attachment and Human Development*, vol. 14, no. 3, pp. 265–88.

Oberklaid, F, Baird, G, Blair, M, Melhuish, E & Hall, D 2013, 'Children's health and development: approaches to early identification and intervention', *Archives of Disease in Childhood*, vol. 98, no. 12, pp. 1008–11.

Organisation for Economic Co-operation and Development (OECD) 2015, *Skills for social progress: the power of social and emotional skills*, OECD, Paris.

Pianta, RC 1999, *Enhancing relationships between children and teachers. School psychology book series*, American Psychological Association, Washington.

Pianta, RC & Steinberg, M 1992, 'Teacher–child relationships and the process of adjusting to school', *New Directions for Child and Adolescent Development*, vol. 1992, no. 57, pp. 61–80.

Pianta, RC, Steinberg, MS & Rollins, KB 1995, 'The first two years of school: teacher–child relationships and deflections in children's classroom adjustment', *Development and Psychopathology*, vol. 7, no. 2, pp. 295–312.

Pianta, RC, DeCoster, J, Cabell, S, Burchinal, M, Hamre, BK, Downer, J & Howes, C 2014, 'Dose–response relations between preschool teachers' exposure to components of professional development and increases in quality of their interactions with children', *Early Childhood Research Quarterly*, vol. 29, no. 4, pp. 499–508.

Riggs, NR, Jahromi, LB, Razza, RP, Dillworth-Bart, JE & Mueller, U 2006, 'Executive function and the promotion of social–emotional competence', *Journal of Applied Developmental Psychology*, vol. 27, no. 4, pp. 300–09.

Rolfe, SA 2004, *Rethinking attachment for early childhood practice: promoting security, autonomy and resilience in young children*, Allen & Unwin, Sydney.

Salvas, MC, Vitaro, F, Brendgen, M & Cantin, SP 2016, 'Prospective links between friendship and early physical aggression: preliminary evidence supporting the role of friendship quality through a dyadic intervention', *Merrill-Palmer Quarterly: Journal of Developmental Psychology*, vol. 62, no. 3, pp. 285–305.

Schindler, HS, Kholoptseva, J, Oh, SS, Shonkoff, JP, Yoshikawa, H, Duncan, GJ & Magnuson, KA 2015, 'Maximizing the potential of early childhood education to prevent externalizing behavior problems: a meta-analysis', *Journal of School Psychology*, vol. 53, no. 3, pp. 243–63.

Shepley, C & Grisham-Brown, J 2019, 'Multi-tiered systems of support for preschool-aged children: a review and meta-analysis', *Early Childhood Research Quarterly*, vol. 47, pp. 296–308.

Shonkoff, JP & Phillips, D 2000, *From neurons to neighborhoods: the science of early childhood development*, National Academy Press, Washington.

Smart, D, Richardson, N, Sanson, A, Dussuyer, I, Marshall, B, Toumbourou, J, Prior, M & Oberklaid, F 2005, *Patterns and precursors of adolescent antisocial behaviour: outcomes and connections*, Australian Institute of Family Studies, Melbourne.

Stanton-Chapman, TL, Walker, V & Jamison, KR 2014, 'Building social competence in preschool: the effects of a social skills intervention targeting children enrolled in head start', *Journal of Early Childhood Teacher Education*, vol. 35, no. 2, pp. 185–200.

Sutherland, KS, Conroy, MA, Algina, J, Ladwig, C, Jessee, G & Gyure, M 2018, 'Reducing child problem behaviors and improving teacher-child interactions and relationships: a randomized controlled trial of BEST in CLASS', *Early Childhood Research Quarterly*, vol. 42, 31–43.

Tremblay, RE 2010, 'Developmental origins of disruptive behaviour problems: the "original sin" hypothesis, epigenetics and their consequences for prevention', *Journal of Child Psychology and Psychiatry*, vol. 51, no. 4, pp. 341–67.

Vancraeyveldt, C, Verschueren, K, Van Craeyevelt, S, Wouters, S & Colpin, H 2015, 'Teacher-reported effects of the playing-2-gether intervention on child externalising problem behaviour', *Educational Psychology*, vol. 35, no. 4, pp. 466–83.

Weissberg, RP, Durlak, JA, Domitrovich, CE & Gullotta, TP 2015, 'Social and emotional learning: past, present, and future', in JA Durlak, CE Domitrovich, RP Weissberg & TP Gullotta (eds), *Handbook for social and emotional learning: research and practice*, Guilford, New York, pp. 3–19.

West, J, Denton, K & Reaney, LM 2001, 'The kindergarten year: findings from the early childhood longitudinal study, kindergarten class of 1998–99, *Education Statistics Quarterly*, vol. 2, no. 4, pp. 25–30.

Yoshikawa, H, Aber, JL & Beardslee, WR 2012, 'The effects of poverty on the mental, emotional, and behavioral health of children and youth: implications for prevention', *American Psychologist*, vol. 67, no. 4, pp. 272–84.

CHAPTER 9

Facilitating children's agency in early childhood education and care

Caroline Scott[1], Andrea Nolan[2] and Anna Kilderry[2]

DOI: https://doi.org/10.37517/978-1-74286-555-3_9
[1] Victoria University
[2] Deakin University

LINKS TO NATIONAL QUALITY STANDARD

Quality Area 1: Educational program and practice
- Standard 1.2: Practice – educators facilitate and extend each child's learning and development.
- Element 1.2.3: Child-directed learning – each child's agency is promoted, enabling them to make choices and decisions that influence events and their world.

LINKS TO EARLY YEARS LEARNING FRAMEWORK

Learning Outcome 1: Children have a strong sense of identity
- Children develop their emerging autonomy, inter-dependence, resilience and sense of agency.

Learning Outcome 2: Children are connected to and contribute to their world
- Children become aware of fairness.

Introduction

Ten years have passed since the concept of 'children's agency' was introduced to early childhood educators in Australia. In the 21st century it is hard to imagine a time where the notion of children's agency was not part of the early childhood education and care (ECEC) discourse (Degotardi 2013; Sairanen & Kumpulainen 2014). This chapter explores educator practice and how it can facilitate children's agency, along with presenting a deeper understanding of children's agency in ECEC. Interest in the topic of children's agency and how educators can support children being agentic arose from observing children in ECEC settings engaging in play and routine activities. This interest resulted in Scott (2019) investigating how children's agency is understood by early childhood educators and how it is facilitated through everyday interactions. It is the findings from this study along with discussion from other research on children's agency that will be the focus of this chapter. We commence with an overview of what the concept of children's agency is all about, followed by an examination of how the concept of children's agency is presented and positioned in the Early Years Learning Framework for Australia (EYLF) (DEEWR 2009), the National Quality Standard (NQS) (ACECQA 2018a) and the *Guide to the national quality framework* (ACECQA 2018b) (the Guide). A revised version of the Guide was released in 2020, however, is not referred to in this chapter due to the analysis being conducted on the contents of the 2018 version.

In Australia, agency is an underpinning principle that informs and guides educator practice through frameworks and policies; such as the EYLF and the NQS. These documents present a particular view of the concept of children's agency and what it looks like for children to enact agency in ECEC settings. Children's agency has been defined within the EYLF (DEEWR 2009, p. 45) as children 'being able to make choices and decisions, to influence events and have an impact on one's world'.

However, research suggests that the concept of agency, particularly as it relates to children in ECEC, is in need of further explanation due to the complex nature of the concept and the important role of the educator (Esser, Baader, Betz & Hungerland 2016; Mentha, Church & Page 2015; Rainio & Hilppö 2017). The research upon which this chapter is based sought to add to the knowledge around children's agency and offer a deeper understanding of the concept. The study investigated practices considered by educators to be effective for facilitating children's agency. Scott (2019) and other researchers (Baraldi & Iervese 2014; Mentha et al. 2015; Sorin 2005) recommend that to effectively support and facilitate children's agency, educators should be encouraged to practice in a way that goes beyond the act of acknowledging children's agency and their ability to engage in decision-making. Instead, research advocates for educators to be mindful that their daily interactions with children have the potential for 'agency enactment', where children are presented with opportunities to exercise authority and to act with initiative (Baraldi & Iervese 2014; Markström & Halldén 2009; Mentha et al. 2015; Sorin 2005).

The potential that early childhood educators have in facilitating or constraining children's agency is a vital aspect to consider when understanding how to provide an enabling context where children can be supported to be agentic. Educators engaging in a range of deliberate and intentional practices can increase the likelihood of children being able to enact their agency. The findings from Scott's research (2019) suggests that the type of deliberate and intentional practices can include: establishing relationships with children based on personal bonds; prioritising children's agency across and beyond the program; enabling children to experience space and freedom within the program; and sharing decision-making with children. Two of these practices, 'enabling children to experience space and freedom within the ECEC program' and 'sharing decision-making with children', are presented in more detail later in this chapter. Also featured are highlights from research showcasing early childhood educators' experiences of how they facilitate children's agency through their practice.

The chapter concludes with an overview of a deeper and more nuanced understanding of children's agency than that which is provided in the EYLF (DEEWR 2009), the NQS (ACECQA 2018a) and the Guide (ACECQA 2018b). Building on the perspective of children's agency contained in these documents, the expanded understanding aims to assist educators to deepen their own knowledge of children's agency and how they might engage in practices that facilitate children's agency in the future.

What is children's agency?

'Agency' has been described as an essential trait or characteristic that humans possess and which, when enacted, enables individuals to pursue outcomes they value, and live a life that is personally meaningful (Robeyns 2003; Sairanen & Kumpulainen 2014). For children, agency is often equated with their ability to make choices and decisions, and to act to influence their world. If young children are able to enact and strengthen their agency throughout childhood, then potentially they will be capable of using that agency throughout adolescence and into adulthood to achieve goals that they value. When individuals act with agency, they are more likely to make choices and decisions that are right for them and that can lead to personally fulfilling outcomes. Research has shown that having strong agency empowers individuals to take more control over their own lives, to pursue more meaningful goals and to potentially achieve greater wellbeing (Robeyns 2003; Sairanen & Kumpulainen 2014; Walker 2006; Wright 2012). In order for individuals to live their own idea of a good life, they must be able to pursue opportunities and realise their desires (Unterhalter, Vaughan & Walker 2007; Fegter & Richter 2014; Sen 2005; 2009).

The concept of children's agency involves the ability of children to make choices and decisions (DEEWR 2009). While children might not be making the type of large-scale decisions that adults do; for example, which university course to study, which career to pursue, whether to start a family etc, the decisions that children make in their day-to-day lives still matter. The choices that children make during their day in an ECEC setting involve them acting with agency as they pursue experiences that are of interest to them. In other words, children are pursuing experiences that they value and that are meaningful. The importance of these choices may be overlooked by adults as they can be seen as small and inconsequential, however, research has found that these choices are important sites for agency enactment and can influence children's wellbeing (Hilppö, Lipponen, Kumpulainen & Rainio 2016; Kellock & Lawthorn 2011).

The importance of making choices and decisions with regard to children's agency cannot be underestimated, however, it is suggested by scholars that making choices and decisions is only one component of the complex concept that is children's agency (Sorin 2005; Wood 2014). Some further discussion about how the EYLF centralises the act of children making choices and decisions without adequately acknowledging the important role that educators play, features next. Following this will be a discussion around how the NQS positions children's agency, where the understanding is broadened to incorporate recognition of educator practice.

Children's agency in the EYLF and NQS

The definition contained in the EYLF (DEEWR 2009) suggests that children can be viewed as capable of making choices and decisions within the ECEC program, with the requirement that educators recognise this ability and ensure children are able to do so. Any reference to the active and deliberate facilitation of agency is largely absent from the EYLF (DEEWR 2009) and accompanying *Educators' guide* (DEEWR 2010). Instead, the idea of agency in these documents is mainly concerned with ensuring children and educators *recognise* children's agency. This view supposes that educators recognise children as having agency, with this agency simply existing within them and naturally unfolding over time irrespective of the environment surrounding them. For example, the practice guidelines and child outcomes related to children's agency include statements such as 'children recognise their agency' (DEEWR 2009, p. 9); 'children develop their emerging autonomy, interdependence, resilience and sense of agency' (p. 21); and 'children have agency … and they have capacities and rights to initiate and lead learning and be active participants and decision makers in matters affecting them' (p. 14). It is evident in these examples that educators recognise children as having agency and that agency develops and strengthens according to the actions and behaviours the child engages in, as compared to any action or behaviour on the part of the educator. The role that the educator plays in children's agency starts to emerge as an important component in the NQS (ACECQA 2018a), originally implemented in 2013, revised in 2018 and again in 2020.

Similar to the EYLF, the concept of children's agency is presented in a particular way in the NQS (ACECQA 2018a) and the Guide (ACECQA 2018b), an accompanying document offering further explanation about practice and providing support for educators. The way in which children's agency is presented in these documents appears to build on the EYLF definition, placing more emphasis on the role that the educator plays in agency facilitation and development. The explanation in these documents moves the concept of children's agency from being understood as simply existing within the individual to being seen as a characteristic that educators can promote or constrain through their practice. For example, in Quality Area 1, Element 1.2.3 of the NQS (ACECQA 2018a), which is concerned with child-directed learning, educators are urged to ensure that 'each child's agency is promoted, enabling them to make decisions and choices that influence events and their world' (ACECQA 2018a). This statement highlights the active role educators are to play in the development of children's agency, providing descriptions of actions; such as *promoting* and *enabling* rather than educators simply recognising that children have agency. Element 1.2.3 is expanded on in the Guide (ACEQCA 2018b) with practice guidelines; such as 'educators promote child-directed learning by encouraging children to make decisions' (p. 117), 'educators support children to make decisions' (p. 117) and suggestions; such as 'when children are given choices and control they begin to understand the connections between actions and consequences' (p. 117). These descriptions explain the practices that educators engage in to ensure that children's agency is able to be enacted in the ECEC setting.

In the years following the EYLF's implementation, an increasing amount of international literature has reflected an emphasis on the important and active role that educators play to support children's agency (see for example Kumpulainen et al. 2014; Mashford-Scott & Church 2011; Rainio & Hilppö 2017; Scott 2019). This reflects a changing perspective, moving away from seeing children as passive and vulnerable, as was the dominant perspective in years past, to viewing children as having agency and rights (Prout & James 2015; UN General Assembly 1989; valentine 2011). The changing role that the educator plays in children's agency is reflected in the EYLF and the NQS, moving from one of acknowledgement that children have agency to one where educators are active in facilitating children's agency through support, promotion and encouragement. However, literature suggests that understanding and facilitating children's agency still needs further investigation and theorisation (Mentha et al. 2015; Rainio & Hilppö 2017). The findings from Scott's research (2019) offer a contribution to advance knowledge around children's agency understanding and facilitation in the ECEC context, and these ideas are discussed here.

Educators facilitating children's agency

Children's agency has been found to be 'relational and contextual', meaning that the environment, including other people who surround the child, has a profound impact on that child's ability to act with agency. Within ECEC settings, educator practice and educator–child interactions can result in children's agency being *facilitated* or *constrained*. Research tells us that the educator's role in children's agency is *active* and *critical*, factors which are not currently emphasised enough in the EYLF or the NQS (Ghirotto & Mazzoni 2013; Mentha et al. 2015; Stoecklin 2013; Sairanen & Kumpulainen 2014; Sorin 2005). As mentioned, it is not enough to view the child as having agency (Sorin 2005), but rather educators need to ensure that children are '*able* to make choices and decisions' [emphasis added] (DEEWR 2009, p. 51). When children engage in decision-making, this does not necessarily equate to them being in control of their experience or being empowered (Wood 2014). Research by Sairanen and Kumpulainen (2014, p. 168) found that in an ECEC setting where recognising and enabling children's agency was valued, children still had very few opportunities to truly act with agency and 'take the initiative to transform their positions and to change the course of activities'. These findings indicate that acknowledging and valuing children's agency and providing opportunities for decision-making in ECEC settings can be improved upon to actually facilitate children's agency. For example, educators can engage in deliberate and intentional practices that actively promote and support children's agency.

Educators share decision-making with children

Understanding the concept of children's agency requires that educators move beyond simply seeing children as able to make choices and decisions, and refocus their attention on the integral role they play in facilitating children's agency. Sorin (2005, p. 19) suggests that the child be viewed as 'a capable actor who shares power with the adult'. Giving children opportunities to exercise power might be a challenging perspective for some early childhood educators to consider, however, there are many ways that this can occur throughout the day in the ECEC setting. One way is for educators to regularly engage in shared decision-making with children. This means that children are given the opportunity to exercise their agency through making a choice or decision that results in change occurring. For example, the child may influence the activities and experiences that are available on any given day, they may choose how, where and with whom they spend their time, or the child's decision may change the timing, duration or location of a routine activity; such as group time or rest time.

Decisions that children can engage in with educators include choosing the experiences, materials and resources that are planned for and made available. Children are acting with agency when they contribute their ideas and choose the materials and resources that best support their play.

Educators can create opportunities within the program for this by ensuring time is spent seeking children's suggestions for experiences, environmental changes, resource availability and so on. Children's suggestions are listened to and taken seriously by educators and are always followed up on. This follow-up action may take the form of the child's suggested experience being planned for, the environment being changed accordingly, the resources being made available or, as importantly, an explanation being provided to the child as to why their suggestion cannot be implemented at that time. Special events and celebrations are another opportunity for children to exercise their agency through shared decision-making. For example, educators can ask children whether they want to participate in events; such as Christmas concerts or Easter parades, or what they might like to do instead. Rather than assigning roles and requiring all children to sing, act or present, educators can engage in discussions with children and invite them to contribute their ideas. These discussions can involve children making decisions as to the format of the celebration, the role they might play and the way in which they wish to contribute; a way that is meaningful and valuable to them.

By engaging in shared decision-making with children, educators are enabling children to exercise their power, act with agency and pursue the outcome, goal or objective that they value. The act of pursuing valued outcomes is a significant component of the deeper understanding of children's agency (Scott 2019). Children act with agency when they are able to pursue the goals that they value (Comim, Ballet, Biggeri & Iervese 2011; Walker 2006; Sen 1999), compared to when agency is constrained, and outcomes are defined by and imposed on children by an outside source. We argue that it is not enough for children to be making choices and decisions from a limited range of options. When offered a limited range of options by an educator; for example, 'Would you like to sit next to Harry or Leila?' or 'You can choose to play with the cars or the blocks', the child's valued outcome might not be part of the choices on offer.

When educators plan for daily experiences and special events and celebrations, they can ensure children are exercising their agency by doing more than listening to a selection of ideas. Instead, educators can plan *with* children rather than *for* them. This is an approach to children's participation in activities that involves educators actively facilitating children's agency. By giving children frequent opportunities to exercise their decision-making to pursue their valued outcomes, educators are facilitating children's agency within the program.

RESEARCH HIGHLIGHT

From policing children to sharing power with them

Sue is an experienced early childhood educator leading a preschool program in a long day care setting who participated in Scott's (2019) research. She explained how a significant shift in her practice occurred after she attended an inspiring professional development session on children's agency. Sue explained how her practice changed from one where she used to 'police the children' to one where she now 'shares power with children'.

In the past Sue explained how her program had been very 'teacher-driven', comprising of a 'rigid boxed program on the wall, [which] changed every fortnight' and this provided few opportunities for children to exercise their decision-making and agency. Whereas now, Sue's program is underpinned by a commitment to children's capabilities and what is meaningful for them, according to the children. Sue and her colleagues work hard to ensure that children's ideas are properly listened to and acted upon.

To facilitate children's agency, Sue maintains that educators should move away from any idea of having power *over* children and instead work *with* children to share decision-making with them. Sue says 'I've been around for years [in the ECEC sector] and I've seen what works and what doesn't and, ultimately, supporting children's agency is what works!'

Educators facilitate opportunities for children to experience space and freedom within the program

Educators enabling children to experience space and freedom to explore and learn within the ECEC setting is considered to be an effective practice for facilitating agency (Scott 2019). Children can be afforded freedom through the practice of supporting them to move freely in the environment and to choose their desired activities and locations for play, as often as possible. Educators can provide children with opportunities to experience a sense of space by deliberately and consciously refraining from engaging in an interaction or intervention. This act gives children the space to act with initiative and make choices and decisions unconstrained by educator suggestions or directions. A significant and essential consideration of this practice is that educators refrain from intervening in a conscious and knowing manner, as opposed to giving children space and freedom by being inattentive and disengaged. Educators are aware of each child's capabilities, actions and movements and give children space and freedom, so they are able to make their own decisions and act unconstrained by unnecessary directions and interventions. Another way in which children are accorded space and freedom is through educators being mindful of the time children are expected to spend in organised activities; such as group times. This results in children being free to act with initiative and pursue their own valued interests, rather than being interrupted and required to attend scheduled activities.

By giving children the experience of space and freedom, educators are creating an environment where children can 'act with initiative'. This is an important characteristic of the expanded definition of agency developed from Scott's (2019) research which states that children's agency involves children acting with initiative to pursue outcomes they value. Acting with initiative involves children acting of their own will (Rainio 2008), which stands in contrast to children having limited and constrained choices within tightly scheduled programs, where there is little time and/or space for them to act with initiative. To act with agency, children need to be able to act unencumbered as far as possible by constraints and directions from others. It is imperative, however, that these opportunities for acting with initiative are appropriate for each child in terms of their abilities and level of maturity, which educators should be aware of at all times.

It is important to understand that giving children space and freedom to act with initiative and make choices and decisions does not mean that children are given *free rein* to do whatever they want, whenever they want, at the expense of other children's agency and rights. Educators who practice in a way that facilitates children's agency also encourage and expect children to act with respect and affiliation towards others (Scott 2019). 'Affiliation' refers to the relationships and connections built between individuals. In developing affiliation, children are encouraged to practise consideration for others and act with a sense of responsibility and empathy (Nussbaum 2003), rather than only being concerned with the outcome they achieve for themselves. Research has shown that individuals develop their agency in a manner which incorporates notions of responsibility and affiliation (Peleg 2013; Reynaert & Roose 2014; Sairanen & Kumpulainen 2014). Unterhalter et al. (2007) explain that individuals develop agency individually as well as in collaboration with those around them. Affiliation is a significant component of the expanded understanding offered by Scott's research (2019) where it is argued that children's agency involves children acting with initiative to pursue valued outcomes with consideration for others. Practices that promote affiliation through encouraging consideration for others include reminding children to be restrained when using resources and materials, ensuring they only take what they need and leave enough for others. Educators assist children to be aware of others using the space and to ensure their actions take into account other children's desires, feelings and agency. There is an expectation that children treat resources with respect and pack them away when finished, making sure the area, the toy or the material is tidy and accessible for other children to use.

RESEARCH HIGHLIGHT

If freedom's gone, we're seeing children wilting

Nina, a participant in Scott's (2019) research, is a diploma-qualified educator, working with children in a kindergarten/preschool setting, who places a very high value on children's experiences of space and freedom, and practises accordingly. While acknowledging the importance of an overarching set of rules and guidelines around children's behaviour, play and movements to ensure the safety and comfort of all children within ECEC, Nina believes that 'there needs to be so much freedom for children … because if that freedom's gone, we're seeing them wilting'.

Nina explained how she practises in a way that means children are able to move freely around the room and engage with experiences when and how they wish, with minimal disruption and direction from staff. She maintains: 'in our room, everything is flexible, the children have the freedom to do whatever they want'.

It is important to note, however, that Nina does not mean that children are simply given free rein to behave how they want with disregard for others or in a manner dangerous to themselves or others. The children are expected to respect other people and the resources and are very good at returning resources to where they belong ready for other children to use. This is partly due to the time that Nina and her colleagues spend early in the kindergarten/preschool year engaged in more direction and intervention, ensuring children are aware of their own capabilities and helping them understand any limitations and rules; such as returning resources to where they belong.

Children are afforded increasing freedom and autonomy as their capabilities evolve and develop in Nina's program. She explained how educators often held back from interactions with children, avoiding intervening in their play and refraining from giving them directions. This results in the facilitation of children's agency through children having freedom to act with initiative to pursue valued outcomes.

Moving forward: an expanded theorisation of children's agency

The practice of sharing decision-making with children and giving children opportunities for space and freedom are effective for facilitating children's agency in ECEC. These practices facilitate agency by creating space for children to act with initiative and pursue the outcomes that they value, two important features of a deeper understanding of children's agency. Following is a full expanded understanding of children's agency developed by Scott (2019, p. 154):

> Children's agency is when children act with initiative to pursue their valued outcomes, with consideration of others. Children's ability to enact their agency is dependent on educator practice. Educators can facilitate children's agency in early childhood education and care settings through prioritising children's decision-making, and agency by engaging in practices which enable children to experience freedom and opportunities to exercise their power, appropriate to their abilities.

Children's agency will no doubt continue to be a key feature of ECEC policy and practice in the future. This chapter has offered an expanded understanding of the concept and suggestions for practices to facilitate children's agency that build upon the notion of agency contained in the EYLF and NQS. This understanding contains key features considered essential for educator knowledge and practice facilitating children's agency. It has been 10 years since the EYLF was introduced and it is hoped that over the next 10 years understanding and facilitation of children's agency will continue to expand and strengthen. Ensuring that children are afforded opportunities to enact their agency throughout their childhood means they will be better able to make choices around goals and objectives that are meaningful for them. Facilitating children's agency can result in children being more able to pursue valued outcomes in their day-to-day lives within the ECEC setting, and more able to do so throughout their lives.

RESEARCH INTO PRACTICE

While considering the following prompts we suggest that you make notes about how you could evaluate your practice as *a series of opportunities*, planned and otherwise, during your time engaging with children.

Think about how you can:
- ensure you are engaging in shared decision-making with children
- incorporate children's interests, abilities and ideas into your program
- give children space and freedom to act with initiative within their everyday opportunities in the early childhood setting
- engage in interactions with children in a way that supports their agency and authentic participation
- engage in critical reflection with regard to aspects of your program which may constrain children's agency and those that facilitate children's agency.

References

Australian Children's Education and Care Quality Authority (ACECQA) 2018a, *The national quality standard,* ACECQA, Sydney. Retrieved from http://www.acecqa.gov.au/national-quality-framework/the-national-quality-standard

Australian Children's Education and Care Quality Authority (ACECQA) 2018b, *Guide to the national quality framework,* ACECQA, Sydney.

Australian Children's Education and Care Quality Authority (ACECQA) 2020, *Guide to the national quality framework,* ACECQA, Sydney. Retrieved from https://www.acecqa.gov.au/sites/default/files/2020-01/Guide-to-the-NQF_2.pdf

Baraldi, C & Iervese, V 2014, 'Observing children's capabilities as agency', in D Stoecklin & JM Bonvin (eds), *Children's rights and the capability approach*, Springer, Dordrecht, pp. 43–64.

Comim, F, Ballet, J, Biggeri, M & Iervese, V 2011, 'Introduction – theoretical foundation and the book's roadmap', in M Biggeri, J Ballet & F Comim (eds), *Children and the capability approach*, Palgrave Macmillan, Basingstoke, pp. 3–21.

Degotardi, S 2013, '"I think – I can": acknowledging and promoting agency during educator–infant play', in OF Lillemyr, S Dockett & B Perry (eds), *Varied perspectives on play and learning: theory and research on early years education,* Information Age Press, Charlotte, NC, pp. 75–90.

Department of Education, Employment and Workplace Relations (DEEWR) 2009, *Belonging, being and becoming: the early years learning framework for Australia*, Commonwealth of Australia, Canberra. Retrieved from https://docs.education.gov.au/node/2632

Department of Education, Employment and Workplace Relations (DEEWR) 2010, *Belonging, being and becoming: educators' guide to the early years learning framework for Australia*, Commonwealth of Australia, Canberra.

Esser, F, Baader, M, Betz, T & Hungerland, B 2016, *Reconceptualising agency and childhood: new perspectives in childhood studies*, Routledge, New York.

Fegter, S & Richter, M 2014, 'Capability approach as a framework for research on children's well-being', in A Ben-Arieh, F Casas, I Frønes & JE Korbin (eds), *Handbook of child well-being*, Springer, Dordrecht, pp. 739–58.

Ghirotto, L & Mazzoni, V 2013, 'Being part, being involved: the adult's role and child participation in an early childhood learning context', *International Journal of Early Years Education*, vol. 21, no. 4, pp. 300–08, doi:10.1080/09669760.2013.867166.

Hilppö, J, Lipponen, L, Kumpulainen, K & Rainio, A 2016, 'Children's sense of agency in preschool: a sociocultural investigation', *International Journal of Early Years Education*, vol. 24, no. 2, pp. 157–71, doi:10.1080/09669760.2016.1167676.

Kellock, A & Lawthorn, R 2011, 'Sen's capability approach: children and well-being explored through the use of photography', in M Biggeri, J Ballet & F Comim (eds), *Children and the capability approach,* Palgrave Macmillan, New York, pp. 137–61.

Kumpulainen, K, Lipponen, L, Hilppö, J & Mikkola, A 2014, 'Building on the positive in children's lives: a co-participatory study on the social construction of children's sense of agency', *Early Child Development & Care*, vol. 184, no. 2, pp. 211–29, doi:10.1080/03004430.2013.778253.

Markström, AM & Halldén, G 2009, 'Children's strategies for agency in preschool', *Children & Society*, vol. 23, no. 2, pp. 112–22, doi:10.1111/j.1099-0860.2008.00161.x.

Mashford-Scott, A & Church, A 2011, 'Promoting children's agency in early childhood education', *Novitas Royal: Research on Youth and Language*, vol. 5, no. 1, pp. 15–38.

Mentha, S, Church, A & Page, J 2015, 'Teachers as brokers: perceptions of "participation" and agency in early childhood education and care', *International Journal of Children's Rights*, vol. 23, no. 3, pp. 622–37.

Nussbaum, M 2003, 'Capabilities as fundamental entitlements: sen and social justice', *Feminist Economics*, vol. 9, no. 2–3, pp. 33–59, doi:10.1080/1354570022000077926.

Peleg, N 2013, 'Reconceptualising the child's right to development: children and the capability approach', *International Journal of Children's Rights*, vol. 21, no. 3, pp. 523–42, doi:10.1163/15718182-02103003.

Prout, A & James, A 2015, 'A new paradigm for the sociology of childhood? Provenance, promise and problems', in A James & A Prout (eds.), *Constructing and reconstructing childhood: contemporary issues in the sociological study of childhood*, Taylor and Francis, Hoboken, NJ, pp. 7–32.

Rainio, AP 2008, From resistance to involvement: Examining agency and control in a play world activity. *Mind, Culture and Activity, 15*(2), 115-40.

Rainio, AP & Hilppö, J 2017, 'The dialectics of agency in educational ethnography', *Ethnography and Education*, vol. 12, no. 1, pp. 1–17, doi:10.1080/17457823.2016.1159971

Reynaert, D & Roose, R 2014, 'Children's rights and the capability approach: discussing children's agency against the horizon of the institutionalised youth land', in D Stoecklin & J Bonvin (eds.), *Children's rights and the capability approach: challenges and prospects*, Springer, Dordrecht, pp. 175–93.

Robeyns, I 2003, *The capability approach: an interdisciplinary introduction*, paper presented at the Third International Conference on the Capability Approach, Pavia, Italy.

Sairanen, H & Kumpulainen, K 2014, 'A visual narrative inquiry into children's sense of agency in preschool and first grade', *International Journal of Educational Psychology*, vol. 3, no. 2, pp. 143–76.

Scott, C 2019, *Children's agency: exploring early childhood educator–child interactions,* unpublished doctoral dissertation, Deakin University, Melbourne.

Sen, A 1999, *Development as freedom*, Oxford University Press, Oxford.

Sen, A 2005, 'Human rights and capabilities', *Journal of Human Development*, vol. 6, no. 2, pp. 151–66, doi:10.1080/14649880500120491.

Sen, A 2009, *The idea of justice*, Harvard University Press, Cambridge, MA.

Sorin, R 2005, *Changing images of childhood: reconceptualising early childhood practice*, University of Melbourne.

Stoecklin, D 2013, 'Theories of action in the field of child participation: in search of explicit frameworks', *Childhood*, vol. 20, no. 4, pp. 441–55.

United Nations General Assembly 1989, *Convention on the rights of the child*, United Nations, New York.

Unterhalter, E, Vaughan, R & Walker, M 2007, 'The capability approach and education', *Prospero*, vol. 13, no. 1, pp. 13–21.

valentine, K 2011, 'Accounting for agency', *Children & Society*, vol. 25, no. 5, pp. 347–58, doi: 10.1111/j.1099-0860.2009.00279.x.

Walker, M 2006, 'Towards a capability-based theory of social justice for education policy-making', *Journal of Education Policy*, vol. 21, no. 2, pp. 163–85, doi:10.1080/02680930500500245.

Wood, E 2014, 'Free choice and free play in early childhood education: troubling the discourse', *International Journal of Early Years Education*, vol. 22, no. 1, pp. 4–18, doi:10.1080/09669760.2013.830562.

Wright, HR 2012, 'Childcare, children and capability', *Cambridge Journal of Education*, vol. 42, no. 3, pp. 409–24, doi:10.1080/0305764X.2012.706256.

SECTION 3

Children as confident and involved learners

Section 3 of this book presents ideas for teaching practices in early childhood settings that have been informed by recent research. The chapters in Section 3 explore evidence pertaining to the Early Years Learning Framework for Australia (EYLF) Learning Outcomes 4 and 5, where children are acknowledged as confident learners and meaning-makers in their own right.

Chapter 10 presents an evidence-informed discussion about children's play and early childhood pedagogies. It discusses the role educators have in providing rich inclusive environments, resources and teaching strategies to promote children's learning and development. The significance of children's learning in nature is raised along with the importance of unstructured and risky play, fostering children's imagination and creativity and the types of physical environments that support children's play.

Chapter 11 acknowledges the importance of language development for young children and the critical role educators play in supporting children's communication skills. The components of oral language are explained, and some of the ways that educators can make a positive difference to children's communication is discussed. Evidence-informed insights shared in this chapter will equip educators with useful insights into how to deepen their understanding of children's oral language development, along with ways their practice can be strengthened.

Chapter 12 discusses early literacy and considers the significance of the educator's role in children's literacy learning. Educators will learn about having a wide range of relevant activities within a play-based program as to support children's literacy development during the early years. An evidence-informed discussion about children's early reading and writing experiences is shared, and ideas around the ways educators can encourage and support young children to develop a literacy focus are provided.

Chapter 13 focuses on STEM (science, technology, engineering and mathematics), a term which is being used more often in early childhood education and care (ECEC). In this chapter, research evidence about the importance of STEM in early childhood is shared, how to identify STEM learning in children's play, along with the types of STEM programs available.

Chapter 14 follows on from the previous chapter, with a STEM focus on mathematics in ECEC. Through evidence-informed literature, readers will explore how children learn mathematics, the important role of educators, and they will learn about EYLF's eight 'powerful mathematical ideas'. Knowing more about these eight ideas and how to incorporate this learning into ECEC programs is 'an important step in supporting young children as powerful mathematicians', according to the authors.

Chapter 15 focuses on children learning through the arts. The chapter presents an evidence-informed discussion about the important role that the arts play in promoting young children's ability to develop higher order and imaginative thinking. Various art forms where children can express themselves and be meaning-makers are described, and a scheme for children's multimodal participation in the arts is presented.

Chapter 16 outlines what it means to be a young child learning in the digital age as well as being an educator in a digital context. The chapter provides an evidence-informed discussion about the importance of digital and multimodal learning for young children, and pedagogical strategies and insights for practice. Readers will explore how new technologies are being used with young children in innovative ways and readers will learn about the emergence of new learning ecologies.

Chapter 17 discusses assessment of children's learning and the role of reflective practice. Readers will be supported to better understand the role of assessment and documentation in ECEC, within the context of their everyday practice. Principles of quality assessment are shared, along with demystifying authentic and holistic assessment, and the importance of collaborating with families.

CHAPTER 10

Play and early childhood pedagogies

Nicole Leggett

DOI: https://doi.org/10.37517/978-1-74286-555-3_10
University of Newcastle

LINKS TO NATIONAL QUALITY STANDARD

Quality Area 3: Physical environment
- Standard 3.2: Use – the service environment is inclusive, promotes competence and supports exploration and play-based learning.
- Element 3.2.2: Resources support play-based learning – resources, materials and equipment allow for multiple uses, are sufficient in number, and enable every child to engage in play-based learning.
- Element 3.2.3: Environmentally responsible – the service cares for the environment and supports children to become environmentally responsible.

LINKS TO EARLY YEARS LEARNING FRAMEWORK

Learning Outcome 4: Children are confident and involved learners
- Children develop dispositions for learning such as curiosity, cooperation, confidence, creativity, commitment, enthusiasm, persistence, imagination and reflexivity.
- Children develop a range of skills and processes such as problem-solving, enquiry, experimentation, hypothesising, researching and investigating.
- Children transfer and adapt what they have learned from one context to another.

Introduction

The Early Years Learning Framework for Australia (EYLF) describes a play-based approach as 'a context for learning through which children organise and make sense of their social worlds, as they engage actively with people, objects and representations'

(DEEWR 2009, p. 46). The role of the educator is to provide rich environments, resources and teaching strategies to promote children's learning and development. This chapter begins by introducing research on the importance of children's play, in particular, how we define and understand play as a significant aspect of children's learning. Vygotsky's (1976; 2004) theoretical ideas regarding play, creativity and the acquisition of knowledge are presented in this chapter, and how play is supported through the provisions of physical environments and resources is further examined in reference to the National Quality Framework (NQF) (ACECQA 2020). Finally, this chapter will explore intentional teaching strategies that will assist children's learning and development while working towards the outcomes of the EYLF.

Children's play and learning

Quite often, how we understand 'play' stems from our own childhood experiences, the types of environments we inhabited and the resources that were available to us. Therefore, the ambiguities of play make it a difficult concept to be defined as play means different things to different people. Moyles (2010) suggests that it is perhaps best to consider play as a process that embraces a wide range of behaviours, dispositions, skills, practices, motivations and opportunities. As they play, children are building theories about how the world works, practising skills for inquiry and negotiation and developing their creativity, abilities and knowledge. Through play, children make their thinking visible.

Play is often described as 'what children do when they follow their own ideas and interests, in their own way and for their own reasons' (Department for Culture, Media and Sport 2004, p. 6). Play is therefore considered as an activity initiated by children, while learning is viewed as a result of a practice initiated by adults (Pramling Samuelsson & Asplund Carlsson 2008). Pramling Samuelsson et al. (2008) explain that in the context of early childhood education, play and learning are often separated by time and space. For example, circle-time, story-time, or music-time are practices of teaching that promote learning; while play-time is regarded as a leisure activity. However, play and learning are not to be viewed as separate entities, rather, play and learning are synonymous for the child. The Action Alliance for Children (2007, p. 2) explains that 'play is not a break from the curriculum; play is the best way to implement the curriculum'. The EYLF supports this view stating that play is a context for learning that:

- allows for the expression of personality and uniqueness
- enhances dispositions such as curiosity and creativity
- enables children to make connections between prior experiences and new learning
- assists children to develop relationships and concepts
- stimulates a sense of wellbeing. (DEEWR 2009, p. 9)

The EYLF recognises that children's learning is 'dynamic, complex and holistic. Physical, social, emotional, personal, spiritual, creative, cognitive and linguistic aspects of learning are all intricately interwoven and interrelated' (DEEWR 2009, p. 9). Through playful interactions, children use all their senses to explore the physical and social worlds around them, constructing new knowledge about people, places and things. Through holistic play experiences children engage in a form of multimodal 'meaning-making' as they make sense of the world around them.

Play, learning and neuroscience

New research techniques including neuroscientific and physiological measures, have indicated strong and consistent relationships between children's playfulness and their cognitive and emotional development (Whitebread 2011; Whitebread et al. 2017). Research provides evidence that learning is something that happens through connections in the brain as a result of external stimuli received through the senses (Doidge 2007; Geake 2009; Goswami 2004). Furthermore, Root-Bernstein (2002, p. 1) suggests that learning is not just *head work* but *heart work* stating that 'one knows what one feels and feels what one knows'. Root-Bernstein (2002) refers to this process as 'synosia', a term derived from Greece. *Synosia* comes from the root words *synaesthesia* (using all one's senses interactively) and *gnosis* (Greek for knowledge). *Synosia* combines the senses with reasoning, or aesthetic abilities with the power of intellect to rationalise what the senses are at a loss to account for (Aretoulakis 2016). When children play, they are fully immersed in a whole-bodied, sensory experience. Through play, children experience real-life events based on their relevant social values, as well as use their imagination in response to physical and emotional stimuli.

Emotions assist in facilitating rational thought by enabling children to apply emotional feedback to their decision-making. While emotions were previously thought of as secondary to cognition in learning, neuroscience is revealing the interconnection between the two (Immordino-Yang & Damasio 2007). Positive affect or mood induced research has found that spontaneity and joy in play is related to divergent thinking. The experience of joy is associated with network changes in the brain and can enhance processes that are linked to creative thinking (Liu et al. 2017).

Figure 10.1 Welcoming spaces for children
Source: Elder Street Early Childhood Centre.

Play can rarely proceed without exhibiting positive effects and ultimately, joy. The connection between joy and learning assists children in developing responses and adapting to experiences of emotion (Burgdorf & Panksepp 2006). Of all the emotional states connected to learning, joy is considered one of the most powerful (Immordino-Yang & Damasio 2007; Liu et al. 2017). Joy, it seems has an important relationship with our propensity to learn. Loris Malaguzzi, founder of the Reggio Emilia approach in Italy maintained that when children are learning and playing these should be viewed as the same matter, as then adults can create the environment from which joy can emerge (Edwards, Gandini & Forman 2011). **Figure 10.1** shows an inviting learning space created by an educator to evoke a positive play experience for children.

Deep knowledge: the relationship between body, nature, time and space

Through play, children learn to believe in their abilities and possess high levels of energy to persist with their ideas. Csikszentmihalyi (1996) refers to this as the 'state of flow'. Characteristics of when a child is in a *state of flow* include involvement, concentration, strong motivation, fascination and total implication. Evidence suggests that an involved child is gaining deep, motivated, intense and long-term learning experience (Fullan & Langworthy 2014). Deep knowledge is concerned with the underlying meanings and principles including the integration of facts and feelings with previous knowledge (Weigel 2002).

To acquire deep knowledge, one needs to pause and dwell in spaces that encourage us to attach and receive meaning from that place (Payne & Wattchow 2009). Payne and Wattchow describe the importance of the body in education with various environments through their *slow (eco)pedagogy of place*. They state that:

> ... experiencing the Australian landscape fosters an embodied sensory-perceptual and conceptual-theoretical *sense* or *possibility* of place, while assisting its participants to understand the relations of their body and nature, in time and space, as they are experienced phenomenologically (Payne & Wattchow 2009, p. 15).

Children develop a sense of wonder and appreciation for the natural world through bringing all their senses to explore nature, taking pleasure in the beauty of nature, and by connecting to and respecting the natural world. **Figure 10.2** features a routine walk, engaging the senses in the natural bush that is adjacent to the children's centre.

The more time children spend engaging with nature, the more likely they are to respect and care for the environment and develop environmentally sustainable practices. However, research indicates that there has been a 50% decrease in outdoor activities and a 35% decrease in free play overall since the 1980s (Barreiro & Howards 2017). Louv (2010) directly links the disconnect from nature in the lives of today's wired

Figure 10.2 Children exploring nature
Source: KU Ourimbah Preschool and Children's Centre.

Figure 10.3 Being in and with nature
Source: KU Ourimbah Preschool and Children's Centre.

generation to disturbing health trends in childhood; such as obesity, attention deficit disorders (ADHD) and depression. Louv has coined the term 'nature-deficit disorder' to highlight the research indicating that direct exposure to nature is essential for healthy development. **Figure 10.3** features children being with nature and developing a sense of belonging to their natural surrounds.

Unstructured play and children's mental health

Mental health conditions in childhood are on the rise with a range of conditions reported, including stress, anxiety, pervasive developmental depression, self-harm, attachment, emotional and behavioural disorders (Costello, Foley & Angold 2006; Lissauer & Clayden 2018; Ogundele 2018). Research indicates that children's lifestyles are changing with new pressures of overscheduling and lack of free-play time outdoors, causing emotional distress in children. Families receive carefully marketed messages that 'good parents' expose their children to a plethora of tools and engage them in organised enrichment activities (Ogundele 2018). In this regard, highly scheduled children have less time for free, child-driven and creative play which offers benefits that may be protective against the effects of pressure and stress (Elkind 2001; Ginsburg 2007; Rosenfeld & Wise 2000).

In the midst of the conflicting advice offered to families and parents for what they should do to prepare children for future careers, many pediatricians are now advocating on behalf of the child's right to play (*see* UNCRC Article 31, UN General Assembly 1989) emphasising the benefits of unstructured play as a healthy, essential part of childhood. Ginsburg (2007) presented a clinical report from the American Academy of Pediatrics, offering advice for pediatricians whose role is to promote the physical, emotional and social wellbeing of children. Strategies that support children to be resilient and to reduce excessive stressors in their lives, include promoting: *free-play* (unstructured, unscheduled, independent, non-screen time); *active play* (discouraging the overuse of passive entertainment, i.e. television and computer games); *active child-centred play*; and, the provision of *conventional toys* or resources (i.e. blocks and natural objects where children use their imagination fully). Play during which children are free to explore, take risks, imagine, create and investigate, assists in developing resilience to stressful events and provides support for psychological processes, learning and emotional wellbeing.

A natural aspect of children's physical play involves engaging in play that is challenging and risky. This type of play often occurs outdoors and is categorised into six areas: play at great heights, play with high speed, play with dangerous tools, play near a dangerous element, rough and tumble play, and play where children can disappear or get lost (Sandseter 2007). How risk is perceived by educators will influence children's opportunities for risky play. It is important to keep in mind that what is perceived as a great height or speed from a child's perspective is very different to that of an adult. Through observing and understanding the interests and strengths of each child, educators are able to assess individual competencies and adjust the boundaries of risky play. Learning skills for risk assessment and risk management in children is an important aspect that enables the child to be better equipped and more resilient in managing challenging and stressful situations later in life. **Figure 10.4** depicts a child negotiating and managing a risky play opportunity in nature.

Figure 10.4 Finding risky play opportunities in nature
Source: KU Ourimbah Preschool and Children's Centre.

RESEARCH HIGHLIGHT

New research techniques have indicated strong and consistent relationships between children's playfulness and their cognitive and emotional development (Whitebread 2012; Whitebread et al. 2017).

Highly scheduled children have less time for free, child-driven, risky and creative play which offers benefits that may be protective against the effects of pressure and stress (Elkind 2001; Ginsburg 2007; Rosenfeld & Wise 2000).

Of all the emotional states connected to learning, joy is considered one of the most powerful forces (Immordino-Yang & Damasio 2007; Liu et al. 2017).

Joy, it seems has an important relationship with our propensity to learn (Liu et al. 2017).

Play, meaning-making, imagination and creativity: drawing from Vygotsky's theory

Vygotsky's (1976; 2004) ideas regarding play are of vital importance to early childhood. 'Play' according to Vygotsky involves three components; children:

1. create an imaginary situation
2. take on roles and act out roles
3. follow a set of rules determined by specific roles. (Bodrova & Leong 2007)

Play therefore has a purpose, is intentional and is multidirectional according to the various players within social-cultural contexts. Vygotsky advocated that play is the leading source of development promoting cognitive, emotional and social development (Bodrova & Leong 2007; Vygotsky 1976; 2004). **Figure 10.5** features two girls engaged in a play scenario where imagination, roles and rules are being enacted.

Through play, young children problem-solve and problem-find, test hypotheses, and draw upon their imaginations and creativity to find and make meaning in their world. Vygotsky (2004) theorised the relationship between creativity and the imagination. He proposed that the imagination serves as an imperative impetus of all human creative activity. Vygotsky claimed that the use of the imagination is 'a function essential to life' (2004, p. 13). 'Imagination' is a psychological function located within the core of learning and development, originating from social interactions as part of the child's cultural-historical moment in development (John-Steiner, Connery & Marjanovic-Shane 2010). Many researchers agree that the most valuable learning occurs when people are engaged creatively

Figure 10.5 Social contexts for creative play
Source: Elder Street Early Childhood Centre.

in activities that enable them to use their imaginations through intellectual, social, artistic and cultural ways (Egan 2005; John-Steiner & Moran 2012; Lobman 2010; Vygotsky 2004). The dialectical relationship between creativity and learning is maintained as:

> ... inseparable from the activity of creating the environment for learning. From this perspective creativity does not reside in the products of learning, but in the dialectical relationship between the process of creating the environment for learning and what is created. (Lobman 2010, p. 202)

Vygotsky's (1976; 2004) socio-cultural and historical framework illustrates the innovative, integrated nature of thought and emotion as well as the multimodal meaning-making and learning that occurs through play and imaginative processes. 'Creativity' is fundamental to learning and development, and the imagination of children is a powerful tool for advancing cognitive growth.

RESEARCH HIGHLIGHT: VYGOTSKY'S THEORY

Vygotsky understood that play is the leading source of development promoting cognitive, emotional and social development (Bodrova & Leong 2007; Vygotsky 1976; 2004).

Vygotsky (2004) theorised the relationship between creativity and the imagination. He wrote that the imagination serves as an imperative impetus of all human creative activity.

Vygotsky (1976; 2004) understood that creativity is fundamental to learning and the use of the imagination is an important tool for advancing cognitive growth in children.

Creative development and social contexts

When children play, they draw from previous experience, knowledge and skills and challenge new ideas employing their imagination. This cognitive flexibility involving the ability to let go of existing views and change one's perspective based on new requirements paves the way for creativity (Liu et al. 2017). Neurologically, it has been recognised that the early years are a prime time for generating pathways in the brain that lay the foundation for future innovators and creative thinkers (Leggett 2017). There is strong evidence suggesting a critical period in the first 10 years of life where young children are considered to be in a creative period of development during the time when the brain is still being wired (Doige 2007; Goswami 2004; Leggett 2017; McCain, Mustard & Shanker 2007). Children in particular from 4 to 6 years of age, are often adventurous, imaginative and spontaneously creative.

Contemporary understandings of children's play embrace the social contexts within which creativity takes place and the collaborative nature of sharing ideas and solving problems together (Carlile & Jordan 2012). Learning Outcome 4 in the EYLF calls for play-based learning opportunities where 'children develop a range of skills and

Strong Foundations

Figure 10.6 Social contexts for play
Source: Elder Street Early Childhood Centre.

processes such as problem-solving, enquiry, experimentation, hypothesising, researching and investigating' (DEEWR 2009, p. 37). Through collaborative social experiences children are able to share their knowledge and transfer and adapt what they have learned from one context to another (DEEWR 2009). Particular attention therefore should be given to the use of physical spaces, the types of resources provided, and the intentional teaching strategies used by educators that support the development of children as confident, involved learners. **Figure 10.6** illustrates children engaged in a social play-based learning activity that provides opportunities for developing a range of skills.

Physical environments

The physical environment is crucial to contributing to children's wellbeing and creativity and to developing a sense of independence. An ECEC setting needs to ensure that the environment is 'inclusive, promotes competence and supports exploration and play-based learning' (ACECQA 2020, p. 88). Environments are inclusive when they are designed to support the interests, preferences and learning styles of all children in the setting. Educators should consider the learning environment as a 'the third teacher' (Rinaldi 1994) with careful consideration for space, organisation, design, colour, lighting and atmosphere. Educators can create flexible, welcoming, home-like environments that are responsive to individual children and their families. The types of environments that support the playfulness of children include the level of stimulation, the affordance of diverse resources and natural play areas, the quality of interactions with adults, and the degree to which independence and autonomy are offered to children concerning their play. **Figure 10.7** features a play-based learning opportunity for children using a range of natural resources.

ECEC settings also play an important role in assisting children to develop an understanding about the interdependence between people, plants, animals and the land in which they belong. Educators should show that they 'care for the environment and support children to become environmentally responsible' (ACECQA 2020, p. 198). Time with nature is essential for children to be able to promote positive attitudes and values towards sustainable practices and caring relationships between people, animals and their natural worlds. The following list summarises key factors to consider when educators are planning for the physical environment.

Figure 10.7 Play environments with natural elements
Source: Elder Street Early Childhood Centre.

Physical environments that can support children's play:

- provide warm, welcoming spaces for children and families, that are vibrant flexible, inviting and responsive to the interests of the children
- create spaces that are home-like, inclusive and accessible, and reflect the cultures of families and the broader community
- create spaces that invite open-ended interactions, conversations between children, educators and families and promote opportunities for building relationships
- incorporate sensory experiences through the arrangement of colour, light and shade, sights and sounds
- include learning spaces that are safe for children, promote competence and support exploration and play-based learning
- include areas that are planned well for easy access and participation of all children
- give children opportunities to be involved in planning, setting up and modifying the environment
- provide opportunities for children to engage in unstructured play
- provide opportunities where children can assess and take appropriate risks
- give children opportunities for individualised and group play
- cater for different learning capacities

- include spaces that capitalise on children's curiosity, awe and wonder in the world around them
- provide engaging, interesting spaces that extend children's thinking, learning and problem-solving
- give children the freedom to be protagonists in constructing their own knowledge
- create spaces where children can be alone or hide
- provide outdoor spaces that reflect the Australian landscape
- provide play spaces in natural environments that include plants, trees, edible gardens, sand, rocks, mud, water and other natural elements
- allow children to explore insects and animals in their habitats and develop an understanding of biodiversity
- create areas that engage children with environmental sustainability
- demonstrate responsive care for the environment and assist in developing healthy relationships between children and their natural world.

Figure 10.8 features an area created by an educator for children where they feel they can escape or hide. **Figure 10.9** represents a physical learning environment that is welcoming, inviting and accessible for families and children.

Resources and learning environments

Resources should reflect the various ages, cultures, interests and capabilities of children that are sharing the environment. Element 3.2.2 of the National Quality Standard (NQS) (ACECQA 2020, p. 195) promotes 'resources, materials and equipment [that] allow for multiple uses, are sufficient in number, and enable every child to engage in play-based learning'. Resources that support exploration and independence in play

Figure 10.8 Spaces for children to be alone or hide
Source: Elder Street Early Childhood Centre.

Figure 10.9 Inviting areas for children
Source: Alkira Early Learning Centre.

include open-ended materials that encourage children to use objects in a variety of different ways. These objects can be moved, carried, combined, and redesigned in any way the children decide. Open-ended materials, such as loose parts, natural materials, commercial and recyclable goods, pose questions leading to investigation and discovery. They provide new encounters where children are able to discover new meanings, and thus develop more complex understandings and skills (Al-Mansour 2018). Children are intrinsically motivated to manipulate, explore, test and learn within environments that provide stimulating resources and opportunities. Using open-ended materials gives children the freedom to choose and create; it encourages imagination, creativity and problem-solving skills so that play can become more complex. **Figure 10.10** shows a young child exploring recyclable materials.

How resources are identified, displayed, organised and utilised within the learning environment will also reflect wider social values. Resources need to represent cultural diversity and be inclusive, along with being able to stimulate visual, auditory, tactile, physical and cultural facets as well as reflect a variety of materials and colours. See **Figure 10.11** for a thoughtful arrangement of resources to promote play-based learning about Indigenous culture and crafts.

Successful interaction and learning opportunities should be facilitated and inclusive of all children, all who have a right to be active participants in play. The following list is a summary of key considerations when providing resources within play-based environments.

Resources that support children's play:

- are sufficient in variety and number to meet the range of interests, ages and abilities of children
- are culturally diverse and inclusive
- are displayed and presented with care and beauty

Figure 10.10 Open-ended resources to encourage children's exploration
Source: Elder Street Early Childhood Centre.

Figure 10.11 Resources reflecting different cultural backgrounds
Source: Elder Street Early Learning Centre.

- are stimulating, of good quality and enable multiple uses
- are novel and provoke children's curiosity
- are flexible, open-ended and encourage children to explore, discover and experiment
- challenge children's thinking and provoke problem-solving
- are accessible, promote independence and enable every child to engage in play-based learning
- are physically challenging
- include a range of sensory objects
- include a range of commercial, natural, recycled and homemade materials to enable children to represent their thinking and express meaning in different ways
- support the use of real tools and the handling of equipment with increasing skill and competence
- provide children with opportunities to experiment with different technologies and media
- include props for children that engage them in pretend play, imaginative play and improvisational creativity
- are presented or introduced in a way that provides provocations to spark children's interests, curiosity and creativity.

Figure 10.12 represents how resources can be presented to promote independence. Shown in **Figure 10.13**, the educator has arranged resources in a way that provokes the interest and curiosity of children.

The role of the educator in children's play

To support children's learning, the EYLF states that 'early childhood educators take on many roles in play with children and use a range of strategies to support learning'

Figure 10.12 Promoting independence
Source: Elder Street Early Childhood Centre.

Figure 10.13 Interesting and novel play spaces
Source: Elder Street Early Childhood Centre.

(DEEWR 2009, p. 15). Playful experiences with an adult can provide an effective context for learning. Ugaste (2007) notes that educators need to use and enrich actual experiences the children have had during play so that the play contains a *personal idea* that is motivating for children. While adults prepare environments for play and use strategies to enhance children's learning, it is important to remember that play is not created by adults for children, but by the children themselves. There needs to be balance between the role of the intentional teacher and the role children play as intentional learners (Leggett & Ford 2013). Intentional learning involves:

> Children using specific strategies that enable them to progress toward their own goals for learning as well as broad outcomes for learning as supported by the educator. Children actively participate as co-constructors in the planning of curriculum and are involved in everyday decisions that impact upon their growth and development. (Leggett 2015, p. 301)

The EYLF suggests that educator guidance and engagement in sustaining play is essential for learning and development within stimulating learning environments (DEEWR 2009). Ridgway and Quinones' (2012, p. 53) research found that it was not only important to consider the 'child playing, but to pay close attention to the complex interactions between the child and the educator'. Through intentional teaching strategies, children should be encouraged and supported to take risks, make mistakes, be spontaneous and self-motivated. Becoming involved in children's play means more than just playing with children or observing them play. It means developing positive dispositions towards learning.

Developing positive learning dispositions in children through play

Our role as educators is to be intentional about how we deliberately, purposefully and thoughtfully interact and develop children's skills, attitudes, values, knowledge, understandings and dispositions (DEEWR 2009). 'Dispositions' can be described as enduring habits of mind and actions, as well as tendencies to respond in characteristic ways to situations. For example, maintaining an optimistic outlook, being willing to persevere, or approaching new experiences with confidence (Carr 2001). Learning dispositions impact children's overall ability to learn and progress. As educators, we can support children in developing positive learning dispositions; such as curiosity, cooperation, confidence, creativity, commitment, enthusiasm, persistence, imagination and reflexivity through active engagement, guidance and support (DEEWR 2009). Educators can also plan for a supportive environment and interactions that will encourage and strengthen positive dispositions through play. The following list provides intentional teaching strategies for educators that will encourage the development of positive learning dispositions in children:

- Include the interests of the child/ren and follow their pathways of thinking.
- Provide children with real world experiences, culturally diverse and inclusive resources and opportunities.
- Provide opportunities for children to develop responsibility.
- Model positive play behaviours.
- Provide new and interesting play experiences.
- Encourage independence and self-reliance by letting children make decisions and be responsible for their own belongings.
- Offer support for choice-making.
- Share your knowledge, expertise and interests with children.
- Give children time to experience a state of flow and to become fully engrossed, sustained, and deeply involved in their learning.
- Listen to children's ideas and respond with thoughtful questions and provocations.
- Encourage children to think of different ways to solve a problem.
- Develop skills of co-inquiry by observing, documenting, reflecting, interpreting and taking action together with children.
- Model a sense of awe and wonder in the natural world.
- Show that you are interested in lots of different things.
- Encourage children's exploration, curiosity, risk-taking, discovery and spontaneity.
- Model positive learning dispositions such as playfulness, courage, confidence, trust, resilience, perseverance and responsibility.
- Show that you value positive dispositions by noticing and commenting on them.
- Provide opportunities for children to develop dispositions (time, space, equipment and encouragement).
- Acknowledge children's feelings, individual differences and preferences.
- Provide assistance and guidance for developing patience, resilience and coping skills.
- Introduce changes gradually and with support.
- Be playful.
- Have fun.

Figure 10.14 shows an educator sharing his knowledge with a young child.

Figure 10.14 Adults sharing knowledge and interests with children

Conclusion

Research findings discussed in this chapter indicate that there is a strong correlation between children's playfulness and their cognitive growth, creativity, dispositions towards learning and their emotional wellbeing. Recent studies highlighted in this chapter have alerted us to the concerns about reducing unstructured play times and the effects of highly structured lifestyles on children's mental health. In particular, it has been suggested by pediatricians that play opportunities, where children are free to explore, take risks, create and investigate may assist in developing resilience to stressful events, offering protection against psychological and emotional harm. The role of the educator is therefore significant in facilitating supportive learning environments for children where play is central. However, it is important that educators not only consider elements; such as time, space, diversity, inclusiveness and resources that stimulate the imagination, creativity and learning processes of children, but also become involved in children's play and experience together the joy of co-researching, co-inquiring and reconnecting with the world around them. In the words of Loris Malaguzzi (1975) there is 'nothing without joy' (as cited in Rinaldi 2013, p. 12).

RESEARCH INTO PRACTICE

While considering the following questions, make notes about how you would evaluate your practice in terms of the opportunities you provide for young children, planned or otherwise.

Consider how you can:

- ensure environments are inclusive, and support children's competence and exploration in play-based learning
- design and plan physical play spaces that are safe and contribute to children's wellbeing and creativity, along with their developing identities and independence
- create open spaces that provide children with opportunities to be involved in self-chosen experiences, that are active or quiet learning or reflective situations
- provide outdoor spaces that are dynamic and flexible, and offer children opportunities to be active and wholly engaged in play
- create inclusive learning environments that reflect diverse cultural backgrounds, interests, abilities and learning styles for all children
- provide diverse resources and materials that provide support for multiple uses, are sufficient in number and enable every child to engage in play-based learning
- assist children in developing their own unique abilities, to take risks, trial and error, experiment, research and investigate within learning environments
- support children to develop a range of skills and processes; such as problem-solving, enquiry, experimentation, hypothesising, researching and investigating

continued…

- develop dispositions for learning; such as curiosity, cooperation, confidence, resilience, commitment, persistence, imagination and reflexivity
- promote and develop children's social and emotional skills including how to develop positive relationships between people, objects and the natural world
- promote sustainable practices and care for the environment
- have fun, engage and participate in inclusive play and learning with children
- take time, be still and enjoy times with the children. When was the last time you lay on the green grass and watched the clouds morph into various wonderful forms …?

References

Action Alliance for Children 2007, *Play in the early ears: key to school success*, a policy brief, Early Childhood Funders, Oakland.

Al-Mansour, MA 2018, 'Young children's journey into a world of play with open-ended materials: a case study of the creative play club', *International Education Studies*, vol. 11, no. 12, pp. 117–32, doi:10.5539/ies.v11n12p117.

Aretoulakis, E 2016, *Forbidden aesthetics, ethical justice, and terror in modern western culture*, Lexington Books, London.

Australian Children's Education and Care Quality Authority (ACECQA) 2020, *Guide to the national quality framework*, ACECQA, Sydney. Retrieved from https://www.acecqa.gov.au/sites/default/files/2020-01/Guide-to-the-NQF_2.pdf

Barreiro, J & Howard, R 2017, 'Incorporating unstructured free play into organised sports', *Strength and Conditioning Journal*, vol. 39, no. 2, pp. 11–19.

Bodrova, E & Leong, D 2007, *Tools of the mind: the Vygotskian approach to early childhood education*, Pearson, Hoboken, NJ.

Burgdorf, J & Panksepp, J 2006, 'The neurobiology of positive emotions', *Neuroscience and Biobehavioural Reviews*, vol. 30, no. 2, pp. 173–87, doi:10.1016/j.neubiorev.2005.06.001.

Carr, M 2001, *Assessment in early childhood settings: learning stories*, Paul Chapman, London.

Carlile, O & Jordan, A 2012, *Approaches to creativity. A guide for teachers*, Open University Press, New York.

Costello EJ, Foley DL & Angold A 2006, '10-year research update review: the epidemiology of child and adolescent psychiatric disorders: II. Developmental epidemiology', *Journal of the American Academy of Child & Adolescent Psychiatry*, vol. 45, no. 1, pp. 8–25, doi:10.1097/01.chi.0000184929.41423.c0.

Csikszentmihalyi, M 1996, *Creativity: flow and the psychology of discovery and invention*, Harper Perennial, New York.

Department for Culture, Media and Sport (DCMS) 2004, *Getting serious about play – A review of children's play*, DCMS, London.

Department of Education, Employment and Workplace Relations (DEEWR) 2009, *Belonging, being and becoming: the early years learning framework for Australia*, Commonwealth of Australia, Canberra. Retrieved from https://docs.education.gov.au/node/2632

Doidge, N 2007, *The brain that changes itself. Stories of personal triumph from the frontiers of brain science*, Penguin, New York.

Edwards, C, Gandini, L & Forman, G (eds) 2011, *The hundred languages of children: the Reggio approach to early childhood education*, Ablex, Norwood, NJ.

Egan, K 2005, *An imaginative approach to teaching*, Jossey-Bass, San Francisco.

Elkind D 2001, *The hurried child: growing up too fast too soon*, 3rd edn, Perseus, Cambridge, MA.

Fullen, M & Langworthy, M 2014, *A rich seam: how new pedagogies find deep learning*, Pearson, London.

Geake, J 2009, *The brain at school: educational neuroscience in the classroom*, Open University Press, Maidenhead, England.

Ginsburg, K 2007, 'The importance of play in promoting healthy child development and maintaining strong parent–child bonds', *American Academy of Pediatrics*, vol. 119, no. 1, pp. 182–91, doi:10.1542/peds.2006-2697.

Goswami, U 2004, 'Neuroscience and education: from research to practice?', *British Journal of Educational Psychology*, vol. 74, no. 1, pp. 1–14.

Immordino-Yang, M & Damasio, A 2007, 'We feel, therefore we learn: the relevance of affective and social neuroscience to education', *Mind, Brain and Education*, vol. 1, no. 1, pp. 3–10, doi:10.1111/j.1751-228X.2007.00004.

John-Steiner, V, Connery, MC & Marjanovic-Shane, A 2010, 'Dancing with the muses', in MC Connery, V John-Steiner & A Marjanovic-Shane (eds), *Vygotsky and creativity: a cultural-historical approach to play, meaning-making, and the arts*, Peter Lang, New York.

John-Steiner, V & Moran, S 2012, *Creativity in the making: Vygotsky's contemporary contribution to the dialectic of development and creativity*, Oxford scholarship online, doi:10.1093/acprof:oso/9780195149005.001.0001.

Leggett, N 2015, *Intentional teaching practices of educators and the development of creative thought processes of young children within Australian early childhood centres*, unpublished doctoral dissertation, University of Newcastle, Newcastle.

Leggett, N 2017, 'Early childhood creativity: challenging educators in their role to intentionally develop creative thinking in children', *Early Childhood Education Journal*, vol. 45, no. 6, pp. 845–53, doi:10.1007/s10643-016-0836-4.

Leggett, N & Ford, M 2013, 'A fine balance: understanding the roles educators and children play as intentional teachers and intentional learners within the early years learning framework', *Australasian Journal of Early Childhood*, vol. 38, no. 4, pp. 42–50.

Lissauer, T & Clayden, G 2018, *Illustrated textbook of paediatrics*, 5th edn, Mosby Elsevier, New York.

Liu, C, Solis, L, Jensen, H, Hokins, E, Neale, D, Zosh, J, Hirsh-Pasek, K & Whitebread, D 2017, *White paper. Neuroscience and learning through play: a review of the evidence*, The LEGO Foundation, Billund, Denmark.

Lobman, C 2010, 'Creating developmental moments: teaching and learning as creative activities', in MC Connery, V John-Steiner & A Marjanovic-Shane (eds), *Vygotsky and creativity. A cultural approach to play, meaning making and the arts*, Peter Lang, New York.

Louv, R 2010, *Last child in the woods. Saving our children from nature-deficit-disorder*, Atlantic Books, London.

McCain, M, Mustard, F & Shanker, S 2007, *Early years study 2: putting science into action*, Council for Early Childhood Development, Toronto.

Moyles, J (ed.) 2010, *The excellence of play*, Open University Press, Milton Keynes, England.

Ogundele, M 2018, 'Behavioural and emotional disorders in childhood: a brief overview for paediatricians', *World Journal of Clinical Paediatrics*, vol. 7, no. 1, pp. 9-26, doi:10.5409/wjcp.v7.i1.9.

Payne, P & Wattchow, B 2009, 'Phenomenological deconstruction, slow pedagogy, and the corporeal turn in wild environmental/outdoor education', *Canadian Journal of Environmental Education*, vol. 14, no. 1, pp. 15–32.

Pramling Samuelsson, I & Asplund Carlsson, M 2008, 'The playing learning child: towards a pedagogy of early childhood', *Scandinavian Journal of Educational Research*, vol. 52, no. 6, pp. 623–41.

Ridgway, A & Quinones, G 2012, 'How do early childhood students conceptualise play-based curriculum?', *Australian Journal of Teacher Education*, vol. 37, no. 12, pp. 45–56.

Rinaldi, C 1994, 'The emergent curriculum and social constructivism: an interview with Lella Gandini', in C Edwards, L Gandini & G Forman (eds), *The hundred languages of children: the Reggio Emilia approach to early childhood education*, Ablex, Norwood, NJ.

Rinaldi, C 2013, *Re-imagining childhood: the inspiration of Reggio Emilia education principles in South Australia*, Government of South Australia, Adelaide. Retrieved from https://www.education.sa.gov.au/sites/default/files/reimagining-childhood.pdf?acsf_files_redirect

Root-Bernstein, RS 2002, 'Aesthetic cognition', *International Journal of the Philosophy of Science*, vol. 16, no. 1, pp. 61–77.

Rosenfeld, AA & Wise, N 2000, *The over-scheduled child: avoiding the hyper-parenting trap*, St Martin's Griffin, New York.

Sandseter, EBH 2007, 'Categorizing risky play – how can we identify risk-taking in children's play?', *European Early Childhood Education Research Journal*, vol. 15, no. 2, pp. 237–52.

Ugaste, A 2007, 'The cultural-historical approach to play in the kindergarten context', in T Jambor & J Gils (eds), *Several perspectives on children's play: scientific reflections for practitioners*, Garant, Philadelphia, pp. 105–18.

United Nations General Assembly, *United Nations convention on the rights of the child*, 20 November 1989, treaty series, vol. 1577, p. 3, United Nations, New York. Retrieved from https://www.refworld.org/docid/3ae6b38f0.html

Van Hoorn, J, Nourot, P, Scales, B & Alward, K 2010, *Play at the center of the curriculum*, 5th edn, Pearson Merrill Prentice Hall, Columbus, OH.

Vygotsky, LS 1976, 'Play and its role in mental development of the child', in J Bruner, A Jolly & K Sylva (eds), *Play: its role in development and evolution*, Basic books, New York.

Vygotsky, LS 1978, *Mind and society: the development of higher psychological processes*, Harvard University Press, Cambridge, MA.

Vygotsky, LS 2004, 'Imagination and creativity in childhood', *Journal of Russian and East European Psychology*, vol. 42, no. 1, pp. 7–97, doi:10.1080/10610405.2004.11059210.

Weigel, Van B 2002, *Deep learning for a digital age: technology's untapped potential to enrich higher education*, Jossey-Bass, San Francisco.

Whitebread, D 2011, *Developmental psychology and early childhood education*, Sage, London.

Whitebread, D 2012, *The importance of play. A report on the value of children's play with a series of policy recommendations*, written for the Toy Industries of Europe, Brussels. Retrieved from https://www.toyindustries.eu/wp-content/uploads/2012/11/Dr-David-Whitebread-The-Importance-of-play-final.pdf

Whitebread, D, Neale, D, Jensen, H, Liu, C, Solis, SL, Hopkins, E, Hirsh-Pasek, K & Zosh, JM 2017, *The role of play in children's development: a review of the evidence*, The LEGO Foundation, Bullund, Denmark.

CHAPTER 11

Supporting oral language development in young children

Louise Paatsch and Andrea Nolan

DOI: https://doi.org/10.37517/978-1-74286-555-3_11
Deakin University

LINKS TO NATIONAL QUALITY STANDARD

Quality Area 1: Educational program and practice
- Standard 1.2: Practice – educators facilitate and extend children's learning and development.
- Element 1.2.1: Intentional teaching – educators are deliberate, purposeful and thoughtful in their decisions and actions.
- Element 1.2.2: Responsive teaching and scaffolding – educators respond to children's ideas and play and extend children's learning through open-ended questions, interactions and feedback.

LINKS TO EARLY YEARS LEARNING FRAMEWORK

Learning Outcome 5: Children are effective communicators
- Children interact verbally and non-verbally with others for a range of purposes.
- Children express ideas and make meaning using a range of media.

Introduction

The development of language in the early years of a child's life is critical. By the time a child begins formal schooling, at the age of around 5 years, they need to have mastered the basic structures of language and be proficient and effective communicators (Vukelich, Christie & Enz 2008). Children learn through language and at the same time they begin to learn about language. This is achieved through rich and meaningful interactions with others, and involves listening to the language of their community and interacting with more sophisticated language users. Most children will learn the spoken language of their community without a great deal of stress or effort through active engagement with those around them (Justice & Pullen 2003; Justice 2004; Dickinson & Tabors 2001).

Children learn about language as they begin to explore how language is used to communicate their needs, wants, feelings and desires. They learn how language works during everyday activities; for example, through play, shared storybook reading, talk and when engaging in daily routines; such as mealtimes, getting dressed, going on visits and the like. Children learn through language when interacting with others including caregivers, siblings, family members and educators. Language is critical for children's literacy, social and academic success, and is a pathway for developing friendships and social relationships (Chow, Ekholm & Coleman 2018).

In the preschool years, educators play a critical role in supporting young children's oral language development. However, in order to provide rich and engaging opportunities for oral language learning, educators need to have strong understandings of the complex and interrelated components of language, and how these impact the development of later literacy, social and behavioural development. In addition, educators need to be aware of their own language and communication skills and how these foster the oral language skills of the young children with whom they work (Law et al. 2019; Whorrall & Cabell 2016).

Components of oral language

Language is a socially and culturally shared code for representing concepts, expressing thoughts, feelings, needs, ideas and interacting with others in our world. Language is a critical process of communication that includes a set of arbitrary but very complex rule-governed symbols that are typically transmitted through verbal and non-verbal modes (Owens 2015; Paatsch & Toe in press). Young children are always refining their language use as they try to work out the rules, structures, word meanings, pronunciations and the social context of the language that surrounds them.

Language has many functions, including its use in getting things done, controlling others, regulating behaviour, expressing thoughts and ideas, formulating and maintaining social relationships, seeking knowledge, finding things out, conveying information and expressing creative thinking (Flint, Kitson, Lowe & Shaw 2017; Halliday 1975; 1978). Language, whether verbal or non-verbal, spoken or sign, is the main means of communication between people. Communication is a cognitive and interactive process whereby two or more people co-construct meaning and develop a shared understanding. For example, in conversation typically there is a listener and a speaker. The speaker must formulate a message and encode it into language then convey this message to the listener. The listener must not only decode the message but must also interpret the intended meaning and act upon it. This communicative process may involve sounds, words, phrases and sentences as well as the use of language in social contexts.

Understanding intended messages also relates to interpreting paralinguistic information; such as duration (speed and rate), intensity (stress and loudness) and pitch (high/low). For example, in the phrase 'Sarah loves chocolates', the intended meaning will vary according to the paralinguistic cues used. Intensity on the word *Sarah* may indicate that the speaker is stressing that it is Sarah and not another person. In contrast, intensity on the word *chocolates* may emphasise that it is chocolates that Sarah loves rather than another object. 'Pitch' (using rising inflection) on the word *chocolates* may indicate that the speaker is asking a question, while duration could be used to show emotions; such as excitement (when spoken quickly) or boredom (when spoken slowly and drawn out). Non-verbal cues; such as gestures, eye contact, body posture and facial expressions are also important in understanding and constructing meaning throughout the communication.

To become a competent and effective language user, children must develop both the 'expressive' and 'receptive' forms of language. *Expressive language* refers to the productive form of oral language and may include verbal and non-verbal cues, while *receptive language* involves listening (and watching) and decoding the language used by others. For example, at birth the newborn baby listens to the sounds around them and is able to distinguish language sounds from other sounds. During this time, they need to be in environments where they can hear sounds and be spoken to regularly by family and other caregivers. This talk between family members and children is critical as the child develops. By the time the child reaches the age of 2–3 months they enjoy listening to familiar voices and pay attention to the speech directed at the child. This 'infant-directed speech' typically involves the adult speaking in a slow, high-pitched voice in an exaggerated way. At around the first year of life, young children pay attention when they are called by their names, engage in repetitive games (e.g. 'round and round the garden') and recognise the names of common objects (Fellowes & Oakley 2014). Family members, caregivers and educators have a critical role in supporting young children's oral language as they engage in rich and abundant talk throughout regular everyday experiences, games and routines with children (Kovach & Da Ros-Voseles 2011).

Language, while complex, can be divided into three major components: 'form', 'content', and 'use' across five subsystems of language that comprise 'syntax', 'morphology', 'phonology', 'pragmatics' and 'semantics' (Bloom & Lahey 1978; Owens 2015). In the landmark work by Bloom and Lahey (1978) the three components of language are represented in a model that shows three overlapping circles as a way of illustrating the interrelatedness and equal emphasis between these components. However, in more recent times, the role of language *use* (pragmatics) has been repositioned to highlight the critical role pragmatics plays in language development and its strong link to social and emotional development (Bara 2010; Toe, Paatsch & Szarkowski 2020).

Figure 11.1 shows an adapted model from Toe, Paatsch and Szarkowski (2020) that repositions the ways the three components of language relate to each other, with *use* encircling *content* and *form* to illustrate its importance in relation to the other two critical components of language.

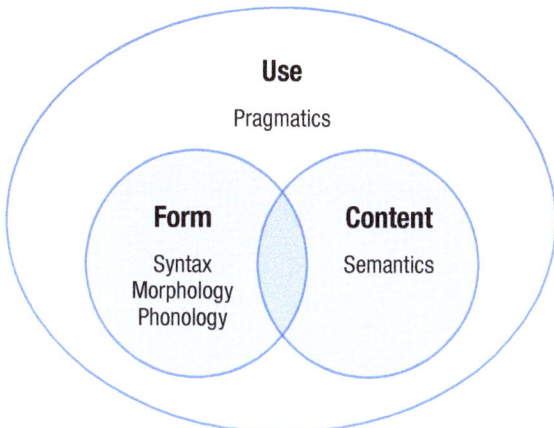

Figure 11.1 Interrelated components of language
Adapted from Toe, Paatsch and Szarkowski (2020).

Form includes *syntax* (the structure of phrases and sentences), *morphology* (organisation and internal structure of words, including adding prefixes and suffixes to mark change in meaning) and *phonology* (distribution and structure of sounds, including understanding how and where sounds are made). *Content* involves *semantics* (meaning of words and word combinations). *Use* includes *pragmatics* (social use of language). For example, if a child wants to tell their educator that they have 'two blue fast cars' they must have the vocabulary (semantics), know the word order (syntax), articulate and sequence the sounds of speech contained in each word (phonology), and know that there is an *s* at the end of the word *car* to denote plural (morphology). In addition, the child must use their language to initiate a conversation with their educator that may commence with a greeting, such as 'Hi', a question, for example 'Guess what I have in my hands?', or a polite initiation, such as 'Excuse me'. The child must also work out the appropriate time to initiate the conversation with the educator by determining whether the educator is busy, is talking to someone else, or has given them eye contact. Once this initiation has taken place, the child may then use eye contact and other non-verbal cues to show interest and excitement, take turns as the educator responds to their initiation, repair the conversation if the educator did not understand, maintain the topic, and use verbal and non-verbal strategies to end the interaction.

All these skills are critical mental processes that relate to the pragmatics subsystem of language. Pragmatics is important for effective communication and for building friendships (Paatsch & Toe 2016). In the first year of life, young children typically are able to request for objects and actions through gestures, vocalisations and single words, and refuse parent and caregivers' requests. They understand and use eye-contact and are able to take turns through routines and games (e.g. peek-a-boo). By 3 years of age children are able to take the perspective of another, make polite requests and can continue a topic and build a list of sequences in their narrative. In the preschool years, children can begin to reason and create imaginary roles as they interact with their peers (Fellowes & Oakley 2014; Paul, Norbury & Gosse 2018). As such, it is important to provide abundant and rich opportunities for young children to interact and converse with a range of partners, including adults and peers. Educators have an important role in fostering these conversations to support children's language and social development.

The connectedness of oral language and literacy development

Strong oral language skills are linked to children's literacy, social and emotional outcomes, and are critical for later educational success and throughout life (Nation, Cocksey, Taylor & Bishop 2010; Pordes-Bowers, Strelitz, Allen, Donkin 2012; Whorrall & Cabell 2016). There is clear evidence showing that children's expressive and receptive vocabularies, the ability to recall and comprehend sentences and stories, and the ability to engage in extended conversations are predictive of early literacy (Dickinson & Porche 2011; Dickinson, Nesbitt & Hofer 2019; Kendeou, van den Brock, White & Lynch 2009; Nation et al. 2010). It is important for children to understand the sounds, words and sentences of their language, and how these are used in social contexts. In addition, children need to understand the rules for how these components of language come together to convey meaning so that they can decode and comprehend the written text.

RESEARCH HIGHLIGHT

Kendeou, van den Brock, White and Lynch (2009) investigated 297 children's oral language and reading comprehension skills at three points in time: 4 years, 6 years and 8 years of age. Results showed that oral language predicted decoding skills at preschool, and both oral language and decoding skills independently predicted a child's reading comprehension by the time the child reached second grade.

Similarly, Dickinson, Nesbitt and Hofer (2019) reported a significant positive correlation between measures of oral language and code-related reading abilities, including phonological awareness, and letter–word knowledge, in a group of 489 African American children from low-income families. In particular, they reported the central role of vocabulary in early reading, as well as the significant association between discourse – an 'ability to comprehend and communicate understanding' – and later language skills (Dickinson, Nesbitt & Hofer 2019, p. 125). These findings support the critical role of oral language as a precondition for literacy.

Research investigating the links between language and early reading has shown that if children enter early childhood environments without well-developed spoken language abilities, these children are more likely to experience literacy problems later in school (Kendeou, van den Brock, White & Lynch 2009; Speaker, Taylor & Kamen 2004; Justice & Pullen 2003). Nation, Cocksey, Taylor and Bishop (2010) used a longitudinal design to investigate the relationship between children's early language and reading skills and later reading comprehension abilities. Results showed that children who were identified as having poor comprehension at the age of 8 years scored towards the lower end of average in receptive and expressive language skills but within normal range for word reading at ages 5, 6 and 7 years. These findings suggest that oral language in the preschool years is a strong predictor of reading comprehension at the age of 8 years.

Similar findings of a causal relationship between oral language and reading comprehension were reported by Clarke, Snowling, Truelove and Hulme (2010) and Fricke et al. (2013) after implementing successful oral language intervention programs with groups of preschool and early years school children. Specifically, these intervention programs resulted in improvements in vocabulary, phonological awareness and reading comprehension. In a more recent study by Duff, Reen, Plunkett and Nation (2015) of 300 British infants assessed in their second year of life and again five years later, results showed that infant vocabulary was a strong predictor of later vocabulary, reading comprehension and phonological awareness.

The findings from these studies support the strong link between a child's oral language development and later literacy achievement, which makes the environment and the interactions that occur within this environment of paramount importance. A young child's environment needs to provide supportive opportunities for receptive and expressive language development in the years before school. These opportunities can include conversational exchanges between adults and children in the contexts of play, storybook reading and shared world experiences. Young children who are exposed to a wide variety of words in meaningful conversations learn new words each day. When adults use a wide variety of descriptive language, children pick up on the words and learn their meaning in appropriate everyday contexts (Bardige & Sega 2004).

Engaging children in conversations about everyday activities expands vocabulary and supports children to acquire the language they need to make sense of print. In addition, there is a large body of research that has shown that rich dialogue during shared book reading improves young children's oral language skills, including sematic and syntactic structures (DeTemple 2001; Duursma 2014; Mol & Bus 2011; Sénéchal, Pagan, Lever & Ouellette 2008) as well as social and emotional understandings, and incorporating pragmatics skills (Rollo & Sulla 2016; Taumoepeau & Ruffman 2006; Ziv, Smadja & Aram 2013). Clearly, educators have a crucial role in fostering these opportunities to support children's oral language, literacy and social skills.

Identifying the issue: children presenting with low levels of oral language

In recent times, research has highlighted that young children are entering school with low levels of language. The developmental levels of children are now able to be assessed through the Australian Early Development Census (AEDC), a national measure of children's development as they enter school. In fact, Australia was 'the first country in the world to collect national data on the developmental health and wellbeing of all children as they start their first year of full-time school' (AEDC 2018, p. 7). The developmental domains measured included:

1. physical health and wellbeing
2. social competence
3. emotional maturity
4. language and cognitive skills (school-based)
5. communication skills and general knowledge. (AEDC 2018)

One domain closely aligned with children's language is the 'language and cognitive skills (school-based)' domain. This domain measures 'basic literacy, advanced literacy, basic numeracy, and interest in literacy, numeracy and memory' (AEDC 2018, p. 32).

The 2018 AEDC report shows that, within this domain, there has been a small but significant increase in the percentage of children who were developmentally vulnerable. Looking across the AEDC data (2015 until 2018), New South Wales and South Australia appear to have experienced a significant increase in vulnerability, whereas the Northern Territory experienced a significant decrease in vulnerability (from 21.5% in 2015 to 19.6% in 2018). What is highlighted within these data is the strong link between socio-economic disadvantage and language and cognitive skills. For example, children were more developmentally vulnerable if they were living in the most socio-economically disadvantaged locations when compared with their peers from less disadvantaged areas. In 2018, children living in very remote areas of Australia were 'more than five times more likely to be developmentally vulnerable on the language and cognitive skills domain compared with children living in major cities, a gap that has been steadily increasing since 2012' (AEDC 2018, p. 33). The gap between Aboriginal and Torres Strait Islander children and their non-Indigenous counterparts also continued to grow in 2018, with Aboriginal and Torres Strait Islander children more likely to be developmentally vulnerable (20.7%) than non-Indigenous children (5.7%). Another widening gap since 2012 is between children with English as an Additional Language (EAL) who were *not* proficient in English, and EAL children who *were* proficient in English. EAL children who were not proficient in English were reported as being more likely to be developmentally vulnerable.

The other domain that is relevant when considering young children's oral language skills is the 'communication skills and general knowledge' domain. This domain measures 'children's communication skills and general knowledge based on broad developmental competencies and skills measured in the school context' (AEDC 2018, p. 37). Findings show that there was a positive trend since baseline, with the percentage of children developmentally vulnerable decreasing and an increase in children considered to be *on track* in this domain. The link between socio-economic disadvantage was again noticeable. For example, 'children living in the most socio-economically disadvantaged locations were three times more likely to be developmentally vulnerable than those in the least disadvantaged areas' (AEDC 2018, p. 38). Unlike the 'language and cognitive skills' domain, the gap in this domain between Aboriginal and Torres Strait Islander children and non-Indigenous children has narrowed. In 2015 the gap was reported as 19.3%, whereas in 2018 it was 18.8%. There has also been an increase in the percentage of Aboriginal and Torres Strait Islander children on track, from 59.5 to 61.6%. A narrowing of the gap with each successive data collection round between children with EAL and children who speak only English at home is also recognised in results on this domain. However, results show that EAL children are still more developmentally vulnerable relative to non-EAL children – 14.8% and 6.4%, respectively. Similar to the 'language and cognitive skills (school-based)' domain, the English proficiency of EAL children continues to influence the vulnerability gap with those displaying good English language skills reported as less vulnerable than those EAL children with no English language. Again, a gap was reported between children living in very remote Australia when compared with children living in major cities. This gap has widened since 2012 (AEDC 2018).

A recent study by Nolan, Paatsch, Stagnitti and Campbell (2018) adds a more localised perspective on the AEDC data. This research study was located in a low socio-economic status (SES) area in Melbourne. Specifically, it was born out of the desire by the school involved to try a different approach to teaching and learning in the first year of formal schooling to improve student outcomes in language, social skills and general knowledge. The study was framed as an inquiry process where teachers were supported to research their own practice in relation to implementing a play-based approach. Specifically, this study investigated the relationship between teacher practice using a play-based approach, and play and language outcomes in a group of 72 Foundation year children (first year of primary school) aged between 4 years 10 months and 6 years 3 months (mean age = 5 years 4 months). Narrative and language assessments were conducted at the beginning of the Foundation year and again at the end of the year, while play assessments were conducted with 30 of the 72 (42%) children at the same time points. Educator experiences and reflections were also collected throughout the study.

Results of oral language skills, as measured by the *Clinical evaluation of language fundamentals: preschool* (CELF:P2) (Wiig, Secord & Semel 2006) showed that 29% of children scored in the low range for receptive language, while 36% scored in the low range for expressive language. In addition, the play abilities of the group of 30 children showed that 70% of the children had low levels of overall elaborate play with 53% of children showing low levels of object substitution, as measured by the *Child-initiated pretend play assessment (ChIPPA)* (Stagnitti 2007). Findings from this study support the AEDC findings that children in low SES communities are more likely to be developmentally vulnerable on measures of language and communication. This points to the need for educators working with young children to have the knowledge and skills to strongly support all children's oral language development, knowing how best to implement a program that scaffolds language learning.

Addressing the issue: building early childhood educator knowledge and practice

Building on the findings from this project, Paatsch and Nolan developed the Supporting Oral Language Development (SOLD) research project (2019), specifically aimed at providing professional learning for early childhood educators across the state of Victoria. This statewide project was a deliberate strategy to address the reported low language levels of many young children attending early childhood settings across Victoria. SOLD was designed to build early childhood educators' knowledge and understandings around oral language development to assist them to critically reflect on their current practice from an evidence-informed stance.

Over the course of four professional learning sessions, all aspects of language were covered, unpacking each subsystem, with educators required to apply what they learned to their practice. Throughout the SOLD project, educators were encouraged to use video in order to make a more nuanced assessment of children's oral language development, and to critique their own practice as well as the children's responses to their pedagogy. Reviewing the video vignettes of practice transports educators back to that moment in time and place to stimulate deeper reflection. In addition, video samples also assist in providing a more comprehensive and complete picture of the complexities of educators' oral language teaching practices as well as the current language levels of the children they teach (Nolan, Paatsch & Scull 2018).

At the commencement of the SOLD project, 77 educator participants from five different urban, regional and rural areas across the state of Victoria were invited to share their understandings of *language*. Educators reflected individually then shared their understandings with the group. Overall, educators understood language as a tool for communication that included sounds, speech, articulation and sentences. Some educators also reported that language involved the use of non-verbal cues; such as eye-contact, body language, gestures and facial expressions and understood that there was order and structure and the need for shared understanding.

These reported understandings suggested that educators were aware of some of the subsystems of language, although they did not use the specific terms for these subsystems; such as semantics and syntax. In addition, the discussions with the educators revealed limited understandings of each subsystem, particularly pragmatics, the interconnected nature of these, and the overall link to communication. One of the main aims of the SOLD professional learning sessions was to deepen educators' understandings of oral language. Specifically, educators were exposed to examples of the components of language, including the five subsystems, and discussed the typical developmental milestones of receptive and expressive language. Educators also used video excerpts of their own practice to analyse the different subsystems that the children were developing and were invited to illustrate their conceptual understandings of how each of the subsystems of language interconnect and contribute to understanding.

Throughout the four professional learning sessions, educators constantly discussed their deepening understandings and reported back to the rest of the group. Educators continued to analyse their own videos of practice as well as those practical suggestions provided throughout the sessions. Specifically, educators reflected on particular strategies they implemented to support children's oral language skills. These strategies included a strong focus on pragmatic skills whereby teachers were encouraged to engage in conversations with the children to develop the more subtle cues of turn-taking; such as pausing, changing topics and eye-gaze. They also role-modelled the ways in which a listener acknowledges another person's contribution to the conversation, and how to seek specific clarification beyond the general strategy of asking 'What?' This involved supporting children to ask questions, to think about the perspective of the other person, how they could enter a group, and how to introduce a topic. At the same time, educators were also encouraged to continue to support children's vocabulary (semantics), with a specific focus on providing multiple meanings of the same word, as well as developing sentence structure (syntax) and articulation (phonology).

At the conclusion of the SOLD project, findings from data collected from end-of-project evaluations as well as from group discussions showed that when educators have a solid understanding of all aspects of oral language, they feel confident to provide rich experiences and pedagogy to support young children's oral language development.

The following two research highlights present details of two of the early childhood educators, Wendy and Roseanne, and their reflections on the importance of supporting oral language, as well as their learnings after participating in the SOLD project.

RESEARCH HIGHLIGHT

Wendy

Wendy holds a degree in early childhood education and works in a preschool setting. Through deepening her knowledge of oral language 'Breaking down the language development into subcategories', Wendy has developed 'a better insight into more areas of language development and its important role'. Wendy came to realise that language comprises more components than just phonics and by breaking it down into the subsystems of language, she could achieve a more detailed understanding of each child's oral language skills and plan accordingly.

continued…

When asked if her understanding of oral language had changed due to her participation in the SOLD project Wendy states: 'Absolutely, breaking down children's language and categorising it into areas of development using receptive and expressive language helps to give a greater understanding of the child's overall language development. I will be using more videos of children's engagement to help with this'.

Exposing Wendy to current research and knowledge about oral language learning strengthened her belief that she, as an educator, plays a major role in supporting the development of children's oral language. 'It's the way we engage children and extend their language that is just as important'.

Wendy is now reflecting on her practice from a more in-depth knowledge base, thinking about how she can encourage and support language development in her program.

RESEARCH HIGHLIGHT

Roseanne

Roseanne holds a certificate qualification in early childhood education and care (ECEC). She came into the SOLD project with no preconceived idea of what this professional learning offering would entail. Roseanne leaves the project with not only new ways of teaching and supporting oral language learning, and ways of assessing oral language, but also changes in her relationships with families and colleagues. With a more detailed understanding of oral language Roseanne feels confident in how she assesses certain language interactions with the children she works with and discusses these assessments with children's families and other colleagues.

Roseanne explains her professional learning experience as changing 'the whole perspective of language and how very important it is. Language has a huge impact on their [children's] lives and their future. I now take more time in conversation with kids, really focusing on all that we have learned'.

Gaining in knowledge and understanding has assisted Roseanne to experience a rise in her professional confidence as she now has a deeper understanding of what oral language comprises, what facilitates and constrains it, and how she can support the oral language learning of young children.

All educators who participated in the SOLD project noted the importance of educators having a more extensive knowledge of oral language development and its relationship to practice. Educators commented:

> *Language is such a big part of what we do and we take it for granted. It's important to understand its usefulness.*

> *Breaking down the language development into subcategories has given me a better insight into more areas of language development and the important role educators play in developing this area.*

> *Language needs much closer attention and more time and opportunity to develop. Language is at the heart of relational pedagogy and as said elsewhere, gives us a strong handle on how to approach social and emotional challenges.*

> *Language is complex but if broken down it is easier to understand and provide help and strategies for the children.*

> *It's not just language and talking – it is so much more and inter-loops with all other areas of development and overall wellbeing.*

The educators reported that their understandings of oral language had become more detailed, in-depth and thorough after attending the SOLD sessions and this directly supported changes to their practice.

> *I am more aware of how to communicate and use more open-ended questions now and talk less over the top of the children.*

> *We now pay more attention to our conversations [with the children]. We are prioritising conversations and recording to try to be accountable on a daily basis in our routine interactions.*

> *I am paying more attention to how I interact with and model to children, concentrating on the different elements of language.*

> *Have undertaken a deeper analysis of children's language skill in play and I am more reflective and considerate of my part in this.*

> *Trying to extend language more within children and to stop myself from wanting to talk when there are pauses in conversations.*

Conclusion

This chapter has highlighted the importance of educators having a solid understanding of all aspects of oral language in order to provide rich experiences and pedagogy to facilitate young children's oral language development. The research outlined in this chapter also illustrates that with a deeper knowledge and understanding of all aspects of oral language, educator confidence in their practice increases. Educators can make a significant difference to children's learning by taking time to build knowledge of oral language development and reflect on practice from an evidence-informed perspective.

RESEARCH INTO PRACTICE

Please use the following questions to reflect on your practice in relation to supporting young children's oral language learning:

- In my practice, how conscious am I about facilitating oral language in the children I work with?
- What strategies do I already know about or use to engage children in sustained conversations?
- How aware am I about the different subsystems of language?
- How could I use my knowledge of the subsystems of language to plan experiences to support children's oral language development?
- What are the different roles I could take up in my daily practice to strengthen children's oral language?

References

Australian Early Development Census (AEDC) 2018, *Australian Early Development Census national report 2018: a snapshot of early childhood development in Australia*, Commonwealth of Australia, Canberra.

Bara, BG 2010, *Cognitive pragmatics: the mental processes of communication*, MIT Press, Cambridge, MA.

Bardige, B & Sega, M 2004, *Building literacy with love: a guide for teachers and caregivers of children from birth through age 5*, Zero to Three, Washington.

Bloom, L & Lahey, M 1978, *Language development and language disorders*, Wiley, New York.

Chow, JC, Ekholm, E & Coleman, H 2018, 'Does oral language underpin the development of later behavior problems? A longitudinal meta-analysis', *School Psychology Quarterly*, vol. 33, no. 3, pp. 337–49.

Clarke, PJ, Snowling, MJ, Truelove, E & Hulme, C 2010, 'Ameliorating children's reading comprehension difficulties: a randomized controlled trial', *Psychological Science*, vol. 2, no. 18, pp. 1106–16.

DeTemple, JM 2001, 'Parents and children reading books together', in DK Dickinson & PO Tabors (eds), *Beginning literacy with language: young children learning at home and school*, P.H. Brookes, Baltimore, pp. 31–51.

Dickinson, DK, Nesbitt, KT & Hofer, KG 2019, 'Effects of language on initial reading: direct and indirect associations between code and language from preschool to first grade', *Early Childhood Research Quarterly*, vol. 49, pp. 122–37.

Dickinson, DK & Tabors, PO (eds) 2001, *Beginning literacy with language*, Brookes, Baltimore.

Dickinson, DK & Porche, MV 2011, 'Relation between language experiences in preschool classrooms and children's kindergarten and fourth-grade language and reading abilities', *Child Development*, vol. 82, pp. 870–86.

Duff, FJ, Reen, G, Plunkett, K & Nation, K 2015, 'Do infant vocabulary skills predict school-age language and literacy outcomes?', *The Journal of Child Psychology and Psychiatry*, vol. 56, no. 8, pp. 848–56.

Duursma, E 2014, 'The effects of fathers' and mothers' reading to their children on language outcomes of children participating in early head start in the United States', *Fathering: A Journal of Theory, Research & Practice about Men as Fathers*, vol. 12, no. 3, pp. 283–302.

Fellowes, J & Oakley, G 2014, *Language, literacy and early childhood education*, Oxford University Press, New York.

Flint, A, Kitson, L, Lowe, K & Shaw, K 2017, *Literacy in Australia: pedagogies for engagement*, John Wiley and Sons, Melbourne.

Fricke, S, Bowyer-Crane, C, Haley, AJ, Hulme, C & Snowling, M 2013, 'Efficacy of language intervention in the early years', *The Journal of Child Psychology and Psychiatry*, vol. 54, no. 3, pp. 280–90.

Halliday, MAK 1975, *Learning how to mean: explorations in the development of language*, Arnold, London.

Halliday, MAK 1978, *Language as social semiotic: the social interpretation of language and meaning*, Arnold, London.

Justice, L 2004, 'Creating language-rich preschool classroom environments', *Teaching Exceptional Children*, vol. 37, no. 2, pp. 36–44.

Justice, L & Pullen, P 2003, 'Promising interventions for promoting emergent literacy skills: three evidence-base approaches', *Topics in Early Childhood Special Education*, vol. 23, no. 3, pp. 99–114.

Kendeou, P, van den Broek, P, White, MJ & Lynch, JS 2009, 'Predicting reading comprehension in early elementary school: the independent contributions of oral language and decoding skills', *Journal of Educational Psychology*, vol. 101, no. 4, pp. 765–78.

Kovach, B & Da Ros-Voseles, D 2011, 'Communicating with babies', *Young Children*, vol. 66, no. 2, pp. 48–50.

Law, J, Tulip, J, Stringer, H, Cockerill, M & Dockrell, J 2019, 'Teachers observing classroom communication: an application of the communicating supporting classroom observation tool for children aged 4–7 years', *Child Language Teaching and Therapy*, vol. 35, no. 3, pp. 203–20.

Mol, SE & Bus, AG 2011, 'To read or not to read: a meta-analysis of print exposure from infancy to early adulthood', *Psychological Bulletin*, vol. 137, no. 2, pp. 267–96.

Nation, K, Cocksey, J, Taylor, J & Bishop, DVM 2010, 'A longitudinal investigation of early reading and language skills in children with poor reading comprehension', *The Journal of Child Psychology and Psychiatry*, vol. 51, no. 9, pp. 1031–39.

Nolan, A, Paatsch, L, Stagnitti, K & Campbell, K 2018, 'Thinking differently about practice: developmental play, report for [name removed for confidentiality] primary school', Melbourne.

Nolan, A, Paatsch, L & Scull, J 2018, 'Video-based methodologies: the affordances of different viewpoints in understanding teachers' tacit knowledge of practice that supports young children's oral language', *International Journal of Research & Method in Education*, vol. 41, no. 5, pp. 536–47.

Owens, RE Jr 2015, *Language development: an introduction*, 9th edn, San Antonio, Pearson, San Antonio, TX.

Paatsch, L & Toe, D 2016, 'The fine art of conversation: the pragmatic skills of school-aged children with hearing loss', in M Marschark and PE Spencer (eds), *The Oxford handbook of deaf studies in language: research, policy and practice*, Oxford University Press, New York, pp. 94–113.

Paatsch, L & Toe, D in press, 'The interplay between pragmatics and reading comprehension in children who are deaf or hard of hearing', in S Estabrooks (ed.), *Oxford handbook of deaf studies in literacy*, Oxford University Press, Oxford.

Paul, R, Norbury, C & Gosse, C 2018, *Language disorders from infancy through adolescence*, 5th edn, Elsevier, St Louis, MO.

Pordes-Bowers, A, Strelitz, J, Allen, J & Donkin, A 2012, *An equal start: improving outcomes in children's centres*, UCL Institute of Health Equity, London.

Rollo, D & Sulla, F 2016, 'Maternal talk in cognitive development: relations between psychological lexicon, semantic development, empathy, and temperament', *Frontiers in Psychology*, vol. 7, p. 394, doi:10.3389/fpsyg.2016.00394.

Sénéchal, M, Pagan, S, Lever, R & Ouellette, GP 2008, 'Relations among the frequency of shared reading and 4-year-old children's vocabulary, morphological and syntax comprehension, and narrative skills', part of a special section entitled, *Parent–Child Interaction and Early Literacy Development*, vol. 19, no. 1, pp. 27–44.

Speaker, K, Taylor, D & Kamen, R 2004, 'Storytelling: enhancing language acquisition in young children', *Education*, vol. 125, ed. 1, pp. 3–14.

Stagnitti, K 2007, *Child-initiated pretend play assessment* (ChIPPA), Coordinates, Melbourne.

Taumoepeau, M & Ruffman, T 2006, 'Mother and infant talk about mental states relates to desire language and emotion understanding', *Child Development*, vol. 77, no. 2, pp. 465–81.

Toe, D, Paatsch, L & Szarkowski A 2020, 'It is more than language: the role of cognition in the pragmatic skills of children who are deaf and hard of hearing', in M Marschark and H Knoors (eds), *The Oxford handbook of deaf studies in learning and cognition*, Oxford University Press, New York, pp. 81–98.

Vukelich, C, Christie, JF & Enz, B 2008, *Helping young children learn language and literacy: birth through kindergarten*, Allyn and Bacon, Boston.

Whorrall, J & Cabell, S 2016, 'Supporting children's oral language development in the preschool classroom', *Journal of Early Childhood Education*, vol. 44, no. 4, pp. 335–41.

Wiig, E, Secord, W & Semel, E 2006, *Clinical evaluation of language fundamentals preschool*, 2nd edn, Pearson, Melbourne.

Ziv, M, Smadja, ML & Aram, D 2013, 'Mothers' mental-state discourse with preschoolers during storybook reading and wordless storybook telling', *Early Childhood Research Quarterly*, vol. 28, no. 1, pp. 177–86.

CHAPTER 12

Early literacy

Bridie Raban

DOI: https://doi.org/10.37517/978-1-74286-555-3_12
University of Melbourne

LINKS TO NATIONAL QUALITY STANDARD

Quality Area 1: Educational program and practice
- Standard 1.2: Practice – educators facilitate and extend children's learning and development.
- Element 1.2.1: Intentional teaching – educators are deliberate, purposeful and thoughtful in their decisions and actions.
- Element 1.2.2: Responsive teaching and scaffolding – educators respond to children's ideas and play and extend children's learning through open-ended questions, interactions and feedback.

LINKS TO EARLY YEARS LEARNING FRAMEWORK

Learning Outcome 5: Children are effective communicators
- Children engage with a range of texts and gain meaning from these texts.
- Children begin to understand how symbols and pattern systems work.
- Children use information and communication technologies to access information, investigate ideas and represent their thinking.

Introduction

This chapter introduces the term 'early literacy', not to be confused with the beginning literacy program that takes place in the early years of primary school.

Before children start school there is much they come to learn and understand about literacy through a wide variety of everyday activities that take place both at home, within their community and at their early childhood setting. These experiences build a strong 'conceptual framework' that supports these children's later understanding of the *item knowledge* (like letters and letter sounds) they will encounter when they start school. This chapter begins by introducing research evidence that informs practice and then continues to give examples of learning experiences. These learning experiences are supported by relevant research and show how both reading and writing can be approached with young children, and embedded within the play-based programs of early childhood settings.

Developing literacy within play-based programs is supported by the definition of literacy found in the Early Years Learning Framework for Australia (EYLF) glossary (DEEWR 2009, p. 46):

> **Literacy**: in the early years includes a range of modes of communication including music, movement, dance, storytelling, visual arts, media and drama, as well as talking, reading and writing.

This chapter will explore how a strong conceptual framework and knowledge about literacy can be developed within a play-based program, without specifically teaching young children to read and write before they start school. Palmer, Bayley and Raban (2013) take this EYLF definition further by giving practical examples of how learning to listen, finding time to talk, moving to music, singing songs and nursery rhymes, story time, learning about print, tuning into sound, and experimenting with writing, all within a play-based program, contribute to developing children's early understandings of literacy.

Early literacy: theoretical underpinnings

Holliday (2013) points out that many teachers and educators believe that literacy learning is best left to the early years of formal schooling, and the years before school need to focus on a play-based environment. But many children arriving at school for the first time have difficulties learning to read and write, falling behind their peers as they progress through the early years (ACARA 2017). It has long been understood that children categorised as low achievers in school have limitations in their prior knowledge rather than any defective learning abilities. But where does this prior knowledge come from? Not from systematic and specific instruction, because that in turn requires prior knowledge. It comes from more general play-based experiences within which their early learning takes place.

The notion of the child as a 'lone scientist' hypothesising about their world and further exploring it on their own, which had been the interpretation of Piaget's work (1955), was extended by these views: first, that children were learning all the time, and second, they learned particularly by being engaged in everyday activities with more knowledgeable and significant others. These developments in thinking made a profound impact on researchers' understanding of early literacy development as they began to take more systematic notice of the play experiences of young children (Dickinson &

Neuman 2014). More recently, a significant amount of early literacy research has been collected by Kucirkova, Snow, Grover and McBride (2017). *The Routledge international handbook of early literacy education* encompasses a wide range of chapters presenting new developments in old debates as well as new approaches to urgent social and cultural challenges.

During the latter part of the 20th century, researchers emphasised the importance of early stimulation for learning, and pointed out the significance of Bruner's statement (1960) that any subject could be taught effectively in some intellectually honest form to any child at any age. These views, in conjunction with those of Vygotsky (1962), which were just becoming known through translation, heralded the way forward to what we now understand as the social constructivist theory of learning and development (Nolan & Raban 2015, pp. 29–30). Vygotsky provided the impetus for this revised view of early childhood learning through his understanding of 'what a child could do with assistance today, they could do for themselves tomorrow' (1978, p. 87).

Early literacy development

Following on from these early studies, which changed the discourse from *pre-reading* to *emergent literacy* and on to *early literacy* development, greater attention is now paid to family literacy practices (Aram 2018; Barratt-Pugh & Rohl 2015; 2016) and to all who support children during the years before formal schooling begins (*see* **Figure 12.1**). By living and participating in environments in which others use print (either on screen or paper) for a variety of purposes, children come to understand and infer the semiotic and functional nature of written language. They begin to build strong 'conceptual' knowledge about literacy before beginning formal schooling (Neuman & Celano 2018).

Figure 12.1 Hazel enjoys looking at her board book

Literacy development during the early years, therefore, involves both social and cognitive dimensions, comprehending the message as well as deciphering the print (Raban & Scull 2013). The social dimension of literacy development consists of young children, through interactions with family and peers, understanding the purpose of reading and writing for both information and for pleasure. Cognitive aspects include coming to understand the many concepts about print, including the alphabetic principle and directionality. **Figure 12.2** shows

Early literacy

Figure 12.2 Name writing across one year of signing in

Figure 12.3 Mum sharing a book with Hazel

examples of one child writing his name in the signing-in book over the course of his 3-year-old preschool program. He progresses from a scribbled line to a recognisable rendition of the three letters in his name.

During the early years, an interested family member or other adult, who clearly loves reading and sharing books, may involve the young learner in what they do and explain their literacy practice as they go along, making what they do explicit (*see* **Figure 12.3**). This will not happen on every occasion, sometimes it will just be enjoying the experience of a good story (Sim & Berthelsen 2014). Stevens, Raban and Nolan (2013) point out that the power of story, for instance, will be a prime motivation for young children wanting to explore books and other resources further, and they will tell you the stories they want read, again and again.

Early literacy: research and evidence

The early years provide opportunities for infants, toddlers and young children to see adults reading and writing in a wide range of circumstances; for example, adults looking up an address, reading a timetable or newspaper, checking ingredients for a recipe, reading and sending emails, paying a bill and reading bedtime stories (Wasik & van Horn 2012). It is an ideal time, when young children enter early childhood settings, to support those who may have limited experiences of this kind in their home environment (Neuman & Wright 2007). Print-rich environments, with posters, books and useful signage that are used daily (*see* **Figure 12.4**), invite young children to engage with reading experiences with the support of their educators (Baroody & Diamond 2016; Roskos & Christie 2017).

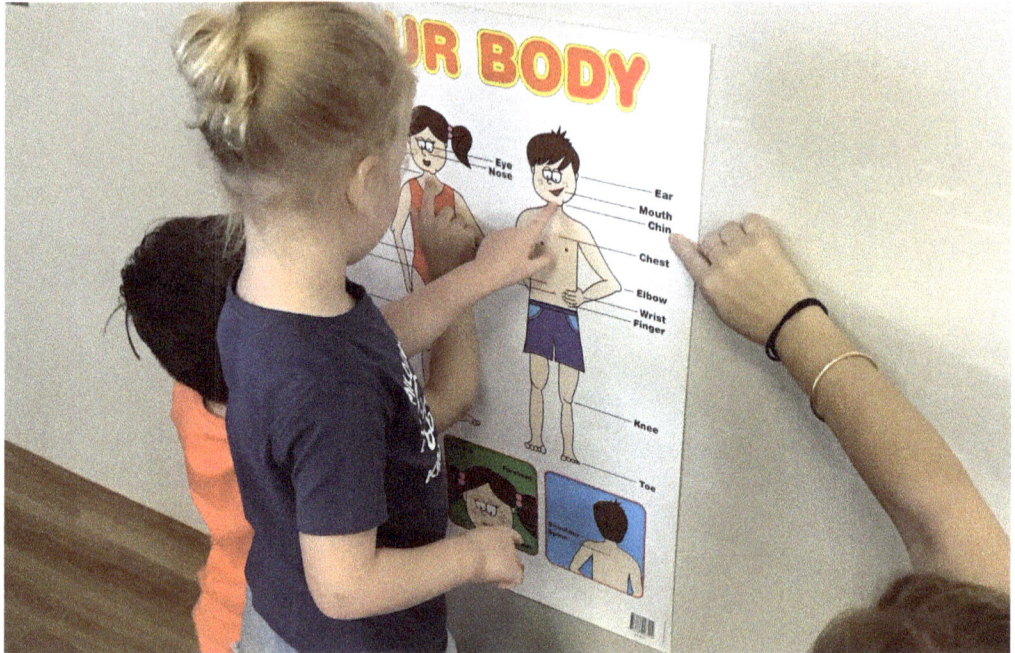

Figure 12.4 Looking at words about different parts of the body

RESEARCH HIGHLIGHT

The opportunity to explore the development of young children's early literacy during the years before school, was taken by Raban and Ure (2000). This Preschool Literacy Project (PLP) worked with educators in 40 Australian early childhood settings. These preschoolers then transitioned into 25 of the lowest performing (with respect to literacy development) primary schools in the state of Victoria at that time.

The purpose of the PLP was to encourage and support early childhood educators in these settings to develop a literacy focus within their established play-based programs. The primary schools that these children later entered were part of a larger Early Years Research Project (ELRP) conducted by Hill and Crevola (2003) The children's data became available as they progressed through the early years of primary school.

The preschools taking part in the PLP were visited regularly, where they discussed their literacy practice with the researchers and new ideas were generated. On subsequent visits, these ideas would be reviewed along with fresh suggestions for further learning experiences.

It was found that children who transitioned to ELRP primary schools from the PLP preschools, still arrived at school unable to read or write, similar to their contemporaries (Raban, Coates & Ure 2016). However, after one year in school, the PLP group of children was ahead of their peers on literacy assessments and maintained this relative progress over subsequent years.

Printed language: conventions and concepts

Through a range of learning experiences, children can be shown the directional aspects of print; by finger pointing and tracking left to right and top to bottom of the page. When adults write with children, they can point out the need to start writing at the top left-hand side of the page, and move from left to right when writing (for the English-language). Cunningham's research (2010), on specific features of children's experiences in the early years, stressed that they need many and varied opportunities for experimenting with writing in order to try out and improve their developing capabilities. Bus and Out (2009) found support, through the use of prompts, cues, modelling and feedback, facilitates early skill development, especially for children experiencing difficulties. Importantly, Mackenzie and Scull (2015) point out that prompting and modelling writing words of a sentence for children are best learned within the context of a real circumstance, where the writing is seen as part of the whole composing experience, including talking and drawing and commenting on a known event.

Early reading experiences

Roskos and Christie (2017) focused on young children's experiences as they entered early childhood settings, as an opportunity to support those who may have limited experiences of literacy in their home environment. Indeed, the single most powerful activity for building knowledge and skills required for later literacy success appears to be reading aloud with children, especially in small, intimate groups (Zrna 2017) where the children can share the storybook and keep close physical contact (*see* **Figure 12.5**). According to Schickedanz (2014), this is also true for infants and toddlers. Furthermore, Beck and McKeown (2007) show that reading with and to young children impacts their language and vocabulary development because children who hear *written* sentences read aloud will experience language constructed in ways that are likely to be different from the spoken language they typically hear around them. Ezell and Justice (2005) point out that in this way they also learn about the pragmatic rules that govern the use of language.

Early writing development

Children do not wait until they start school to learn how to write (Aram & Levin 2016) and the EYLF (DEEWR 2009) supports the provision of early writing along with other literacy experiences during the years before formal schooling begins. Young children, once they know it is physically possible and appropriate to do so, leave messages and stories in mixtures of marks, scribbles and drawings. This is because, for many young children, writing things down is part of their family life (McLachlan et al. 2013). For instance, these children will be included in writing shopping lists, emailing family members, writing and sending texts, sending cards, leaving notes and post-its on the fridge door. However, Raban (2018) shows that the combined complexities of knowing what to write (composing) and knowing how to write (concepts about print and written language as opposed to spoken forms) can be overwhelming obstacles for some children.

Figure 12.5 Small group of children sharing a book with their educator

Figure 12.6 Scribbles of a 2-year-old

Early writing for children under the age of 3 years old has received very little research attention (McFarland 2018, p. 47). However, McFarland shows how the youngest children can be supported in their early writing in a variety of ways within the birth to 2 years' settings. Providing resources and opportunities for mark-making is an important first step. Lancaster (2007, p. 149) reports that children under 3 years of age 'have the capacity to use graphic marks in highly intentioned and reasoned ways', thus suggesting that the marks we observe are far from random. While acknowledging that fostering language is a very important first step in writing, McFarland (2018) argues for the additional importance of developing both early gross and fine motor skills, and supporting experiences with a range of writing and painting tools for scribbling and mark-making (with or without meanings attached). **Figure 12.6** shows the scribbles of a 2-year-old who screwed up his drawing and hid it in the fridge when he didn't want to go home, so everyone had to spend time looking for it!

Researchers have found that the progression from scribble to recognisable writing appears to be *task dependent*. The young children observed in Ferreiro and Teborosky's (1983) landmark study used advanced writing features for easier writing tasks (i.e. writing their name) but resorted to more basic features like scribble or drawing when the writing task proved more challenging. The researchers argue that young children's knowledge regarding their names is more advanced than their other writing, probably because they write it more frequently.

Literacy in play-based activities

Christie and Roskos (2015) show how early literacy learning takes place for babies, toddlers and young children while engaging in play-based activities. During these learning experiences they are being supported to understand what is going on and helped to take part in reading and writing for themselves. Reading with toddlers (Kaefer, Pinkham & Neuman 2017) and older children (Sim & Berthelsen 2014) promotes supportive contexts for learning, and regular engagement in this activity correlates with early literacy development. Incorporating a writing table into a play area can also engage children's curiosity (Raban 2018) (*see* **Figure 12.7**).

Dialogic reading/interactive read-alouds

Evans and Shaw (2008) show that shared storybook reading is a good place to start with young children, infants and toddlers, who may be unfamiliar with book reading at a personal level (one-on-one). The more detailed and specific work of sharing a story is referred to as 'dialogic reading' (Cohen, Kramer-Vida & Frye 2012), or interactive 'read-alouds' (Lennox 2013; Sim & Berthelsen 2014). This is a technique that involves the elaboration of a story by asking questions throughout the reading process, thereby involving children during the reading. Recent research focusing on interactive read-alouds point out that reading aloud to infants stimulates their brains to create new learning pathways and strengthen existing ones.

Kotaman (2013) reminds us that one of the main reasons underlying the benefits of reading aloud *with* children (not *to* children) is that the child is engaged together in the learning experience with the person reading the story. Too frequently the opportunity to share a story takes place with the whole group rather than with individual children or small groups, and this does not enable the individual focus to be capitalised on. The quality and reading style, when reading aloud with children, has been shown to be as important as the frequency of this literacy-promoting experience (Demir et al. 2011). This finding has been supported by the work of Mol, Bus and de Jong (2009)

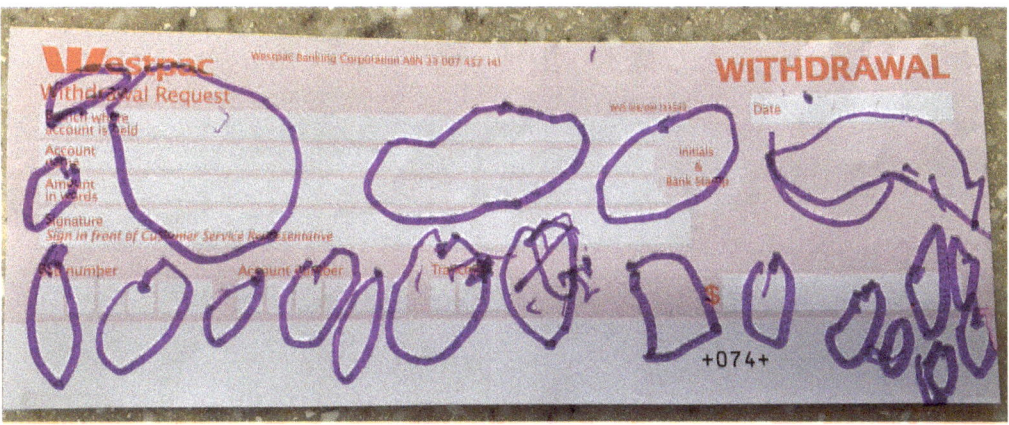

Figure 12.7 Found on the writing table

and Roberts, Jurgens and Burchinal (2005). Phillips, Norris and Anderson (2008) have noted that sharing storybooks with young children will enhance oral language development, with this opportunity frequently focusing on the illustrations and the flow of the story. However, to achieve early learning about literacy, time needs to be taken to occasionally point out special words, by running fingers under text, pointing to each word as it is read, coupled with discussion of word meanings. This is achieved most effectively when sharing a storybook in small groups with an infant and/or two or three toddlers or older children.

Print referencing

'Print referencing' has been found by Justice et al. (2009) to be another important way of enhancing the quality of the shared reading experience with young children, and supporting the development of alphabet knowledge. Justice and Pullin (2003) for instance, describe print referencing as an educator's use of nonverbal and verbal cues to direct a child's attention to the forms, features and functions of written language. These cues are embedded into the shared storybook reading interactions with young children. An example of print referencing is to ask questions; such as 'Do you know where I should start reading', and non-verbal behaviours; such as tracking the print with a finger while reading. Skibbe, Thompson and Plavnick (2018) found that young children's total *fixation duration* to print was greatest when print was read aloud and highlighted, even when the text was digitally presented.

Environmental print

'Environmental print' refers to items such as signs, billboards, food labels and toy packaging. McMahon and Wellhousen (2010), and Neumann, Hood and Ford (2013) claim that environmental print is typically large, bold and presented in all different shapes, colours and sizes; characteristics that can draw and hold a child's attention. Neuman and Dickinson (2011) illustrate how drawing attention to print in the environment is an important experience for young children in forming understandings about the purpose of print in daily life. Reading environmental print is an activity which children often engage in before reading print in books, as they accompany family members on shopping excursions and the like.

Gross and fine motor skill development

Dinehart (2015) explores the research concerning infants', toddlers' and young children's need to participate in a variety of learning experiences, intentionally designed to promote gross and fine motor control. Grasping objects one at a time, moving to music, picking up toys and engaging purposefully with both the indoor and outdoor environments give many opportunities for the development of gross and fine motor skills.

Caletti, McLaughlin, Derby and Rinaldi (2012) used tracing as a technique with young children to help letter formation. Using the letters of their name, children were supported by being shown where to start tracing each letter and being told which way to go, with this being systematically faded as less and less support was required. However, learning experiences like this require the child to be writing recognisable letters and many may not be at that point of fine motor development, even experiencing difficulty holding a pencil or texta.

Pencil grip can be strengthened through other experiences that can involve using scissors, using a plastic dropper (with a squeezy top), tongs, painting a picture or pattern, doing up buttons and the like. One study by Lust and Donica (2011) used whole body activities, directional games and playing with letters, all of which improved the children's dexterity beyond a control group who did not receive the intervention. Learning opportunities outlined by Huffman and Fortenberry (2011) help to develop young children's upper body strength and to strengthen their arm muscles. These experiences included making large circular movements with arms, hand and finger games, as well as using utensils to interact with other objects. Finger play rhymes were also found to be useful.

Writing as communication

Through discussion, Mackenzie (2011) shows how children can talk about their drawing. In response, the educator can write what they say (exactly what they say) and display the drawing and writing for others to view as a complete composition. Rowe and Neitzel (2010) find that through these experiences, children come to understand that what they think about and what they say can be transported over time and shared with others. In addition, Puranik, Phillips, Lonigan and Gibson (2018) identify the significant role of families in supporting early writing understandings and development. Bingham et al. (2018) point out that because their spoken words have been re-presented (written down for them), they can *read* them and share their composition with others. In addition, children develop concepts about print including words, letters and print displays, along with directionality and spacing.

Name writing

Treiman et al. (2007) maintain that because the printed name is synonymous with identity, children's names are often their first stable written form with meaning, and this represents an important benchmark in young children's early literacy understandings and development. In addition, focusing on a child's name provides a culturally and socially relevant activity connecting both home and other settings.

RESEARCH HIGHLIGHT

In a study of 4-year-old children's name writing, reported by Welsch, Sullivan and Justice (2003), one third of them (33%) could make marks, not distinguishable as letters, but 15% could write their name correctly. This range of name-writing ability across this sample correlated positively with young children's other developing knowledge about literacy. Those who could write their name correctly and separate it from a picture of themselves, also achieved higher scores relating to rhyme and beginning sounds of words, alphabet knowledge, concept of a word, and print knowledge generally.

Names, with a photograph are often placed by each child's shelf, cupboard or peg as a reminder of the significance of this special word. Puranik and Lonigan (2012) show that later, name writing serves an ongoing role, helping children make connections to letters, words, sounds and other reading and writing concepts. The report of the National Early Literacy Panel (2009) suggests that by writing their own name, children begin the process of naming objects in writing (*see* **Figure 12.8**).

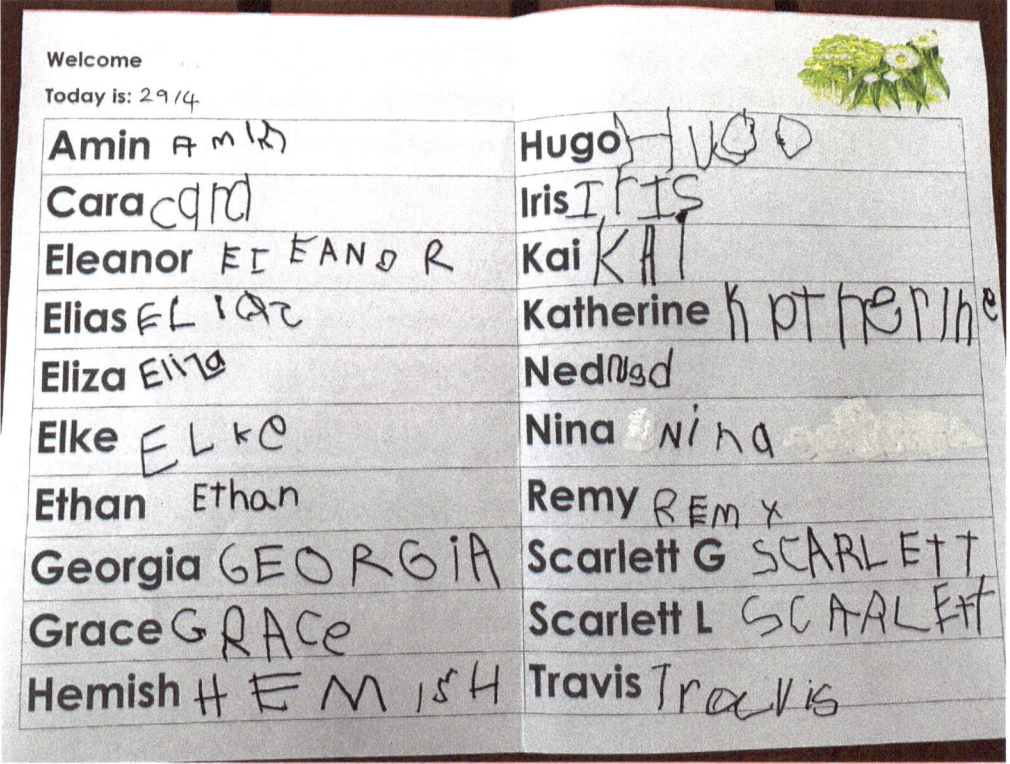

Figure 12.8 Page from a signing-in book

Bennett et al. (2018) review culturally responsive literacy practices. Among a range of learning experiences, they identify an important aspect of early writing for children learning English as an Additional Language (EAL) will be helping them write their name in English as well as their home language. For instance, ask the family of the child whose first language is not English, for a written example of their child's name in their home language. Display this name card where that child keeps their belongings, and place it alongside their name in English. The child's name may be in Arabic or Swahili, languages with very different marks from English letters. There is much for these children to learn and their name will be a good place to start.

Conclusion

The interactive nature of the relationships between young children and their families and other adults is essential to the formation of the developing brain and to early language and literacy development. Positive adult–child shared experiences in the early years of life help to build healthy brain architecture and the formation of concepts that will prepare a child well for the demands of formal schooling. Sharing rhymes, songs, storybooks and stories every day with children from birth are nurturing and responsive learning opportunities that foster positive development in the early years.

In addition, Mol, Neuman and Strouse (2014) are mindful of the developing digital environment which is increasingly a given for the lives of many families. Digital technologies within the Australian ECEC sector are explored by Zabatiero et al. (2018), and Laidlaw, O'Mara and Wong (2015) where they argue that the multimodal affordances of new digital devices offer children accessible communication tools and practices. Neumann (2018), and Harrison and McTavish (2018) focus on the impact of digital technologies into the lives of babies and young children. In contrast, Quinn and Bliss (2019) review over 400 apps designed to assist young children with their writing, and they sound warnings concerning their poor quality. However, the continuing support from communities, families, early childhood educators and teachers, as well as exposure to quality experiences, on and off screen, can help all children to gain the foundational skills for subsequent successful learning of language and literacy when they begin formal schooling.

RESEARCH INTO PRACTICE

While considering the following questions, make notes about how you would evaluate your practice as opportunities, planned and otherwise, emerge during your time with the children.

How can you:

- learn about each child's knowledge, strengths, ideas, culture, abilities and interests with respect to early literacy?
- plan and implement literacy experiences that are relevant and engaging for each child?
- use conversations and interactions with children during storybook reading, making them enjoyable and meaningful opportunities?
- reflect on the range of intentional teaching strategies suggested in the EYLF to support children's literacy development?
- arrange activities, routines and the physical environment to support children's literacy development?
- work collaboratively with each family to share information about children's literacy development and how they participate in the different activities they experience?
- critically reflect on those aspects of your program that support young children's literacy development?

References

Aram, D 2018, 'Promoting early literacy of children from low socioecononmic backgrounds in preschools and at home', in A Bar-On & D Ravid (eds), *Handbook of communication disorders*, De Gruyter, Berlin, pp. 415–36.

Aram, D & Levin, I 2016, 'Mother–child joint writing as a learning activity', in J Perera, M Aparici, E Rosado & N Salas (eds), *Literacy studies: perspectives from cognitive neuroscience, linguistics, psychology and education*, Springer, New York, pp. 29–45.

Australian Curriculum and Assessment Reporting Authority (ACARA) 2017, *National assessment program: literacy and numeracy*, national report, ACARA, Sydney.

Baroody, AE & Diamond, KE 2016, 'Association between preschool children's classroom literacy environment, interest and engagement with literacy activities', *Journal of Early Childhood Research*, vol. 14, no. 2, pp. 146–62.

Barratt-Pugh, C & Rohl, M 2015, 'Better beginnings has made me make reading part of my everyday routine: mothers' perceptions of a family literacy program over four year', *Australasian Journal of Early Childhood*, vol. 40, no. 4, pp. 2–12.

Barratt-Pugh, C & Rohl, M 2016, 'Transforming research into practice: implications of a family literacy program for early childhood professionals' in J Scull & B Raban (eds), *Growing up literate: Australian literacy research for practice*, Eleanor Curtain, Melbourne, pp. 13–35.

Beck, IJ & McKeown, MG 2007, 'Increasing low-income children's oral vocabulary repertoire through rich and focused instruction', *The Elementary School Journal*, vol. 107, no. 3, pp. 251–71, doi:10.1086/511706.

Bennett, S, Gunn, AA, Gayle-Evans, G, Barrera IV, ES & Leung, CB 2018, 'Culturally responsive literacy practices in an early childhood community', *Early Childhood Education Journal*, vol. 46, no. 2, pp. 241–48.

Bingham, GE, Quinn, MF, McRoy, K, Zhang, X & Gerde, HK 2018, 'Integrating writing into early childhood curriculum: a frame for intentional and meaningful writing experiences', *Early Childhood Education Journal*, vol. 46, no. 1, pp. 1–11.

Bruner, JS 1960, *The process of education,* Harvard University Press, Cambridge, MA.

Bus, AG & Out, D 2009, 'Unraveling genetic and environmental components of early literacy: a twin study', *Reading and Writing*, vol. 22, no. 3, pp. 293–306, doi:10.1007/s11145-008-9115-0.

Caletti, E, McLaughlin, TF, Derby, KM & Rinaldi, L 2012, 'The effects of using visual prompts, tracing and consequences to teach two preschool students with disabilities to write their names', *Academic Research International*, vol. 2, no. 3, pp. 265–70.

Christie, JF & Roskos, KA 2015, 'How does play contribute to literacy?', in JE Johnson, SG Eberle, TS Henricks & D Kuschner (eds), *The handbook of the study of play*, vol. 2, Rowman & Littlefield, Lanham, MD, pp. 412–24.

Cohen, LE, Kramer-Vida, L & Frye, N 2012, 'Implementing dialogic reading with culturally, linguistically diverse preschool children', *NHSA Dialog*, vol. 15, no. 1, pp. 135–41, doi:10.1080/15240754.2011.639965.

Cunningham, D 2010, 'Relating preschool quality to children's literacy development', *Early Childhood Education Journal*, vol. 37, no. 6, pp. 501–07.
Demir, OE, Applebaum, L, Levine, SC, Petty, K & Goldin-Meadow, S 2011, 'The story behind parent–child book-reading interactions: specific relations to later language and reading outcomes', in N Danis, K Mesh, & H Sung (eds), *Proceedings of the 35th annual Boston University conference on language development*, vol. 1, pp. 157–69, Cascadilla, Somerville, MA.
Department of Education, Employment and Workplace Relations (DEEWR) 2009, *Belonging, being and becoming: the early years learning framework for Australia*, Commonwealth of Australia, Canberra. Retrieved from https://docs.education.gov.au/node/2632
Dickinson, DK & Neuman, SB 2014, *Handbook of early literacy research*, Routledge, New York.
Dinehart, L 2015, 'Handwriting in early childhood education: current research and future implications', *Journal of Early Childhood Literacy*, vol. 15, no. 1, pp. 97–118, doi:10.1177/1468798414522825.
Evans, MA & Shaw, D 2008, 'Home grown for reading: parental contributions to young children's emergent literacy and word recognition', *Canadian Psychology*, vol. 49, no. 2, pp. 89–95, doi:10.1037/0708-5591.49.2.89.
Ezell, HK & Justice, LM 2005, *Shared storybook reading: building young children's language and emergent literacy*, Paul Brookes, Baltimore, MD.
Ferreiro, E & Teberosky, A 1983, *Literacy before schooling*, Heinemann, Exeter.
Harrison, E & McTavish, M 2018, 'iBabies: infants and toddlers emergent language and literacy in a digital culture of iDevices', *Journal of Early Childhood Literacy*, vol. 18, no. 2, pp. 163–88.
Hill, PW & Crevola, CAM 2003, 'The literacy challenge in Australian primary schools', in V Zbar & T MacKay (eds), *Leading the education debate*, Incorporated Association of Registered Teachers of Victoria, Melbourne, pp. 100–11.
Holliday, M 2013, 'Formal learning: yes or no?', *Every Child*, vol. 19, no. 3, pp. 8–9.
Huffman, JM & Fortenberry, C 2011, 'Developing fine motor skills', *Young Children*, vol. 66, no. 5, pp. 100–103.
Justice, LM, Kaderavek, J, Fan, X, Sofka, A & Hunt, A 2009, 'Accelerating preschoolers' early literacy development through teacher–child storybook reading and explicit print referencing', *Language, Speech, and Hearing Services in Schools*, vol. 40, no. 1, pp. 67–85.
Justice, LM & Pullen, P 2003, 'Promising interventions for promoting emergent literacy skills: three evidence-based approaches', *Topics in Early Childhood Special Education*, vol. 23, no. 3, pp. 99–114.
Kaefer, T, Pinkham, AM & Neuman, SB 2017, 'Seeing and knowing: attention to illustrations during storybook reading and narrative comprehension in two-year-olds', *Infant and Child Development*, vol. 26, no. 5, doi:10.1002/icd.2018.
Kotaman, H 2013, 'Impacts of dialogical storybook reading on young children's reading attitudes and vocabulary development', *Reading Improvement*, vol. 50, no. 4, pp. 199–204.
Kucirkova, N, Snow, CE, Grover, V & McBride, C (eds) 2017, *The Routledge international handbook of early literacy education*, Routledge, London.
Laidlaw, L, O'Mara, J & Wong, S 2015, 'Daddy, look at the video I made on my iPad: reconceptualising "readiness" in the digital age', in JM Iorio & W Parnell (eds), *Rethinking readiness in early childhood education*, Palgrave Macmillan, New York, pp. 67–76.
Lancaster, L 2007, 'Representing the ways of the world: how children under three start to use syntax in graphic signs', *Journal of Early Childhood Literacy*, vol. 7, no. 2, pp. 123–54, doi:10.1177/1468798407079284.
Lennox, S 2013, 'Interactive read-alouds – an avenue for enhancing children's language for thinking and understanding: a review of recent research', *Early Childhood Education Journal*, vol. 41, no. 5, pp. 381–89, doi:10.1007/s10643-013-0578-5.
Lust, CA & Donica, DK 2011, 'Effectiveness of a handwriting readiness program in head start: a two-group controlled trial', *The American Journal of Occupational Therapy*, vol. 65, no. 5, pp. 560–68.
Mackenzie, N 2011, 'From drawing to writing: what happens when you shift teaching priorities in the first six months of school?', *Australian Journal of Language and Literacy*, vol. 34, no. 3, pp. 322–40.
Mackenzie, N & Scull, J 2015, 'Literacy: writing', in S McLeod & J McCormack (eds), *Introduction to speech, language and literacy*, Oxford University Press, Melbourne, pp. 398–445.
McFarland, L 2018, 'Preparing children for writing', in N Mackenzie & J Scull (eds), *Understanding and supporting young writers from birth to 8*, Routledge, New York, pp. 30–49.
McLachlan, C, Nicholson, T, Fielding-Barnsley, R, Mercer, L & Ohi, S 2013, *Literacy in early childhood and primary education*, Cambridge University Press, Melbourne.
McMahon GR & Wellhousen TK 2010, 'Children write their world: environmental print as a teaching tool', *Dimensions of Early Childhood*, vol. 38, no. 3, pp. 23–29.
Mol, SE, Bus, AG & de Jong, MT 2009, 'Interactive book reading in early education: a tool to stimulate print knowledge as well as oral language', *Review of Educational Research*, vol. 79, no. 2, pp. 979–1007.
Mol, SE, Neuman, SB & Strouse, GA 2014, 'Profiles of infants' home media environments in the first two years of life', *Early Child Development and Care*, vol. 184, no. 8, pp. 1250–66, doi:10.1080/03004430.2013.862531.
National Early Literacy Panel 2009, *Developing early literacy: report of the national early literacy panel*, National Institute for Literacy, Washington.
Neumann, MM 2018, 'Using tablets and apps to enhance emergent literacy skills in young children', *Early Childhood Research Quarterly*, vol. 42, no. 1, pp. 239–46.
Neumann, MM, Hood, M & Ford, RM 2013, 'Using environmental print to enhance emergent literacy and print motivation', *Reading and Writing*, vol. 26, no. 5, pp. 771–93, doi:10.1007/s11145-012-9390-7.
Neuman, SB, Dickinson, DK (eds) 2011, *Handbook of early literacy research*, vol. 1, The Guildford Press, New York.

Neuman, SB & Celano, D 2018, 'Enhancing children's access to print' in CM Cassano & SM Dougherty (eds), *Pivotal research in early literacy: foundational studies and current practices,* The Guilford Press, New York, pp. 279–96.

Neuman, SB & Wright, T 2007, *Reading to your young child,* Scholastic, New York.

Nolan, A & Raban, B 2015, *Theories into practice: understanding and rethinking our work with young children and the EYLF,* Teaching Solutions, Blairgowrie.

Palmer, S, Bayley, R & Raban, B 2013, *Foundations of early literacy: a balanced approach to language, listening and literacy in the early years,* Teaching Solutions, Blairgowrie.

Phillips, ML, Norris, SP & Anderson, J 2008, 'Unlocking the door: is parents' reading to children the key to early literacy development?', *Canadian Psychology,* vol. 44, no. 2, pp. 82–88, doi:10.1037/0708-5591.49.2.82.

Piaget, J 1955, *The child's construction of reality,* Routledge & Kegan Paul, London.

Puranik, CS & Lonigan, CJ 2012, 'Name-writing proficiency, not length of name, is associated with preschool children's emergent literacy skills', *Early Childhood Research Quarterly,* vol. 27, no. 2, pp. 284–94, doi:10.1016/j.ecresq.2011.09.003.

Puranik, CS, Phillips, BM, Lonigan, CJ & Gibson, E 2018, 'Home literacy practices and preschool children's emergent writing skills: an investigation', *Early Childhood Research Quarterly,* vol. 42, no. 1, pp. 228–38, doi:10.1016/j.ecresq.2017.10.004.

Quinn, M & Bliss, M 2019, 'Moving beyond tracing: the nature, availability and quality of digital apps to support children's writing', *Journal of Early Childhood Literacy.* Retrieved from https://journals.sagepub.com/doi/abs/10.1177/1468798419838598

Raban, B 2018, 'Writing in the preschool', in N Mackenzie & J Scull (eds), *Understanding and supporting young writers from birth to 8,* Routledge, Oxon, pp. 50–70.

Raban, B & Ure, C 2000, 'Literacy in the preschool. An Australian case study', in J Hayden (ed.), *Landscapes in early childhood education: cross-national perspectives on empowerment – a guide for the new millennium,* Peter Lang, New York, pp. 375–92.

Raban, B & Scull, J 2013, 'Young learners: defining literacy in the early years – a contested space', *Australasian Journal of Early Childhood,* vol. 38, no. 1, pp. 100–106.

Raban, B, Coates, H & Ure, C 2016, 'The Preschool Literacy Project in Victoria', in J Scull & B Raban (eds), *Growing up literate: Australian literacy research for practice,* Eleanor Curtain, Melbourne, pp. 51–63.

Roberts, J, Jurgens, J & Burchinal, M 2005, 'The role of home literacy practices in preschool children's language and emergent literacy skills', *Journal of Speech Language and Hearing Research,* vol. 48, no. 2, pp. 345–59.

Roskos, KA & Christie, JF (eds) 2017, *Play and literacy in early childhood: research from multiple perspectives,* 2nd edn, Routledge, New York.

Rowe, DW & Neitzel, C 2010, 'Interest and agency in 2 and 3 year old's participation in emergent writing', *Reading Research Quarterly,* vol. 45, no. 2, pp. 169–95.

Schickedanz, JA 2014, 'Re-thinking story reading in US preschools: making story comprehension and social-emotional understanding the priority', *Asia-Pacific Journal of Research in Early Childhood Education,* vol. 8, no. 2, pp. 5–25.

Sim, S & Berthelsen, D 2014, 'Shared book reading by parents with young children – evidence-based practice', *Australasian Journal of Early Childhood,* vol. 39, no. 1, pp. 50–55.

Skibbe, LE, Thompson, JL & Plavnick, JB 2018, 'Preschoolers' visual attention during electronic storybook reading as related to different types of textual support', *Early Childhood Education Journal,* vol. 46, no. 4, pp. 419–26.

Stevens, J, Raban, B & Nolan, A 2013, *Storytelling and storymaking in the early years,* Teaching Solutions, Blairgowrie.

Treiman, R, Cohen, J, Mulqueeny, K, Kessler, B & Schechtman, S 2007, 'Young children's knowledge about printed names', *Child Development,* vol. 78, no. 5, pp. 1458–71.

Vygotsky, LS 1962, *Thought and language,* MIT Press, New York.

Vygotsky, LS 1978, *Mind and society: the development of higher psychological processes,* Harvard University Press, Cambridge.

Wasik, BH & van Horn, B 2012, 'The role of family literacy in society', in BH Wasik (ed.), *Handbook of family literacy,* Routledge, New York, pp. 3–18.

Welsch, JG, Sullivan, A & Justice, LM 2003, 'That's my letter: what preschoolers' name writing representations tell us about emergent literacy knowledge', *Journal of Literacy Research,* vol. 35, no. 2, pp. 757–76.

Zabatiero, J, Mantilla, A, Edwards, S, Danby, S & Straker, L 2018, 'Young children and digital technology: Australian early childhood education and care sector adult's perspectives', *Australasian Journal of Early Childhood,* vol. 43, no. 2, pp. 14–22.

Zrna, JL 2017, *I'm a reader: engaging young children's voices about their reading in preschool and the first year of school,* unpublished doctoral dissertation, University of South Australia, Adelaide.

CHAPTER 13

Learning about STEM

Coral Campbell

DOI: https://doi.org/10.37517/978-1-74286-555-3_13
Deakin University

LINKS TO NATIONAL QUALITY STANDARD

Quality Area 1: Educational program and practice
- Standard 1.2: Practice – educators facilitate and extend children's learning and development.
- Element 1.2.1: Intentional teaching – educators are deliberate, purposeful and thoughtful in their decisions and actions.
- Element 1.2.2: Responsive teaching and scaffolding – educators respond to children's ideas and play and extend children's learning through open-ended questions, interactions and feedback.

LINKS TO EARLY YEARS LEARNING FRAMEWORK

Learning Outcome 4: Children are confident and involved learners
- Children resource their own learning through connecting with people, place, technologies and natural and processed materials.

Learning Outcome 5: Children are effective communicators
- Children begin to understand how symbols and pattern systems work.

Introduction

The term 'STEM' (science, technology, engineering and mathematics) has a number of different interpretations, ranging from a strong disciplinary focus in one area, with elements of the other three involved, through to a wholly integrated approach to STEM learning which covers all elements in a holistic manner. Not only is the meaning of

STEM contentious, but as a model for learning, it has different interpretations. In particular, engineering does not sit in the curriculum at pre-university levels, rather the problem-solving and design process inherent in the engineering field can be found in *The Australian Curriculum: the technologies* (ACARA 2020). This raises another issue of interpretation, as most people follow the world view that technology refers only to digital technologies. However, in the curriculum of Australia (and many European countries), technology refers to a broader definition that includes design technologies, related to the idea of designing a solution for a purpose, and includes digital technologies as one aspect of technology.

Defining STEM learning

At its simplest form, 'STEM learning' could include all or some of the four elements of STEM. What is important is that it is appropriate to the context of the child's play-based learning. Children start exploring the world around them from birth, so are already engaged in forms of STEM learning. During their play, children will be presented with instances where knowledge or understanding are the key aspects of their STEM learning, whereas in other play instances, learning how to apply skills, such as observation will dominate. As a child is motivated to explore further, aspects of thinking come to the fore. Currently there are different ways to define STEM learning (*see* **Table 13.1**).

Table 13.1 Different ways to define STEM learning

Content knowledge	*Science* concepts – physical, chemical, biological and earth and space sciences *Technology* concepts – design/produce knowledge and digital learning *Engineering* concepts – problem-solving around an identified need *Mathematics* concepts – spatial sense, structure and pattern, number, measurement
Process skills	Observing, describing, categorising, predicting, communicating 21st century skills: collaboration and teamwork, creativity and imagination, critical thinking, problem-solving
Thinking skills	Thinking associated with scientific and engineering practices: raising questions, problem-solving, analysing and interpreting, mathematical and computational thinking, explaining and designing solutions, reasoning with evidence

Note: Adapted from Milford and Tippett (2015).

Importance of STEM in early childhood

National and international interest in STEM has increased significantly in recent years, with Australia's Chief Scientist endorsing the critical role of STEM education in the future of Australia (Office of the Chief Scientist 2016). When current 4-year-old children are making career choices at secondary school (in the next 5–10 years), 75% of the fastest growing occupations will require STEM-related skills and experience (Sayers 2015). This is a significant factor in the future of our young children and cannot be dismissed or taken lightly. Research undertaken by the Office of the Chief Scientist (2016) indicates a declining interest in pursuing these areas through schooling or into future careers, yet the increasing need for knowledge and understanding in STEM, provides a justification for all educational systems to revisit their actions around STEM learning and engagement. It is essential that educators seek ways to engage children in STEM from the earliest years.

Research asserts that STEM learning should start in preschool (McClure et al. 2017; Milford & Tippet 2015; Moomaw 2012). The recently released *National STEM school education strategy*, 'recognises the importance of a focus on STEM in the early years and maintaining this focus throughout schooling' (Education Council 2015, p. 5). Significant research, addressing the question of why STEM is important in early childhood, highlighted that 'high-quality STEM experiences provide young children with opportunities to develop critical thinking, executive functioning, and problem-solving skills that cut across subject areas' (Early Childhood STEM Working Group 2017, p. 6). STEM in early childhood can increase children's *disciplinary talk*, engage them in foundational concepts and skills, and help develop their confidence and interest in STEM.

International studies of 4-year-old children's engineering capabilities (Bagiatia & Evangelou 2016, p. 67) found that young children could demonstrate 'goal-oriented design, problem-solving thinking, innovation stemming out of synthesis of multiple designs, pattern repetition (PR) and design testing (DT)'. Similarly, Tippett and Milford (2017), using an observation protocol, found that children demonstrated capability in the following skills: observing, describing, categorising, predicting and communicating. If we acknowledge that children often enter preschool with different experiences and abilities, research suggests that intentionally including STEM experiences in early childhood practice can prevent early learning gaps in STEM areas from persisting into later schooling. Much of the research literature (Hobbs et al. 2017) indicates that young children are influenced negatively about STEM from adults (family and friends), so 'providing positive opportunities early to shape their attitudes and beliefs about their ability to succeed in STEM matters all the more' (Early Childhood STEM Working Group 2017, p. 6).

Emerging research findings in Australia (MacDonald & Carmichael 2017) indicate that the early years are becoming increasingly important for foundational learning in STEM because the skills learned are transferable to other subjects at different times. STEM in the early years enables children to make those vital connections between everyday life and the STEM discipline areas (National Science Foundation [NSF] 2019). Research supported by the NSF (2019) concludes that young children benefit from learning STEM subjects, because these disciplines play a fundamental role in setting the foundations for future learning. In considering the individual discipline areas of STEM, early childhood science and mathematics promote positive attitudes and a better foundation for later understanding (Eshach & Fried 2005; Sackes, Trundle, Bell & O'Connor 2011), enhance a child's self-belief in their ability to learn and promote greater interest (Patrick, Mantzicopoulos & Samarapungavan 2009). Children need to feel competent and capable in STEM to want to do it later in school. While we know from research that young children's understanding of the world around them forecasts achievement in their later science, mathematics and literacy learning, international research by Gerde, Pierce, Kyungsook and Van Egeren (2017) provides evidence to suggest that children's opportunities for engagement in STEM are varied at best.

What the research is telling us about current STEM teaching practices

High-quality research, which guides the establishment of effective practice in early childhood STEM, is ongoing. Earlier research focused on the specific discipline areas of STEM, although technology or engineering were not frequently or consistently studied. Given the complexity of the ideas surrounding holistic learning in early childhood, emergent curriculum through child-instigated activities, and the more recent focus on STEM, it is not difficult to understand why there is limited large-scale research in this area of an integrated STEM learning focus. There is a dearth of information for educators to implement STEM into their early childhood settings, however, according to the *Early STEM matters report* (University of Chicago 2017, p. 4), there are a number of important considerations needed to achieve a goal of effective practice. These are:

- understanding the role that adults (family, teachers and other significant others) play in guiding children's understanding
- how STEM is represented and communicated
- the effect that adults' beliefs have on children's response to STEM
- the awareness that STEM education is not culturally neutral.

In a recent analysis of research in STEM education strategies across all levels of education (preschool, primary and secondary), Murphy, MacDonald, Danaia and Wang (2019) found that there were inconsistencies across the Australian STEM education field. Their analysis highlighted the importance of developing STEM capabilities in children and achieving this through research-supported educational practices, such as 'inquiry-based learning'. Another significant point they made related to improving educator knowledge and confidence as a key element of STEM education. They found that there was insufficient attention paid to STEM education in early childhood and to the idea of maintaining learning across transitions (as in preschool to primary). Inquiry-based learning is a form of active learning that starts with the child, or teacher, asking a question which needs solving. Inquiry-based learning incorporates many current learning approaches (e.g. project-based) depending on the ages and abilities of children, the key question and resources.

To support the development of STEM understandings in early childhood, we need to know what is currently happening in early childhood settings. What do early childhood educators do to include STEM into their practice? What strategies do they use? How do they enhance children's current understandings?

Australian research and the implication for future STEM practice

In the past few years in Australia, there has been a much stronger recognition of the importance of STEM learning in early childhood, such that five programs have recently been supported nationally by governments and philanthropic organisations. Since 2016, the Australian Government has provided funding for the provision of three significant programs:

- Early Learning STEM Australia (ELSA)
- Let's Count
- Little Scientists.

The Australian Research Council (ARC) recently provided substantial funding for research into a new way of thinking about STEM learning for young children through Fleer's Conceptual PlayLab (2019). Also, the development of the Curious Young Minds – STEM Literacy Program was supported by the Ardoch Foundation (Campbell & Speldewinde 2018).

The 'ELSA' program focuses on a play-based digital learning environment across its pilot years 2018 and 2019. Using a heuristic 'experience, represent, apply' (ERA) (Lowrie & Larkin 2019) it sets up specific STEM learning through children undertaking STEM experiential activities, representing what they learn through digital form (using apps on an iPad) and then using a digital tool to apply their new learning to a new situation. Evaluation from the educators showed that they 'were able to embrace the cyclic nature of the ERA heuristic and ensure that the time spent on the tablet (Represent) was connected to contextualised learning opportunities (Experience and Apply)' (Lowrie, Leonard & Fitzgerald 2018, p. 14). In addition, the adoption of STEM Habits of Mind (Simoncini & Lasen 2018) provided teachers with a framework of both STEM skills and appropriate language to use when working with children in STEM.

The ELSA educators trialled STEM Habits of Mind, a tool that provides a useful framework relevant to contemporary teaching and learning. It was developed in response to an identified need for a model and common language for teachers, educators, families and children to articulate STEM learning. Linking with the research relating to children's early literacy needs, the STEM Habits of Mind provide a shared thinking about the language, skills and dispositions of STEM. In particular, the descriptive language underpinning the model instantly positions children at the forefront of STEM inquiry-based learning. The Habits of Mind (University of Canberra n.d.) describe children as:

- *Inquirers* – when they wonder why things happen and how things work
- *Observers* – when they watch closely, things in nature and the world around them

- *Describers* – when they describe what they see and do using precise language
- *Encoders* – when they represent what they see and do with drawings and symbols
- *Decoders* – when they make meaning of representations and symbols
- *Engineers* – when they design, build and make things
- *Pattern sniffers* – when they search and find patterns in words, number and the world
- *Experimenters* – when they try and test things to learn how things work and what might happen
- *Measurers* – when they measure and count things
- *Predictors* – when they predict what might happen next.

The STEM Habits of Mind align with the Early Years Learning Framework for Australia (EYLF) relating to Learning Outcome 4: Children are confident and involved learners and Learning Outcome 5: Children are effective communicators (DEEWR 2009, pp. 33, 38).

The 'Let's Count' program is an early childhood mathematics program designed to help educators in low socio-economic areas to work with children and families to provide positive mathematical experiences for children 3–5 years old. A 2012–14 longitudinal evaluation undertaken by Gervasoni, Perry and Parish (2015, p. 259) provides evidence that 'Let's Count children's everyday home and pre-school experiences provided them with a flying start as they made the transition to learning mathematics at school'. Children's mathematical skills had grown significantly and families' involvement in their children's mathematical learning had increased. The newly funded initiative of Let's Count is an online version providing professional learning modules for educators. It has been evaluated across 2017–18, however, the results have yet to be released.

The 'Little Scientists' program (Froebel 2019) was developed in Europe and was brought to Australia in 2015. It is a not-for-profit professional development program, using an inquiry-based approach to science learning, incorporating aspects of mathematics and engineering into its existing units. The workshops offer educators opportunities to engage in STEM inquiry-based learning experiences, while connecting theory and practice to build confidence to recognise STEM in children's play. The program uses a train-the-trainer approach to deliver the professional development where local networks appoint a trainer to carry out the workshops with their early childhood educators.

Fleer's 'Conceptual PlayWorld' is a new initiative which has been firmly grounded in theoretical studies over a period of 10 years (Fleer & Pramling 2015). The ideas underpinning the new initiative provide teachers with a specific strategy, which leverages the power of playful learning and STEM concepts inherent in specific play situations. It allows opportunities for educators to be involved in the imaginative play and experience the children's thinking through articulated dialogue in play. Over the next five years, the pilot will be closely followed with research that looks at the relationship between imaginary situations and STEM conceptual abstractions. It holds promise for rethinking what STEM teaching in early childhood settings could look like.

'Curious Young Minds – STEM Literacy Program' (Campbell & Speldewinde 2018) is based on the success of Ardoch Foundation's previous Early Language and Literacy Program (Campbell & Speldewinde 2018). The program was developed around current researched understanding of STEM in early childhood, children's learning and teacher understandings. Aimed at providing STEM activities for children, guided by volunteers, the program needed to be specific enough in its STEM content to enable children's learning, while catering for the diverse backgrounds of the volunteers. Research undertaken (Campbell & Speldewinde 2019) at the conclusion of the pilot program highlights that the program was successful in providing volunteers with the tools for successful engagement of the children: concept awareness, effective questioning, and appropriate follow-up activities. Children's learning was not assessed directly, however the volunteers' perception was that children were highly motived by, and engaged in the program.

RESEARCH HIGHLIGHT

Each of the five programs mentioned have their own strengths and weaknesses. Ongoing research indicates that the programs are successful in improving educator understandings in STEM and this in turn increases STEM activity with young children. An evaluation report (Dandola Partners 2020, p. 3) highlighted key findings:

- Programs and activities successfully reached their target audiences.
- Most were positively received.
- Most achieved their objectives through increased STEM confidence and engagement in the target audiences.

There were some limitations noted: Dandola Partners (2020) found that there was a lack of measurement of child engagement and achievement; and that the IT resources (both human and infrastructure) for early childhood settings were often inadequate for complete engagement. Another common aspect of all projects was that they rely on significant input by educators and intensive training in background understandings in science and STEM areas.

STEM literacy

The STEM components of knowledge, process (skills and capabilities) and thinking are important for the development of STEM literacy (*see* **Figure 13.1**).

It is the development of STEM literacy in our children's (and adults') understanding of the world which is considered necessary for Australia's future prosperity. In addition to the growing development of STEM literacies, children's learning in early childhood is governed by child-instigated play, and intentional teaching by the educator,

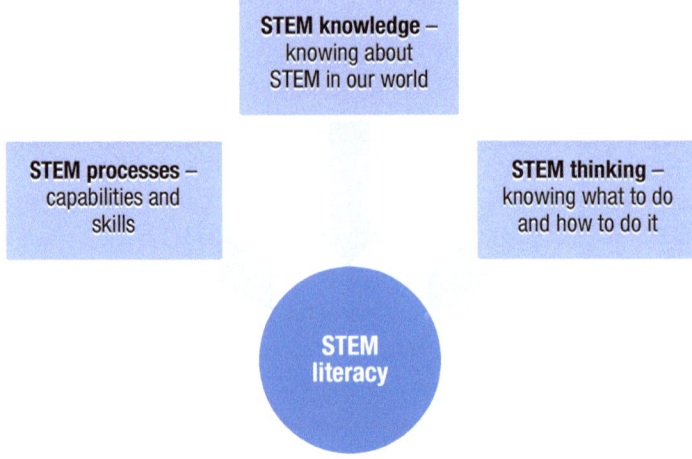

Figure 13.1 STEM literacy
Source: Campbell and Speldewinde (2018).

through planned activities and scaffolding an emergent curriculum. In most early childhood settings, the emergent curriculum for STEM is holistic. However, research (Campbell & Speldewinde 2018) indicates that some educators' documented planning is related to specific learning areas (science, mathematics or digital technologies) but there appears to be little planning for design technologies, engineering or integrated STEM learning.

Young children develop basic understandings (knowledge) of observed phenomena and processing skills, with competency increasing with age (Eshach & Fried 2005). When educators provide children with opportunities for interaction with STEM supported through scaffolding, they enable children to develop basic understandings of a wide range of familiar phenomena in STEM, as well as the STEM skills of *observation*, *exploration*, *inferring*, *questioning* and *reasoning* (Eshach & Fried 2005, pp. 332–3). While educators' attitudes towards children's learning in STEM are positive, their confidence to engage with STEM remains low (Campbell & Speldewinde 2018; Edwards & Loveridge 2011). In early childhood education, integrated STEM opportunities arise naturally in children's play due in part to contextualised, problem-based and interconnected learning. As there is no common national STEM curriculum, a locally developed curriculum (emergent and planned) can be tailored to the needs of learners through the integration of the STEM disciplines within meaningful contexts. Given the tendency for local development of early childhood programs, STEM-related teaching and learning approaches vary according to the structures and priorities of individual settings and the needs of children and educators' knowledge and pedagogy (Campbell & Speldewinde 2018).

Enhancing children's understanding: the role of the educator

Children's developing understanding of the world can be influenced by the experiences they have and how these interconnect. Communication and explication of ideas are the key foundations for children's ability to develop cognitive understanding of many science, mathematical, engineering and technological ideas. Children are able to construct meaning through their intentional interaction with the world, exploring and investigating actively. Through play, children use their existing understanding to link with new ideas to develop ever-increasing complex schema or conceptual links. Young children are capable of theorising and managing their own learning. **Figure 13.2** illustrates how children construct meaning in science, linking their initial ideas with multiple interactions and experiences.

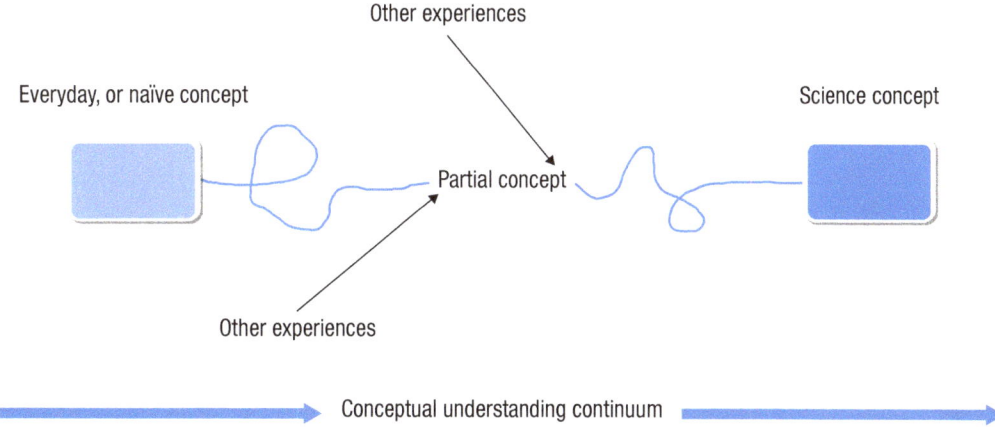

Figure 13.2 Continuum of developing conceptual understanding
Source: Campbell (2018).

In addition, Hedges and Jones (2012, p. 36) discuss children's meaning-making in terms of what they call 'working theories' which represent 'the tentative, evolving ideas and understandings formulated by children (and adults) as they participate in the life of their families, communities, and cultures'. In developing working theories, children engage with others to '… think, ponder, wonder, and make sense of the world in order to participate more effectively within it' (Hedges & Jones 2012, p. 36).

In consideration of our understanding of how children learn, the role of the adults in helping children develop meaning-making or working theories is quite clear. Educators need to provide opportunities for new experiences; they need to participate in receptive and engaging dialogue, and respectful co-learning with children. All these strategies enhance children's opportunities for richer development of their tentative, evolving ideas.

Figure 13.3 highlights the disproportionate scaffolding in science areas, whereby some science areas are favoured over others, leading to a loss of potential learning in physical science.

RESEARCH HIGHLIGHT

In a recent study in New Zealand, Backshall (2016) found that most children's activities revolve around physical science, but educators tend to scaffold biological sciences, something they were more familiar and comfortable with.

Table 13.2 Teacher-scaffolding in science areas

Science area	Percentage of children's play	Percentage of educator's scaffolding
Physics (physical world)	45–66%	25%
Material world (chemistry)	9–17%	10%
Living world	14–32%	60%
Earth and beyond	3–14%	5%

Source: Backshall (2016).

Inquiry-based learning in early childhood settings

Early childhood educators and families have an important role in supporting the development of children's STEM skills, activities and inquiry-based play. Inquiry-based learning, which centres on solving a problem or answering a question, is a form of *active learning* where children are central to the investigations. In early childhood, inquiry-based learning can be established through a child raising a question about something they want an answer to. For example, a child might ask, 'How far can a bee fly?' The inquiry-based learning, facilitated by the educator, might be that the child (or children) observe individual bees to follow their flight pattern, then expand their understanding by informally measuring the distance and comparing it to another insect, like an ant. Educators can also facilitate children's inquiry-led investigations by relating a question to an interest displayed by a child. However, the educator needs to be confident that the child can actively seek and arrive at an answer. For example, a child's question 'Can snails smell things?' may not lead to a satisfactory investigation as there is little a child can do to actively find out the answer. Research using secondary sources; such as books or the internet may help, but these are not considered inquiry-based as they are not *activity based*. Examples of inquiry-based approaches are illustrated in **Figure 13.3** and **Table 13.3**.

Figure 13.3 Inquiry cycle for an inquiry-based approach

Table 13.3 An example of an inquiry-based approach

Inquiry-based learning	What the child does	What the educator does
Ask	Asks questions about objects or things around them	Listens to the child and supports the inquiry-based learning
Investigate	Observes using their senses, focuses on interesting aspects, explores ideas and observes the results	Facilitates and guides the child through supporting discussion and through effective questioning Encourages children to share ideas

continued...

Table 13.3 (continued)

Inquiry-based learning	What the child does	What the educator does
Create	Generates new ideas (ideation) through comparing, sorting, describing observable characteristics, and draws conclusions	Supports the child's ideation through providing resources, ideas or modelling thought processing
Discuss	Shares their ideas, observations and results with others and listens to others' ideas as well Processes new information and evaluates its meaning	Questions children strategically and helps them make connections between prior understanding and new ideas
Reflect	Links their new experiences with their previous understandings to construct new meaning Sometimes applies new knowledge to a new context	Provides opportunities for children to demonstrate their new understanding through communicating with others, e.g. children, family and/or through documenting it for future referral

Seeing the STEM in children's play

There is already a lot of STEM happening in children's own investigations of the world. However, sometimes it remains invisible to the educator who interprets the activity through a different lens. For example, children climbing a tree might be interpreted from the lens of body awareness or physical fitness, whereas a STEM perspective may see the science of force, gravity, friction and mathematics in spatial awareness. Through explicit noticing (looking for STEM), educators can start to see the STEM inherent in children's play and will feel more confident that they can build on those experiences. In particular, the development of a STEM language enables them to make connections between children's everyday STEM experiences and STEM learning (*see* **Table 13.4**).

Table 13.4 Educators taking a STEM perspective

Common play activities	Seeing the STEM
Puppets	Light and shadows (physics)
Climbing a tree	Friction of shoes (physics) Holding a branch (gravity) Spatial awareness (mathematics)
Building roads in the sandpit	Design and construction (design technology/engineering)
Making mud pies or mixtures	Mixing (chemistry)
Water play	Floating or sinking, buoyancy (physics)
Observing small garden animals	Observation (inquiry skill)
Building homes for small animals	Habitat awareness (biology) Construction (design technology/engineering)

Everyday language linked to STEM phenomena

Everyday STEM language can be considered from children's investigations in STEM through the things they do and the way they do them ('STEM phenomena'); for example, children climbing a tree, or floating things in water. Areljung (2016) suggested that these everyday practices or phenomena, usually described using everyday language, could be used to help educators identify STEM key ideas. If an educator is watching children mixing mud and comments, 'Look, Jill and Amy are mixing water and soil', the word *mixing* indicates that the children are engaging with a chemical science activity and, more precisely, with reversible physical change. With a knowledge of these verbs, educators can more effectively identify the STEM in play. Areljung (2016, p. 235) noted:

> Starting from verbs appears to help teachers to recognise the scientific phenomena in everyday practice. Further, the verbs guide the formulating of questions that can be answered by scientific inquiry, such as: 'What matters to how something melts/rolls/mixes?'

Similarly, when educators observe a child categorising rocks by shape, colour or size, they realise that a child is dealing with mathematics; classifications and patterns. In **Table 13.5**, the use of descriptive verbs enables educators to identify the STEM elements of children's play.

Table 13.5 STEM phenomena words

	Concept area	Phenomena verbs
Science	Physics, forces	spinning, rotating, rolling, pulling, pushing, braking, accelerating, falling, throwing, bouncing, floating, sinking, flying
	Physics, light and sound	glowing, reflecting, shading, sounding
	Chemistry	dissolving, mixing, separating, gluing, sticking, wetting, absorbing, dyeing, melting, freezing, evaporating, boiling, condensing, rusting
Technology	Investigating materials	suitable, comparing, best, worst
	Designing solutions	thinking, problem-solving, generating, new, creative, novel
	Producing	joining, fixing, constructing, building, making
	Evaluating	it works, it fits
Engineering	Define the problem	asking questions
	Ideation	suggesting an answer
	Plan	drawing or listing ideas
	Create	building or constructing
	Test and evaluate	trying it out
	Modify	changing
	Communicate	telling others
Mathematics	Position	inside, outside, above, below, beside, next to, left, right, middle, top, bottom, before, after, between
	Comparing	enough, more, less, fewer
	Size, measurement	long, short, tall, light, heavy, wide, narrow, big, small
	Classification	same, different, before, after, between
	Patterns	repeat, same again, next
	Time	days of the week, seasons, clock times
	Fractions	parts of
	Money	how much
	Processes (+, −, /, ×)	add together, join, plus, sum, altogether take-away, minus, reduce share between, split group, groups of, altogether, times, twice, double

Note: Adapted from Areljung (2016).

Connecting language with STEM

STEM learning relies on the opportunity for communication (speaking and listening) and cognitive development – the opportunity to think through (reason) with evidence. It is important to provide opportunities for children to communicate, through rich and meaningful interactions with other children or a trusted adult. As children engage in child-instigated STEM activities, the role of the educator is important to engage children in communicating their ideas, raising questions and listening to ideas and responses from others. Lind (2005, p. 130) states that for children's developing understanding of mathematics and science, communication, connections in language, and reasoning, form a 'significant part of the child's early learning'. In terms of STEM, adults can:

- ask children questions in appropriate language
- use everyday STEM words when first introducing a concept or skill – moving on to canonical language only after the concept has been gained.

As children develop their STEM vocabulary, it is important to extend the understanding of these words to ensure that children have multiple experiences and examples for the same word. In particular in STEM, words often have multiple meanings: the everyday use of a word and a scientific/mathematical meaning. For example, the word *energy* has a concise scientific definition but can be used to describe a child's energy in play. There are many other examples. When working with STEM activities, it is necessary to use children's common words and gradually introduce more complex language.

Young children are keen to try new words and will often mimic adults around them, without necessarily understanding the meaning underpinning the word. For that reason, it is very important that the educator introduces new concepts in everyday science words, until the child understands the meaning. The educator can intentionally introduce and use new or different words in authentic contexts; for example, when children are interested in a particular topic or investigating a particular idea (*see* **Table 13.6** for examples).

Table 13.6 Educator practices to enhance language development

New language	Learning experience
Labelling nouns	When talking about shadows, the educator says, 'The shadow is there because your body is blocking the sun's rays.'
Using verbs	When making animal movements the educator uses action words: 'Let's waddle like a duck.'
Comparing	Children comparing personal attributes: 'My hair is longer than Jill's.'

continued…

Table 13.6 (continued)

New language	Learning experience
Describing	When reading a book about camels in the desert the educator comments, 'See the hump on the back? That helps camels survive without water for a long time.'
Pretending	The educator comments on a child's play, 'So you are pretending to be a jet plane flying at a super-sonic speed?'
Creating	Child comments, 'I am building a bigger cubby house so Jill can come in too.'
Using prepositions	Using prepositions in games or when giving instructions: 'Put sunscreen on your face, when you go outside.'

Note: Adapted from the Queensland Curriculum and Assessment Authority (2014).

As part of the educator's communication, asking effective questions is one way to extend children's STEM language and understanding. Effective questioning is about asking the right question at the right time to elicit a response from a child that encourages extended thinking. Asking effective questions can help an educator understand what the child already knows and can engage the child in a more thoughtful interchange, drawing out ideas and helping a child construct meaning. When responding to questions, it is not helpful if a child answers 'yes' or 'no' as it tells the educator nothing about what the child knows or thinks. Effective questions include (Deakin University 2003):

- *Productive questions*, which encourage children's investigation and discussion; for example, 'Have you noticed ...' 'What happens when ...?' 'How can you make ...?'
- *Person-centred questions*, which focus on the children's ideas; for example, 'Why/what do *you* think ...?'
- *Subject-centred questions*, which focus on a subject or object and where questions start with 'What does ...?' 'Why do ...?' These questions will often intimidate children as they think an adult is seeking the right answer, so they are not appropriate for use with very young children.
- *Promoting-thinking questions*, which promote thinking or action and find out what children already know; for example, 'How do you think the sound of the siren travels from over there to your ear?'
- *Questions used to develop processing skills;* such as*:*
  - Observing: 'What do you notice?'
  - Hypothesising: 'Why do you think that happened?'
  - Predicting: 'Can you predict what would happen if ...?'
  - Investigating: 'What will you do to do find out?'
  - Interpreting, finding and drawing conclusions: 'What is the same/different between these two things?'

- Communicating: 'How are you going to show/tell/draw this so others can understand?'

To enhance children's understanding and ask questions that promote children's hypothetical, tentative and exploratory talk, educators use open-ended *productive* and *person-centred* questions. Educators should also encourage children to ask questions. When children ask their own questions, it can stimulate their cognitive strategies, there is a sharing of intellectual control, it may raise children's self-esteem through the interaction with others and educators can monitor children's understandings. Chouinard (2007, p. 113) investigated the role of children's own questions on their learning and cognitive development, commenting that 'the ability to ask questions is a powerful tool that allows children to gather information they need in order to learn about the world and solve problems in it'.

Using picture books to support young children's STEM learning

Picture books that contain both narrative and expository text, with accurate and accessible text are the best books to facilitate STEM learning as they enable children to make observations, raise questions and form conclusions from evidence. Picture books representing accurate activities or ideas in STEM provide children with close-up pictures of things that may be unavailable to them in normal situations; for example, seeing the minute detail of a caterpillar or the size of a super-sonic jet fighter. A picture book brings the outside world into the room in a supportive, familiar environment and enables children to return to the same picture, repeatedly, reinforcing their memory of the detail and providing confirmation of prior knowledge. The text can support the picture in a structured way, enabling the child to create a moving mental image through descriptive words. Explanations can extend a child's understanding and build their appreciation of the STEM aspects in the activity.

Conclusion

Educators can expand children's STEM experiences by the addition of rich resources and authentic experiences in the early childhood setting and can build on child-instigated inquiries. Educator practices, such as actively looking for STEM in children's everyday play, scaffolding at the point of need, effective questioning to enhance thinking, and connecting everyday language with STEM experiences, will build children's STEM knowledge and understanding. By considering what research has been undertaken, educators can make professional judgements about fundamental STEM understandings and how these can best be achieved.

RESEARCH INTO PRACTICE

While considering the following questions, make notes about how you would evaluate your practice as *opportunities*, planned or otherwise, emerge during your time with the children.

How can you:

- follow up on children's STEM ideas and interests with open-ended questions and discussion?
- encourage children to further explore their interests and stimulate their thinking using an inquiry-based approach?
- plan and implement experiences that support STEM learning?
- critically reflect on those aspects of your program that support young children's STEM development?
- use spontaneous teachable moments and incidental opportunities to enhance children's play and scaffold their learning?

References

Australian Curriculum, Assessment and Reporting Authority (ACARA) 2020, *The Australian curriculum: the technologies,* ACARA, Sydney. Retrieved from https://www.australiancurriculum.edu.au/f-10-curriculum/technologies/

Areljung, S 2016, 'Science verbs as a tool for investigating scientific phenomena – a pedagogical idea emerging from practitioner–researcher collaboration', *Nordina*, vol. 12, no. 2, pp. 235–45.

Backshall, B 2016, *A culture for science in early childhood education: where cultures meet cultures*, unpublished doctoral dissertation, University of Waikato, New Zealand.

Bagiatia, A & Evangelou, D 2016, 'Practicing engineering while building with blocks: identifying engineering thinking', *European Early Childhood Education Research Journal*, vol. 24, no. 1, pp. 67–85, doi:10.1080/1350293X.2015.1120521.

Campbell, C 2018, 'Learning theories', in C Campbell, W Jobling & C & Howitt (eds), *Science in early childhood,* 3rd edn, Cambridge University Press, Melbourne.

Campbell, C & Speldewinde, C 2018, *Curious young minds – STEM literacies program*, Invergowrie Foundation, Melbourne. Retrieved from https://www.ardoch.org.au/programs/curious-young-minds/

Campbell, C & Speldewinde, C 2019, *The role of volunteers in early childhood STEM,* presentation at the Australasian Science Education Research Association Conference, Queenstown.

Chouinard, M 2007, 'Children's questions: a mechanism for cognitive development', with commentary from M Michelle, PL Harris & Michael P Maratsos, *Monographs of the Society for Research in Child Development*, vol. 72, no. 1, pp. vii-ix, 1–129.

Chubb, I 2015, 'Foreword' in C Campbell, W Jobling & C Howitt (eds), *Science in early childhood,* 2nd edn, Cambridge University Press, Melbourne.

Dandolo Partners 2020, *Evaluation of early learning and schools initiatives in the national innovation and science agenda*, Department of Education, Canberra. Retrieved from docs.education.gov.au/system/files/doc/other/nisa_evaluation_report_january_2020.pdf

Deakin University 2003, *Categorising questions*, material developed for Department of Education, Canberra.

Department of Education, Employment and Workplace Relations (DEEWR) 2009, *Belonging, being and becoming: the early years learning framework for Australia*, Commonwealth of Australia, Canberra. Retrieved from https://docs.education.gov.au/node/2632

Early Childhood STEM Working Group 2017, *Early STEM matters*, University of Chicago. Retrieved from http://ecstem.uchicago.edu/

Education Council 2015, *National STEM school education strategy*, Council of Australian Governments, Canberra. Retrieved from http://www.educationcouncil.edu.au

Edwards, K & Loveridge, J 2011, 'The inside story: looking into early childhood teachers' support of children's scientific learning', *Australasian Journal of Early Childhood*, vol. 36, no. 2, pp. 28–35.

University of Canberra n.d., Early learning STEM Australia (ELSA), STEM Education Research Centre University of Canberra. Retrieved from https://elsa.edu.au

Eshach, H & Fried, M 2005, 'Should science be taught in early childhood?', *Journal of Science Education and Technology*, vol. 14, no. 2, pp. 315–36.

Fleer, M & Pramling, N 2015, *A cultural-historical study of children learning science: foregrounding affective imagination in play-based settings*, Springer Dordrecht, doi:10.1007/978-94-017-9370-4.

Fleer, M 2019, *Fleer's Conceptual PlayWorld*, Monash University, Melbourne. Retrieved from https://www.monash.edu/conceptual-playworld/home

FROEBEL Australia 2019, *Early childhood development in STEM*, Little Scientists, Melbourne. Retrieved from https://littlescientists.org.au/

Gerde, H, Pierce, K, Kyungsook, L & Van Egeren 2017, 'Early childhood educators' self-efficacy in science, math, and literacy instruction and science practice in the classroom', *Early Education and Development*, vol. 29, no. 1, pp. 70–90, doi:10.1080/10409289.2017.1360127.

Gervasoni, A, Perry, B & Parish, L 2015, 'The impact of Let's Count on children's mathematics learning', in M Marshman, V Geiger & A Bennison (eds), *Mathematics education in the margins: proceedings of the 38th Annual Conference of the Mathematics Education Research Group of Australasia (MERGA38)*, Mathematics Education Research Group of Australasia, Adelaide, pp. 253–60.

Hedges, H & Jones, S 2012, 'Children's working theories: the neglected sibling of Te Whāriki's learning outcomes', *Early Childhood Folio*, vol. 16, no. 1, pp. 34–39.

Hobbs, L, Jakab, C, Millar, V, Prain, V, Redman, C, Speldewinde, C, Tytler, R & van Driel, J 2017, *Girls' future – our future. The Invergowrie Foundation STEM report*, Invergowrie Foundation, Melbourne.

Lind, K 2005, *Exploring science in early childhood education*, 4th edn, Thomson Delmar Learning, New York.

Lowrie, T, Leonard, S & Fitzgerald, R 2018, 'STEM practices: a translational framework for large-scale STEM education design', *EDeR. Educational Design Research*, vol. 2, no. 1, pp. 1–2, doi:10.15460/eder.2.1.1243

Lowrie, T & Larkin, K 2019, 'Experience, represent, apply (ERA): a heuristic for digital engagement in the early years', *British Journal of Educational Technology*, vol. 50.

Milford, T & Tippett, C 2015, 'The design and validation of an early childhood STEM classroom observational protocol', *International Research in Early Childhood Education*, vol. 6, no. 1, pp. 24–37.

McClure, ER, Guernsey, L, Clements, DH, Bales, SN, Nichols, J, Kendall-Taylor, N & Levine, M H 2017, *STEM starts early: grounding science, technology, engineering, and math education in early childhood*, The Joan Ganz Cooney Centre at Sesame Workshop, New York.

MacDonald, A & Carmichael, C 2017, 'Early mathematical competencies and later achievement: insights from the longitudinal study of Australian children', *Mathematics Education Research Journal*, vol. 30, no. 4, 429–44, doi:10.1007/s13394-017-0230-6.

Moomaw, S 2012, 'STEM begins in the early years', *School Science & Mathematics*, vol. 112, no. 2, pp. 57–58.

Murphy, S, MacDonald, A, Danaia, L & Wang, C 2019, 'An analysis of Australian STEM education strategies', *Policy Futures in Education*, vol. 17, no. 2, pp. 122–39, doi:10.1177/1478210318774190.

National Science Foundation (NSF) 2019, *USA inspiring STEM learning*, National Science Foundation, Arlington, VA. Retrieved from https://www.nsf.gov/about/congress/reports/ehr_research.pdf

Office of the Chief Scientist 2016, *Australia's STEM workforce: science, technology, engineering and mathematics*, Commonwealth of Australia, Canberra.

Patrick, H, Mantzicopoulos, P & Samarapungavan, A 2009, 'Motivation for learning science in kindergarten: is there a gender gap and does integrated inquiry and literacy instruction make a difference', *Journal of Research in Science Teaching*, vol. 46, no. 2, pp. 166–91.

Sackes, M, Trundle, K, Bell, R & O'Connell, A 2011, 'The influence of early science experience in kindergarten on children's immediate and later science achievement: evidence from the early childhood longitudinal study', *Journal of Research in Science Teaching*, vol. 48, no. 2, pp. 217–35.

Sayers, I 2015, *Demand for STEM skills will generate the next wave of growth report*, Price Waterhouse Cooper, Canberra. Retrieved from https://www.pwc.com.au/press-room/2015/stem-skills-apr15.html

Simoncini, K & Lasen, M 2018, 'Ideas about STEM among Australian early childhood professionals: how important is STEM in early childhood education?', *International Journal of Early Childhood*, vol. 50, no. 3, pp. 353–69, doi:10.1007/s13158-018-0229-5.

The Smith Family 2020, *Let's Count early mathematics program*, The Smith Family, Sydney. Retrieved from https://letscount.thesmithfamily.com.au/

Tippett, C & Milford, TM 2017, 'Findings from a pre-kindergarten classroom: making the case for STEM in early childhood education', *International Journal of Science and Mathematics Education*, vol. 15, no. 1, pp. s67–86, doi:10.1007/s10763-017-9812-8.

University of Chicago STEM 2017, *Early STEM matters report*, Early Childhood STEM Working Group, University of Chicago. Retrieved from http://ecstem.uchicago.edu/

CHAPTER 14

Learning about mathematics

Bob Perry and Sue Dockett

DOI: https://doi.org/10.37517/978-1-74286-555-3_14
Charles Sturt University and Peridot Education Pty Ltd

LINKS TO NATIONAL QUALITY STANDARD

Quality Area 1: Educational program and practice
- Standard 1.1: Program – the educational program enhances each child's learning and development.
- Element 1.1.2: Child-centred – each child's current knowledge, strengths, ideas, culture, abilities and interests are the foundation of the program.
- Standard 1.2: Practice – educators facilitate and extend children's learning and development.
- Element 1.2.1: Intentional teaching – educators are deliberate, purposeful and thoughtful in their decisions and actions.
- Element 1.2.2: Responsive teaching and scaffolding – educators respond to children's ideas and play and extend children's learning through open-ended questions, interactions and feedback.
- Element 1.2.3: Child-directed learning – each child's agency is promoted, enabling them to make choices and decisions that influence events and their world.
- Standard 1.3: Assessment and planning – educators and coordinators take a planned and reflective approach to implementing the program for each child.
- Element 1.3.1: Assessment and planning cycle – each child's learning and development is assessed or evaluated as part of an ongoing cycle of observation, analysing learning, documentation, planning, implementation and reflection.
- Element 1.3.2: Critical reflection – critical reflection on children's learning and development, both as individuals and in groups, drives program planning and implementation.

> **LINKS TO EARLY YEARS LEARNING FRAMEWORK**
>
> **Learning Outcome 2: Children are connected with and contribute to their world**
> - Children develop a sense of belonging to groups and communities and an understanding of the reciprocal rights and responsibilities necessary for active community participation.
> - Children become aware of fairness.
>
> **Learning Outcome 4: Children are confident and involved learners**
> - Children develop dispositions for learning such as curiosity, cooperation, confidence, creativity, commitment, enthusiasm, persistence imagination and reflexivity.
> - Children develop a range of skills and processes such as problem-solving, inquiry, experimentation, hypothesising, researching and investigating.
> - Children transfer and adapt what they have learned from one context to another.
>
> **Learning Outcome 5: Children are effective communicators**
> - Children begin to understand how symbols and pattern systems work.

Introduction

Young children are capable of complex and sophisticated mathematical thinking and they often demonstrate this capability through their play (Clements & Sarama 2009; Gervasoni & Perry 2015; Ginsburg, Lee & Boyd 2008; Perry & Dockett 2008). Young children can be *powerful mathematicians*. Similarly, educators of young children can be *powerful mathematicians*, although many may feel that their experiences with mathematics have not prepared them well for this role:

> ... low levels of content knowledge and the resulting lack of confidence about mathematics limit [early childhood] teachers' ability to maximise opportunities for engaging children in the mathematical learning embedded within existing activities (Anthony & Walshaw 2007, p. 47).

Similarly, young children's families often do not feel that they are particularly *powerful mathematicians* but reflection on the mathematics they use in their daily lives can go a long way towards countering that argument (The Smith Family 2015). This chapter is built on the premise that, at least in the early childhood space, we are all *powerful mathematicians*.

Note about age and stage

Early childhood education is sometimes characterised in terms of the ages (or stages) of young children. For example, children are labelled as 2-year-old or 5-year-old or infants, toddlers and preschoolers. Following this, activities and experiences are often designated as being suitable for one of these stages but not suitable for other stages. In this chapter, neither ages nor stages will be designated for activities and experiences.

This position derives from evidence that children's mathematical knowledge, skills and dispositions are the result of their experiences rather than their age. Some activities and experiences will clearly be more suited to younger children, not because of the mathematics involved but because of other experiential aspects. For example, a 5-year-old may not understand a mathematical idea understood by a 2-year-old and vice versa. One thing that is clear is that young children (of all ages) can deal with whatever mathematical idea or question they are confronted with, perhaps by ignoring it, or by engaging with the idea at their level. The asking of the question or the offering of the experience is not the issue for educators; but expecting a certain answer can be, both for the educator and the children. As you engage with this chapter, we encourage you to reflect upon how the various mathematical experiences provided might be interpreted in different ways by different children in different contexts.

Notice, explore and talk about

As they facilitate young children's mathematical development, a key role for educators is to 'notice' what mathematics occurs within the children's play. While educators may not always choose to refer explicitly to the mathematics they notice – possibly so as not to interrupt the play – there are many times when noticing can be the start of engaging with children about both their mathematics and their play. For example, joining the play or asking questions within the play context can help set the scene for ongoing discussion and future planning. Noticing, exploring and talking about children's mathematics are the key strategies of the *Let's Count*™ program (The Smith Family 2015).

RESEARCH HIGHLIGHT

Let's Count™

'*Let's Count* is a preschool mathematics intervention implemented by The Smith Family from 2012 to the present in 'disadvantaged' communities across Australia. It is based on current mathematics and early childhood education research and aligns with the Early Years Learning Framework (EYLF) (DEEWR 2009). *Let's Count* has been shown to be effective in enhancing mathematics learning and dispositions of young children, early childhood educators and families ... *Let's Count* is ... designed to assist family members to help their young children aged 3–5 years play, investigate and learn powerful mathematical ideas. Through this play and investigation, the aim is for the children and adults to develop positive dispositions to learning as well as mathematical knowledge and skills. *Let's Count* relies on family members providing the opportunities for children to engage with the mathematics present in their everyday lives, talk about it, document it, and extend it in ways that are relevant ... *Let's Count* involves professional learning for educators that aims to enhance mathematics learning and teaching and strengthen partnerships between educators and families. The key message in the *Let's Count* program is Notice, Explore and Talk about Mathematics' (Perry, Gervasoni, Hampshire & O'Neill 2016, pp. 75–6).

The *Let's Count* mantra: 'notice, explore and talk about mathematics' emphasises the importance of both educators and families observing children's play and other activity to see the mathematics involved in their actions and thinking. While this noticing requires some familiarity with the mathematical ideas involved, it mostly requires strong observation skills and a willingness to see and listen carefully to children. Once the mathematics has been noticed, the adult can provoke further exploration of the ideas by the children through astute questioning, introduction of new materials or contexts and playful interactions which make the play more complex and stimulate further thinking. Throughout all of this, interactive language is critical. Children and adults need to talk about what they are doing and what they are learning. The application of this mantra through *Let's Count* has been shown to enable young children's mathematics learning to thrive (Gervasoni & Perry 2016).

Powerful mathematical ideas

Powerful mathematicians deal with powerful mathematical ideas. Eight 'powerful mathematical ideas' are listed in the EYLF (DEEWR 2009, p. 38):

- spatial sense
- structure and pattern
- number
- measurement
- data
- argumentation
- connections
- exploring the world mathematically.

In this chapter, we describe each of these ideas and share some examples of young children engaging with them.

Spatial sense

Young children engage with shapes and space every day. They see shapes in their environment; they have favourite toys, perhaps because of the shape but also because of smell, touch, and taste; they learn that inside and outside of their cot are different places; and they see movement through space. There are two major aspects of 'spatial sense' that are developed during early childhood: 'shapes and transformations' and 'spatial thinking' (Clements 2011). Shapes and transformations include 2D and 3D shapes, their properties and how they can be compared and changed. Spatial thinking considers orientation, position, maps and spatial visualisation. Both are important in the early childhood years.

These representations usually involve standard forms. For example, as shown in **Figure 14.1**, triangles are almost always equilateral and presented with the base horizontal, and squares almost always have their base horizontal as well (think of the windows in the television program *Play school* as an example).

Figure 14.1 Triangle and square **Figure 14.2** Rotated square

How would you react, as an early childhood educator, if a child, when presented with the shape in **Figure 14.2**, said, 'It would be a square if only it was turned around?' What does this say about how the child has learned shape names and developed a concept of a square? It may well be worth presenting this child with many other squares which are oriented other than in the standard way.

Building with blocks can provide young children with many different experiences with 3D shapes, where they need to consider not only the shapes but also the sizes and how various shapes fit together. There are plenty of opportunities for educators to point out various properties of shapes (*see* **Figure 14.3**) and to introduce language of position: on top of, beside, next to etc, as children are building using blocks like *Lego®*, *Magna-Tiles®* and other materials, as in the following example:

'I have made a tall building with lots of different shapes.'

'What shapes have you used?'

'Long boxes, square boxes, circular boxes.'

'Which ones work best when you are building something tall?'

'The ones with flat sides that fit together.'

'Tell me about your building.'

Through using mirrors, folding paper, investigating shapes in nature, or using drawing programs on a device, young children can gain an understanding of both rotational and reflection symmetry. They will often use symmetrical patterns in their artwork. These provide a wide range of opportunities for educators to notice patterns, explore children's thinking about how and why they made them, and talk about them with the children.

An important realisation for educators is that children experience many shapes which are perhaps more interesting than circles, squares, triangles and rectangles. Inkblots, trees and clouds are some examples. Noticing, exploring and talking about the shapes children see and imagine can provide opportunities for exploring mathematical ideas using children's interests as the starting point.

Figure 14.3 'Tell me about your building.'

Position and location are also components of a developing spatial sense. One interesting activity is to show pictures of only the noses of animals with the rest of the picture covered and ask the children to identify the animals. Then try tails or feet. Ask the children to draw their own animals and test the educators out in the same way. Using maps or giving directions also provide experience in orientation. Some children might like to draw a plan of their room, of the preschool or yard. The important elements for educators in these experiences are to notice the thinking going into these drawings, ask some questions, and talk about how they could be made more interesting, more accurate or more useful.

Structure and pattern

Mathematics has been characterised as the study of patterns and, in the early childhood years, this is apparent in counting patterns, spatial patterns and generalisations or rules which grow out of multiple experiences and reflections on these experiences. For example, many preschool children learn that you need an even number of children in order to break into two equal teams. It does not matter what the number of children is: if it is even, then you can have two equal teams. Later, this generalisation or rule is stated 'Only even numbers can be divided by 2 with no remainder' – always true, regardless of the particular numbers involved: a result of the structure of the number system.

> Virtually all mathematics is based on pattern and structure ... mathematical *pattern* involves any predictable regularity involving number, shape, or measure. Examples include friezes, number sequences, measurement, and geometrical figures. By *structure*, we mean the way in which the various elements are organized and related. (Mulligan & Mitchelmore 2013, p. 30)

For young children, pattern is often the product of repetition of sound, number, action, colour and/or shape. There can also be patterns that are generated by some rule.

The game of 'peek-a-boo' involves a pattern of the child being able to see the adult's face followed by not being able to see the face when it is hidden behind an object; such as a cloth or hands. As children enjoy the fun of the game, they are learning about repetition of patterns. Peek-a-boo is an example of what is called an ABAB pattern; a pattern made up of repetitions of two states: *see, don't see, see, don't see* and so on. There can be AA patterns or ABCABC patterns. Can you think of examples of these which might be created with or by young children? The collection of objects or actions which is repeated is called the *unit of repeat*. There cannot be a repeating pattern until there is a unit of repeat.

Alison has generated a pattern in her artwork which she explained as 'Purple squiggle, green squiggle, purple squiggle, green squiggle'. Strictly speaking the squiggles are not identical, but the pattern could just be *purple, green, purple, green*. Alison could be asked about her pattern, why she chose the pattern and how she would continue it

Strong Foundations

Figure 14.4 Alison's squiggles

if she had more paper. She could be asked to describe the unit of repeat: *purple, green* (see **Figure 14.4**).

Young children make many patterns during their play and the astute educator will notice these and provoke discussion about the unit of repeat, possible changes to the pattern and where the pattern might end. Children can also be asked to continue patterns that have already been started and can be as blue to explain what comes next in the pattern and why? (*See* **Figure 14.5**.)

An educator had been playing with some small teddies when Rohan joined her.

'What are you doing, Jenny?'

'I think I am making a pattern, but you could help if you like. What do you think will come next?'

'I think a white teddy?'

'Why?'

'Because it goes white teddy, blue teddy, white teddy, blue teddy, and next will be white. After every blue teddy there is a white one.'

Figure 14.5 Jenny and Rohan's teddy patterns

Rohan's final response introduces a rule about the pattern, not just a description of the unit of repeat. This rule or *generalisation* forms the basis of much later mathematics.

Children not only experience repeating patterns. They may also meet *growing* patterns. The most common growing pattern in number is the counting sequence: 1, 2, 3, 4, 5 … where each item is *one more than* the previous one. You can find the next term in the pattern by counting right through the sequence or by using the *one more than rule* no matter where you are in the sequence. For instance, two girls were talking about birthdays. Rosie wasn't sure how old she would be on her next birthday. Alex said, 'If you count up to your number, then you count the next one to find out how old you are'. Alex had devised a general rule which would work for all ages. Listening to this exchange, an educator might want to ask if the girls could work out how old she will be at her next birthday. Even if the numbers are outside the scope of the children's experience, they could still start by applying the rule and the conversation can carry on from there.

Structure and pattern are central to much mathematical development leading to notions of equality, sequence and generalisation which are useful for young children as well as being very helpful in their later, perhaps more abstract, mathematical learning.

> [E]ffective mathematical reasoning involves the ability to note patterns and structure in both real world situations and symbolic objects; such reasoning enables the formation of generalizations in which the abstraction of ideas and relationships can take place. (Mulligan & Mitchelmore 2013, p. 30)

Number

Counting

Young children encounter numbers in almost every aspect of their lives. They sing the counting rhyme, firstly without much meaning but later using it to count collections of objects and compare quantities. 'Counting' is not the whole story, however. The beginnings of the development of a 'number sense' is 'a person's general understanding of numbers and operations along with the ability and inclination to use this understanding in flexible ways to make mathematical judgments' (McIntosh, Reys & Reys 1997, p. 322) and is often observed in young children. When children are competent and confident in their use of numbers, they will be able to use number flexibly to help them solve everyday challenges.

Children are able to recite the counting words in sequence through many experiences with their families and friends; such as repeating them as they go up steps. Often, children like to play with numbers and make up their own rhymes about them. As well, there are many rhymes and stories that use numbers either incidentally or as a focus. There are some favourites; 'One two, three, four, five; once I caught a fish alive', for example, but there are many others from many cultures. Early childhood educators can ask families about rhymes they say at home in their own language, learn them, and sing them around the setting.

Counting is not just about the words used. There are also some important principles that ensure that collections of objects can be counted accurately and consistently. These principles are:

- the *stable order principle* – when counting collections of objects, always use the number word sequence in its correct order
- the *one-one principle* – to each item in the collection, there must be one and only one number attached
- the *cardinality principle* – the last number counted is the number of objects in the collection
- the *abstraction principle* – any collection of separate objects can be counted
- the *order irrelevance principle* – counting can be done in any order and will give the same result. (Cross, Woods & Schweingruber 2009, p. 135)

Through their experiences, young children will gradually learn about these principles. In the early years, they do not need to be taught explicitly, although the explanations of the principles can be used in conversations with children. These principles emphasise that counting is not a simple task and not one that can be taken for granted.

A note about materials and symbols

Young children may need concrete objects to count and manipulate and there are plenty of these in any early childhood setting. However, they also need to manipulate ideas mentally and should be encouraged to do so through provocations from educators as well as from other children. A question, such as 'What were you thinking just before you said that number?' can be very powerful.

There is no need to rush into situations where children are required to write *correct* mathematical symbols; such as numerals and signs. The time to do this is when the children feel the need to communicate their ideas in ways that other people might understand them. In the meantime, encourage children to use oral language and their own, made-up, written symbols. So long as they know what the symbols mean and can explain them, all is well.

Measurement

If counting is the process we use to find out 'How many?', then 'measurement' is the process we use to find out 'How much?' Measurement encourages young children to utilise other powerful mathematical ideas by connecting them with quantities and shapes. The essence of all measurement is *comparison*. Sometimes comparisons can be made *directly*; such as when two sticks are placed next to each other to compare their lengths, or balance scales are used to compare the mass of two objects. Sometimes, comparisons need to be made *indirectly*, using an intervening object; such as with Emma and Alfredo. In **Figure 14.6** and **14.7**, Emma and Alfredo wanted to bring the wood

Figure 14.6 Collecting wood for the fire

Figure 14.7 Measuring with a stick

in for the fire in their outdoor home corner. But how were they to decide which pieces of wood would fit into the wood box? Alfredo said that they could take all of them in on the wheelbarrow and just see which fitted. Emma saw that as a lot of extra work. She said, 'Let's find a stick as long as the box. Then we can make sure we only bring in wood that is shorter than the stick'.

An educator observing this interaction could check on Emma and Alfredo's understanding of how to use indirect comparison by setting other challenges; such as whether the chair might fit into the wood box or whether the tractor being used to carry the wood is as long as the children's favourite home toys. There is a lot of comparative language involved in measurement. Initially, children might talk about objects being *big* or *little* and will learn to refine these descriptions through the use of comparative language such *is longer than* or *holds less than*. Before measurement can be undertaken, children need to understand the particular attributes of the object which they are measuring; such as length, mass, area, capacity, time and temperature. They consolidate their understandings of each of these attributes through interactive play and the language used in this play.

Water play can be a great introduction to the language of capacity. Notions of *empty* and *full* and *how many cupfuls* are needed to fill a drink bottle can be explored. When measuring jugs are used, some children may notice the measurement marks on the side and ask about them (*see* **Figure 14.8**).

Figure 14.8 Notions of empty and full

The marks on the side of the measuring jug represent units which are used to standardise measurement. Some educators are reluctant to introduce so-called *formal* or *standard* units of measurement before the children have had lots of experience with *informal* units; such as sticks for length, cups for capacity, and stones for mass. There is evidence that suggests that, while children enjoy playing with measurement ideas using units that they create themselves, they also can enjoy using instruments and units which they see in their worlds or hear adults talking about. Early childhood educators might consider introducing formal and informal units simultaneously rather than sequentially in order to provoke challenging conversations with children (Peter-Koop 2001).

One of the key aspects of measurement which can begin to be developed with young children is 'estimation'. Adults often use estimation when accurate measurement is either not necessary or even possible. Whenever children ask or are asked comparison questions; such as 'Who is taller – you or Ronald?' or 'How many cups of water will fill the bucket?', they can estimate. Use the word *estimate* in such activities to distinguish it from a *guess*. While initially an estimate may not be much more than a guess, the aim is to have children apply their knowledge of comparison and of units in order to make their estimate. In time, estimation will improve both the estimate and the accuracy of the measurement.

Data

'Data' is information; we are all surrounded by it. Data can be numerical; for example, in answer to a question; such as 'What ages are the children in the preschool room today?' Or they can be non-numerical; for example, in answer to a question like 'What are the names of the children in the preschool class today?' Much of the information we see and attempt to interpret comes to us through various representations of data, such as tables and graphs. Children need to develop a sense of all aspects of data, including its collection, analysis, representation, and communication. This type of thinking and questioning can commence during the early childhood years.

Collection

Data help answer questions posed by the children or by adults. While questions posed by an educator, such as 'What is your favourite toy?', might be a starting point for data collection, children can also be encouraged to pose their own questions and seek ways to collect data to answer them. For instance, Jackson comes from a family with five children, including himself. He was talking to educator Ashton and asked him how many children were in his family.

'Three', answered Ashton.

'I wonder if there are other people here with three or five children?' asked Jackson.

'Let's find out.'

Ashton gave Jackson a list of names of the children and adults in the room. Jackson went and asked all of them, although Manuel and Harriet were not in the room that day. He carefully wrote down numbers next to each name. Some of the other children told him which name was theirs so that he could write the numbers in the right place.

Analysis

Analysis of data is a way of organising the data so that it is more helpful for answering the question posed, for instance, in Jackson's case, 'Are there other people with three or five children?' This component of the process may need support from educators, although many children will be quite capable of dealing with it themselves. Educators might support children in their recording by supplying tally sheets, coloured paper shapes or blocks, photo cards of each child, or beads or buttons to help them sort and organise their data.

Continuing the episode above, Jackson sought Ashton's help: 'Everyone has told me their number, but I still don't know the answer'.

'Well, let's have a look. Who had one child only in their family?'

Jackson went through his list to find that Matthew and Amy were the only two. 'OK, I can do the other numbers now.' He tried to count how many children had families of two children but lost count fairly quickly. After repeated attempts to count he was losing interest. Ashton intervened with some square Post-it notes, and suggested Jackson write the names of those with two children, one on each note. Jackson did not want to write all of the names but did agree to write the first letter of the name. He did this and put them in a pile. Then he continued with the other numbers.

Representation

Adults represent data in many different ways, particularly through a variety of graphs and tables, but also through narratives or stories. There is no need to rush young children into more formal representations if they have other ways which they find more suitable. A first question from educators might be 'Tell me what you have found'.

Jackson had separate piles of notes, for one child, two children, three, four, five and six. He counted each pile and he found that two children had one child in their family, six had two, four had three, four had four, two had five and one had six. He wrote these numbers on the top note for each pile. Ashton reminded Jackson of his question: 'I wonder if there are other people here with three or five children?' Jackson looked at his piles and was able to answer, 'Four with three children and two with five'.

Communication

Jackson wanted to tell his friends what he had found out. He did this through a story but then he wondered whether other people, like his mum and other mums might want to know.

Ashton took the two notes representing the children with one child in their family and stuck them on the whiteboard, one under the other. He then walked away. Jackson looked at the column and then took another pile of notes and arranged them in a column next to the one Ashton had done. This continued until all the notes had been stuck to the board. Jackson ran to show Ashton what he had done. Ashton gave a puzzled look towards the columns and asked, 'What does this tell you?' and 'How do we know which column shows which families?' Jackson was puzzled. Further provocation from Ashton led to numbers being placed under each column to represent family size.

Not every question will lead to a complete series of steps from collection through to communication of data. Children will choose how far they want to pursue the activity, whether they want assistance from peers or adults, and how they want to play with the data. However, by offering experiences with data, the children will gradually develop their own data sense.

Argumentation

One of the key features of mathematics is the need to justify your own mathematical thinking and to understand when one person's thinking is the same or different to another's. The process of such justification is called 'argumentation'. The powerful mathematical idea of *argumentation* leads directly to *mathematical proof*, one of the distinguishing characteristics of mathematics. Early childhood educators can foster young children's skills in argumentation by asking the question 'How do you know that?' in response to a mathematical claim.

On a crowded train, a boy was standing near the carriage door with his mother. His father was further into the carriage.

The boy looks at his mother and then across to his father.

'Who's tallest? You or Dad?'

'Dad.'

'How old is Dad?'

'38.'

'How old are you?'

'27.'

'OK, so that's why he's taller.'

In this example, the boy has connected age to height; the older you are, the taller you are. While this is interesting enough, it is not always correct. A family member or educator who notices this reasoning might want to provide some experiences to lead the boy to question his thinking. Perhaps he can meet some older, shorter, and some younger, taller people. Noticing his argumentation provides the stimulus to explore and talk about it later.

Young children are quite capable of justifying their mathematical approaches and solutions, often in ways that are not expected by adults. Encouraging children to justify and explain their thinking contributes to their understanding of argumentation.

Connections

Mathematics is connected to other areas of learning and knowledge in many different ways. Not only do these other areas provide opportunities for mathematics to emanate from real-life experiences, but mathematics also provides a conceptual vehicle through which many of these areas can be better understood. Other areas of children's learning where mathematics is integral include music and movement, art, and children's rhymes and stories. The 'Research into practice' section at the end of this chapter invites readers to make connections between mathematics and children's literature.

Exploring the world mathematically

The term 'exploring the world mathematically' is derived from an earlier notion of 'mathematisation' which was coined in the 1960s 'to signify the process of generating mathematical problems, concepts and ideas from a real world situation and using mathematics to attempt a solution to the problems so derived' (Perry & Dockett 2008, p. 81).

We have all experienced the process of mathematisation often in our lives. Each time we plan a meal, there are real-life challenges around quantities, times and spatial arrangements which will have their solutions in mathematics. Young children also have experiences which require the process of mathematisation. One example of exploring the world mathematically can be seen in the following learning story excerpt (Department for Education and Child Development 2015, p. 41).

Jolie found a quiet moment in the cubby. She placed four chairs around the table and matched a plate to each of the chairs. She had brought a bucket of bark into the cubby with her. Jolie stood at the stove stirring the bark. She took a measuring cup, filled it with bark from the pot and poured it onto one of the plates. She did this for each plate. Jolie noticed that there was still some bark in the pot. She took her measuring cup, but this time only half filled it before repeating the serving she did previously. This time Jolie was satisfied with each serve. When asked what she had been doing, Jolie explained that she was going to have three friends visit and that she had shared the soup so they would all have the same. The other chair was for her.

Jolie had a *real-life*, pretend play challenge around preparing lunch for her friends. She met this challenge through numerous pieces of mathematical thinking. First, she used addition or counting to determine that she needed four chairs and four plates for her three friends and herself ($3 + 1 = 4$). Second, she devised a sharing approach to ensuring that each of her friends, and herself, had equal portions of soup (measurement using the cup as a unit). Then, upon noticing that she still had some soup in the pot, Jolie reflected on the situation and estimated that there would not be enough for another full cup for each person, leading to a fractional solution. All the soup had been used and each person had an equal share. Even though not expressed in the story, Jolie also probably needed to make some calculations about temperature and time required to heat the soup. The process of exploring the world mathematically and a lot of mathematical knowledge has been used to meet the real-life challenge.

The role of adults in children's mathematics learning

Adults, particularly educators and families, have important roles to play in young children's mathematical learning. Through their interactions, adults can support children as they persevere with problems and challenges, provoke children to extend their experiences and make their play (and the mathematics involved) more complex, consider possible connections with other mathematics or real-life situations, and help celebrate and document children's progress.

Early childhood educators can employ the full range of pedagogies highlighted in the EYLF and ensure that children have opportunities to experience all of the powerful mathematical ideas through their play and other experiences. This will mean that educators will need to consider how they plan for these mathematical opportunities as well as being able to notice what mathematics can arise naturally from children's play and how they might extend this. While it is always helpful if the educators are fluent in their own mathematical concepts and skills and can assist children to see where some of their ideas might lead, what is also important is for these educators to have the dispositions to enable them to stimulate the children's thinking, even though this thinking might take the educator into uncharted territory.

Conclusion

Young children can be competent mathematicians as they build 'the capacity, confidence and disposition to use mathematics in daily life' (DEEWR 2009, p. 38). In a range of ways and across contexts, they use and engage with mathematics as part of their everyday lives. Play-based early childhood programs provide an interesting and challenging context where children can try out and extend their mathematical understandings, and where observant and responsive educators can support and extend these. Recognising the eight 'powerful mathematical ideas' and children's use of these is an important step in supporting young children as powerful mathematicians.

RESEARCH INTO PRACTICE

Choose a favourite children's picture book – one of our long-time favourites is *Wombat stew* (Vaughan & Lofts 1984). As you read the book, think about the mathematical ideas you encounter, and consider how you might use the book to introduce or reinforce the ideas with young children.
Read the story again with some children and see what happens.
I What mathematics do the children notice? Do they notice the same things you did?
I How might you provoke their learning by pointing out, or questioning, things in the book?
I What ideas or questions could be used to plan follow-up activities?
I What might guide you as you engage with the children, the story and their mathematical understandings?

One of the challenges in activities such as this, is balancing the pleasure of reading/hearing the story with efforts to highlight specific concepts. What might guide you as you engage with the children, the story and their mathematical understandings?

References

Anthony, G & Walshaw, M 2007, *Effective pedagogy in mathematics/pāngarau,* Ministry of Education, Wellington. Retrieved from https://www.educationcounts.govt.nz/__data/assets/pdf_file/0007/7693/BES_Maths07_Complete.pdf

Clements, DH 2011, 'Geometric and spatial thinking in early childhood education', in DH Clements, J Sarama & AM DiBiase (eds), *Engaging young children in mathematics: standards for early childhood mathematics education,* Lawrence Erlbaum, Mahwah, NJ, pp. 267–97.

Clements, DH & Sarama, J 2009, *Learning and teaching early math: the learning trajectories approach,* Routledge, New York.

Cross, CT, Woods, TA & Schweingruber, H (eds) 2009, *Mathematics learning in early childhood: paths toward excellence and equity,* The National Academies Press, Washington.

Department for Education and Child Development 2015, *Implementation guidelines for indicators of preschool numeracy and literacy in government preschools,* Government of South Australia, Adelaide. Retrieved from https://www.education.sa.gov.au/doc/implementation-guidelines-indicators-preschool-numeracy-and-literacy-government-preschools

Department of Education, Employment and Workplace Relations (DEEWR) 2009, *Belonging, being and becoming: the early years learning framework for Australia,* Commonwealth of Australia, Canberra. Retrieved from https://docs.education.gov.au/node/2632

Gervasoni, A & Perry, B 2015, 'Children's mathematical knowledge prior to starting school and implications for transition', in B Perry, A MacDonald & A Gervasoni (eds), *Mathematics and transition to school – international perspectives,* Springer, Dordrecht, pp. 47–64.

Gervasoni, A & Perry, B 2016, 'The impact on learning when families and educators act together to assist young children to notice, explore and discuss mathematics', in T Meaney, O. Helenius, ML Johansson, T Lange & A Wernberg (eds), *Mathematics education in the early years,* Springer, Dordrecht, pp. 115–35.

Ginsburg, HP, Lee, JS & Boyd, JS 2008, 'Mathematics education for young children: what it is and how to promote it', *Society for Research in Child Development Social Policy Report,* vol. 22, no. 1, pp. 1–24.

McIntosh, A, Reys, BJ & Reys, RE 1997, 'Mental computation in the middle grades: the importance of thinking strategies', *Mathematics Teaching in the Middle School,* vol. 2, no. 5, pp. 322–27.

Mulligan, JT & Mitchelmore, MC 2013, 'Early awareness of mathematical pattern and structure', in LD English & JT Mulligan (eds), *Reconceptualizing early mathematics learning,* Springer, Dordrecht, pp. 29–45.

Perry, B & Dockett, S 2008, 'Young children's access to powerful mathematical ideas', in LD English (ed.), *Handbook of international research in mathematics education,* 2nd edn, Routledge, New York, pp. 75–108.

Perry, B, Gervasoni, A, Hampshire, A & O'Neill, W 2016, 'Let's Count: improving community approaches to early years mathematics learning, teaching and dispositions through noticing, exploring and talking about mathematics', in B White, M Chinnappan & S Trenholm (eds), *Opening up mathematics education research,* proceedings of the 39th annual conference of the Mathematics Education Research Group of Australasia, MERGA, Adelaide, pp. 75–84.

Peter-Koop, A 2001, Authentische zugänge zum umgang mit größen (Authentic access to quantities), *Grundschulzeitschrift,* vol 15, no. 141, pp. 6–11.

The Smith Family 2015, *Strengthening early numeracy learning: the Let's Count program,* The Smith Family, Sydney. Retrieved from https://www.thesmithfamily.com.au/programs/numeracy/lets-count

Vaughan, M & Lofts, P 1984, *Wombat stew,* Scholastic, Sydney.

CHAPTER 15

Learning through the arts

Susan Wright and Jan Deans

DOI: https://doi.org/10.37517/978-1-74286-555-3_15
University of Melbourne

LINKS TO NATIONAL QUALITY STANDARD

Quality Area 1: Educational program and practice
- Standard 1.2: Practice – educators facilitate and extend children's learning and development.
- Element 1.2.1: Intentional teaching – educators are deliberate, purposeful and thoughtful in their decisions and actions.
- Element 1.2.2: Responsive teaching and scaffolding – educators respond to children's ideas and play and extend children's learning through open-ended questions, interactions and feedback.

LINK TO EARLY YEARS LEARNING FRAMEWORK

Learning Outcome 5: Children are effective communicators
- Children express ideas and make meaning through a range of media.

Introduction

This chapter discusses young children's engagement in 'the arts' in terms of learning about self, others and the world. It draws attention to the important role that the arts play in promoting young children's ability to develop 'higher order' and 'imaginative' thinking. *The arts* are introduced as innately occurring creative and expressive ways of meaning-making and giving voice; first appearing in children's play and becoming more sophisticated over time. Three modes of children's artistic/creative learning and the interrelations between them are featured, with summaries of various arts disciplines, and the role of the teacher overviewed and presented in diagrammatic form. Finally, ways of 'knowing-thinking-feeling through the arts' are summarised diagrammatically by showing links between sensorial, imaginative and kinaesthetic aspects of play.

Teaching and learning through the arts: featuring the senses and imagination

It is widely recognised that the world of the young child is permeated with extensive opportunities for discovery through first-hand experiential processing. The physical and social environment is a qualitative space made up of wide-ranging stimuli that excite the senses, drawing individuals into complex sensorial explorations that rely on seeing, touching, hearing and smelling. The young child is innately programmed to explore this world, relying in the first instance on the sensory system to begin to make meaning of the complexity of the socio-cultural world into which they were born. To fully understand the role of the arts in early childhood education we must begin with the recognition that in the early years of life children learn through their senses, which is noted by Eisner (2002, p. 2) to be the 'first avenues to consciousness'. Sensory exploration is the means through which development occurs and this, coupled with the human fascination for learning through play, supports growing understandings that are further shaped and refined by culture, language, relationships and the sciences of the physical world.

Young children experience joy and pleasure as they manipulate and explore the features and available materials in the environment. This exploration can be described as artistic endeavour from the perspective of the fact that imagination, sensory perception and aesthetic sensibilities are stimulated as discoveries and connections are made and new knowledge and skills acquired through creative problem-solving. The child draws on information coming in through the senses and quickly learns that the world is filled with colour, shape, movement, sound and textures; stimuli that excite a desire to represent and re-represent as a way of meaning-making in the world. This is where the connection between sensory explorations of the physical and social world meet the notion of artistic expression.

Many renowned scholars (Arnheim 1954; Dewey 1934; Eisner 2002; Gardner 1983; Langer 1953; Read 1943) note that the arts play an important role in refining the senses and enlarging and cultivating the imagination. They have often been referred to as a 'universal language' employed by individuals to express thoughts, ideas and emotions. Thus, they can be understood as an important form of creative communication with the process of representation providing an opportunity for ongoing experimentation and discovery which results in the transformation and externalisation of ideas. As Eisner (2002, p. 240) notes, 'humans grow through their ability to experiment with aspects of the world that they encounter' and, for the young child, engagement with the arts serves to heighten the imagination and ignite make-believe worlds.

The arts and play

The concept of 'play-based learning' is widely accepted and documented in early childhood literature (Edwards & Cutter McKenzie 2011; Fleer 2017; Mavers 2011), having been originally endorsed by the well-known early philosophers and educators Jean-Jacques Rousseau (1712–78), Fredrick Froebel (1782–1852) and Maria Montessori (1870–1952). Within early childhood education 'learning through play' is the phrase frequently used to describe a particular pedagogical approach to teaching and learning. It has been defined in the Early Years Learning Framework (EYLF) (DEEWR 2009, p. 46) as 'a context for learning through which children organize and make sense of their social worlds as they engage actively with people, objects and representations'.

The idea of linking play with the arts is not new. A number of authors (Kress 1997; Maranović-Shane & Beljanski-Ristić 2008; Sansom 2011) have noted the integral relationship that exists between the two, recognising that they share similar attributes when it comes to exploratory, improvisational and imaginative sensory processing. As Eisner (2002, p. 4) states:

> The arts have an important role to play in refining our sensory system and cultivating our imaginative abilities. Indeed, the arts provide a kind of permission to pursue qualitative experience in a particularly focused way and to engage in the constructive exploration of what the imaginative process may engender. In this sense, the arts in all their manifestations are close in attitude to play.

Similarly, prominent theorists (Dockett & Fleer 1999; Elkind 2007; Vygotsky 1978) all emphasise that imagination and fantasy, improvisation and freedom, choice and control, are key features of children's play and that different forms of play can be identified at different stages of development. Matthews (1999, p. 24) further explains by noting that 'play is implicated in the development of all forms of representation' and it is through playful inquiry that children explore the wide range of symbols and culturally accepted meanings that are available to them. They bring to their play their personalised, interpretative meaning-making which is coloured by their imagination, fantasy and creativity.

For young children, the arts are 'a serious form of interacting with the world' (Sunday 2018, p. 32). Children explore, create and communicate ideas through visual, aural/musical, and physical/dance/dramatic modes that offer 'limitless possibilities for finding and expressing answers to questions that they themselves find most compelling' (Sunday 2018, p. 32). Improvisational playful inquiry through drawing, dancing, making music and engaging in dramatic play, enables children to 'connect multiple experiences of time and space, blurring geographical, cultural, and temporal boundaries to arrive at new meaning' (Sunday 2018, p. 32). Through these art forms, children make connections between thought, object, emotion and action and provide evidence of their sophisticated grasp of complex and abstract ideas (Wright & Deans 2020).

Governed by innate natural curiosity and a desire to explore and learn about the world, children demonstrate a significant capacity to live in and through their playing. Play is acknowledged to be a creative act and it is through play that much of children's learning is achieved (Niland 2012). As noted in the EYLF (DEEWR 2009, p. 15):

> Play provides opportunities for children to learn as they discover, create, improvise and imagine. When children play with other children, they create social groups, test out ideas, challenge each other's thinking and build new understandings. Play provides a supportive environment where children can ask questions, solve problems, and engage in critical thinking. Play can expand children's thinking and enhance their desire to know and learn. In these ways play can promote positive dispositions towards learning. Children's immersion in their play illustrates how play enables them to enjoy being.

From this perspective, the strong relationship between play and artistic activity is further affirmed with the improvisational processing of ideas, forms, materials, sounds and movements, having the capacity to produce new interpretations or impressions. Through engagement in the arts, children have ongoing opportunities to 'self-scaffold' their learning, enlivening and enlarging their imaginations; to find out, in turn, leads to meaning-making.

The arts for the expression of child voice

Another way of understanding the important role the arts play for young children is to acknowledge artistic learning for its capacity to support the expression of 'child voice'. The catalyst of this trend has been the highly influential human rights charter, the United Nations Convention on the Rights of the Child (UNCRC) (UN 1989), which recognises the right of children to be heard and consulted on matters that affect them. In particular, Article 13, which endorses the importance of children having the opportunity to express their ideas in a variety of ways. It states:

> The child shall have the right to freedom of expression; this right shall include freedom to seek, receive and impart information and ideas of all kinds, regardless of frontiers, either orally, in writing or in print, in the form of art, or through any other media of the child's choice (UN 1989).

Embedded within the principles of the UNCRC is an image of the child as strong, competent and capable. This enlightened image of the child highlights the capacities of young children to construct valid meanings about the world and their place in it; a position that supports the notion of children as 'active agents' (Smith 2007) who are capable of influencing and directing their own learning and making an impact on the environment. It also affirms the significance of children's artistic explorations and expressions and specifically the many possibilities that are contained within the arts as expressive languages of childhood. Many authors have commented that, when young children are given an opportunity to express their views, they develop a sense of autonomy and self-determination (Tobin 2005), and from this perspective, the arts provide a powerful semiotic tool for the expression of voice.

Semiotic meaning-making through the arts

'Semiotics' is the study of signs, including gestures, movements, words and visual symbols (a sign being something that stands for something else). The field of semiotics looks at meanings and messages in a variety of forms and a variety of contexts (Innis 2012). Within early childhood arts education, semiotics is understood to be the capacity of children to use a variety of symbolic domains (language, drawing, modelling, music-making and body movement) for thinking, reflecting, and expressing ideas and feelings. These symbolic domains provide a means of growing and preserving knowledge. Like language, play, art, music and dance are valuable semiotic systems in their own right (Wohlwend 2011).

Hence the various art forms can be viewed as vehicles of symbolisation that the child can access to mobilise meaning-making. Signs are used as semiotic tools for 'investigating, deciphering, documenting and explaining the what, why and how' of lived experience (Wright 2007, p. 12). Malaguzzi (1998, p. 93) notes 'symbols have profound associations with emotions, feelings and many other things that cannot be qualified through observation'. Hence, thinking through the arts supports the child's developing ability to experience, understand and organise the world through thinking processes that enable the transformation of concepts and their associated meanings into new and unique forms. As noted by Eisner (2002, p. 24) through explorations in the arts, 'sensibilities are refined, distinctions are made more subtle, the imagination is stimulated, and skills are developed to give form to feeling'.

Kinaesthetic ways of knowing through the arts

For the purposes of this chapter, three modes of young children's artistic/creative learning and interrelations between them are featured:

- visual-kinaesthetic (e.g. visual art)
- physical-kinaesthetic (e.g. movement, dance, drama)
- aural-kinaesthetic (e.g. music).

The term 'kinaesthetic' is used to foreground how each of these art forms derives from embodied (kinaesthetic) ways of experiencing and understanding the self and others. For instance, when drawing, making music, dramatising or dancing, there is a strong connection between imagination, bodily experience and spatial-temporal reasoning. Children's artistic meaning-making becomes 'narrated through embodied actions' (Kim & Kim 2017, p. 578) and enacted through graphic, musical, dramatic and dance-based creation and communication.

The notion of 'narration' requires further explanation. How, for instance, can a child's dance, drawing, dramatisation or musical improvisation be considered a narrative? By way of example, within the domain of art, Wright (2007; 2010) coined the term 'graphic-narrative-embodied play' to describe how children unite mind, body and emotion when drawing and simultaneously *telling* the narrative of their drawing through imaginative depictions of people/characters, objects and events and the use of expressive gestures and vocalisms. Similarly, children create dance, music and dramatic narratives, but not necessarily with words. Although these creative expressions may resemble a storyline, the unfolding is not necessarily in a linear sense, and the plot is not necessarily literal. Instead, children's improvised dances, musical and dramatic enactments often function at a metaphoric level, for instance, where an idea/emotion is applied to an object or action, such as when dancing with a 'droopy' body to stand for a wilting plant.

As Egan (1997) notes, children are especially good at creating metaphors, and they do so by using 'felt understanding and the ability to translate this understanding to words or other expressions. The metaphor mediates between body, experience and language' (Nielsen 2009, p. 90). Indeed, the arts often are beyond the reach of words and offer an understanding that is far richer, deeper and more abstract than what can be communicated in words alone (Eisner 2002; Gardner 1983; Langer 1953). This is often due to the metaphoric cross-over from one mode to another, such as when a child sings a painting, or dances a story. Such 'multimodal' experiences enable the communication to function poetically.

RESEARCH HIGHLIGHT

Research reported in Deans and Wright (2018) illustrates how a group of 4-year-old children enacted an image from a children's book through dramatic/dance play. The core character was a tree (who was encased in a material body tube from ankles to neck) and fireflies flew to and from the tree (holding long thin ribbons of various colours, which they touched on the branches of the tree as they rested). The teacher modelled flying and resting in response to the musical aspects of the recorded music (e.g. fast/slow rhythm, high/low pitch), inviting them to fly at the beginning of the musical phrase, and to rest at the end of the phrase. She altered her voice to suit the level of energy required for particular movements and to encourage the children to enact the *movement qualities* of the fireflies and to experience a sense of 'ensemble' through the group dance. At the end of the dance encounter, the children drew what they remembered from the experience. Two examples show how children depicted diagonal lines to demonstrate convergence on the tree. The tree stands apart and appears larger than the fireflies, which are depicted as dots and swirling movement lines (*see* **Figure 15.1** and **15.2**).

continued…

Strong Foundations

Figure 15.1 'The fireflies are fluttering around the tree because it's almost night and the people are dancing home.'

Figure 15.2 'This cross is spreading the drawings apart (dividing the space). That's the tree from the story and that's the firefly.'

Table 15.1 presents a succinct summary of the various modes involved when learning in/through the arts; the environmental conditions that are required to support participation in these modes; the types of resources and methods that are supportive of young children's learning, and the form in which various modalities are expressed. In addition, the types of mediation that are applicable across each of the modes and artforms is summarised. It must be recognised that this table is not meant as a checklist, nor is it inclusive of a number of other qualities that might have been added. Rather, it is a schematic reminder to those working with young children of the various dimensions of participation in the arts, and a means for thinking beyond a narrow interpretation of particular art forms, in and of themselves. Each of the three types of arts-based play are discussed in greater detail here.

Table 15.1 A schematic of the potential for multimodal participation in the arts

	Dance/dramatic play	**Drawing play**	**Musical play**
Mode	Physical-kinaesthetic	Visual-kinaesthetic	Aural-kinaesthetic
Environment	Movement	Light	Acoustics
Resources	Musical instruments, dance props, recorded music, voice	Paper, pencils, felt pens, chalks, paint, charcoal, clipboard	Hand percussion, body percussion, xylophones/metallophones, voice, song

Table 15.1 (continued)

	Dance/dramatic play	**Drawing play**	**Musical play**
Method	Individual or group dance, improvise, observe, perform, critique, dance-draw	Observe, imagine, graphic-narrative-embodied play, play-draw	Improvise, call and response, ostinatos, rhyme, sing, move, music-draw
Form	Body, space, force, time, flow, character, mime, narrative	Composition, line, shape, texture, colour, media techniques	Beat, rhythm, pitch, melody, form, duration, tempo, timbre, meter, dynamics
Socio-constructivist mediation (adult–child; child–child)	Scaffolding, questioning, appreciating, demonstrating, modelling, collaborating, motivating, hypothesising, leading, responding, empathising, affirming, reflecting, developing vocabulary and skills		

Dance and dramatic play

Closely aligned with sensorial knowing is the notion of kinaesthetic learning – experiencing and understanding the body through sensation, emotion and cognition. As noted, 'kinaesthetics' has to do with the sensory perception of body movement and can be further explained as the *muscle sense*; it detects weight, body position, and relationships between movements and body parts; such as sitting, bending, reaching, rolling or falling. For young children, kinaesthetics play a prominent role in learning in every part of the curriculum, from scientific explorations, to climbing on monkey bars, to painting a self-portrait, to dramatising or dancing an idea or feeling. Children kinaesthetically capture forms of meaning through their bodies, improvising, imitating and enacting the world and emotions, imaginatively and metaphorically.

'Proprioception' is the sense that tells the body where it is in space and the effort being employed. The movement principles as identified by Rudolf Laban (1879–1958), specifically, 'space, force, time and flow' (Laban 1963), are widely acknowledged as the four basic elements of educational dance (Sansom 2011; Schiller & Meiners 2003, Stinson 1993). These elements also translate readily into the teaching of drama and are metaphorically applicable to music and art as well. They are simply understood in terms of what action is being performed, what body parts are involved, where in space the actions begin, travel to and end, how the actions use time and force and in which ways the actions are connected to other people or objects. The principles, when combined, provide access to an open-ended movement vocabulary that enables the expression of the mind/body/spirit connections, which are deemed to be the core of artistic pursuit.

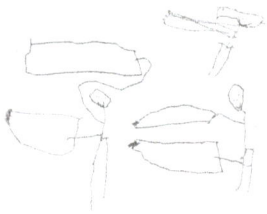

Figure 15.3 'That's us punching the monsters.' **Figure 15.4** 'Those are our strong arms.'

Figure 15.3 illustrates a trio of children dramatically dance-playing *punching the monsters* to highly energised music that they named the 'Harry Potter music' (Deans & Wright 2018). Following the dance experience, one of the children metaphorically represents, through drawing-telling, the physical strength and energy of the dance by exaggerating the size of the arms and capturing the jabbing thrust of punching movements (*see* **Figure 15.4**). As illustrated, the children embraced characterisation freely, embodying the qualities of strength and perseverance to ward off the imagined threatening event.

This example illustrates how children channel the proprioceptive sense while engaging in improvisational dance-dramatic play (Zachest 2015) and are able to seamlessly trans-mediate from one mode (physical/dance) to another (visual/graphic) (Suhor 1984).

RESEARCH HIGHLIGHT

Kress (1997) studied his own children's ability to 'transmediate' (shift) between modes of representation as they played. He noted that representations could take on many forms and purposes, and a shift in modes during play liberated the children to select whichever mode suited their purposes the best (e.g. a child's drawing of an airplane, when cut out of the page, enabling it to be flown by/through the child's enactment). Kress (1997, p. 350) argued that 'children act multi-modally, both in the things they use, the objects they make, and the engagement of their bodies; there is no separation of body and mind'.

Musical play

In musical play, children engage in explorations of, for instance, beat, tempo, rhythm, pitch, melody and timbre using body percussion, musical instruments and the voice. Notably body movement and music exploration are inseparable. Full-body movement is innately accessed to explore the rhythm, mood and style of the music being experienced. Often children create onomatopoeia to accompany their play-based gestures (for instance, sounds or made-up words that function similarly to sound effects in film, to punctuate the action). Children also engage in musical improvisations with others, which often involves playing musical instruments with fine-tuned precision, where hand movements are monitored in relation to effort (e.g. time, force, energy) to create a desired musical effect (e.g. languid sounds, percussive explosive sounds).

Music is considered to be integral to the young child's development (Barrett 2005; de Vries 2006; Nyland, Ferris & Deans 2005). Music is an expressive, culturally bound art form that assists children to develop a stronger sense of self, aural awareness and skills, and importantly, collaborative meaning-making. Individual and group singing is central to the world of the young child 'often being singled out as an activity that promotes emotional wellbeing and communicative competence' (Nyland, Acker, Ferris & Deans 2015, p. 60). From birth, young children are naturally drawn to song and understand musicality on a deeply embodied level. Nursery rhymes, singing games, musical chants, action songs and listening to a wide variety of music are part of the child's lived socio-cultural experience (Flohr 2004; Niland 2012).

Drawing play

Dewey (1934) described artmaking, or *thinking in symbols*, as one of the most sophisticated modes of thinking. It brings into play a creative process that enables the expression of personal experience, thought and imaginative problem-solving. This ability to capture a personally meaningful moment through graphic symbolisation sheds light on the young child's focus, interests, intention, mood and emotions (Wright 2010), thus opening another window into the nature of the young child's learning and development. Drawing when combined with verbal narration (drawing-telling) is often accompanied with expressive gestures and vocalisms; a process that affords a mutually beneficial integration of thinking and feeling modalities. Cox (2005, p. 123) notes that 'talk and drawing interact with each other as parallel and equally transformative processes' and these processes work effectively to help children crystallise their understandings of experience. Through the combination of these forms, children access both non-verbal and verbal languages (bodily gesture, drawing and speaking) and the interconnectedness between these symbolic languages propels the learning much further than would be anticipated.

The Reggio Emilia philosophy incorporates the idea that young children communicate using many different *languages* for expressive communicative purposes. Children are acknowledged as having a 'hundred ways of knowing, feeling and understanding' (Edwards, Gandini & Forman 1998; Malaguzzi 1996, p. 1). It is through the utilisation of the visual and performing arts that they build knowledge and concepts. Drawing, painting, singing, making music, enacting, poetry, story and dance are just a few of the *hundred languages* for learning.

The literature surrounding the notion of the hundred languages draws attention to the capacity of the child to move seamlessly through a range of forms of representational thinking and to systematically organise both abstract and concrete thoughts, ideas and feelings both non-verbally and orally. The multimodal communication of graphic-narrative-embodied play, for instance, often includes a combination of words, physical gestures, onomatopoeia, and broadly-based symbols that reflect objects, events, people; graphic-narrative-embodied play may also include naming, labelling and writing (Wright 2007).

To enrich and recall the children's communications, their words may be transcribed. The adult's role as *empathetic scribe* requires taking responsibility for the establishment of a shared dialogue. The intention is for the adult, or *interlocuter* (Wright, 2010), to record verbatim the words children use to describe their drawing; an activity that requires active listening followed by faithful recording of each child's thinking and understandings. Ideally, such transcriptions will be recorded on a separate page rather than on the child's drawing, as the adult's written symbols detract from the child's visual symbols. At times, however, the child may request the adult to contribute writing to their work, or occasionally the adult may ask permission to provide the drawing with a title, for instance, or to label some significant content within the work.

The role of the educator

The literature has often described teaching as an art (Eisner 2002; Lemov 2010). It is understood that to be a successful educator, foundational attitudes, skills and knowledge need to come together to ensure the best possible outcomes for children's learning. Educators are required to become familiar with the discipline content of each of the arts areas and to employ a range of teaching strategies that support effective learning.

In his influential work *The psychology of art*, Vygotsky (1971, p. 249) proposed that 'Art is the social within us ... the social technique of emotion, a tool of society that brings the most personal aspects of our being into the circle of social life'; it is the means through which individuals learn about self and others more fully. As an extension of this idea, the Zone of Proximal Development (ZPD) has been widely embraced by educational communities as the primary pedagogical tool to guide the practice of teaching. Vygotsky (1978, p. 86) states:

> What we call the Zone of Proximal Development ... is the distance between the actual developmental level as determined by independent problem solving, and the level of potential development as determined through problem solving under adult guidance or in collaboration with more capable peers.

This idea draws attention to the important role that adults and/or peers play in the learning process. Vygotsky's view, that learning leads development, gives support to a teaching and learning construct that provides opportunities for young children to form strong relationships. Through relationships with educators and peers, children engage in problem-solving. This enables individuals and groups to move beyond the known, to push past prior capabilities and to achieve new understandings.

As well as open-ended scaffolding strategies, direct teaching or intentional teaching through verbal explanation or modelling can be employed by educators to help the children to grasp and master content and skills of each of the art forms. Direct teaching approaches that include imitation, practise, shaping and reinforcement, work hand in hand with learning processes that involve back and forth verbal exchanges between educators and children and children and children. This provides opportunities for shared sustained thinking (Siraj-Blatchford 2009) and individual, small and large group explorations of 'big ideas' (Ritchhart, Church & Morrison 2011) that expand thinking and give permission for individuals to engage in imaginative problem-solving and communicating.

Conclusion

Through the arts, children 'stand a head taller' (Vygotsky 1971). In other words, they understand, feel and communicate knowledge and emotions that seem to be above what would be expected from such young children. The outcomes produced through children's first literacies – the arts – can sometimes astound us, because of the deep insights and emotions that are represented. Through artistic, aesthetic and creative expression, children are able to *say* what is often difficult to communicate through words (McArdle & Wright 2014). In the process of such meaning-making, children discover more about themselves and their worlds. Through the types of activities identified in this chapter, children create their own ZPD, alone or with others. It is the open-endedness of the semiotic tools of music-making, dramatising, dancing and art-making that liberates children's independent discovery through imaginative, kinaesthetic and sensorial learning and development. These principles are summarised in **Figure 15.5**.

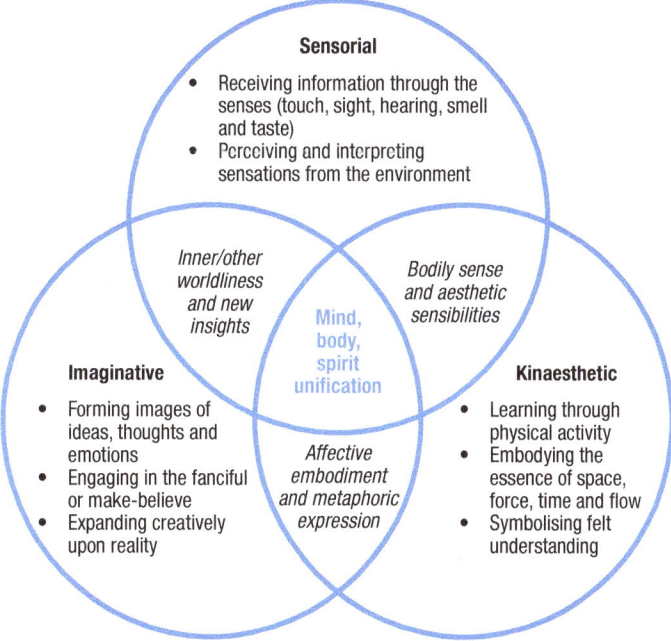

Figure 15.5 Linking the sensorial, imaginative and kinaesthetic aspects of play

Figure 15.5 is quite simplistic, even visually poetic, which makes the content more easily remembered, sort of like a mnemonic device. The terms 'imaginative', 'kinaesthetic' and 'sensorial' within the figure are adjectives to describe these fundamental aspects of play. Under each of these three terms are definitions, which are phrased as verbs (i.e. *ing* words). The italicised words in the bubbles link the constructs (sensorial-imaginative, imaginative-kinaesthetic and kinaesthetic-sensorial). These phrases describe the essence of what occurs when two parts intersect or are combined.

RESEARCH INTO PRACTICE
After reading this chapter, consider how you can:
- provide learning environments that encourage play-based learning through the arts
- plan, implement and evaluate children's learning across three modes of children's artistic/creative development within a socio-constructivist theoretical framework
- identify and adopt a range of intentional teaching strategies to ensure that imaginative, kinaesthetic and sensorial learning in/through the arts is optimised
- critically reflect on your program to ensure that artistic and expressive thinking is catered for
- make children's learning in/through the arts visible for children and families.

References

Arnheim, R 1954, *Art and visual perception*, Faber and Faber, London.
Barrett, M 2005, 'Musical communication and children's communities of practice', in D Miell, R MacDonald & D Hargreaves (eds), *Musical Communication*, Oxford University Press, Oxford, pp. 261–80.
Cox, S 2005, 'Intention and meaning in young children's drawings', *Journal of Arts and Design Education*, vol. 21, no. 2, pp. 115–25.
de Vries, P 2006, 'Being there: creating music-making opportunities in a childcare centre', *International Journal of Music Education*, vol. 24, no. 3, pp. 255–70.
Deans, J & Wright, S 2018, *Dance-play and drawing-telling as semiotic tools for young children's learning*, Routledge, New York.
Dewey, J 1934, *Art as experience*, Capricorn Books, New York.
Department of Education, Employment and Workplace Relations (DEEWR) 2009, *Belonging, being and becoming: the early years learning framework for Australia*, Commonwealth of Australia, Canberra. Retrieved from https://docs.education.gov.au/node/2632
Docket, S & Fleer, M 1999, *Play and pedagogy in early childhood: bending the rules*, Harcourt Brace, Melbourne.
Edwards, S & Cutter-MacKenzie. AN 2011, 'Environmentalising early childhood education curriculum through pedagogies of play', *Australasian Journal of Early Childhood*, vol.36, no. 1, pp. 51–59.
Edwards, C, Gandini, l & Forman, G (eds) 1998, *The hundred languages of children: the Reggio Emilia approach to early childhood education*, Ablex, Westport, CT.
Egan, K 1997, *The educated mind: how cognitive tools shape our understanding*, The University of Chicago Press.
Eisner, E 2002, *The arts and the creation of mind*, Yale University Press, New Haven, CT.
Elkind, D 2007, *The power of play: learning what comes naturally*, De Capo, Boston, MA.
Fleer, M 2017, *Play in the early years*, 2nd edn, Cambridge University Press, Melbourne.
Flohr, J 2004, *The musical lives of young children*, Prentice Hall, Upper Saddle River, NJ.
Gardner, H 1983, *Frames of mind: the theory of multiple intelligences*, Basic Books, New York.
Innis, RE 2012, 'Meaningful connections: semiotics, cultural psychology, and the form of sense', in J Valsiner (ed.), *The Oxford handbook of culture and psychology*, Oxford University Press, Oxford, pp. 255–76.
Kim, K & Kim, K 2017, 'Multimodal play-literacy: a preschooler's storytelling, drawing, and performing of dinosaur extinction theories', *Early Child Development and Care*, vol. 187, no. 3–4, pp. 568–82.
Kress, G 1997, *Before writing: rethinking the paths to literacy*, Routledge, London.

Laban, R 1963, *Modern educational dance,* 2nd edn, revised by L Ullmann, MacDonald and Evans, London.
Langer, SK 1953, *Feeling and form: a theory of art developed from philosophy in a new key,* Scribners & Routledge & Kegan Pau, London.
Lemov, D 2010, *Teach like a champion: 49 techniques that put students on the path to college,* Jossey-Bass, San Francisco.
Malaguzzi, L 1996, 'The hundred languages of children: narrative of the possible', in the catalogue, *Hundred languages of children exhibition*, Reggio Emilia, Italy.
Malaguzzi, L 1998, 'History, ideas and basic philosophy: an interview with Lella Gandini', in C Edwards, L Gandini & G Forman (eds), *The hundred languages of children: advanced reflections*, Ablex, London.
Maranović-Shane, A & Beljanski-Ristić, L 2008, 'From play to art–from experience to insight', *Mind, culture and activity*, vol. 15, no. 2, pp. 93–114.
Matthews, J 1999, *Helping children to draw and paint in early childhood,* Hodder and Stoughton, London.
Mavers, D 2011, *Children's drawing and writing: the remarkable in the unremarkable,* Routledge, Oxon.
McArdle, F & Wright, S 2014, 'First literacies: arts, creativity, play, constructive meaning-making', in G Burton (ed.), *Literacy in the arts: retheorising learning and teaching,* Springer, New York, pp. 21–37.
Nielsen, CS 2009, 'Children's embodied voices: approaching children's experiences through multi-modal interviewing', *Phenomenology & Practice*, vol. 3, no. 1, pp. 80–93.
Niland, A 2012, 'Exploring the lives of songs in the context of young children's musical cultures', *Min-Ad: Israel Studies in Musicology*, vol. 10, pp. 27–46. Retrieved from http://www.biu.ac.il/hu/mu/min-ad/12/4%20Niland.pdf
Nyland, B, Ferris, J & Deans, J 2005, 'Music as experience: from Dewey to Rogoff', *International Journal of Early Childhood*, vol. 11, no. 1, pp. 125–39.
Nyland, B, Acker, A, Ferris, J & Deans, J 2015, *Musical childhoods: explorations in preschool years*, Routledge, Taylor & Francis, London.
Read, H 1943, *Education through art*, Faber and Faber, London.
Ritchhart, R, Church, M & Morrison, K 2011, *Making thinking visible: how to promote engagement, understanding, and independence for all learners,* Jossey-Bass, San Francisco.
Sansom, AN 2011, *Movement and dance in young children's lives: crossing the divide*, Peter Lang, New York.
Schiller, W & Meiners, J 2003, 'Dance – moving beyond steps to ideas', in S Wright (ed.), *Children, meaning-making and the arts*, Pearson, Sydney, pp. 91–116.
Siraj-Blatchford, I 2009, 'Conceptualising progression in the pedagogy of play and sustained shared thinking in early childhood education: a Vygotskian perspective', *Educational & Child Psychology*, vol. 26, no. 2, pp. 77-89.
Smith, AB 2007, 'Children's rights and early childhood education. Links to theory and advocacy', *Australian Journal of Early Childhood*, vol. 32, no. 3, pp. 1–8.
Stinson, S 1993, *Dance for young children: finding the magic in movement*, The American Alliance for Health, Physical Education, Recreation and Dance, Reston, VA.
Suhor, C 1984, 'Towards a semiotic-based curriculum', *Journal of Curriculum Studies*, vol. 16, no. 3, pp. 247–57.
Sunday, K 2018, 'When drawing proliferates: toward an onto-epistemological pedagogy of children's drawing', *Visual Arts Research*, vol. 44, no. 2, pp. 31–42.
Tobin, J 2005, 'A right to be no longer dismissed or ignored: children's voices in pedagogy and policy making', *International Journal of Equity and Innovation in Early Childhood*, vol. 3, no. 3, pp. 4–18.
United Nations (UN) 1989, *Convention on the rights of the child,* Office of the United Nations High Commissioner of Human Rights, Geneva.
Vygotsky, LS 1971, *The psychology of art,* Massachusetts Institute of Technology, Cambridge, MA.
Vygotsky, L 1978, *Mind in society. The development of higher psychological processes*, Harvard University Press, Cambridge, MA.
Wohlwend, K 2011, 'Mapping modes in children's play and design: an action-oriented approach to critical multimodal analysis', in R Rogers (ed.), *An introduction to critical discourse analysis in education*, 2nd edn, Lawrence Erlbaum, Mahwash, NJ, pp. 242–66.
Wright, S 2007, 'Graphic-narrative play: young children's authoring through drawing and telling', *International Journal of Education and the Arts*, vol. 8, no. 1, pp. 1–28.
Wright, S 2010, *Understanding creativity in early childhood: meaning-making and children's drawing*, Sage, Washington.
Wright, S & Deans, J 2020, 'The role of movement, dynamics and expression on children's drawings of dancing', in C Svendler Nielsen & S Burridge (eds), *Dancing across borders: perspectives on dance, young people and change,* Routledge, London, pp. 157–69.
Zachest, K 2015, *Drama for early childhood*, Currency Press, Sydney.

CHAPTER 16

Play and learning in the digital age

Nicola Yelland

DOI: https://doi.org/10.37517/978-1-74286-555-3_16
University of Melbourne

LINKS TO NATIONAL QUALITY STANDARD

Quality Area 1: Educational program and practice
- Standard 1.2: Practice – educators facilitate and extend children's learning and development.
- Element 1.2.1: Intentional teaching – educators are deliberate, purposeful and thoughtful in their decisions and actions.
- Element 1.2.2: Responsive teaching and scaffolding – educators respond to children's ideas and play and extend children's learning through open-ended questions, interactions and feedback.

LINKS TO EARLY YEARS LEARNING FRAMEWORK

Learning Outcome 4: Children are confident and involved learners
- Children develop a range of skills and processes such as problem-solving, inquiry, experimentation, hypothesising, researching and investigating.

Learning Outcome 5: Children are effective communicators
- Children express ideas and make meaning using a range of texts.
- Children use information and communication technologies to access information, investigate ideas and represent their thinking.

Introduction

This chapter focuses on children's learning in the digital age and the educational practices that can support new learning in early childhood settings. It illustrates evidence-informed practices that consider the ways in which young children incorporate new technologies into their playful explorations, and discusses the ways in which educators can create learning ecologies to ensure that every child is viewed as a capable learner. In reading this chapter you will gain an understanding about contemporary discussions regarding the use of new technologies by young children that will form the basis of deciding how to incorporate them effectively into early childhood learning programs. An overview of the contested views about the role new technologies play in our lives, and their use by young children and their families, is considered. Case studies of exemplary practices that incorporate new technologies are presented and linked with the notion of quality provision as well as the Learning Outcomes stated in the Early Years Learning Framework for Australia (EYLF) (DEEWR 2009).

Definition of terms

A clear definition of the terms being used in this chapter is needed at the beginning. The terms 'new technologies', 'digital technologies' and 'digital artefacts' are used interchangeably to include computers, tablets, smart phones and indeed any electronic and internet-connected items (toys, cameras, whiteboards, scanners, musical instruments, printers etc) as well as the apps that are available to use on them.

'New learning' (Kalantzis & Cope 2012) is a response to changes in our contemporary society, just like at previous critical junctures in our civilisation; for example, the Renaissance and the advent of the printing press. The contemporary changes, and challenges in our lives are a consequence of the prevalence of new technologies and the advent of globalisation, which has caused major movements of people so that our societies are much more multicultural and diverse. New learning considers alternative ways of knowing and organising knowledge that enable multimodal learning and meaning-making. New learning also requires that children are critical and creative in their thinking, effective communicators and collaborative learners. *New* learning can be contrasted to *old* learning, which put a premium on knowledge as content and being able to recall it for specific uses in often narrowly defined contexts; for instance, tests and examinations. New learning is authentic learning that is deeply engaging for children since they usually define the parameters of their investigations. Further, because it is authentic, it is shared in communities of practice (Lave & Wenger 1991) and not just produced for a teacher.

'Multimodal learning' involves linguistic, visual, aural, oral and kinaesthetic representations and forms of communication (e.g. Kress & Jewitt 2003). New technologies have both enhanced and changed each of these modalities and in many ways created an additional modality to represent and share ideas.

'Deep learning' (Fullan & Langworthy 2014) is viewed as occurring when children are engaged with ideas and materials (digital and non-digital) so that they learn and shape their own ideas about the world.

New technologies in the early childhood years

Research about the use of new technologies with young children takes place in differing inter-disciplinary contexts beyond education, such as media studies and communications (Livingstone, Mascheroni & Staksrud 2018; Salomaa & Mertala 2019), sociology (Mascheroni 2018) and computing (Manches & Plowman 2017).

There is an increasing body of research evidence that reveals the ways in which young children are fluent in the use of new technologies as part of their everyday experiences (Huber, Highfield & Kaufman 2018; Marsh et al. 2015; Marsh et al. 2018; Plowman & Stephen 2005; Yelland & Gilbert 2017; 2019). Much of this work has been focused on a consideration of the ways in which the use of new technologies can support and indeed enhance learning and transform teaching. It has taken place in both home and educational contexts (Arnott 2018; Arnott, Palaiologou & Gray 2019; Johnston, Highfield & Hadley 2018; Plowman, McPake & Stephen 2010; Plowman, Stephen & McPake 2010; Plowman, Stevenson, Stephen & McPake 2012; Scott & Marsh 2018; Yelland 2018; Yelland & Gilbert 2017; 2019).

RESEARCH HIGHLIGHT

There has also been research that has surveyed children and their families about the extent of their use of new technologies (Commonsense Media 2013; Livingstone 2011; Rideout, Foehr & Roberts 2010) which not only revealed a wide range of types of activities, but also that children still played with, and enjoyed, *traditional* materials (e.g. books, dolls, blocks, board games) alongside the new technologies.

The Internet of Toys

The emergence of the 'Internet of Toys' (IoToys), whereby young children play with internet-connected items in their homes, and to a more limited extent in early childhood settings, has also enabled new conceptualisations about the ways in which digital items are incorporated into play. The IoToys provides contexts to think about how a variety of complimentary materials are included in play-based scenarios that facilitate multimodal meaning-making and learning. This led Arnott et al. (2019, p. 402) to suggest that 'play in the digital world should be viewed through a social ecology lens in an effort to understand the *wholeness* of children's play and learning at home and in ECE [early childhood education]'. In this way conceptualisations of play have been revised so that playing with technologies is included in any consideration of play as well as the fact that playful explorations (Yelland 2011) can be supported and extended with careful guided instruction by educators and indeed any adults (Verenikina & Kervin 2011).

Play and new technologies

We need to consider that in order to advise and support educators, families and children with examples that might act as exemplars for the incorporation of new technologies, we inadvertently privilege the digital, rather than emphasise the dynamic ways in which the digital and material items complement each other. It is this emphasis that enables young children to learn in new and dynamic ways to support multimodal learning and meaning-making (Hatzigianni & Kalaitzidis 2018; Johnston et al. 2018; Marsh et al. 2018; Yelland 2016; 2018). Additionally, while we are acutely aware of the 'digital disconnect' between home and school (Edwards et al. 2017) we have tended to conceptualise the differences as being in deficit for early childhood education. However, Arnott et al. (2019, p. 411) view home and early childhood education settings as places of opportunity to experience IoToys 'across multi-layered and multi-dimensional social worlds that children inhabit'. These are exciting learning spaces in which evolving identities and meaning-making are made possible in dynamic ways (Plowman 2016). They attribute increasing agency for the young child in their learning and they provide learning ecologies that can be scaffolded by adults to ensure playful explorations of the most profound kind.

Palaiologou (2016a) has suggested that many of the anxieties that exist around young children's use of new technologies might be attributed to the binary nature of discussions that position digital against traditional materials used by young children in their play. With the IoToys apps there is an opportunity to think more holistically about the place of media more generally in young children's lives.

Screen time

Certainly, the advent of touch-screen technologies (smartphones and tablets) have meant that the use of new technologies by young children has become ubiquitous. Commensurately there seem to have been increased concerns voiced about the amount of time young children are spending engaged in 'screen time'. Again the discussions have been framed as binary – either/or scenarios – rather than focusing on the ways in which both digital and non-digital experiences need to be moderated, scaffolded and viewed as complementary.

There seems to be a propensity to quantify the appropriate *screen time* that children should be exposed to each day (Blum-Ross & Livingstone 2018; Hiniker, Radesky, Livingstone & Blum-Ross 2019). As previously stated, the use of *new* versus *traditional* technologies is frequently framed as a binary, emphasising the positive or the negative, as if in competition rather than a consideration of how they might be combined and create new opportunities for learning. These concerns about the amount of screen time young children were experiencing were manifested in the American Academy of Pediatrics (2013) initial directive that children under 3 years of age should have no screen time at all, which they modified to the following statement in 2016:

> Parents of children 18–24 months of age who want to introduce digital media should choose high-quality programming, and watch it with their children to help them understand what they're seeing. (American Academy of Pediatrics 2016)

In Australia, it is recommended that children under 2 years of age have no screen time at all while those from 2 to 4 years of age should only have approximately one hour of screen time a day. They also advocate for a minimum of 3 hours of physical activity (Australian Government 2017). In their study of home ownership and use of new technologies, Huber, Highfield and Kaufmann (2018, p. 830) found that 'children are using screens more than policies advise'. They advise that parents need to be able to make informed choices when choosing screen time for their children and additionally participate with them in these play activities rather than encouraging a passive screen-time experience.

New learning ecologies

There is also a recognition that children do not learn in a vacuum, nor just in early childhood settings and schools. As a result of a broader approach that considers a variety of different sites and contexts as learning ecologies, it has been postulated that *traditional* and *new* technologies can co-exist. They can be utilised by the learner when they make decisions about what resources they need in order to complete their designed task (Plowman & Stephen 2007; Plowman, Stephen & McPake 2010). Yelland (2016; 2018) has contended that the difference about learning in the 21st century is that while learning has always been multimodal, it has incorporated linguistic, visual spatial, aural and kinetic dimensions. Digital technologies have affected these modalities in significant ways and additionally can be regarded as a modality on their own. In essence, research and discussions have moved beyond questioning the developmental appropriateness of technologies for young children in both home and schooling contexts (Donohoe 2015). We have moved towards the realisation that new technologies are an inevitable part of contemporary childhoods and our lives more generally.

With the enhanced capabilities of the latest tablets there are a variety of apps that encourage creativity and engagement, and enable parents to play along with their children (Blaisdell, Arnott, Wall & Robinson 2019; Neumann & Neumann 2015). The same can be said for early childhood educators whereby activities with digital technologies can be part of multimodal learning ecologies that encourage deep learning and meaning-making. Marsh et al. (2018) surveyed 2000 parents about their children's use of apps and how the apps might foster creativity. They also conducted six family case studies. Their results revealed that children from birth to 5 years of age were using a wide variety of apps, not all of which were designed for that age group. They contended that the design of the apps, and their use by the children, had the potential to promote play and creativity when they, for example, enabled children to produce new and original texts and artefacts.

They did, however, also note that many apps promoted 'rule-bound' (Marsh et al. 2018, p. 878) play rather than free play because of their design. For example, some of the apps that claimed to foster creativity did so, 'in a way that constrained children's choice and agency' (Marsh et al. 2018, p. 879). This included a paint app where there was a restriction on the number of colours available and did not enable mixing of colours. Thus, it was in the *open ended* apps (creative with many possibilities) in which the children could create their own original artefacts where creative practices were made possible. They also found some examples where the children had subverted the aims of an app by playing with it in a way that it was not designed for. In this way they were being very creative and showing a high level of competence to understand the original rules and replace them with a new set that they determined to be more appropriate, or fun.

Pedagogial strategies

Pedagogial strategies play an important role in the use of new technology in early childhood settings (Bird Early Childhood Educators & Edwards 2015). Plowman and McPake (2013) noted that educators' professional decisions have a significant impact on what is learned in early childhood settings. Factors such as personal anxiety, lack of encouragement by leaders, lack of opportunity and professional learning sessions are just some of many identified by Palaiologou (2016b) as being inhibitors to the use of new technologies.

RESEARCH HIGHLIGHT

Hatziglanni and Kalaitzidis (2018) found that educators of children under 3 years of age, were more confident about using technology for their own work but less confident about using them with young children. However, they noted that their views were evolving and moving more towards increasing confidence. With the portability of tablets and their ease of use, it has become increasingly apparent that their use is more relevant to children's explorations, whereby they are able to take photographs of their *'wonderings'* (Yelland in press) and document their play-based constructions for later discussions. This has increasingly meant that children have been active contributors to pedagogical documentation, which in turn is more valuable to deep learning as they provide sites of reflection and the relaunching of ideas and new explorations.

With regard to the use of new technologies in education contexts, there has been research about how the use of new technologies impacts young children's lives and learning (Plowman, Stephen & McPake 2010), in relation to transformative pedagogies that can facilitate learning with new technologies (Fleer 2017; 2018). As previously stated, some studies have focused on the home use of new technologies and comparisons between home and school use (Huber et al. 2018). Other studies have focused on defining what digital play is and how it might be incorporated into play-based programs (Arnott 2016; Hatzigianni, Gregoriadis, Karagiorgou & Chatzigeorgiadou 2018; Marsh et al. 2016; Mustola, Koivula, Turja & Laakso 2018). There is also a considerable body of work that reflects and describes a new conceptualisation of literacies that incorporate the basic premise of multimodality and the social capital that accrues from being fluent and multiliterate (Flewitt, Messer & Kucirkova 2015; Harrison & McTavish 2016; Sefton-Green, Marsh, Erstad & Flewitt 2016; Yelland 2018).

Case studies of play and learning in the early childhood years

Here we explore three cases, or examples, of the use of technologies embedded in active explorations by young children in preschool (ages 3–4 years) and the first year of entry into public schooling (5–6 years) to illustrate evidence-informed practice regarding the use of new technologies in early childhood education settings. All the examples are from research projects conducted by the author over the past decade. They all took place in early childhood settings and primary school classrooms with the researchers collaborating with the educators, teachers, children and families to co-design and explore activities and explorations that enabled us to think creatively about the ways in which new technologies could be incorporated into young children's learning and to extend educators' pedagogical repertoire. The cases were chosen to illustrate the range of contexts, pedagogical strategies and learning opportunities that were created. They resonate with the National Quality Standard (NQS) and the EYLF Learning Outcomes highlighted at the beginning of this chapter, which stipulate that children should use new technologies to investigate their ideas and to represent their thinking, and be exposed to intentional teaching that supports and encourages their use in meaning-making and for the acquisition of foundations skills.

The pedagogical strategies included: scaffolding and guided learning, encouraging problem-posing and problem-solving processes, as well as the documentation of learning ecologies in multimodal formats. Children's agency was at the forefront of the research design process. The pedagogical strategies were designed to create learning ecologies in which the children could feel confident to explore and be supported in their investigations. This way they can use their specific knowledge-building scaffolding techniques that would broaden their approaches to novel encounters. In this process the educators' pedagogical repertoire was extended to include the use of the new technologies and what they afforded in the learning of young children. These included a deliberate focus on multimodal learning and literacies as well as the use of pedagogical documentation, not only for planning but for deep reflections on learning and for re-launching ideas and investigations. Thus, the three cases illustrate:

Play and learning in the digital age

1. the use of apps to support the acquisition of foundational skills that will support playful explorations and investigations. They will be considered in context of the use of some traditional materials, to illustrate the ways in which multimodal learning occurs
2. examples of multimodal representations and conversations to scaffold knowledge building and meaning-making
3. pedagogical documentation panels that reflect learning conversations and provide the impetus for reflection about learning and re-launching ideas.

CASE STUDY 1

Learning to count and recognise numbers

On entry to school in Australia (5 years of age), children are assessed with a number of diagnostic tests that are aimed at determining their skill level in some foundational areas of literacy and numeracy. For example, in numeracy, aspects of *number* are important and detailed in the National Curriculum (ACARA 2012). Information is obtained about each child's ability to count to 20 in sequence, to recognise the numerals and number names, and to show and count a selection of items accurately.

In one study there were 11 children, out of a group of 68, who were not able to do this at the mid-year point of their first year at school. Accordingly, we worked with the teachers to design a sequence of activities over a 5-week time span to support their number learning with us in small groups (two groups, of five and six respectively). Alongside apps that we thought might teach and reinforce number and counting skills (*see* **Figure 16.1**), we also had other materials, including blocks of various sizes, and everyday items; such as buttons, bottle tops and bread tags. We had playdough to create numerals, we used number rhymes and we went outside in the playground to count steps and items; such as how many fence posts were in one section of the school fence.

a) Counting ants
b) Color by Number

continued...

c) Tally Tots	d) Drawing the number 6

Figure 16.1 Apps to support counting and number knowledge

We had apps such as *TallyTots*, *Bugs and Buttons*, *Bugs and Numbers*, I Can Write (numerals), *Play School Art Maker* and *Book Creator*. For example, when using *TallyTots* (see **Figure 16.1c**) children can gain fluency with the numerals up to 20. When a number is selected a voice counts to the number. The teacher can count with the child or leave them to work individually. The child is required to count the items in the example – and then completes an activity; such as feeding the number of acorns to a squirrel. The child can also see the numeral before and the numeral that follows and select one of them. Even though the children in this group were not able to demonstrate their understanding of numbers to 20, in *TallyTots* they could follow the counting sequence verbally and indicate which numeral matched the spoken number. There were some instances when a child would press 2 for 12, but apart from this they were very accurate.

What was even more evident was their excitement at using the tablets as well as their enthusiasm for completing the tasks successfully. One of the teachers commented on how she noticed that the children's faces 'lit up' when they came back from the tablet sessions. Over a period of 5 weeks, in one 20-minute session a week, we were able to work with the group so that when they were retested all but two of them were able to demonstrate they could do these types of activities and move on to the numbers beyond 20. The combination of materials and small group focus facilitated this process. This was important because, as Yelland (2018) noted, if children do not possess these foundational skills they are unable to embark on investigations for which the skills are an essential part. Fluency in these skills ensures that children can explore their world systematically and communicate and document their findings effectively. We were not exploring the acquisition of early number here, but on the request of the teachers, we were working with the children with multimodal materials with the goal of supporting them to reach the number benchmarks for the Foundation year of schooling in Australia.

In a previous study with children in preschool (4 years old) we wanted to see what type of apps they spontaneously chose when given a range of choices. In many instances the apps regarded as being appropriate for this age group were focused on early learning skills with letters, numbers, shapes and colours. One day we observed Jack as he played with *Counting Train*. In this app the user has to select the correct numeral, out of a choice of three, to complete a number sequence that is presented as the train chugs by. Jack was able to drag the correct numeral from the bottom of the screen and place it in the correct position on the number train in all instances observed. For example, he moved the numeral 4 and placed it in between 3 and 5. He was always very pleased when he got the correct answer: 'I got it right!' he said excitedly and smiled when the app congratulated him. After playing this app for about 2–3 minutes Jack exited by pushing the home button and then selected to play another number app, *TallyTots*. In this counting game the player selects a number from 1 to 20 and then counts to that number as well as completing a task; such as putting 10 acorns in a squirrel's mouth. Jack started at the number 2 and continued to touch the numerals in sequence and complete each number task until he reached 10. After he completed each number activity associated with the number, he again seemed very pleased with his own efforts – exclaiming 'I did it!' excitedly. After completing the activity for 10, he advanced straight to number 20 and completed that activity. At the end of the activity, fireflies create the numeral 20 and Jack exclaimed 'I made the number!' He then counted down from 20 to 16.

CASE STUDY 2

Multimodal representations

Yelland (2016; 2018) has shown that explorations can be enriched when multimodal representations of ideas are presented and used as a catalyst to discuss theories and meaning-making. This might take the form of making, drawing, mapping or studying (*see* **Figure 16.2** and **16.3**).

a) Reading maps   b) Mapping the garden

Figure 16.2 Multimodal representations

continued…

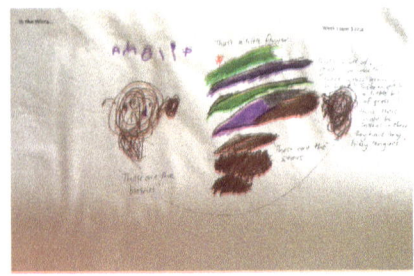

a) Tiny flowers in the Wirra

b) Drawing leaves

c) Studying plants

Figure 16.3 Children considering and representing the Wirra in different modalities

In **Figure 16.2 and 16.3** children are considering and representing their observations and ideas in different modalities. For example, in **Figure 16.3** a group of preschool and early-primary children were exploring in a space adjacent to their buildings that they called 'the Wirra'. They were able to take photos in the area as well as make sketches with pencil and paper while they were located there. Additionally, when they returned to their rooms they were able to document their investigations, by drawing a map of the Wirra and including the items that they had observed. Their explorations of the Wirra also extended into further studies about the butterflies that they had observed. The teacher brought some butterfly samples in from a local museum and the children created some scientific drawings, with appropriate labelling of body parts, to show their understandings about butterflies.

In thinking about their investigations the children were generating theories about the inhabitants of the Wirra and sharing their ideas in different modalities of representations. They were able to pose questions and follow up their explorations with extended resources to answer these questions. In the process the teacher was scaffolding their learning by challenging them with questions and supporting their meaning-making and language development with materials and ideas about how they could share their findings.

These examples reflect a pedagogy of multiliteracies (New London Group 1996) in which literacy is viewed as more than being fluent in reading and writing print-based texts. A pedagogy of multiliteracies recognises the *what* and *how* of literacies in contemporary times. The *what* becomes the learning design, and the *how* the pedagogies. This view of curriculum as a design for social futures is characterised by diversity and multimodality. It broadens the definition of literacy beyond the linguistic (spoken and written) and creates a context to enable new ways of thinking and making meanings about our world.

CASE STUDY 3

Pedagogical documentation

One of the most important aspects of learning is having the opportunity to articulate what you have learned and share it with others. In this way, the notion of pedagogical documentation has become significant not only for educators to record their learning planning and outcomes but also for children as sites of communication of ideas and reflection. Pedagogical documentation has its origins in the work of the *pedagogistas* in Reggio Emilia, Italy and has evolved to create contexts for not only sharing new knowledge and ideas but also as re-launching sites for new explorations.

The children began to notice their shadows while exploring the outdoor environment. Curious about the position and movement of shadows, they began to question. Together the educators and the children entered into deep conversation about shadows and *how* they move. We listened and actively responded to the children's voices to support their emerging theories. We documented and tested their theories and relaunched ideas and actions to deepen the learning through the inquiry process.

Deepening child-led learning ... exploring children's theories

Eric's theory was that the movement of shadows occurred due to the movement of the sun. The educators relaunched this idea through a series of questions that responded to his emerging theories.

How and why did the sun move Eric?
'Cos it's winter, some days it's winter.
The Earth spins around and the sunshine at different locations that means, different places.
So, how sun moves? Sometimes the sun moves in a day and each day the sun moves.'

Why does the sun move each day?
'Maybe because the night, when it moves to a different place and it stops at daytime. Sometimes day it moves. It drives. I think it moves and moves and moves ... it looks like a different place for the sun. I can see sun in a different place. I think it follows the car when you are driving ... it follows you.'

How does the sun follow you?
'Maybe the moon moves and then ... the sun goes to the same place. The moon follows my car at night. I think IT moves ... moves to places. Maybe ... to different countries. I think it always follows you. It stops in different places.'

'The moon moves and the sun comes up at the same location' – Thomas

'The sun is going down and the moon is coming up. Follows your car. The sun went to a different window.'

It moves, the sun moves ... cos ... it moves all around and ... moves to different places – Zarliah

Figure 16.4 Shadows and the sun

continued...

In one example, a group of preschool children were having a conversation about their shadows and how they changed during the day. The educator talked with them and helped them to take photographs of their shadows at various times during the day. They then had a conversation about their shadows and drew and talked about their theories about shadows. The educator made this into a documentation panel (*see* **Figure 16.4**), which was displayed on the wall. In doing this, it was available as a point of reflection about the day the group thought about shadows. It also acted as a stimulus for further investigations as they reflected about the experience some time after the initial exploration and relaunched the shadows investigation by creating a sundial in the playground.

Creating books of events also acts as pedagogical documentation (Kucirkova, Littleton & Cremin 2017). On the day a new scooter arrived in the preschool, the children decided to see who was the fastest scooter-rider in the group. They each took turns to scoot around the concrete path bounding the playground while the educator made a video of their journey and recorded the time it took. The educator then made a table of the times, each with a photo of the child next to it. It was then possible to figure out who had the fastest time and declare that child the winner. Later the educator used *Book Creator* to make a book of all the children's efforts and embedded the videos on each page. Additionally, she decided to print the book out as a big book (A3) (*see* **Figure 16.5**) so that it could be accessed in the reading corner as both an eBook and a hard copy. Later we added QR codes to the printed book so that the children could use it in conjunction with the iPad and scan it to hear the story of the scooter race as told by each child. This switching of modalities and the conversations around the events enabled the children to think about the events of the scooter race and recall them in different ways. It also provided them with a memory of a happy day!

Figure 16.5 The scooter race

Conclusion

These examples provided the impetus for working with educators to create new learning contexts that were dynamic and encouraging of deep learning. They were characterised by active learning in which the children were given agency to direct their learning via explorations that were of interest to them and, as a consequence, stimulated their curiosity about the things around them. It involved moving beyond the walls of the setting into the playground or areas nearby. The teachers incorporated new technologies as part of a suite of resources that facilitated investigations and could be used as a medium for sharing findings and communicating ideas and theories. Children were encouraged to wonder about the phenomena around them and give voice to their ideas. The educators, teachers and children used new technologies and other materials (pencil and paper for drawing maps, diagrams and writing) to document their findings. Being able to communicate these observations and their subsequent ideas about the world was a vital part of the learning experiences. The documentation consisted of panels, movies, drawings, pottery artefacts and many more forms, with the goal being to systematically capture their ideas and theories and share them in an authentic way so that they could be built on in subsequent investigations. This type of multimodal learning and representations is the essence of new learning.

References

American Academy of Pediatrics 2013, 'Children, adolescents & the media', *Pediatrics*, vol. 132, no. 5, pp. 958–61. Retrieved from https://pediatrics.aappublications.org/content/pediatrics/132/5/958.full.pdf

American Academy of Pediatrics 2016, *American Academy of Pediatrics announces new recommendations for children's media use*. Retrieved from https://www.aap.org/en-us/about-the-aap/aap-press-room/Pages/American-Academy-of-Pediatrics-Announces-New-Recommendations-for-Childrens-Media-Use.aspx

Australian Curriculum and Assessment Reporting Authority (ACARA) 2012, *Australian Curriculum – mathematics*, ACARA, Sydney. Retrieved from http://www.australiancurriculum.edu.au/Mathematics/Curriculum/F-10

Australian Government Department of Health (DoH) 2017, *Australia's physical activity and sedentary behaviour guidelines*, DoH, Canberra. Retrieved from https://www1.health.gov.au/internet/main/publishing.nsf/Content/health-pubhlth-strateg-phys-act-guidelines

Arnott, L 2016, 'An ecological exploration of young children's digital play: framing children's social experiences with technologies in early childhood', *Early Years*, vol. 36, no. 1, pp. 271–88.

Arnott, L 2017, 'Framing technological experiences in the early years', in L Arnott (ed.), *Digital technologies and learning in the early years*, Sage, London, pp. 7–19.

Arnott, L 2018, 'Children's negotiation tactics and socio-emotional self-regulation in child-led play experiences: the influence of the preschool pedagogic culture', *Early Child Development and Care*, vol. 188, no. 7, pp. 951–65.

Arnott, L, Palaiologou, I & Gray, C 2019, 'Internet of Toys across home and early childhood education: understanding the ecology of the child's social world', *Technology, Pedagogy and Education*, vol. 28, no. 4, pp. 401–12.

Blaisdell, C, Arnott, L, Wall, K & Robinson, C 2019, 'Look who's talking: using creative, playful arts-based methods in research with young children', *Journal of Early Childhood Research*, vol. 17, no. 4, pp. 26378.

Bird, J & Edwards, S 2015, 'Children learning to use technologies through play: a digital play framework', *British Journal of Educational Technology*, vol. 46, no. 6, p. 149.

Blum-Ross, A & Livingstone, S 2018, 'The trouble with 'screen time' rules', in G Mascheroni (ed.), *Digital parenting: the challenges for families in the digital age*, Nordicom, Gothenborg, pp. 179–87.

Commonsense Media 2013, *Zero to eight: children's media use in America 2013*, Commonsense Media, San Francisco. Retrieved from https://www.commonsensemedia.org/research/zero-to-eight-childrens-media-use-in-america-2013

Department of Education, Employment and Workplace Relations (DEEWR) 2009, *Belonging, being and becoming: the early years learning framework for Australia*, Commonwealth of Australia, Canberra. Retrieved from https://docs.education.gov.au/node/2632

Donohoe, C 2015, *Technology and digital media in the early years: tools for teaching and learning*, Routledge, New York.

Edwards, S, Henderson, M, Gronn, D, Scott, A & Mirkhil, M 2017, 'Digital disconnect or digital difference? A socio-ecological perspective on young children's technology use in the home and the early childhood centre', *Technology, Pedagogy and Education*, vol. 26, no. 1, pp. 1–17, doi:10.1080/1475939X.2016.1152291.

Fleer, M 2017, 'Digital pedagogy: how teachers support digital play in the early years', in L Arnott (ed.), *Digital technologies and learning in the early years*, Sage, London, pp. 114–26.

Fleer, M 2018, 'Digital animation: new conditions for children's development in play-based setting', *British Journal of Educational Technology*, vol. 49, no. 5, pp. 943–58.

Flewitt, R, Messer, D & Kucirkova, N 2015, 'New directions for early literacy in a digital age: the iPad', *Journal of Early Childhood Literacy*, vol. 15, no. 3, pp. 289–310.

Fullan, M & Langworthy, M 2014, *A rich seam: how new pedagogies find deep learning*, Pearson, London.

Harrison, E & McTavish, M 2016, 'iBabies: infants' and toddlers' emergent language and literacy in a digital culture of devices', *Journal of Early Childhood Literacy*, vol. 18, no. 2, pp. 163–88.

Hatzigianni, M, Gregoriadis, A, Karagiorgou, I & Chatzigeorgiadou, S 2018, 'Using tablets in free play. The implementation of the digital play framework in Greece', *British Journal of Educational Technology*, vol. 49, no. 5, pp. 928–42.

Hatzigianni, M & Kalaitzidis, I 2018, 'Early childhood educators' attitudes and beliefs around the use of touchscreen technologies by children under three years of age', *British Journal of Educational Technology*, vol. 49, no. 5, pp. 883–95.

Hiniker, A, Radesky, JS, Livingstone, S & Blum-Ross, A 2019, 'May, moving beyond the great screen time debate in the design of technology for children', paper presented at the CHI 2019, Glasgow.

Huber, B, Highfield, K & Kaufman, J 2018, 'Detailing the digital experience: parent reports of children's media use in the home learning environment', *British Journal of Educational Technology*, vol. 49, no. 5, pp. 821–33.

Johnston, K, Highfield, K & Hadley, F 2018, 'Supporting young children as digital citizens: the importance of shared understandings of technology to support integration in play-based learning', *British Journal of Educational Technology*, vol. 49, no. 5, pp. 896–910.

Kalantzis, M & Cope, WW 2012, *New learning: elements of a science of education*, 2nd edn, Cambridge University Press, Melbourne.

Kress, G & Jewitt, C (eds) 2003, *Multimodal literacies*, Peter Lang, New York

Kucirkova, N, Littleton, K & Cremin, T 2017, 'Young children's reading for pleasure with digital books: six key facets of engagement', *Cambridge Journal of Education*, vol. 47, no. 1, pp. 67–84.

Lave, J & Wenger, E 1991, *Situated learning: legitimate peripheral participation*, Cambridge University Press, Cambridge.

Livingstone, S 2011, 'Critical reflections on the benefits of ICT in education', *Oxford Review of Education*, vol. 38, no. 1, pp. 9–24.

Livingstone, S, Mascheroni, G & Staksrud, E 2018, 'European research on children's internet use: assessing the past and anticipating the future', *New Media & Society*, vol. 20, no. 3, pp. 1103–22, doi:10.1177/1461444816685930.

Manches, A & Plowman, L 2017, 'Computing education in children's early years: a call for debate', *British Journal of Educational Technology*, vol. 48, no. 1, pp. 191–201.

Marsh, J 2017, 'Russian dolls and three forms of capital: ecological and sociological perspectives on parents' engagement with young children's tablet use', in C Brunnett, G Merchant, A Simpson & M Walsh (eds), *The case of the iPad*, Springer, Singapore, pp. 31–47.

Marsh, J, Plowman, L, Yamada-Rice, D, Bishop, J, Lahmar, J & Scott, F 2018, 'Play and creativity in young children's use of apps', *British Journal of Educational Technology*, vol. 49, no. 5, pp. 870–82.

Marsh, J, Plowman, L, Yamada-Rice, D, Bishop, J & Scott, F 2016, 'Digital play: a new classification', *Early Years*, vol. 36, no. 3, pp. 242–53, doi:10.1080/09575146.2016.1167675.

Marsh, J, Plowman, L, Yamada-Rice, D, Bishop, JC, Lahmar, J, Scott, F & Davenport, A 2015, *Exploring play and creativity in pre-schoolers' use of apps: final project report*. Retrieved from http://www.techandplay.org/reports/TAP_Final_Report.pdf

Mascheroni, G 2018, 'Datafied childhoods: contextualising datafication in everyday life', *Current Sociology*, doi.org/10.1177/0011392118807534.

Mustola, M, Koivula, M, Turja, L & Laakso, ML 2018, 'Reconsidering passivity and activity in children's digital play', *New Media & Society*, vol. 20, no. 1, pp. 237–54.

New London Group 1996, 'A pedagogy of multiliteracies', *Harvard Educational Review*, vol. 60, no. 1, pp. 66–92.

Neumann, MM & Neumann, DL 2015, 'The use of touch-screen tablets at home and pre-school to foster emergent literacy', *Journal of Early Childhood Literacy*, vol. 17, no. 2, pp. 203–20.

Palaiologou, I 2016a, 'Teachers' dispositions towards the role of digital devices in play-based pedagogy in early childhood education', *Early Years: An international journal of Research and Development*, vol. 36, no. 3, pp. 305–21.

Palaiologou, I 2016b, 'Children under five and digital technologies: implications for early years pedagogy', *European Early Childhood Education Research Journal*, vol. 24, no. 1, pp. 5–24.

Plowman, L 2016, 'Rethinking context: digital technologies and children's everyday lives', *Children's Geographies*, vol. 14, no. 2, pp. 190–202, doi:10.1080/14733285.2015.1127326.

Plowman, L & McPake, J 2013, 'Seven myths about young children and technology', *Childhood Education*, vol. 89, no. 1, pp. 27–33, doi:10.1080/00094056.2013.757490.

Plowman, L, McPake, J & Stephen, C 2008, 'Just picking it up? Young children learning with technology at home', *Cambridge Journal of Education*, vol. 38, no. 3, pp. 303–19, doi:10.1080/03057640802287564.

Plowman, L, McPake, J & Stephen, C 2010, 'The technologisation of childhood? Young children and technology in the home', *Children & Society*, vol. 24, no. 1, pp. 63–74, doi:10.1111/j.1099-0860.2008.00180.x.

Plowman, L & Stephen, C 2007, 'Guided Interaction in pre-school settings', *Journal of Computer Assisted Learning*, vol. 23, no. 1, pp. 14–26.

Plowman, L & Stephen, C 2005, 'Children, play, and computers in pre-school education', *British Journal of Educational Technology*, vol. 36, no. 2, pp. 145–57.

Plowman, L, Stephen, C & McPake, J 2010, 'Growing up with technology: young children learning in a digital world', research report, The University of Stirling, Scotland. Retrieved from https://ewds.strath.ac.uk/Portals/50/Digital%20Families/Christine-Stephen-presentation.pdf

Plowman, L, Stevenson, O, Stephen, C & McPake, J 2012, 'Preschool children's learning with technology at home', *Computers & Education*, vol. 59, no. 1, pp. 30–37, doi:10.1016/j.compedu.2011.11.014.

Rideout, VJ, Foehr, UG & Roberts, DF 2010, *Generation M2: media in the lives of 8 to 18 year olds*, Kaiser Family Foundation: Menlo Park, CA. Retrieved from https://www.kff.org/other/report/generation-m2-media-in-the-lives-of-8-to-18-year-olds/

Salomaa, S & Mertala, P 2019, 'An education-centred approach to digital media education', in I Palaiologou & C Gray (eds), *Early learning in the digital age*, Chapter 11, Sage, London.

Scott, F & Marsh, J 2018, 'Digital literacies in early childhood. Curriculum and pedagogy', in *Oxford Research Encyclopedia of Education*, doi:10.1093/acrefore/9780190264093.013.97.

Sefton-Green, J, Marsh, J, Erstad, O & Flewitt, R 2016, *Establishing a research agenda for the digital literacy practices of young children*, a white paper for COST (Cooperation in Science and Technology), action IS1410, European Union, Brussels. Retrieved from http://digilitey.eu/wp-content/uploads/2015/09/DigiLitEYWP.pdf

Verenikina, V & Kervin, L 2011, 'iPads, digital play and pre-schoolers', *He Kupu*, vol. 2, no. 5, pp. 4–16.

Yelland, NJ 2011, 'Reconceptualising play and learning in the lives of children', *Australasian Journal of Early Childhood*, vol. 34, no. 2, pp. 4–12.

Yelland, NJ 2015, 'Playful explorations and new technologies', in J Moyles (ed.), *The excellence of play*, Open University Press, Milton Keynes, pp. 225–36.

Yelland, NJ 2016, 'Tablet technologies and multimodal learning in the early years', in S Garvis & N Lemon (eds), *Understanding digital technologies and young children*, Routledge, London, pp. 122–38.

Yelland, NJ 2018, 'A pedagogy of multiliteracies: young children and multimodal learning with tablets', *British Journal of Educational Technology*, vol. 49, no. 5, pp. 84758.

Yelland, NJ in press, 'STEM learning ecologies: supporting the transition from preschool to school in productive partnerships', in S Garvis & C Cohrssen (eds), *Embedding STEAM in ECE*, Palgrave, London.

Yelland, NJ & Gilbert, CL 2017, 'Re-imagining play with new technologies', in L Arnott (ed.), *Digital technologies and learning in the early years*, Chapter 3, Sage, London.

Yelland, NJ & Gilbert, CL 2019, 'Digital technologies and literacy contexts for young indigenous children. Global policies and issues', in A Tatnall (ed.), *Encyclopedia of education and information technologies*, Springer, Cham. Retrieved from https://doi.org/10.1007/978-3-319-60013-0

CHAPTER 17

Assessment and documentation for children's learning and development

Bronwyn Reynolds

DOI: https://doi.org/10.37517/978-1-74286-555-3_17
University of Tasmania

LINKS TO NATIONAL QUALITY STANDARD

Quality Area 1: Educational program and practice
- Standard 1.3: Assessment and planning – educators and coordinators take a planned and reflective approach to implementing the program for each child.
- Element 1.3.1: Assessment and planning cycle – each child's learning and development is assessed or evaluated as part of an ongoing cycle of observation, analysing learning, documentation, planning, implementation and reflection.
- Element 1.3.2: Critical reflection – critical reflection on children's learning and development, both as individuals and in groups, drives program planning and implementation.
- Element 1.3.3: Information for families – families are informed about the program and their child's progress.

LINKS TO EARLY YEARS LEARNING FRAMEWORK

Learning Outcomes 1, 2, 3, 4, 5
- Children have a strong sense of identity.
- Children are connected with and contribute to their world.
- Children have a strong sense of wellbeing.
- Children are confident and involved learners.
- Children are effective communicators.

Introduction

Strongly acknowledged and understood is the value of high-quality early childhood education and care (ECEC) programs in developing the potential and raising the attainment of infants, toddlers and young children (Arthur et al. 2018; Page & Tayler 2016). As emphasised in The Early Years Learning Framework for Australia (EYLF) (DEEWR 2009) for children from birth to 5 years, and the National Quality Standard (NQS) (ACECQA 2020), this means undertaking effective assessment, rich documentation, collaborating with children and families, critical reflection and constructive planning to achieve the best outcomes for children. This chapter will explore the need to observe, document and reflect on observations to gauge and plan effectively for young children's holistic learning and development as this takes place in authentic contexts. Capturing children's knowledge, skills, attitudes and dispositions, along with their interests and capabilities is central for planning appropriate experiences and to move young children's learning and development forward. The value and importance of working with families, and viewing children as active agents and decision-makers of their learning will be considered alongside this work.

Assessment and documentation

As explained in the EYLF, 'Assessment for children's learning refers to the process of analysing and gathering information as evidence about what children know, can do and understand' (DEEWR 2009, p. 17). By collecting diverse forms of information about each child, greater insights will be gained and, as a result, inform planning for environments and experiences to further support children's learning. The notion of assessment for learning through documentation, interpretation, reflection and planning encapsulates a sound cyclic framework. Documentation is then the nucleus of a continuous and evolving cycle of professional learning. As highlighted by Raban (2011), a critical element is to gain a more profound understanding for why we need to observe, document, interpret and synthesise the various forms of information and how best to link this knowledge to plan effectively for young children's learning.

What is assessment and when does it become documentation?

Assessment is a word that has varied meanings and understandings (Szarkowicz 2006). Smidt (2015) argues also that assessment is a loaded word and what needs to be distinguished is that it is not testing or examining. In early childhood settings, as Drummond (2003) suggests, it refers to the ways that we, as professionals, monitor and attempt to understand children's learning in their daily practices and how this knowledge is demonstrated. Some people, however, are hesitant to embrace the term *assessment* in early childhood, perhaps due to a lack of understanding about what it involves, connotations of it being prescriptive and simply a 'tick the box' exercise. A constructive way to view 'assessment' is to embrace it as an essential element of the planning cycle. We need to ascertain what a child is learning and if the experiences and teaching strategies implemented are making a difference to a child's development (Smidt 2015). Without assessment information concerning children's learning and development their progress will not be determined, and opportunities may not be fully realised.

When observing young children, it is valuable also to record what is happening so that the learning becomes visible (Edwards, Gandini & Foreman 2012). When it is recorded, assessment becomes documentation and for those working in early childhood, with so many time constraints, this may appear problematic. It needs to be acknowledged that a great deal of time and effort can be afforded to documentation, so it ought to be managed with insight to be productive. Furthermore, Szarkowicz (2006) asserts that not all happenings and experiences are recorded, because many informal assessments of children occur as a response to their engagements in everyday activities. The reality is that not all assessment will become documentation, because informal observations occur naturally and continually as educators notice children going about their daily routines and experiences (Carr 2001). This type of assessment, Carr (2001) explains, is important for children's learning, but it is also imperative that some observations are written or recorded, because documentation is visible and available to others to reflect upon. As stated in the NQS (ACECQA 2020) it is essential that children's experiences are captured through documentation for quality practice.

During the past few decades there has been a shift from the term 'observation' to 'documentation' or 'pedagogical documentation' (DEEWR 2009; ACECQA 2020). Fleet et al. (2011) point out that a focus on reflection and interpretation is what differentiates *pedagogical documentation* from *observation*. Arthur et al. (2018, p. 279) suggest that this move is reflective of journeying from the notion that observations need to be 'objective and scientific truth about children towards more open-ended and collaborative forms of documentation'. The evolving nature of supporting children's learning from observation to documentation, and the importance of drawing on all voices including children, families and professionals in recording, sharing and celebrating children's achievements needs to be valued. Knowing why and how to observe, and recognising the usefulness and benefits of different forms of assessment and documentation, is a fundamental competence for both professionals and students. It means being open to change with a mindfulness of always moving children's learning forward.

Principles of quality assessment

To ensure that assessment equates to quality practice, early childhood professionals and students need to think about the following forms of assessment.

Authentic assessment

In early childhood the concept of 'authenticity' is when we strive for an accurate account of the child's capabilities within the context of everyday (Ure & Raban 1996). Nilsen

(2004) adds that assessment needs to be viewed as authentic because observations are best if conducted as infants, toddlers and children engage in everyday activities. It is essential, therefore, that educators conduct assessments as these occur in children's everyday settings and as they go about their daily routines, play episodes and experiences. As Worthen (2008, p. 13) notes, assessments are 'contextual in that they emerge from the child's accomplishments'. We need to show ways to gather rich and meaningful information that depict children's learning in their environments, identify their development and describe their progress (DEEWR 2009).

Unbiased assessment

When educators first begin to observe children, it can be challenging to choose words appropriate to describe the happenings and behaviours. As Szarkowicz (2006) explains, when observing children, we need to consciously endeavour to describe what we see and hear and not what we may feel or think. In other words, we need to strive for professional judgement. 'Unbiased' language means noting what you see and hear, rather than using subjective words and being biased about the behaviour and responses to a situation, although avoidance of judgement cannot be absolute. For example, to support children's sense of 'belonging, being and becoming' (DEEWR 2009, p. 7) when observing and recording children's experiences and behaviours, the words below align well with the EYLF elements:

- Identity – engage, contribute, reflect, display, model.
- Community – notice, care, initiate, connect, participate.
- Wellbeing – smile, sigh, giggle, shout, negotiate, share.
- Learning – focus, explore, match, manipulate, create.
- Communication – pause, repeat, clap, listen, sing, view.

Quality assessment

Ultimately, by using a plethora of observation techniques we are more likely to see the reality of the happenings and to avoid instead seeing what we want to see, including assumptions (Palaiologou 2016). Szarkowicz (2006) argues that skilful observers are mindful of their partialities, which may include their impression of the child. 'Quality assessment' also means noticing and capturing all areas of a child's learning and development (Arthur et al. 2018), and these domains are encapsulated in the EYLF (DEEWR 2009) as the five Learning Outcomes. It means observing and documenting information about children from a holistic lens and a strength-based perspective. With a focus on what children can do, along with their interests, strengths, capabilities and competencies, they are being honoured. Being *competent* with a task does not necessarily mean that further improvement cannot be explored. Educators need to provide opportunities for young children to develop even more complex skills and understandings and document these over time (Szarkowicz 2006).

It is beneficial for children to be observed without interrupting the flow of their engagements. One of the keys to capturing children's ways of knowing and doing is to be quiet and non-intrusive and this respect for children while observing them will more likely seize authentic moments. Flexibility is another feature associated with observations as these can be brief or detailed and certain behaviours or actions can be a single or multiple focus (Szarkowicz 2006).

The rights of the child and families

Educators need to work collaboratively with children, families and other team members to ascertain how best to capture, document and ensure that children's daily ways of going about their work, along with their experiences, views and suggestions, are respected and that consideration is given to their privacy (ECA 2016). Observations must be conducted professionally for they need to be non-threatening and this means openly communicating with children and gaining their assent, if they are able to give it. As stated in the United Nations Convention on the Rights of the Child (UNCRC), Article 12 highlights that if children have the ability to construct their own views then they have the right to voice these in all matters concerning them (UNICEF 2018). We need to ensure that children are not silenced as learners and that they feel empowered with their learning (Smidt 2015). This aligns well with the NQS (ACECQA 2020) and the EYLF (DEEWR 2009) perspective of children being capable and competent. Accordingly, children need to be encouraged to actively participate with matters concerning their learning and development, appropriate to their age and abilities, and this includes assessment and documentation.

With new and engaging technological formats and the ease of sharing information on the internet, we must be mindful of each child's digital footprint for the future (ACECQA 2020). As professionals this means being aware of the challenges regarding technologies, including photography, video recording and the privacy settings on social media, especially in terms of ethics and confidentiality. Many families, for instance, are comfortable for photographs to be taken of their child and included in a personal portfolio. For various reasons, however, they may be reluctant to have their child's image included in public documentation, and so feel uncomfortable about their child being photographed and their image displayed. What is critical is that we must honour their decisions and understand that ethical documentation means asking children and inviting parents to sign a permission form (or not) so that staff know which children can be photographed freely.

There are now secure online environments with EYLF software and platforms, such as Storypark, Kinderloop and EarlyWorks, that ECEC settings are using to interactively stream data to families about their child. These platforms enable educators and families to record and communicate information about a child's learning. This can be achieved through photographs, videos and observations and instant feed-forward can be given to help with future learning pathways and to extend a child's sense of 'belonging, being and becoming'.

Different types of assessment

In gaining an understanding about how to write quality observations, it is necessary to think about the different types and ways that observations might be presented based on the need and situation at a given time. Through regular and varied assessment, a collection of evidence can be gathered to construct a story of the child's learning and development journey. As highlighted in the NQS (ACECQA 2020) observing and understanding children's learning and development is paramount for educators to plan quality programs.

Formative assessment

Absolum (2006) claims that we should think about assessment as being informative and therefore making assessment *for* learning. A distinguishing feature about 'formative' or qualitative assessment is that it is conducted while the children are engaged in their daily routines, play episodes and experiences (Barnes 2012). Carr (2001) explains that formative assessment involves narrative approaches, and that these can provide rich evidence for capturing deep learning to inform planning for children. As educators we can employ a range of formative or qualitative assessments to document children's progress; such as anecdotal, diary and running records, learning stories, work samples, photographic records and video footage. Subsequent information provides examples of some of these observations.

Setting the scene for writing observations

A sound knowledge of how to write quality observations includes knowing how to set the scene (Szarkowicz 2006), and this means consideration for what needs to be written in the observation format. Podmore (2006) maintains that when observations include background details, the information can be viewed over specific time frames and this can be helpful to form a more holistic and complete data collection. She considers that background contexts should be evident for most written observations. In addition, photographs can be collected over time, showing how a child has developed during a certain period. For example, in **Figure 17.1**, a few months earlier Freya was not able to sit up by herself, hold the tambourine with one hand and tap it with the other hand. A photograph of her attempting to hold this instrument previously could have been taken and kept as a record. These two photographs could then be used to compare her progress over time.

Anecdotal records

'Anecdotal' observations tend to be short, focused, descriptive records that depict excerpts of, or episodes of happenings or interactions (Bentzen 2009). They are written in the past tense, brief in detail and only document speech that is central to the record. For these reasons anecdotal records can be convenient, useful and flexible for they are written after the event (Nilsen 2004). Sharing anecdotal conversations and records with families should also be a focus, for this two-way process means that insights can

Figure 17.1   Example of a photographic record

be gained to help make sense of a child's world, their interests and strengths. For example, Freya's mother mentioned how her daughter of 9 months enjoyed different engagements with a beach ball. She commented:

> Yesterday, Freya touched, patted and rolled a rubber spiked beach ball. She giggled the whole time and then turned and looked up at her twin brother, Harvey, to get a response. It was encouraging to watch because they both took turns to giggle at one another.

Narratives and running records

An important aspect when reviewing different types of documentation is to know that the difference between a narrative description and a running record is slight. Bentzen (2009) explains that 'narrative description' requires prior thinking about the time, location, the format and the reason for the observation. He claims that 'running records'

Running record	**Name of child**: Rex **Age**: 4 years, 5 months **Date**: 3.06.19 **Context**: Computer area in preschool room **Child initiated**: ✔ or Adult initiated: **Individual experience**: ✔ Group experience: **Purpose for documenting**: Social interactions **Documented by**: Meme	
Time	**Events**	**Comments**
9.20 am 9.22 am	After asking the educator if he could have a turn, Rex walks over to a computer and sits down on the chair. He manipulates the chair by pulling the seat forward with both hands, so that it fits closer to the monitor. He turns the egg timer over to start his turn. On the screen is a beginning maths number program, with numerals, dots and images. Rex says, smiling, 'Oh good, it's the one with dots and ants'. He moves his left arm and then places his fingers from both hands on the keyboard and with his middle right finger presses a key on the right-hand side. Still looking at the monitor he says, 'Now I'm ready to play my favourite game' (an educational maths program). He then moves his head slightly left to look at the child sitting next to him and he says, 'Hey Zac! Computers are cool!'. Zac replies, 'Yeah'. Rex says, 'Would you like to play this game with me? I like playing with you because you're my friend'. Zac moves his chair close to Rex and looks at him with a smile.	Rex chooses the computer area to play in. He knows from previous experience that when the chair is free, he can have a timed turn at the computer (for 6 minutes). He sees the maths number program which he remembers as his favourite. Rex invites Zac, the child sitting close by, to play it with him. Rex shows awareness and interest in being with others.
Interpretation: *(What does this documentation tell us? Links to the EYLF can be included in the interpretation and/or planning sections.)* Rex seems to enjoy playing with the educational number program on the computer, and says it is his 'favourite'. He communicates with Zac, approaching and asking him to play the 'game' with him. *EYLF Learning Outcome 1: Identity – shows an interest in and engages in shared play with other children;* *EYLF Learning Outcome 4: Confident and involved learners – extends his own interest and is enthusiastic about his learning*		
Planning for the future Provide opportunities for Rex to extend his learning through other maths programs or manipulatives. Also provide opportunities for Rex to explore on his own, to play with Zac, and with others in small groups. *EYLF Learning Outcome 4: Confident and involved learners – uses ICT to investigate and problem-solve*		

Figure 17.2 Example of a running record

tend to be spontaneous, written in the present tense and concerned with the moment, rather than planned. Irrespective, running records and narrative techniques describe in a continuous format and in detail how children interact with others or objects and what they say at a given time. Bentzen (2009) reiterates that the main purpose of a narrative is to record an unbiased and descriptive account of each child's behaviour in sequence and without making any inference and interpretation in the actual record of events (*see* **Figure 17.2**).

Learning stories

Carr (2001) explains that a 'learning story' is a structured narrative that documents a child's progress through storytelling to describe the experience and the learning that occurred. Learning stories can be documented in different ways, including handwritten narratives, examples of children's work, computer generated stories, video footage and digital photographs (Lee, Hatherly & Ramsey 2002). Learning stories can capture as much information as possible, including conversations and interactions, the happenings, the child's reactions and interactions with others and the experience (Carr 2001; Podmore 2006). These types of observations are written in the past tense and focus on tracking children's strengths and interests. As Gould and Pohio (2006) point out, as a form of pedagogical documentation, learning stories are most inclusive as they can foster shared conversations and dialogue.

An appropriate format for a learning story is to include a section for relevant background details; such as the child's name, the recorder and date, along with other contextual information: the story, which is the main body; an interpretation; and areas for future planning. In this way, they are not dissimilar to other observations. They may differ, however, because of a focus on multi-learnings, skills and dispositions; whereas other observations tend to centre on a specific aspect. In more recent times, in Australia, the five Learning Outcomes from the EYLF (in brief: identity, connections and contributions to their world, sense of wellbeing, confident and involved learners and effective communicators) have underpinned learning stories, as seen in the example in **Figure 17.3**.

Assessment as learning

'Assessment *as* learning' in early childhood occurs when young children are active participators and monitors of their learning and development. In this way, children are asked and encouraged to reflect on their learning and the use of strategies to decide what they know and are able to do, and how best they can move forward (Barnes 2012). An educator, for example, may ask a 3-year-old to talk about a sequence of photographs that show them constructing a rocket with cardboard boxes, including the process and the end product. In this way, children can become empowered with their learning and gain a sense of agency.

Summative assessment

Summative assessment, however, is widely known as assessment *of* learning and it seems that there are educators who remain confused about this term. It needs to be highlighted that summative assessments in early childhood are about undertaking checklists, logs and rating scales (Szarkowicz 2006), rather than standardised formal

Assessment and documentation for children's learning and development

Learning story	
Child's name: Harvey **Date**: 3.01.20 **Time**: 9.30–9.33 am	**Place**: Children's playroom **Recorder**: Bonnie

EYLF Learning Outcomes in brief	A story from a grandparent
EYLF LO 1: *Identity*	
EYLF LO 2: *Connections and contributions to the world*	a) Harvey looking at book b) Harvey reading book
EYLF LO 3: *Sense of wellbeing*	
EYLF LO 4: *Confident and involved learners*	Harvey, today when you were crawling around the playroom floor, moving past and looking at different toys, you suddenly stopped when spotting a book that we have been reading together for the past few days, *Never touch a koala*. I have never witnessed you crawl so fast before as you moved over to the book. You sat down with a big smile on your face, turned the book over to the front cover and while making an 'Ah' sound stroked the koala's furry nose. You then proceeded to slowly turn over each page, looking, touching and then stroking the koala's nose.
EYLF LO 5: *Effective communicators*	

Interpretation – short term review *(What learning is going on here?)*

Harvey explored his environment by crawling around the playroom floor looking at different toys.
He showed a sustained interest and enjoyment in the book, *Never touch a koala*, by sitting down, turning over each page of the book with a smile and stroking the furry nose on the koala.

LO 4: ability to resource his learning through connecting with materials.
LO 2: demonstrates a sense of belonging, connectedness and comfort in his environment and demonstrates an empowerment to make choices.

Future planning – pathways and possibilities

Provide opportunities for a variety of books, perhaps the same series, but with different main characters and textures to explore.
Read these books with Harvey, model appropriate interactions relevant to the stories and encourage him to also interact with the books.

EYLF LO 4: uses senses to explore different materials.
EYLF LO 5: children engage in a variety of texts and gain meaning from these texts.

Figure 17.3 Example of a learning story

testing. These types of assessments generally happen after children have performed or been engaged in a specific activity, performance, task, or involved in a sequence of play events (Barnes 2012). In other words, summative assessments take place at the end of a task, experience or time period. Observations do not always need to be recorded in large amounts of detail; for example, a checklist would be appropriate to assess a child's ability to name and match colours and shapes.

Incorporated with other types of observations, summative assessments can be used as a valuable tool to accompany formative assessments and to provide further guidance for quality planning and children's learning and development. The role of summative assessment needs to be acknowledged, because these types of records can help educators gain insights about certain behaviours and abilities. Raban (2011) notes that summative records can also be beneficial in determining any gaps with documentation gathered about a child. By gaining a varied collection of assessments over time professionals can build a better understanding of children's learning, strengths and capabilities.

Interpreting observations and documentation

Documentation is more than undertaking and displaying observations for it involves interpretation. Rather than just making the actions visible, educators also need to be mindful that the *learning* is also visible (Wien, Guyevskey & Berdoussis 2011). This involves analysing the documentation to interpret the children's wonderings, happenings and learning processes. Deeper understandings of interpretations, and collaborations with children, families and other team members can be helpful, too, in gaining different perspectives about what is involved in the actual learning experience. Collectively, the information gathered about children's documented evidence can be used to inform individual and group planning for the future. When interpreting a child's records using the EYLF Learning Outcome as a perspective, it is important to look for each child's range of strengths and interests, for these can be the foundation for programming and extending the children's knowledge, understandings and skills (DEEWR 2009).

Collaborating with families

In the EYLF (DEEWR 2009) the five Learning Outcomes (which are also noted at the beginning of this chapter) have been carefully considered to guide educators. It is critical, therefore, that children's holistic learning and development is respectfully communicated with families and other significant professionals as they, too, collaborate and foster each child's progress. The cliché that families know their children best, needs to be valued, for they see them in cultural and linguistic contexts (Smidt 2015). Enriching children's potential means collaborating with families and recognising and valuing the rich insights afforded to educators about a child's interests, abilities and areas for improvement.

Dewey (Boydon 1988) wrote at length about the significance of learning happening in purposeful, real-life contexts, and after a century we still need to fully realise the many authentic opportunities that exist in the home, school and community (Murdoch & Wilson 2004). As educators, if we espouse Dewey's (1934) notion of authenticity, then it is imperative that we embrace multiple voices in the documentation and sharing of young children's learning. As the proverb states: 'It takes a village to raise a child'. What is important is that families have intimate funds of knowledge of their child's experiences and their generated theories of the world around them (Rinaldi 2006).

RESEARCH HIGHLIGHT

An opportunity to explore families' perceptions about sharing children's learning through pedagogical documentation was explored.

Reynolds and Duff's research (2016) employed an in-depth structured questionnaire. Thirty-seven families were involved with young children aged from 3 to 5 years old. All children attended the same early childhood setting in northern Tasmania. The documentation included hard copy and digital formats of the children's learning with the intent of capturing their voices and explorations.

It was found that the sharing of documentation encouraged family conversations about children's learning and that this created stronger connections between the setting, home and extended family. Another highlight was that families considered their children gained a sense of pride and a positive sense of identity through sharing the documentation with them.

Critical reflection

At different times during teaching and the children's learning and development journey, educators need to reflect on how children have progressed and how they have participated and engaged with more complex experiences and ideas (DEEWR 2009). Contemporary means of documentation (using reflective practice), involve collaborations with children, families and other early childhood team members, who use these reflections to interpret the happenings and to inform planning (Arthur et al. 2018). Furthermore, evidence of critical reflection shows a sense of professionalism and as stated in the EYLF 'ongoing learning and reflective practice' is one of the five principles for high-quality practice (DEEWR 2009, p. 13).

An important understanding is that critical reflection is about supporting educators to move forward with their thinking and actions. It is about a dispositional attitude and a frame of mind that considers multiple perspectives, and reflects on these to gain greater insights. As Schon (1987) explains, critical reflection is a skill and it means professionals seeking and thinking beyond what they already know and understand. In this way, support and encouragement may be needed to think about and apply new questions and enquiries relating to theories, practices and assumptions (Brookfield 1995). Without consciously knowing, practices can become automatic and without engaging in a more profound level of reflection, professional learning may be hindered (Raban et al. 2007). This is a sound reason for educators to engage in rich conversations with more knowledgeable others, targeted professional learning, and reading literature about evolving theories and emerging evidence. Engaging a mentor or critical friend can also be an effective way to challenge one's views and understandings as they can encourage multiple perspectives and ways of thinking to enable further insights (Rouse 2020).

From observation and assessment ... to planning

Ultimately, well-written and recorded observations can provide valuable insights for intentional teaching and constructive planning. 'Children's learning is dynamic, complex and holistic' (DEEWR 2009, p. 9), so when assessing and documenting children's engagements and experiences educators need to foster children's emotional, personal, spiritual, social, cognitive and linguistic ways of knowing and understanding, as these domains are intricately interwoven.

We know that children are spontaneous discoverers who like to explore, question, hypothesise and theorise about different matters (Rinaldi 2006). To capture these moments in narrative formats and to interpret these, helps professionals to support and build on children's knowledge and understandings of the world. Knowing children and understanding their world, helps us to engage in meaningful conversations with them and, in this way, we are better able to scaffold their learning within what Vygotsky terms the 'zone of proximal development' (Vygotsky 1978), and plan effectively. As educators it is paramount to acknowledge that assessment and documentation provides a catalyst to support further planning for children to progress. By gaining a varied collection of assessments, over time, a more in-depth understanding of children's learning and development can be identified, including:

- strengths, capabilities, challenges, interests, attitudes and dispositions
- attachment patterns and relationships
- learning and development progress
- emotional wellbeing and physical health
- planning needs to extend learning
- needs for additional assessment and/or intervention
- how effective the curriculum and planned experiences are for individuals and groups. (Adapted from Harley 2006)

Reviewing and reflecting on programs to ensure high-quality teaching and learning is paramount. Children are inquisitive explorers and researchers and their generated theories constantly change and resultantly their learning and development is extended. Early childhood programs need to adapt to children's often unexpected ways of knowing and understanding and constantly review their short-term goals and long-term plans. This means reflecting on the resources and experiences available to facilitate further learning and to respond to the children's interests, wishes, competencies and capabilities (Raban 2011).

Apparent throughout this chapter is the connectedness of assessment, documentation, interpretation, collaboration, reflection and planning for effective teaching and children's learning and development. This cyclic trajectory, although not static, can provide educators with constructive insights to inform pedagogical decisions (Sharmahd & Peters 2019). In Reggio Emilia centres in Italy, along with in Scandinavia, and now in Australia, pedagogical documentation underlines important links between interpretations and reflections on documentation to plan effectively for children's learning (Arthur et al. 2018). Plans also need to be flexible to encapsulate evolving evaluations and accordingly, changes made based on the interpretation.

Conclusion

ECEC programs are crucial to developing the potential and raising the attainment of children, for they have been found to have both short- and long-term gains (Muijs, Aubry, Harris & Briggs 2004). The best way to provide beneficial ECEC programs for children is to reflect on the critical importance of assessing and documenting young children's learning and development to augment the assessment cycle that includes planning, engaging, documenting, reflecting and assessing (Raban 2011).

RESEARCH INTO PRACTICE

Through observing and documenting young children's experiences and capabilities, along with what is seen and heard we can begin to ask some key questions. These enquiries can be helpful to interpret the photograph in **Figure 17.4**. For example:

- What are the babies doing or interested in? How do I know this or how can I gain more information?
- What experience might the babies have of this encounter? How do I know? How can I find out more information? Who could I consult?
- What prior knowledge do the babies have about this? How do I know?
- What do the babies feel about this experience? How do I know? (Adapted from Smidt 2015, p. 18)

Figure 17.4 Young children in the garden

RESEARCH INTO PRACTICE

While pondering the following questions consider and record how you would plan rich and inclusive experiences and intentional teaching strategies for children.

How might you:

- learn about each child's knowledge, competencies, strengths, ideas, culture, and interests in relation to their learning and development?
- assess and document to gain rich information about each child?
- ensure that conversations and exchanges with children are well considered, so that children may model these rich interactions and engagements?
- reflect on the range of intentional teaching strategies suggested in the EYLF to support children's holistic learning and development?
- ensure that daily routines, transitions, learning experiences and projects support children's holistic learning and development?
- encourage each family to share information about children's experiences and their day-to-day engagements?
- critically reflect on aspects of your program and your teaching that support young children's holistic learning and development?

References

Absolum, M 2006, *Clarity in the classroom: using formative assessment to build learning-focused relationships*. Auckland, New Zealand: Hodder Education.

Australian Children's Education and Care Quality Authority (ACECQA) 2020, *Guide to the national quality framework*, ACECQA, Sydney. Retrieved from https://www.acecqa.gov.au/sites/default/files/2020-01/Guide-to-the-NQF_2.pdf

Arthur, L, Beecher, B, Death, E, Dockett, S & Farmer, S 2018, *Programming and planning in early childhood settings*, 7th edn, Cengage Learning, Melbourne.

Barnes, S 2012, *Provocations on assessment in early childhood education*, PSC National Alliance, NSW Children's Services Central, Department of Education, Employment and Workplace Relations, Sydney.

Bentzen, W 2009, *Seeing young children: a guide to observing and recording behavior*, Delmar Learning, New York.

Boyden, JA (ed.) 1988, *The later works of John Dewey*, vol.13: 1938–1939, Southern Illinois University Press, Carbondale, IL.

Brookfield, SD 1995, *Becoming a critically reflective teacher*, Jossey Bass, San Francisco.

Carr, M 2001, *Assessment in early childhood settings*, Learning stories, Sage, London.

Department of Education, Employment and Workplace Relations (DEEWR) 2009, *Belonging, being and becoming: the early years learning framework for Australia*, Commonwealth of Australia, Canberra. Retrieved from https://docs.education.gov.au/node/2632

Dewey, J 1934, *Art as experience*, Capricorn Books, New York.

Drummond, MJ 2003, *Assessing children's learning*, David Fulton, London.

Early Childhood Australia (ECA) 2016, *Code of ethics*, ECA, Canberra.

Edwards, C, Gandini, L & Foreman, G 2012, *The hundred languages of children: the Reggio Emilia experience in transformation*, Praeger, Santa Barbara.

Fleet, A, Honig, T, Robertson, J, Semann, A & Shepherd, W 2011, *What's pedagogy anyway: using pedagogical documentation to engage with the early years learning framework*, Children's Services Central, Sydney. Retrieved from https://childaustralia.org.au/wp-content/uploads/2017/02/Whats-Pedagogy-Anyway.pdf

Fraser, S, and Gestwicki, C 2011, *Authentic childhood: exploring Reggio Emilia in the classroom*, Nelson Education, New York.

Gould, K & Pohio, L 2006, 'Stories from Aotearoa/New Zealand', in A Fleet, C Patterson & J Robertson (eds), *Insights: behind early childhood pedagogical documentation*, Pademelon, Sydney, pp. 77–86.

Harley, E 2006, 'Assessment in the early years. Birth to 8 years', *Assessment in the Early Years Newsletter*, vol. 1, pp. 1–4, Department of Education, Adelaide.

Lee, W, Hatherly, A & Ramsey, K 2002, 'Using ICT to document children's learning', *Early Childhood Folio 6*, pp. 10–16.

Murdoch, K & Wilson, S 2004, *Learning links: strategic teaching in the learner centred classroom*, Curriculum Corporation, Melbourne.

Muijs, D, Aubrey, C, Harris, A & Briggs, M 2004, 'How do they manage? A review of the research on leadership in early childhood', *Journal of Early Childhood Research*, vol. 2, no. 2, pp. 157–69, doi:10.1177/1476718X04042974.

Nilsen, B 2004, *Week by week. Documenting the development of young children*, Thomson Delmar Learning, Clifton Park, NY.

Page, J & Tayler, C 2016, 'Learning and teaching in the early years', in J Page & C Tayler (eds), *Learning and teaching in the early years*, Cambridge University Press, Melbourne, pp. 5–25.

Palaiologou, I 2016, *Child observation: a guide for students of early childhood*, Learning Matters, London.

Podmore, V 2006, *Observation: origins and approaches to early childhood research and practice*, NZCER Press, Wellington.

Raban, B 2011, *Assessment for learning: documentation and planning for the EYLF*, Teaching Solutions, Melbourne.

Raban, B, Nolan, A, Waniganayake, M, Brown, R, Deans, J & Ure, C 2007, *Building capacity: strategic professional development for early childhood practitioners*, Thomson, Melbourne.

Reynolds, B & Duff, K 2016, 'Families' perceptions of early childhood educators' fostering conversations and connections by sharing children's learning through pedagogical documentation', *Education 3–13*, vol. 44, no. 1, pp. 93–100.

Rinaldi, C 2006, *In dialogue with Reggio Emilia: listening, researching and learning*, New York.

Rouse, E 2020, *Partnerships in the early years: building connections and supporting families*, Oxford University Press, Melbourne.

Schon, D 1987, *Educating the reflective practitioner*, Jossey-Bass, San Francisco.

Sanisi, L & Edgington, M 2015, *Developing high quality observation, assessment and planning in the early years: made to measure*, Routledge, New York.

Sharmahd, N & Peeters, J 2019, 'Critical reflection, identity, interaction: Italian and Belgian experiences in building democracy through pedagogical documentation', in J Formosinjo & J Peeters (eds), *Understanding pedagogic documentation in early childhood education: revealing and reflecting on high quality learning and teaching*, Routledge, London, pp. 52–66.

Smidt, S 2015, *Observing young children: The role of observation and assessment in early childhood settings*, Routledge, New York.

Szarkowicz, D 2006, *Observations and reflections in childhood*, Thomson, Melbourne.

UNICEF 2018, *United Nations convention on the rights of the child*, United Nations, New York. Retrieved from https://www.unicef.org.au/Upload/UNICEF/Media/Our%20work/childfriendlycrc.pdf

Ure, C & Raban 1996, *Assessing young learners: an introduction to methods of assessing new school entrants*, Board of Studies, Melbourne.

Vygotsky, L 1978, *Mind in society: the development of higher psychological processes*, Harvard University Press, Cambridge, MA.

Wien, C, Guyevskey, V & Berdoussis, N 2011, 'Learning to document in Reggio-inspired education', *Early Childhood Research in Practice*, vol. 13, no. 2, pp. 1–12.

Worthen, SC 2008, *Assessment in early childhood education*, Pearson, Upper Saddle River, NJ.

SECTION 4

Children and society: building positive futures

Section 4 enables educators and early childhood professionals to step back and reflect on the larger issues that impact their work. The broader topic of children and society is considered, linking to the National Quality Standard (NQS) Quality Areas. This section considers what the research evidence is telling us, and the implications for daily practice in early childhood education and care (ECEC).

Chapter 18 discusses the ways in which children and families make early years transitions, for example, transitions to and within early childhood settings, school and school-age care, and how these transitions can be supported by educators. Early years transitions have been conceptualised in this chapter as an ongoing process, requiring continuity and change occurring within social and cultural contexts. The issue of how children and families can be supported while making transitions, and how critical collaborative relationships are during transitions is made in the light of evidence-informed practice.

Chapter 19 focuses on research evidence about the importance of families and communities in relation to children's learning. Questions raised in this chapter ask: what has been learned from major longitudinal studies, such as the Australian Institute of Family Studies (AIFS) *Growing up in Australia: longitudinal study of Australian children* study – and what are the implications for early childhood educators and professionals? Evidence-informed understandings about building positive relationships with families and communities are discussed.

Chapter 20 explores the importance of leadership in the early years. This chapter considers evidence in terms of leading practice in early childhood education. Educators will be able to identify different types of leadership; such as pedagogical, ethical or distributive leadership, and will be able to identify their own role within the complex organisational structure of contemporary ECEC settings.

Chapter 21 offers readers with innovative ideas on how to rethink research in ECEC; ways that give rise to new perspectives to contribute to meaning-making. By rethinking research practices in early childhood by (re)turning familiar ideas and approaches, the authors aim to generate new questions, ways of knowing, doing and acting. Questioning familiar topics and unsettling dominant discourses, they put forward the notion of thinking *with*, rather than thinking *about* phenomena and what this could look like in practice.

Chapter 22 completes the book by embracing change in the early childhood sector, and returning to the big picture of ECEC. The author draws on surfing and ocean metaphors, as she argues that similar to the sea, the contexts in which early childhood professionals live and work will not remain still. The policy demands and fragmentation in ECEC, which early childhood teachers and educators may find overwhelming at times, is acknowledged and discussed. On an uplifting note, it is maintained that ECEC professionals can make a positive difference – they can do more than survive during these times of rapid change, and instead they can thrive.

CHAPTER 18

Early years transitions

Sue Dockett and Bob Perry

DOI: https://doi.org/10.37517/978-1-74286-555-3_18
Charles Sturt University and Peridot Education Pty Ltd

LINKS TO NATIONAL QUALITY STANDARD

Quality Area 6: Collaborative partnerships with families and communities
- Standard 6.2: Collaborative partnerships – collaborative partnerships enhance children's inclusion, learning and wellbeing.
- Element 6.2.1: Transitions – continuity of learning and transitions for each child are supported by sharing information and clarifying responsibilities.

LINKS TO EARLY YEARS LEARNING FRAMEWORK

Learning Outcome 2: Children are connected with and contribute to their world
- Children develop a sense of belonging to groups and communities and an understanding of the reciprocal rights and responsibilities necessary for active community participation.

Learning Outcome 3: Children have a strong sense of wellbeing
- Children become strong in their social and emotional wellbeing.

Learning Outcome 4: Children are confident and involved learners
- Children transfer and adapt what they have learned from one context to another.

Introduction

This chapter focuses on the roles of early childhood professionals in supporting children and families making early years transitions. Young children and their families make many transitions, often including the transition to early childhood settings, as well as the transition to school. When they start school, children and families often make further transitions as they navigate school-age care.

This chapter explores the research base underpinning transitions in the early years and considers what is meant by 'effective transitions'. By the end of this chapter, early childhood professionals and students will understand research evidence about the nature of transitions and how transitions have the potential to create challenging and supportive environments, for all involved.

The importance of early years transitions

Both the National Quality Standard (NQS) (ACECQA 2020) and The Early Years Learning Framework for Australia (EYLF) (DEEWR 2009) note the importance of 'transitions in the early years', and the responsibilities of educators to facilitate positive transitions for all. The emphasis underpinning the NQS is about building collaborations that support children's continuity of learning. 'Transition', as outlined in the EYLF, is a broad construct, describing the processes involved as children move between and across early childhood settings and home, as well as from their early childhood settings to school. A similar focus is evident in *My time, our place: framework for school-age care in Australia* (DEEWR 2011), which acknowledges the importance of transitions as children and families move between home, school and school-age care.

As noted in the NQS, the EYLF and in *My time, our place*, children make many transitions during their early years. These can include the transition to early childhood settings, school and school-age care. Children's actions and first-hand reports suggest mixed feelings about such transitions – often feelings of excitement are tinged with a little uncertainty about what exactly will happen and how they will be expected to respond (Balaban 2011; Dockett, Einarsdóttir & Perry 2019; Dockett & Perry 2016a; Lago & Elvstrand 2019). For example, many children anticipate challenges as they make the transition to school. Most children look forward to such challenges and expect that they will have appropriate support to manage these. Some children are overwhelmed by the changes and challenges – but also expect to be able to call on a range of support as they work through these. However, children are not the only ones involved in transitions, and they are also not the only ones to experience changes and challenges, as well as excitement.

There are some consistent themes in recent transitions research that highlight potential implications for children, their families and educators, as well as their strategies for managing change. These themes indicate that children's transition experiences influence their engagement in the new community, as well as their educational outcomes. For example, Australian and international research reports that children's transition to school influences their learning and development, not only as they begin school, but also as they progress through school (Claessens, Duncan & Engel 2009; Magnuson, Ruhm & Waldfogel 2007; Sayers et al. 2012).

RESEARCH HIGHLIGHT

One research theme highlights the importance of children's own perspectives of their transition experiences. Over the past two decades, there has been a noticeable increase in the number of studies engaging with young children to report their own experiences of transition. These studies have used a range of methods to promote the engagement of young children in research, recognising their competence, as well as their rights to share their views on matters that are important for them (Alderson 2012; Clark & Moss 2001; Palmadóttir & Einarsdóttir 2015; Sandberg 2017). As a result, a nuanced discussion of the importance of incorporating children's perspectives, strategies to achieve this, and examination of the purposes and outcomes of considering these, has emerged (e.g. Dockett, Einarsdóttir & Perry 2019).

In some instances, recognition of the importance of positive transitions has underpinned strategies to enhance these experiences for children and families living in disadvantaged circumstances. Examples include specific transition to school programs for children who have English as an Additional Language (EAL); whose families experience life stressors; who may have additional education requirements; or whose early experiences have involved trauma. It is possible that children and families in these circumstances may find the transition to new environments more challenging than others (Rosier & McDonald 2011; Smart et al. 2008). However, it is also possible that sensitive, responsive and collaborative educators can build on the strengths and knowledge all children and families bring with them to promote effective transitions, regardless of the backgrounds of those involved (Dockett 2014; Perry 2014).

While transitions are important times in the lives of all involved, and while much can be done to promote effective transitions (Dockett & Perry 2014a), the outcomes of transition are influenced by the social and cultural contexts in which they occur. Peters (2010, p. 2) notes that 'almost any child is at risk of making a poor or less successful transition if their individual characteristics are incompatible with the features of the environment they encounter'. This is an important finding, as it focuses on the match between environments and suggests that by conceptualising effective transitions it requires us to look beyond individual child characteristics.

Relationships are critical elements of effective transition approaches. Relationships can provide the continuity referenced in the NQS Quality Area 6.2.1: Transitions (ACECQA 2018a). Relationships also contribute to the sense of *belonging* emphasised in the EYLF (DEEWR 2009). Conceptualising transitions in terms of relationships highlights the importance of people and connections. For example, children's relationships with their family, peers and educators will all influence their transition experiences. Parents' relationships with their child, with other family members, other families, as well as educators and the broader communities in which they live, will also influence transition. Educators' relationships with children, families, other educators, education systems or organisations, and the community, also impact what happens in transition. Rimm-Kaufman and Pianta (2000, p. 492) highlighted the importance of relationships in the transition to school when they noted that 'links among child, home, school, peer, and neighborhood factors create a dynamic network of relationships that influence children's transition to school both directly and indirectly'. Further, they emphasised 'how relationships among these contexts change over time', influencing transition outcomes and children's engagement with school. Similar principles apply across other early transitions (Balaban 2011; Coelho et al. 2019; Lago & Elvstrand 2019; van Laere & Boudry 2019).

Defining transition

With 'transition' being recognised as an important time for all involved, it is essential to define the term and the ways in which it is used. The working definition that underpins our research approach comes from the work of Rogoff (2003, p. 150), who describes transitions as times when 'individuals change their role in their community's structure'. This broad definition enables us to consider the many transitions people make throughout their lives; not only in education. When we think of transitions in this broad way, we consider the nature of changes associated with events; such as becoming a teacher, changing jobs, or moving to a different community, as well as educational transitions such as starting early childhood settings, school, school-age care, high school or further education.

Each of these transitions involves changes in identity, agency, role and status (Beach 1999). For example, as children start school, they adopt the role and identity of a school *student*. This role change is marked by the wearing of a school uniform, access to school equipment and resources, as well as the adoption of the language and interaction patterns associated with school. As they start school, children also begin to construct their school identity – including their sense of who they are at school, how they fit in at school, and what is expected of them at school (Broström 2003). At the same time, children experience changes in their sense of agency as they enter a new environment, such as school. In some ways, they expect to be able to exercise agency at school – they feel *bigger* and often equate this with increasing independence (Sirkko, Kyrönlampi & Puroila, 2019). They are also aware of the rules of school and very clear about the significance of transgressing those rules. Children's status also changes as they start school. For example, from being the *biggest* in preschool, children may move to being the *smallest* in the school context (Dockett, Griebel & Perry 2017).

The broad definition of transition as *changing roles in community structure* locates transition within social and cultural contexts. In other words, transition does not occur in a vacuum; nor does it only impact the individual. Rather, transitions are socially situated and impact a range of people across different contexts. This emphasis on context is supported by 'bio-ecological theory' (Bronfenbrenner & Morris 2006), which highlights the interplay of the contexts that constitute the *microsystem* (the immediate environment); the *mesosystem* (connections among and between microsystems); the *exosystem* (indirect environments); *macrosystem* (social and cultural values) and the *chronosystem* (interactions and changes over time). Considering interactions between systems also facilitates focus on the many different people and contexts involved in transitions. It is not only children who experience change as they start preschool or school – families, educational settings and educators also experience change.

Relationships, and changes in relationships, have multiple roles in transition: they can be one of the catalysts for transitions; one of the major supports during transition; and one of the markers of effective transitions. Effective transition practices have, as their base, a commitment to building secure, respectful and reciprocal relationships (Dockett & Perry 2014a). When such relationships exist, all participants regard themselves, and are regarded by others, as valued members of the community.

Horizontal and vertical transitions

Some transitions, such as starting preschool or school for the first time, occur only once. They are conceptualised as *moving up* the educational ladder and, because of this, are referred to as 'vertical transitions'. 'Horizontal transitions' occur on a regular basis, as children move between contexts. These might include the daily transitions from home to early childhood settings and then home again; or from school to school-age care and back home. They could also include transitions from outdoor to indoor environments, or from one classroom context to another. Horizontal transitions signify that individuals are members of more than one community and that such memberships often overlap (Hughes, Greenbough, Yee & Anderson 2010; Lago & Elvstrand 2019; Petriwskyj, Thorpe & Tayler 2005).

Continuity and change

While constructing a preschool or school identity is an important element of early educational transitions, so too is maintaining a home identity. When children start preschool or school, or some other new educational setting, they do not cease to be members of families or other communities. Rather, they are expected to manage moves between different environments and to adjust to the differing demands and contexts of each.

Our definition conceptualises 'transitions' as ongoing processes involving both continuity and change occurring within social and cultural contexts. Transition involves change: if nothing changes, there is no need for transition. Transition also involves some elements of continuity. For example, a child starting school may experience changes as an individual, as well as changes in settings, expectations, curricula and pedagogy. At the same time, they may live in the same house or same area, maintain family connections, attend the same out-of-school events, engage in the same social or cultural communities, or have the same interests as they had before starting school. In summary, there will be some elements of continuity, as well as elements of change that contribute to transition experiences (Dockett & Einarsdóttir 2017).

In many instances, much of this continuity derives from the family context (Pelletier & Brent 2002). However, families also experience both change and continuity as children start preschool or school. This has been highlighted by Griebel and Niesel (2013), who describe parallel changes occurring at the individual, interactional, and contextual levels for both children and families as children start school. They describe how becoming the parent of a school student involves individual changes in role, identity, agency and status for parents; changes in interactions as some relationships are lost and new ones are created with a new group of educators; and changes in contexts as routines and responsibilities shift to integrate family, work and school lives.

It is important to recognise the changes that are associated with educational transitions; such as the transition to early childhood settings or school. Doing so enables us to reflect on the many discontinuities that exist between contexts, and to consider how and why these impact on transitions experiences (Dockett & Einarsdóttir 2017). However, focusing only on the changes or discontinuities can draw us into *deficit views*, which position some children, families and communities in terms of *lack* of knowledge or experience, or *inability* to access specific curricula, pedagogies or resources.

While discontinuities can generate tension, it is also important to reflect on the continuities that exist and to build on these during transition, as these provide the basis for strengths-based approaches. Strengths-based approaches to transition draw on recognition of strengths as a means for promoting positive change. These approaches do not ignore challenges; rather, they emphasise the importance of 'working collaboratively for solutions, instead of dwelling on problems' (Hopps-Wallis, Fenton & Dockett 2016, p. 104). Strengths-based approaches to transition move 'from a focus on what a child brings with them to school, to a focus on what educators and children can achieve: how can we help all children achieve their potentials' (Dockett & Perry 2016b, p. 151).

The timing of transitions

What is the time frame for early years transitions? In some instances, the timing of some elements of transition are defined by age; for example, there is an age (or age range) during which children are required to start school; some preschool programs are designated as 3-year-old preschool or 4-year-old preschool; and school-age care is generally only available for children aged 5–12 years. Children's attendance in a new environment is certainly part of transition, but transition involves much more than the 'first day' experience.

Across our research, we have defined transition as a process that begins when those involved start to think about the transition. For example, when children and/or family members start to think about which early childhood setting or school they will attend, the processes of transition has begun (Dockett & Perry 2007). This may occur well before the actual first day is spent within a new environment.

When does transition end? Again, we utilise a broad definition, noting that transition concludes when all involved (children, families, educators and possibly, others) feel that they *belong* in the new setting. It is hard to put a time limit to this, as different individuals and different contexts influence the time it takes for a sense of belonging to develop.

To help understand this process it is useful to draw on the anthropological research of van Gennep (1960), who described significant life events in terms of 'rites of passage'. In applying this model to early transitions, several researchers have outlined three phases of transition: separation, transition and incorporation (Ackesjö 2013; Garpelin 2014; Peters 2014). This framework starts with 'separation' – where individuals separate from one context. In the early childhood years, this could involve a child separating from (leaving) family day care, before attending preschool, or separating from preschool before attending school. The next phase is entitled 'transition', but is also referred to as a period of 'betwixt and between' (Turner 1969, p. 95). This is particularly noticeable when considering the transition to school, when children leave early childhood settings at the end of a particular year, but do not start school until several weeks (or months) later (Huser, Dockett & Perry 2016). During this time, they are neither a preschooler nor a school student. The final phase of 'incorporation' marks the changed identity of individuals as they feel that they belong in the new environment.

Considering this model of transition has a number of implications for educational settings, including: recognising the importance of leaving a particular community (Ackesjö 2014) and the strategies that are used to support this; knowing that children may be confused as they enter the 'betwixt and between' phase; and understanding that the settings from which children come and the ones they go to, make important contributions to children's transitions.

Defining transition as a time when individuals change their role in a community's structure; recognising the changes in role, status, agency and identity; and acknowledging that the time frame for transitions can vary considerably, all contribute to the conceptualisation of transition as a process, rather than a set of skills.

Transition and readiness

The terms 'transition' and 'readiness' are often conflated, with the result that discussion of transition may focus strongly on the skills and attributes of individual children. For example, there is much attention directed towards perceptions of children's school readiness during the transition to school (Dockett & Perry 2013). This focus on individual child skills and/or knowledge continues to attract research interest, even though there are broad definitions of readiness that acknowledge the influences of family, school and community contexts on children's readiness (Ackerman & Barnett 2005; Dockett & Perry 2009).

Broad definitions of readiness recognise many of the challenges associated with assessing children's skills and knowledge, noting that early assessments may not be strong predictors of later adjustment or achievement (Meisels 1999; Pianta & La Paro 2003). In considering family contexts, broad definitions also acknowledge the family as an educational context and encourage reflection on the ways in which families support children's health and wellbeing as well as their learning. Attention to community elements of readiness addresses the resources and connections available within communities and the ways in which these may be accessed by children, families and educational settings. Ready schools (and other educational contexts) are responsive in their support for children and families, promote collaborative relationships, are committed to providing high-quality educational environments, and support the ongoing professional development of their educators (Dockett 2016).

The skills, knowledge and understandings that children have as they enter new environments will influence their transition experiences – supporting the view that children's readiness is important. However, and in keeping with the bio-ecological theory described previously, focusing on the processes of transition enables us to adopt a broader perspective, and to consider the impact of family, educational setting, and community on transition experiences. In the following section of the chapter, we outline one example of efforts to reframe conversations around readiness and transition to school.

Transition to school: position statement

Cognisant of the differing perspectives around children's readiness and transition, a group of international researchers met in Australia in 2010, with the aims of exploring and synthesising research directions and developing a position statement that could inform research, policy and practice around transition to school. A draft position statement was workshopped with policymakers and early childhood professionals, resulting in a consensus document that re-framed transition to school (Dockett & Perry 2014b). The *Transition to school: position statement* (ETC Research Group 2011, p. 1):

> reconceptualises transition to school in the context of social justice, human rights (including children's rights), educational reform and ethical agendas, and the established impact of transition to school on children's ongoing wellbeing, learning and development.
>
> Transition to school is taken to be a dynamic process of continuity and change as children move into the first year of school. The process of transition occurs over time, beginning well before children start school and extending to the point where children and families feel a sense of belonging at school and when teachers recognise this sense of belonging.

Further, the statement characterises transition to school in terms of:

> *Opportunities* – including those for all involved to support change and continuity; to build relationships; extend their understandings through

interactions and to recognise starting school and school-age care as a significant event in the lives of children and families.

Aspirations – as all look forward to positive engagement with school and positive outcomes, both social and educational; professional partnerships are formed, and communities provide support and resources to promote positive engagement with school.

Expectations – as all enact high expectations for all participants in the transition; multiple participants are recognised and respected for their role in contributing to children's education; and children meet challenges with the support of friends and responsive adults.

Entitlements – as high-quality services are provided for all children and families; families and communities are confident that access and equity are promoted; respect is demonstrated for existing competencies, cultural heritage and histories; and personal and professional regard is afforded to those involved in the transition to school and school-age care.

Transition to school and school-age care

This characterisation of transition to school also underpins a resource developed to support effective transition to school and school-age care (Dockett & Perry 2014a). Based on extensive national consultation, eight effective transitions practices were identified:

- connecting with children
- connecting with families
- connecting with professionals
- connecting with communities
- flexible and responsive transition programs
- recognising strengths
- reflective practice
- building relationships.

RESEARCH HIGHLIGHT

Several examples of practice based on these principles are included in the resource (Dockett & Perry 2014a). Many of these are used by educators across different settings. However, we argue that it is important to reflect on the general practices and consider how these might be relevant in specific contexts, rather than suggesting that any one practice might be universally applicable. With this caveat in mind, it is possible to identify several strategies that have been used across settings, and nominated as effective by those involved (children, families and educators) in those settings.

Connecting with children
- Developing buddy programs, where children can connect with peers as well as with children who have had more experience in the setting
- Engaging in personal communication with the child before they start school. This may involve meeting them in their existing setting (i.e. their early childhood settings), inviting them to visit the new setting, and/or sending them a letter or card introducing the teacher and the setting
- Having conversations with children
- Visiting the school and school-aged care settings. Where these are easily accessible, visits to different parts of the school, or for different events, can help children become familiar with what schools look like, sound like and even smell like.

Some strategies that have been identified as effective across a range of settings include:

Connecting with families
- Examining ways to welcome families to new settings
- Sharing information with families in appropriate and meaningful ways
- Inviting families to visit settings
- Actively listening to families and respecting their knowledge about their children.

Connecting with professionals
- Promoting collaboration among educators and across settings
- Engaging in professional networks
- Supporting professional development opportunities
- Encouraging reciprocal visits among educators.

Connecting with communities
- Engaging regularly in community events
- Inviting community engagement in settings
- Sharing information with communities
- Working with communities to recognise the importance of the transition to school.

Transition programs

Transitions programs across Australia and internationally incorporate several of these strategies, albeit in different ways, to reflect different social and educational contexts. In some instances, transition programs are developed with the aim of *smoothing out* the discontinuities between and across contexts. This might lead to actions; such as sharing information across settings (e.g. 'transition statements' written by educators being shared with school teachers); the incorporation of familiar materials or resources across settings; or building common pedagogical approaches. It might also lead to strategies that serve to *push down* school curriculum and pedagogies into early childhood settings (Moss 2013).

While *smoothing the way* is an admirable aim, it is important to acknowledge that settings differ. The transition across settings will involve recognition of the elements of both continuity and change for all involved. One of the ways educators can support children and families at times of educational transition is to help them develop or strengthen strategies for managing change (Dockett & Einarsdóttir 2017).

There are many activities that can be incorporated into transition programs (Dockett & Perry 2014a). Several of these activities will involve orientation to the new setting. They might include tours of the setting; showing children and families the location of specific facilities; such as toilets, the office, lockers, and the like. Orientation activities are important. However, on their own, they do not constitute transition programs. One of the major changes in approaches to transition over the past few decades has been this recognition, that orientation – while important – is not the same as the building of relationships that underpins transition processes (Dockett & Perry 2001; 2014a).

Conclusion

Our ongoing work with children, families and teachers (Dockett & Perry 2014a) defines transition as a process involving both continuity and change. Transition is more than a set of activities. Transition to preschool is a process of children becoming preschoolers; parents becoming parents of a preschool child; and educators becoming the educators of a particular group of preschoolers, in a particular time and place. Similar processes are involved for children, families and educators during transitions to school and school-age care.

A critical element of these early transitions is the relationships that are formed and maintained to support all involved. Effective transitions are characterised by positive relationships between and among all involved: children, families, educators and communities.

Transitions start long before the first day experience at the new setting. For some children and families, transitions can also extend well into the educational year. While they may make the transition to the new setting as a group, children's individual experiences, expectations and approaches will vary considerably; as will those of their families. Recognising and responding to this variation, rather than assuming that all children have the same experiences, is critical if educators are to develop and implement appropriate strategies to support transition

Early educational transitions can be both an exciting and challenging time for everyone. Strong, positive relationships among all involved – educators, families, children and communities – are the basis for effective transitions. When all feel a sense of belonging and connection within educational settings, all kinds of positive educational outcomes are achievable.

RESEARCH INTO PRACTICE

Think about some of the major transitions you have made in your educational career. How did these transitions influence your role within the community structure, your agency, status and identity? When did you feel that your transition started and concluded? How might reflection on your own educational transitions influence the ways you consider young children's transitions?

Make a list of the things you regard as important for children as they start school. Working through the list, consider whether the elements you have listed relate to *transition* or to *readiness*. What difference does it make to your expectations if you focus on readiness or transition?

Transitions are times of both continuity and change for all involved. What changes occur for families when children make the transition to:

- child care
- preschool
- school
- school-age care?

As an educator, what are your roles and responsibilities towards children and families at these times of transition?

In your professional practice, how might you regard transitions as times of opportunities, aspirations, expectations, and entitlements for children, families, educators and communities? What practices are in place to reflect these?

References

Australian Children's Education and Care Quality Authority (ACECQA) 2020, *Guide to the national quality framework,* ACECQA, Sydney. Retrieved from https://www.acecqa.gov.au/sites/default/files/2020-01/Guide-to-the-NQF_2.pdf

Ackerman, D & Barnett, W 2005, *Prepared for kindergarten: what does readiness mean?* NIEER policy report, The State University of Jersey, Rutgers University, New Brunswick, NJ. Retrieved from http://nieer.org/policy-issue/policy-report-prepared-for-kindergarten-what-does-readiness-mean

Ackesjö, H 2013, 'Children crossing borders: school visits as initial incorporation rites in transition to preschool class', *International Journal of Early Childhood*, vol. 45, no. 3, pp. 387–410.

Ackesjö, H 2014, 'Children's transitions to school in a changing educational landscape: borders, identities and (dis-)continuities', *International Journal of Transitions in Childhood*, vol. 7, pp. 3–15. Retrieved from https://extranet.education.unimelb.edu.au/LED/tec/pdf/journal7_2014/international_journal_of_transitions_in_childhood_7_2014_Ackesjo.pdf

Alderson, P 2012, 'Right-respecting research: a commentary on "The right to be properly researched: research with children in a messy, real world"', *Children's Geographies*, vol. 10, no. 2, pp. 233–39.

Balaban, N 2011, 'Transition to group care for infants, toddlers, and families', in DM Laverick & MR Jalongo, MR (eds), *Transitions to early care and education*, Springer, Dordrecht, pp. 7–19.

Beach, K 1999, 'Consequential transitions: a sociocultural expedition beyond transfer in education', *Review of Research in Education*, vol. 24, no. 1, pp. 101–39.

Bronfenbrenner, U & Morris, P 2006, 'The bioecological model of human development', in W Damon & RM Lerner (eds), *Handbook of child psychology, vol.1, Theoretical models of human development*, 6th edn, Wiley, New York, pp. 993–1023.

Broström, S 2003, 'Problems and barriers in children's learning when they transit from kindergarten to kindergarten class in school', *European Early Childhood Education Research Journal Monograph Series*, vol. 11, no. 1, pp. 51–66, doi:10.1080/1350293X.2003.12016705.

Claessens, A, Duncan, G & Engel, M 2009, 'Kindergarten skills and fifth-grade achievement: evidence from the ECLS–K', *Economics of Education Review*, vol. 28, no. 4, pp. 415–27.

Clark, A & Moss, P 2001, *Listening to young children: the mosaic approach*, National Children's Bureau, London.

Coelho, V, Barros, S, Burchinal, MR, Cadima, J, Pessanha, M, Pinto, A, Peixoto, C & Bryant, D 2019, 'Predictors of parent-teacher communication during infant transition to childcare in Portugal', *Early Child Development and Care*, vol. 189, no. 13, pp. 2126–40, doi:10.1080/03004430.2018.1439940.

Department of Education, Employment and Workplace Relations (DEEWR) 2009, *Belonging, being and becoming: the early years learning framework for Australia*, Commonwealth of Australia, Canberra. Retrieved from https://docs.education.gov.au/node/2632

Department of Education, Employment and Workplace Relations (DEEWR) 2011, *My time, our place: framework for school-age care in Australia*, DEEWR, Canberra.

Dockett, S 2014, 'Transition to school: normative or relative?', in B Perry, S Dockett & A Petriwskyj (eds), *Transitions to school – international research, policy and practice*, Springer, Dordrecht, pp. 187–200.

Dockett, S 2016, *Transition to school or readiness for school – what's the difference and why does it matter?*, Research Institute for Professional Practice, Learning and Education, Charles Sturt University, Albury. Retrieved from https://www.aracy.org.au/publications-resources/command/download_file/id/292/filename/ARACY-EYC-webinar-August-2016.pdf

Dockett, S, Einarsdóttir, J & Perry, B (eds) 2019, *Listening to children's advice about starting school and school age care*, Routledge, London.

Dockett, S & Einarsdóttir, J 2017, 'Continuity and change as children start school – the current state of play', in N Ballam, B Perry & A Garpelin (eds), *Pedagogies of educational research. European and Antipodean research*, Springer, Dordrecht, pp. 133–50.

Dockett, S, Griebel, W & Perry, B (eds) 2017, *Families and the transition to school*, Springer, Dordrecht.

Dockett, S & Perry, B (eds) 2001, *Beginning school together: sharing strengths*, Australian Education Consultant Alliance, Canberra.

Dockett, S & Perry, B 2007, *Starting school: perceptions, expectations and experiences*, UNSW Press, Sydney.

Dockett, S & Perry, B 2009, 'Readiness for school: a relational construct', *Australasian Journal of Early Childhood*, vol. 34, no. 1, pp. 20–26.

Dockett, S & Perry, B 2013, 'Trends and tensions: Australian and international research about starting school', *International Journal of Early Years Education*, vol. 21, no. 2–3, pp. 163–77, doi: 10.1080/09669760.2013.832943.

Dockett, S & Perry, B 2014a, *Continuity of learning: a resource to support effective transition to school and school age care*, Australian Government Department of Education, Canberra. Retrieved from https://docs.education.gov.au/system/files/doc/other/pdf_with_bookmarking_-_continuity_of_learning-_30_october_2014_1_0.pdf

Dockett, S & Perry, B 2014b, 'Research to policy: transition to school position statement', in B Perry, S Dockett & A Petriwskyj (eds), *Transitions to school – international research, policy and practice*, Springer, Dordrecht, pp. 277–94.

Dockett, S & Perry, B 2016a, 'Supporting children's transition to school age care', *Australian Education Researcher*, vol. 4, no. 3, pp. 309–26, doi:10.1007/s13384-016-0202-y.

Dockett, S & Perry, B 2016b, 'Imagining children's strengths as they start school', in W Parnell & JM Iorio (eds), *Disrupting early childhood education research: imagining new possibilities*, Routledge, New York, pp. 139–53.

Educational Transitions and Change (ETC) Research Group 2011, *Transition to school: position statement*, Charles Sturt University, Albury. Retrieved from https://arts-ed.csu.edu.au/education/transitions/publications/Position-Statement.pdf

Garpelin, A 2014, 'Transition to school: a rite of passage in life', in B Perry, S Dockett & A Petriwskyj (eds), *Transitions to school – international research, policy and practice*, Springer, Dordrecht, pp. 117–28.

Griebel, W & Niesel, R 2013, 'The development of parents in their first child's transition to primary school', in K Margetts & A Kienig (eds), *International perspectives on transition to school: reconceptualising beliefs, policy and practice*, Routledge, London, pp. 101–10.

Hopps-Wallis, K, Fenton, A & Dockett, S 2016, 'Focusing on strengths as children start school: what does it mean in practice?', *Australasian Journal of Early Childhood*, vol. 41, no. 2, pp. 103–11.

Hughes, M, Greenbough, P, Yee, W & Andrews, J 2010, 'The daily transition between home and school', in K Ecclestone, G Biesta & M Hughes (eds), *Transitions and learning through the lifecourse*, Routledge, London, pp. 16–31.

Huser, C, Dockett, S, Perry, B 2015, 'Transition to school: revisiting the bridge metaphor', *European Early Childhood Education Research Journal*, vol. 24, no. 3, pp. 439–49, doi:10.1080/1350293X.2015.1102414

Lago, L & Elvstrand, H 2019, 'Pupils' everyday transitions in school as a condition for social relations and activities in leisure time centres', *Early Years*, vol. 39, no. 2, pp. 163–74, doi:10.1080/09575246.2017.1371675.

Magnuson, KA, Ruhm, C & Waldfogel, J 2007, 'The persistence of preschool effects: do subsequent classroom experiences matter?', *Early Childhood Research Quarterly*, vol. 22, no. 1, pp. 18–38.

Meisels, SJ 1999, 'Assessing readiness', in RC Pianta & M Cox (eds), *The transition to kindergarten: research, policy, training, and practice*, Paul H Brookes, Baltimore, pp. 39–66.

Moss, P 2013, 'The relationship between early childhood and compulsory education: a proper political question', in P Moss (ed.), *Early childhood and compulsory education: reconceptualising the relationship*, Routledge, London, pp. 2–49.

Palmadóttir, H & Einarsdóttir, J 2015, 'Young children's views of the role of preschool educators', *Early Child Development and Care*, vol. 185, no. 9, pp. 1480–94.

Pelletier, J & Brent, J 2002, 'Parent participation in children's school readiness: the effects of parental self-efficacy, cultural diversity and teacher strategies', *International Journal of Early Childhood*, vol. 34, no. 1, pp. 45–60.

Perry, B 2014, 'Social justice dimensions of starting school', in B Perry, S Dockett & A Petriwskyj (eds), *Transitions to school – international research, policy and practice*, Springer, Dordrecht, pp. 175–86.

Peters, S 2010, *Literature review: transition from early childhood education to school*, Ministry of Education, Auckland. Retrieved from http://www.educationcounts.govt.nz/publications/ECE/98894/Executive_Summary

Peters, S 2014, 'Chasms, bridges and borderlands: a transitions research "across the border" from early childhood education to school in New Zealand', in B Perry, S Dockett & A Petriwskyj (eds), *Transitions to school – international research, policy and practice*, Springer, Dordrecht, pp. 117–28.

Petriwskyj, A, Thorpe, K & Tayler, C 2005, 'Trends in the construction of transition to school in three western regions, 1990–2004', *International Journal of Early Years Education*, vol. 13, no. 1, pp. 55–69.

Pianta, RC & La Paro, KM 2003, 'Improving early school success', *Educational Leadership*, vol. 60, no. 7, pp. 24–29.

Rimm-Kaufman, S & Pianta, R 2000, 'An ecological perspective on the transition to kindergarten: a theoretical framework to guide empirical research', *Journal of Applied Developmental Psychology*, vol. 21, no. 5, pp. 491–511, doi:1016/S0193-3973(00)00051-4.

Rogoff, B 2003, *The cultural nature of human development*, Oxford University Press, Oxford.

Rosier, K & McDonald, M 2011, *Promoting positive education and care transitions for children*, Australian Institute of Family Studies, Melbourne. Retrieved from http://www.aifs.gov.au/cafca/pubs/sheets/rs/rs5.html

Sandberg, G 2017, 'Different children's perspectives on their learning environment', *European Journal of Special Needs Education*, vol. 32, no. 2, pp. 191–203, doi:10.1080/08856257.2016.1216633.

Sayers, M, West, S, Lorains, J, Laidlaw, B, Moore, T & Robinson, R 2012, 'Starting school: a pivotal life transition for children and their families', *Australian Institute of Family Studies*, vol. 90, pp. 45–56.

Sirkko, R, Kyrönlamoi, T & Puroila, AM 2019, 'Children's agency: opportunities and constraints', *International Journal of Early Childhood*, doi:10.1007/s13158-019-00252-5.

Smart, D, Sanson, A, Baxter, B, Edwards, B & Hayes, A 2008, *Home-to-school transitions for financially disadvantaged children: summary report,* The Smith Family and Australian Institute of Family Studies, Sydney. Retrieved from https://www.thesmithfamily.com.au/-/media/files/research/reports/home-school-summary-2008.pdf

Turner, V 1969, *The ritual process: structure and anti-structure*, Routledge & Kegan Paul, London.

van Gennep, A 1960, *The rites of passage,* BV Minika & GL Caffee (trans), Routledge & Kegan Paul, London.

van Laere, K & Boudry, C 2019, *Enabling well-being and participation of children and families living in poverty during transition periods across home, childcare and kindergarten*, case study, Verlag Barbara Budrich GmbH, Ghent, Belgium, doi:10.6092/unibo/amsacta/6222.

CHAPTER 19

Building positive relationships with families and communities

Laura McFarland

DOI: https://doi.org/10.37517/978-1-74286-555-3_19
Charles Sturt University

LINK TO NATIONAL QUALITY STANDARD

Quality Area 6: Collaborative partnerships with families and communities
- Standard 6.1: Supportive relationships with families – respectful relationships with families are developed and maintained and families are supported in their parenting role.

LINKS TO EARLY YEARS LEARNING FRAMEWORK

Learning Outcome 1: Children have a strong sense of identity

Learning Outcome 2: Children are connected with and contribute to their world
- Children develop a sense of belonging to groups and communities and an understanding of the reciprocal rights and responsibilities necessary for active community participation.

Learning Outcome 5: Children are effective communicators

Introduction

Families are children's first teachers and have a major influence on their learning and wellbeing (Beyond Blue 2019). When children begin attending early education or formal schooling, they bring with them a rich history of family, culture and community (Bronfenbrenner & Evans 2000). Educators must embrace this history and work to develop collaborative partnerships with families and communities. The diversity of family and community backgrounds must be respected in order to promote the best outcomes for children and create a sense of belonging (Dockett & Perry 2008). Given the positive impacts of collaborative partnerships with families and communities in the early education setting, it is important to understand the ways in which policies and practices can support these partnerships (Borgonovi & Montt 2012; Daniel 2015).

Different from the concept of parent involvement, 'collaborative partnerships' with families in the early education context involves sharing responsibility between people who work together towards a common goal. Collaborative partnerships are based on mutual trust and respect, where each person is valued and contributes their own views, skills and knowledge (DEEWR 2008). Within collaborative partnerships, communication is open, decisions are made together, and diversity is celebrated (Beyond Blue 2019).

In recent years, Australian early childhood policy has recognised the importance of families and communities in children's early education (Murray, McFarland-Piazza & Harrison 2015). The Early Years Learning Framework for Australia (EYLF) (DEEWR 2009) outlines principles and practice for educators to implement in order to support children's learning and wellbeing. One of the EYLF principles, 'partnerships', emphasises the importance of developing respectful partnerships with families. This principle states that educators should 'create a welcoming environment where all children and families are respected and actively encouraged to collaborate with educators about curriculum decisions to ensure that learning experiences are meaningful', and educators and families should 'communicate freely and respectfully with each other' (DEEWR 2009, p. 12). There is no doubt that early childhood education and care (ECEC) professionals need to have the skills to build positive relationships with families and communities in order to maintain high-quality early education environments (Murray et al. 2015). However, research confirms that ECEC professionals often feel inadequately prepared to understand diverse family dynamics and ways of interacting positively with families (Bennet, Katz & Beneke 2006; McFarland & Lord 2008).

The chapter begins by introducing some of the key theoretical underpinnings of the influence of families and communities on children's outcomes. This chapter will outline what has been learned from a range of research including *Growing up in Australia: the longitudinal study of Australian children* conducted by the Australian Institute of Family Studies (AIFS) (Soloff, Millward, Sanson & LSAC 2003). The implications for the future work of ECEC professionals will be explored based on the research findings. By the end of this chapter ECEC professionals and students will have insights into the role of the ECEC professional in building positive relationships with families and communities and be aware of a range of strategies to support their work in this area.

Theoretical underpinnings

The impact of family and community on children's learning and wellbeing and the importance of forming collaborative relationships with families can be explained through a variety of theoretical lenses. This section will give an overview of three of the most prominent theories in current research on family and community partnerships in schools and early childhood settings. Bronfenbrenner's 'social ecology' model (Bronfenbrenner 1979; 2001; 2005), Epstein's model of 'school, family and community partnerships' (Epstein 1985; 1996; 2011) and Bourdieu's theory of 'social and cultural capital' (Bourdieu 1977) will be discussed in the following sections.

Bronfenbrenner's social ecology model

Bronfenbrenner's social ecology model suggests that each child's individual development is impacted directly and indirectly by the 'enduring environment' in which they live (Bronfenbrenner 1979, p. 2). This enduring environment has been conceptualised to consist of five nested systems of interaction:

1. Microsystem – the settings, interactions and activities in which the child is immediately involved. The microsystem includes a child's family, peers and educators.
2. Mesosystem – relationships between microsystems and/or connections between contexts. The mesosystem involves relationships between different microsystems or connections between contexts.
3. Exosystem – social settings in which the child does not have an active role, but which influence experiences in the immediate context. Examples of the exosystem include a parent's workplace or mass media.
4. Macrosystem – the broad ideological and institutional patterns of the child's culture.
5. Chronosystem – the environmental events and transitions that occur over the child's life course.

All of these systems both influence and are influenced by the individual child. Thus, the child is not a passive recipient of experiences within the systems. Rather, the child is an active participant in constructing these settings.

Bronfenbrenner's social ecology model suggests that children's development is influenced by a broad range of family, school and community factors. As relevant to partnerships with families and communities, research using a social ecology approach suggests that a strong home–school mesosystem is related to a child's learning and success in school and enhanced mental health (Sheridan & Wheeler 2017). Thus, for young children, the early childhood setting and home setting mesosystem is particularly significant to the child's learning and wellbeing. To build this important mesosystem, Bronfenbrenner (1979) suggests that there should be frequent supportive communication between the home and early childhood settings.

Epstein's model of school, family and community partnerships

Epstein's model of school, family and community partnerships locates the child at the centre, surrounded by three spheres of influence: home, school and community (Epstein 1986). This model suggests that increasing the overlap between these three spheres provides a more supportive developmental environment for children. Epstein states, 'When parents, teachers, students, and others view one another as partners in education, a caring community forms around students and begins its work' (Epstein 1995, p. 701). This notion of overlapping spheres of influence is similar to Bronfenbrenner's notion of the home–school mesosystem (Bronfenbrenner 1979).

Epstein (1995) also proposed a model of 'parent involvement' that is relevant to building relationships with families and communities. This model suggests that family involvement in their children's education can be represented in a variety of ways:

- Parenting – where families establish supportive home environments for children as learners.
- Communicating – between home and school about children's learning and wellbeing.
- Volunteering – where families assist in setting/school activities.
- Learning at home – to support educational objectives.
- Decision-making – on educational policies and management.
- Collaborating – with the community, drawing on local resources and services. (Epstein 2011)

Epstein's model of parent involvement emphasises the proactive role of schools in facilitating family involvement and promoting partnerships with families and communities. Epstein's theoretical frameworks continue to form the foundation of current family–school partnership policies and practices (DEEWR 2008; Emerson, Fear, Fox & Saunders 2012).

Bourdieu's theory of social and cultural capital

Bourdieu's theory of cultural and social capital has been used to explain why family involvement and relationships with family and community are important for children's educational and developmental outcomes (Berthelson & Walker 2008). As outlined by Bourdieu (1977), Coleman (1988) and Lareau (1987) (as cited in Yamauchi, Ponte, Ratliffe & Traynor 2017), partnerships between families and the educational setting offer opportunities for families to increase their access to social capital, including resources, support, information and networks. 'Social capital' includes economic resources gained by being a part of social networks (e.g. employment, clubs). Social capital includes non-economic resources; such as knowledge, skills and education, which enable social mobility (Bourdieu 1977).

Social capital is represented by family involvement in the organisational and social aspects of the life of the educational setting (Lareau & Horvat 1999). As families and educators develop relationships, families learn important information about the policies and practices of the educational setting. They also meet other families, who provide information and insight about the expectations of the educational setting (Berthelsen & Walker 2008). Another example of social capital is when families talk with their children about what is happening in the educational setting and monitor children's engagement in the setting. When families show an interest in their children's educational activities, the message that education is important is conveyed (Berthelsen & Walker 2008).

'Cultural capital' can be explained by the nature of direct family involvement in the educational process (Lareau 1987). Bourdieu (1977) argued that inequalities exist in the amounts of cultural capital that individuals either hold or can obtain. A person can acquire more cultural capital through access to relevant resources over time, which increases the likelihood of accessing additional capital. From a social and cultural capital perspective, partnerships that support and link families to resources may decrease family economic and social stressors. As a result, there are opportunities for partnerships between families and educational settings to enhance social equity and support diverse communities (Yamauchi, Ponte, Ratliffe & Traynor 2017). Families with more social and cultural capital are likely to be more involved in the educational setting because these families are more comfortable with the educational system and are more likely to have supportive social networks. This enables them 'to construct their relationships with the school with more comfort and trust' (Lareau & Horvat 1999, p. 44).

Research evidence

Outcomes for children and families

The research evidence has clearly established that collaborative partnerships with families and communities in educational settings have positive outcomes for children and families (Epstein & Sheldon 2006; Mitchell & Furness 2015). In early childhood settings, collaborative partnerships help to support a positive transition to school for children (Mitchell et al. 2015; Peters 2010) and may also be associated with later academic outcomes (Epstein & Sheldon 2006). Research has also found benefits for families as a result of engagement in the educational setting, including increased social support and stress reduction (Benseman 2008). Positive outcomes for families have been found across various types of early childhood settings (e.g. McDonald, O'Byrne & Prichard 2015; Mitchell et al. 2015; Needham & Jackson 2014). Mitchell and Furness (2015, p. 2) suggest that 'such improvements in parents' lives may in turn contribute to child outcomes'.

RESEARCH HIGHLIGHT

There have been recent discoveries in neurobiology indicating that the first 1000 days of life strongly influence a child's ability to learn and relate to others. In fact, research finds that the child's brain develops most rapidly and has the highest plasticity during the last trimester of pregnancy and the first two years of life. The degree and focus of a child's structural brain development during these early years is influenced not only by factors such as stimulation and physical care, but also by the quality of relationships with those who provide comfort, nurture and emotional support (Cusick & Georgieff n.d.).

An understanding of these new discoveries in early brain development can be useful in developing collaborative family–educator partnerships. Although an educator is not expected to be able to change the child's past experience, awareness of the child's early experiences within the family and the potential influence on where the child is now, is important as background knowledge for the educator to build partnerships with families.

Patterns of relationships with families and community

Understanding the patterns of relationships with families and communities in different sociocultural contexts can support the development of partnership strategies that better respond to the diverse needs of families (Borgonovi & Montt 2012). In fact, the Organisation for Economic Co-operation and Development (OECD) identified the need to investigate 'the extent and forms of parental involvement in children's education according to gender, socio-economic and ethnic background' in different sociocultural contexts (Borgonovi & Montt 2012, p. 30). There have been a few large-scale studies in Australia examining patterns of family and community partnerships within educational settings (Berthelsen & Walker 2008; Daniel 2015; Murray, McFarland-Piazza & Harrison 2015; Saulwick-Muller Social Research 2006; Walker & Berthelsen 2010).

Growing up in Australia: the longitudinal study of Australian children is the first nationally representative study following the development of 10 000 children and young people and their families from all regions of Australia. It is conducted in a partnership between the Department of Social Services (DSS), the AIFS and the Australian Bureau of Statistics (ABS). The study began in 2003 with a representative sample of children from urban and rural areas of all states and territories in Australia. The broad aims of the study are to examine children's health and development over time in relation to the varied social, economic and cultural environments of the families and communities in which they live (Soloff, Millward & Sanson 2003). Data are collected from two cohorts every two years. The first cohort of 5000 children was aged birth to 1 year in 2003–04, and the second cohort of 5000 children was aged 4–5 years in 2003–04.

Murray et al. (2015) analysed the data to examine various aspects of family and community partnerships with early childhood settings compared to the early years of school. The authors firstly examined family involvement with children's early childhood settings and school settings. Factors considered included the different types of parent involvement, as well as family–educator communication strategies, and the extent to which these changed when children move from early childhood settings to school. The study also examined how various aspects of family social and cultural capital (family socio-economic status [SES], language spoken at home, Aboriginal and Torres Strait Islander family background, and family involvement in educational activities at home) related to patterns of parent involvement and family–educator communication for early childhood and school settings (Murray et al. 2015).

Results from Murray et al. (2015) indicated that family involvement was lower in the early years of school compared to the early childhood setting. Specifically, direct family involvement; such as participation in excursions, committees and classroom activities was much more common in early childhood settings compared to schools. Additionally, there was less frequent family–educator communication occurring in schools compared to early childhood settings. Specifically, the frequency of daily informal talks between families and educators decreases significantly as children move from early childhood settings to school settings. Although there is little empirical research comparing these aspects of family–educator relationships in both settings, these findings are consistent with those of Rimm-Kaufman and Pianta (1999; 2005), who found similar patterns in early childhood settings compared to schools.

Although families' direct contact with educators and direct involvement in the educational setting was infrequent in schools, other examples of family engagement; such as talking with other parents and attending other school events, was more frequently reported. It is likely that the nature of family involvement and the strategies used by educators to communicate with families and build partnerships change as children get older due to structural differences in the early childhood settings and schools. It is also a possibility that families may not feel that direct involvement in the educational setting is as necessary in school settings compared to early childhood settings, due to the children being older and more independent (Murray et al. 2015).

Murray et al. (2015) also reported on the various strategies that educators use to promote family involvement. It was found that formal meetings between educators and families were more commonly implemented in school settings, whereas social activities and parent newsletters were more commonly implemented in early childhood settings. There were also some differences in the effectiveness of family–educator communication, as rated by parents. Educators in early childhood settings were rated as more effective on informing parents about the child's progress, helping them to understand the child's development and providing information about services in the community. Alternatively, educators in schools were rated as more effective on advising families about how to extend children's learning at home and providing information about how families can get involved at school. Results reported by Murray et al. (2015) suggest that the effectiveness of particular types of communication strategies differs between early childhood settings and school settings. It remains unclear, however, whether or not the differences in strategies reflect differences in the changing needs of families as children get older, or if improvement is needed to expand the variety of communication strategies used by educators.

Murray et al. (2015) also examined a range of social and cultural capital factors as they relate to family–educator partnerships, such as socio-economic position (SEP), language spoken at home and Indigenous status. In this nationally representative sample, educators in both early childhood settings and in schools reported using fewer strategies to promote parental involvement for families with lower SEP. SEP is the combined measure of parents' education level, income and occupational status. Other research has found that on average, educators have lower expectations for students with low SES and minority status (Auwarter & Aruguete 2008; de Boer, Bosker &

van der Werf 2010; Hinnant, O'Brien & Ghazarian 2009). It is possible that such educators also have lower expectations for families of lower SES and minority status in general, however, further investigation is needed to understand these results. Families with lower SEP were less involved in their child's education in both school and early childhood settings (Murray et al. 2015). Other studies have also found that lower parental education is related to lower parent involvement (Kohl, Lengua & McMahon 2000). One reason for this association may be that parents with low levels of education may feel that they are not as well equipped to be involved in their children's education (Rimm-Kaufman & Pianta 2005). However, another possibility is that educators need to implement more effective strategies to support a diverse range of families to be engaged.

Similar to SEP, families' language spoken at home was also related to parent involvement and parent–educator communication (Murray et al. 2015). In early childhood settings, educators rated families who had English as an Additional Language (EAL) as being less involved; engaged in less frequent informal talks with the educator; and self-reported as less likely to be engaged as a volunteer in the room. These families also gave lower ratings of the educator's effectiveness of communicating information.

In Australia, being of Aboriginal or Torres Strait Islander background has been identified as a cultural capital variable, which can impact relationships between educators and families. Aboriginal and Torres Strait Islander families can be among the most disadvantaged and marginalised in educational settings. Research by Dockett, Mason and Perry (2006), and Grace and Trudgett (2012) suggests that being of Aboriginal or Torres Strait Islander background can act as a barrier in early childhood and school settings. The reasons for this are certainly varied. One possibility is that some non-Indigenous educators and families are unfamiliar with Aboriginal and Torres Strait Islander Peoples and customs. Views of family engagement in educational settings tend to privilege the white middle-class way of doing things. Research suggests that Aboriginal and Torres Strait Islander families may not be as visible in their involvement with their children's education, but may be involved in less visible, but equally important ways, such as home-learning activities (Anderson & Minke 2007; Ewing 2009). Murray et al. (2015) did examine Aboriginal and Torres Strait Islander background as a cultural capital variable, but it was not found to be related to parent involvement or parent–educator communication.

Other studies drawing on the *Growing up in Australia: the longitudinal study of Australian children* data examined patterns of family–school partnerships, the early years of schooling, and the impact of social and cultural capital variables (Daniel 2015). Although there were reductions in home, school and community-based parent involvement as children got older, the majority of families still engaged in family–school partnerships, indicating a relatively high level of family engagement overall.

Similar to the findings of Murray et al. (2015), Daniel (2015) found differences in the experiences of family–school partnership related to family socio-economic and cultural background in the Australian context. Families from lower socio-economic backgrounds experienced less involvement in their child's education in Year 3. However, in Year 1 there were no significant differences in any form of parent involvement.

Berthelsen and Walker's work with the data has also identified that parent engagement in their child's education lessens as children move through the early years of school (Berthelsen & Walker 2008; Walker & Berthelsen 2010). These findings indicate an opportunity for educators to build stronger relationships with families that might help maintain ongoing partnerships (Daniel 2015).

RESEARCH HIGHLIGHT

Connecting to the home environment is an often-overlooked aspect of building relationships with families and communities. However, the quality of the home environment has also been identified as an important part of a family's social capital related to involvement in their child's education (Epstein 1996). Researchers have investigated the importance of the home environment in the first European longitudinal study of the effectiveness of early years education, called the Effective Provision of Pre-School Education (EPPE). Major results of the study indicate that the quality of the home learning environment (HLE) strongly related to children's intellectual and social development (Siraj-Blatchford 2010). High-quality HLEs were reflected in engagement in learning activities, including reading and singing songs with children, playing with letters and numbers, painting and drawing, taking children to libraries, and supporting children to play with friends (Sylva, Melhuish, Sammons, Siraj-Blatchford & Taggart 2004).

This research finds that the quality of the HLE is associated with other social capital factors; such as parental occupation and education level. This suggests that families with more resources may be better equipped to provide educationally engaging environments for their children (Siraj-Blatchford et al. 2002).

In Australia, using the *Growing up in Australia: the longitudinal study of Australian children* data, Murray et al. (2015) found that families who engaged with their children in home learning activities were more involved in their child's early childhood setting and communicated more with educators. These findings from both studies suggest that early childhood educators have a powerful role in collaborating with families in order to meet educational aims.

Strategies to build relationships with families and communities

Before any discussion of specific strategies educators can use to promote collaborative relationships with families and communities, it is important to outline the 'strengths approach' to working with families and communities. The strengths approach is currently advocated as a key factor in collaborative work with families and communities in early childhood settings (Fenton & McFarland 2018; Fenton & McFarland-Piazza

2014). The strengths approach is an ecologically based, solution-focused philosophy for supporting individuals, families, groups, organisations and communities (O'Neil 2005).

Rather than focusing on deficits, the strengths approach recognises the multiple contexts that influence peoples' lives, as well as the resilience, potentials, strengths, interests, abilities, knowledge and capacities of individuals (McCashen 2005). Social justice principles of self-determination, empowerment and transparency form the basis of the strengths approach. Using a strengths approach, change is achieved by *power with* stakeholders rather than *power over* them. Saleebey (1996, p. 297) states that a strengths approach requires 'a different way of looking at individuals, families and communities'. Using the strengths approach when working with families in early childhood settings can encourage collaborative partnerships, whereas deficit approaches, which focus on families' and children's weaknesses, may result in stigma (Dockett et al. 2011). With a strengths approach, families are genuinely believed to be the experts on their children. Given the diversity and complexity of families that early childhood educators are likely to work with, the strengths approach is a useful cross-cultural framework for supporting the formation of collaborative partnerships.

There are a variety of strategies that educators can use to develop and maintain collaborative partnerships with families and communities. Effective communication, whether it be verbal, written or electronic, is at the heart of this process. Educators should be aware of the various communication preferences of families and use a range of communication strategies to suit families' needs (Knopf & Swick 2007). Regular and intentional collaborative communication with families about their child's learning, behaviour, play and interactions enable educators to draw on and benefit from the world views, knowledge, capacities and diversity of families. In turn, families are enabled to gain vital information to support their children's learning and development (DEEWR 2008).

Verbal communication can be used at drop-off and pick-up times, at parent–educator interviews, home visits or phone calls (Knopf & Swick 2008). Written communication can also be used in the form of newsletters, daily journals, letters to families and noticeboards. Additionally, some families may prefer electronic communication; such as email, text messages, social media and digital portfolios. Effective strategies for promoting communication with families require both one-way and two-way communication opportunities (Berger & Riojas-Cortez 2016). It is also important to be aware that there is no one-size-fits-all approach to effective communication between educators and families. Educators must recognise the 'cultural and social diversity of families and communities' (Saulwick-Muller Social Research 2006, p. 1). What matters most is that families feel welcomed in the environment, are respected, see themselves as part of the learning community and feel included and empowered in their child's experience (Stonehouse 2012).

RESEARCH HIGHLIGHT

In a recent analysis of findings from studies examining relationships with families and communities in early childhood settings, Mitchell and Furness (2015) identified six key principles for productive collaborations, particularly in communities experiencing disadvantage:

1. Hold a strengths-based view of children, families and communities – deficit positioning works against collaboration. Respectful relationships need to be at the heart of interactions with family and community members.
2. Work with an ecological understanding of the child in the context of their family and community. Engage with families and their wider community to understand aspirations and aims for children, draw on cultural knowledge and expertise, and work together to design solutions.
3. Develop services that are culturally congruent with those of family and community members. Connect families through intergenerational links.
4. Provide opportunities for families to say what desirable outcomes for their children would look like to them.
5. Enable equitable opportunities for engagement – this means communicating in ways and at times that suit family and community members. We know that collaboration involves active participation and partnership towards shared goals.
6. Offer professionals facilitating conditions to support collaboration – for example, access to external researchers/advisers to offer tools for self-review, to help critical reflection, to evaluate outcomes. (Mitchell & Furness 2015, p. 11)

Conclusion

Building and maintaining collaborative partnerships with families and communities is certainly challenging work. However, given the range of benefits of such partnerships, it is well worth the effort (Stonehouse 2012). Guided by the EYLF (DEEWR 2009), educators must go beyond simply reporting on children's learning and asking families to be involved in the setting to develop rich and complex collaborations to support children's development and wellbeing. Stonehouse (2012, p. 1) states that:

> Partnerships and collaboration are created and strengthened during quick and unconscious daily interactions and communications, as well as in practices that are grounded in thoughtful statements of philosophy and enacted through carefully considered policies and procedures. Real collaboration with families arises not from specific activities or strategies, but rather from a pervasive attitude and perspective that educators bring to every aspect of service operation.

It is critical that educators understand the uniqueness of each child's family background and community context in order to develop collaborative partnerships. Strategies to promote communication and family engagement need to be individualised and adapted based on the interests and needs of each family. It is through valuing and respecting the strengths and cultural customs that each family brings to their child's education, that true collaboration will be built. Most families, regardless of background or circumstance, want the best for their child. Educators searching to connect with this desire will be most successful.

RESEARCH INTO PRACTICE

Certainly, most early childhood settings will have policies and philosophies that reflect a strong commitment to building relationships with families and communities. However, it is essential to reflect regularly on how these ideas are enacted and put in place a continuous improvement plan. Educators can use the following reflective questions to think deeply about how they are building collaborative and meaningful partnerships with families and communities (Stonehouse 2012):

- Does the physical environment create a sense of welcome and belonging when families walk in the door?
- In what ways do families see their own culture and community reflected in the environment?
- Am I working to develop relationships with ALL families? How can I adapt my communication strategies to do so?
- In what ways do I communicate acceptance for a range of family practices?
- How am I connecting to the local community as a way of understanding children and families?

References

Anderson, KJ & Minke, KM 2007, 'Parent involvement in education: toward an understanding of parents' decision making', *The Journal of Educational Research*, vol. 100, no. 5, pp. 311–23.

Auwarter, AE & Aruguete, MS 2008, 'Effects of student gender and socioeconomic status on teacher perceptions', *The Journal of Educational Research*, vol. 101, no. 4, pp. 242–46.

Australian Children's Education and Care Quality Authority (ACECQA) 2020, *Guide to the national quality framework*, ACECQA, Sydney. Retrieved from https://www.acecqa.gov.au/sites/default/files/2020-01/Guide-to-the-NQF_2.pdf

Benseman, J 2008, 'Foundation learning and family literacy: the Manukau family literacy programme experience', in J Benseman & A Sutton (eds), *Facing the challenge: foundation learning for adults in Aotearoa New Zealand*, Dunmore, Wellington, pp. 110–21.

Bennett, T, Katz, L & Beneke, S 2006, *Teachers evaluate their training retrospectively*, unpublished manuscript.

Berger, EH & Riojas-Cortez, MR 2016, *Parents as partners in education: families and schools working together*, 9th edn, Merrill, Upper Saddle River, NJ.

Berthelson, D & Walker, S 2008, 'Parents' involvement in their children's education', *Family Matters*, vol. 79, pp. 34–41.

Beyond Blue 2019, *What partnerships look like*, Beyond Blue, Melbourne.

Bourdieu, P 1977, 'Cultural reproduction and social reproduction', in J Karabel & A Halsey (eds), *Power and ideology in education*, Oxford University Press, New York, pp. 487–511.

Borgonovi, F & Montt, G 2012, 'Parental involvement in selected PISA countries and economies', *OECD education working papers*, no. 73, Organisation for Economic Co-operation and Development, Paris.

Bronfenbrenner, U 1979, *The ecology of human development: experiments by nature and design*, Harvard University Press, Cambridge, MA.

Bronfenbrenner, U 2001, 'The bioecological theory of human development', in NJ Smelser & PB Baltes (eds), *International encyclopedia of the social and behavioral sciences*, vol. 10, pp. 6963–70, Elsevier, New York.

Bronfenbrenner, U 2005, 'The developing ecology of human development: paradigm lost or paradigm regained', in U Bronfenbrenner (ed.), *Making human beings human: bioecological perspectives on human development*, Sage, Thousand Oaks, CA, pp. 94–105.

Bronfenbrenner, U & Evans, GW 2000, 'Developmental science in the 21st century: emerging questions, theoretical models, research designs and empirical findings', *Social Development*, vol. 9, no. 1, pp. 115–25, doi:10.1111/1467-9507.00114.

Coleman, JS 1988, 'Social capital in the creation of human capital', *American Journal of Sociology*, vol. 94, pp. s95–120.

Cusick, S & Georgieff, MK n.d., *The first 1000 days of life: the brain's window of opportunity*, UNICEF, Geneva.

Daniel, G 2015, 'Patterns of parent involvement: a longitudinal analysis of family–school partnerships in the early years of school in Australia', *Australasian Journal of Early Childhood*, vol. 40, no. 1, pp. 119–28. Retrieved from https://researchoutput.csu.edu.au/en/publications/patterns-of-parent-involvement-a-longitudinal-analysis-of-family-.

de Boer, H, Bosker, RJ & van der Werf, MPC 2010, 'Sustainability of teacher expectation bias effects on long-term student performance', *Journal of Educational Psychology*, vol. 102, no. 1, pp. 168–79.

Department of Education, Employment and Workforce Relations (DEEWR) 2008, *Family school partnerships framework: a guide for schools and families*, Commonwealth of Australia, Canberra.

Department of Education, Employment and Workplace Relations (DEEWR) 2009, *Belonging, being and becoming: the early years learning framework for Australia*, Commonwealth of Australia, Canberra. Retrieved from https://docs.education.gov.au/node/2632

Dockett, S, Mason, T & Perry, B 2006, 'Successful transition to school for Australian Aboriginal children', *Childhood Education*, vol. 82, no. 3, pp. 139–44.

Dockett, S & Perry, B 2008, 'Starting school: a community endeavour', *Childhood Education*, vol. 85, no. 5, pp. 274–80, doi:10.1080/00094056.2008.10523024.

Dockett, S, Perry, B, Kearney, E, Hampshire, A, Mason, J & Schmied, V 2011, *Facilitating children's transition to school from families with complex support needs,* Research Institute for Professional Practice, Learning and Education, Charles Sturt University, Albury.

Dyson, LL 2001, 'Home–school communication and expectations of recent Chinese immigrants', *Canadian Journal of Education*, vol. 26, no. 4, pp. 455–76.

Emerson, L, Fear, J, Fox, S & Sanders, E 2012, *Parental engagement in learning and schooling: lessons from research,* a report by the Australian Research Alliance for Children and Youth (ARACY), Family–School and Community Partnerships Bureau, Canberra.

Epstein, JL 1986, 'Parents' reactions to teacher practices of parent involvement', *Elementary School Journal*, vol. 86, no. 3, pp. 277–94.

Epstein, JL 1995, 'School/family/community partnerships: caring for the children we share', *Phi Delta Kappan*, vol. 76, no. 9, pp. 703–07.

Epstein, JL 2011, *School, family, and community partnerships: preparing educators and improving schools*, Westview Press. Philadelphia.

Epstein, JL & Dauber, SL 1991, 'School programs and teacher practices of parent involvement in inner-city elementary schools', *The Elementary School Journal*, vol. 9, no. 3, pp. 289–305. Retrieved from http://www.jstor.org/stable/1001715

Epstein, JL & Sheldon, S 2006, 'Moving forward: ideas for research on school, family and community partnerships', in C Conrad & R Serlin (ed.), *The Sage handbook for research in education. Engaging ideas and enriching inquiry,* Sage, Thousand Oaks, CA, pp. 117–37.

Ewing, BF 2009, 'Torres Strait Islander parents' involvement in their children's mathematics learning: a discussion paper', *First Peoples Child & Family Review Journal*, vol. 4, no. 2, pp. 119–24.

Fenton, A & McFarland, L 2018, 'Building early childhood educators' capacity to apply a strengths approach to working with families', *New Zealand International Research in Early Childhood Education Journal*, vol. 21, no. 2, pp. 19–31.

Fenton, A & McFarland-Piazza, L 2014, 'Supporting early childhood pre-service teachers in their work with children, families, and communities with complex needs: a strengths approach', *Journal of Early Childhood Teacher Education*, vol. 35, no. 1, pp. 22–38, doi:10.1080/10901027.2013.874384.

Grace, R & Trudgett, M 2012, 'It's not rocket science: the perspectives of Indigenous early childhood workers on supporting the engagement of Indigenous families in early childhood services', *Australasian Journal of Early Childhood*, vol. 37, no. 2, pp. 10–18.

Hinnant, JB, O'Brien, M & Ghazarian, SR 2009, 'The longitudinal relations of teacher expectations to achievement in the early school years', *Journal of Educational Psychology*, vol. 10, no. 3, pp. 662–70.

Knopf, HT & Swick, KJ 2007, 'How parents feel about their child's teacher/school: implications for early childhood professionals', *Early Childhood Education Journal*, vol. 34, no. 4, pp. 291–96.

Knopf, HT & Swick, KJ 2008, 'Using our understanding of families to strengthen family involvement', *Early Childhood Education Journal*, vol. 35, no. 5, pp. 419–27.

Kohl, GO, Lengua, LJ, McMahon, RJ & the Conduct Problems Prevention Research Group 2000, 'Parent involvement at school: conceptualizing multiple dimensions and their relations with family and demographic risk factors', *Journal of School Psychology*, vol. 38, no. 6, pp. 501–23.

Lareau, A 1987, 'Social-class differences in family–school relationships: the importance of cultural capital', *Sociology of Education*, vol. 60, no. 2, pp. 73–85.

Lareau, A & Horvat, EM 1999, 'Moments of social inclusion and exclusion: race, class, and cultural capital in family school relationships', *Sociology of Education*, vol. 72, no. 1, pp. 37–53.

McCashen, W 2005, *The strengths approach*, St. Luke's Innovative Resources, Bendigo.

McDonald, M, O'Byrne, M & Prichard, P 2015, *Using the family partnership model to engage communities: lessons from Tasmanian Child and Family Centres*, Centre for Community Child Health at the Murdoch Children's Centre and the Royal Children's Hospital, Melbourne.

McFarland, L & Lord, A 2008, 'Bringing professional experience to the rural university classroom: learning and engagement with communities', *Education in Rural Australia*, vol. 18, no. 1, pp. 23–42.

Mitchell, L, Cowie, B, Clarkin-Phillips, J, Davis, K, Glasgow, A, Hatherly, A, Rameka, L, Taylor, L & Taylor, M 2015, *Continuity of early learning: learning progress and outcomes in the early years*, overview report on data findings, Ministry of Education New Zealand, Wellington.

Mitchell, L & Furness, J 2015, *Importance of collaboration among parents, early years professionals and communities: discussion paper for Goodstart*, Goodstart, Brisbane. Retrieved from https://www.goodstart.org.au

Mitchell, L, Meagher-Lundberg, P, Caulcutt, T, Taylor, M, Archard, S, Kara, H & Paki, V 2014, *ECE participation programme evaluation*, delivery of the ECE participation initiatives: stage 2, Ministry of Education, Auckland. Retrieved from http://www.educationcounts.govt.nz/publications/ECE/148513

Murray, E, McFarland-Piazza, L & Harrison, LJ 2015, 'Changing patterns of parent–teacher communication and parent involvement from preschool to school', *Early Child Development and Care*, vol. 185, no. 7, pp. 1031–52, doi:10.1080/03004430.2014.975223.

Needham, M & Jackson, D 2014, 'Stay and play or play and chat; comparing roles and purposes in case studies of English and Australian supported playgroups', *European Early Childhood Education Research Journal*, vol. 20, no. 2, pp. 163–76, doi:10.1080/1350293X.2012.681133.

O'Neil, D 2005, 'How can a strengths approach increase safety in a child protection context?', *Children Australia*, vol. 30, no. 4, pp. 28–32.

Peters, S 2010, *Literature review: transition from early childhood education to school* Ministry of Education, Auckland. Retrieved from https://www.educationcounts.govt.nz/publications/ECE/98894/Executive_Summary

Rimm-Kaufman, SE & Pianta, RC 1999, 'Patterns of family–school contact in preschool and kindergarten', *School Psychology Review*, vol. 28, no. 3, pp. 426–38.

Rimm-Kaufman, SE & Pianta, RC 2005, 'Family–school communication in preschool and kindergarten in the context of a relationship-enhancing intervention', *Early Education and Development*, vol. 16, no. 3, pp. 287–316.

Saleebey, D 1996, 'The strengths perspective in social work practice: extensions and cautions', *Social Work*, vol. 41, no. 3, pp. 296–305.

Saulwick-Muller Social Research 2006, *Family–school partnerships project: a qualitative and quantitative study*, a report prepared for the Department of Education, Science & Training, Australian Council of State School Organisations, Australian Parents Council, Commonwealth of Australia, Canberra.

Sheridan, SM & Wheeler, LA 2017, 'Building strong family–school partnerships: transitioning from basic findings to possible practices', *Family Relations*, vol. 66, no. 4, pp. 670–83.

Siraj-Blatchford, I 2010, 'Learning in the home and at school: how working class children "succeed against the odds"', *British Educational Research Journal*, vol. 36, no. 3, pp. 463–82.

Siraj-Blatchford, I, Sylva, K, Muttock, S, Gilden, R & Bell, D 2002, *Researching effective pedagogy in the early years*, research report RR. 356, Department for Education and Skills, London.

Soloff, C, Millward, C, Sanson, A & LSAC Consortium Advisory Group and Sampling Design Team 2003, *Growing up in Australia: the longitudinal study of Australian children* – discussion paper no. 2, proposed study design and wave 1 data collection, Australian Institute of Family Studies, Canberra. Retrieved from https://growingupinaustralia.gov.au/data-and-documentation/discussion-papers

Stonehouse, A 2012, 'Collaborating with families: not a problem!', *Every Child*, vol. 18, no. 1, pp. 28–29.

Sylva, K, Melhuish, E, Sammons, P, Siraj-Blatchford, I & Taggart, B 2004, *The effective provision of pre-school education (EPPE) project: final report: a longitudinal study funded by the DfES 1997–2004*, Department for Education and Skills, London.

Walker, S & Berthelsen, D 2010, 'Social inequalities and parent involvement in children's education in the early years of school', in V Green & S Cherrington (eds), *Delving into diversity: an international exploration of issues of diversity in education*, Nova Science Publishers, New York, pp. 139–49.

Yamauchi, LA, Ponte, E, Ratliffe, KT & Traynor, K 2017, 'Theoretical and conceptual frameworks used in research on family–school partnerships', *School Community Journal*, vol. 27, no. 29, pp. 9–34.

CHAPTER 20

Leading practice in early childhood education

Jo Bird and Angel Mok

DOI: https://doi.org/10.37517/978-1-74286-555-3_20
University of New England

LINKS TO NATIONAL QUALITY STANDARD

Quality Area 7: Governance and leadership

- Standard 7.2: Leadership – effective leadership builds and promotes a positive organisational culture and professional learning community.
- Element 7.2.1: Continuous improvement – there is an effective self-assessment and quality improvement process in place.
- Element 7.2.2: Educational leadership – the educational leader is supported and leads the development and implementation of the educational program and assessment and planning cycle.
- Element 7.2.3: Development of professionals – educators, coordinators and staff members' performance is regularly evaluated and individual plans are in place to support learning and development.

Introduction

In the early childhood education and care (ECEC) sector, strong leadership has a direct correlation to the quality of the service provided (Davis, Krieg & Smith 2015; Gibbs, Press & Wong 2019, p. 174). The importance of leadership is also signalled in the National Quality Standard (NQS) Standard 7.2: Leadership, putting forward that 'effective leadership builds and promotes a positive organisational culture and professional learning community' (ACECQA 2020, p. 91). ECEC has gone through significant reform over the past decade with changes such as the introduction of the

Early Years Learning Framework for Australia (EYLF) (DEEWR 2009) and the NQS and ongoing changes to educator–child ratios (ACECQA 2019). Other issues such as 'marketisation, accountability and performativity' are also putting pressure on ECEC leaders to ensure their service meets requirements from all stakeholders and regulatory bodies (Ward 2018, p. 1).

The need to understand ECEC leadership is important for qualified educators entering the field and is an ongoing area of professional learning needed for all educators. Considering leadership from different lenses, this chapter has been structured based on Waniganayake, Cheeseman, Fenech, Hadley and Shepherd's (2017) three basic elements of leadership, comprising the 'person, the place and the position' (pp. 13–14). Beginning broadly and then narrowing down to the individual, this chapter is broken into three sections: 'contexts and theories'; 'early childhood leaders'; and 'individual leadership'.

Contexts and theories

Leadership in early childhood

ECEC leadership is socially constructed and is reinforced by the beliefs and values of the community in which it occurs (Hujala, Waniganayake & Rodd 2013). Leadership roles are assigned, and are also the expectation for professional practice of every educator (Denee & Thornton 2018; ECA 2016). ECEC leadership is a professional issue often sparking debate, not only in the various settings and contexts, but also within local communities and stretching to governments who oversee the regulatory requirements (Rodd 2013). Highlighted in the Early Childhood Australia's (ECA 2016) Code of Ethics, advocating for children, families and the ECEC profession is part of every educator's role. Strong leadership supports high-quality service provision (Davis et al. 2015; Gibbs et al. 2019) and plays an important part in promoting ECEC 'as a credible profession with unique expertise that is different from yet equal to other professions' (Rodd 2013, p. 1).

Organisational structures

There are many types of ECEC settings in Australia, including: long day care, preschool (year or two before formal schooling), family day care, outside school hours care, occasional care, multifunction Aboriginal and Torres Strait Islander children's services, mobile children's services and playgroups (Waniganayake et al. 2017). Each of these settings can be viewed as a professional landscape, each made up of multilayered contexts, influenced by government policies, the management or governance structure, the philosophical stance of staff, and the influence of any affiliations the setting may have (McCrea 2015, p. 60). Each type of setting can be organised differently, and so can the way each service meets legislative or quality requirements. Consider a preschool; it might be a one-room service that has two full-time groups. The director might work part-time with children and the other time completing director duties. Another setting might have two groups with a full-time director and two qualified early childhood teachers (ECTs), each responsible for a group. A co-worker may work across the two groups or there might be two separate co-workers. The combination of director, ECTs and co-workers can be quite different even though the setting provides the same educational structure.

Considering the structure of each ECEC setting, individual settings at a minimum would be made up of staff of varying roles and qualifications, with the number being determined by the size of the service and the director. The preschool with one room and a teaching director mentioned here may only have two staff members; the teaching director and an assistant. A service may also contain a management body; for example a local council, an organisation, a church body or a company. The ECEC sector has many for-profit settings and therefore the organisational structure of these settings would also contain owners who fund and may have a say in the operation of the setting. All of these structures influence the running and leading of the setting.

The complexity of early childhood settings

Due to the complexity of organisational structures within ECEC, each leader, and their role can also be very different. It is a 'complex milieu of people, policy and practice' (Gibbs et al. 2019, p. 173). Differences in qualifications, experience, time allocated to leading and perhaps teaching, and the type of service, all result in every leader's job description and role being distinctive. Recognised within the literature, leadership is 'enacted within a complex landscape comprising complicated legislation, a volatile workforce, comprehensive standards of practice and a diversity of children and families' (Gibbs et al. 2019, p. 174).

Part of the issue surrounding the ECEC sector is the lack of understanding of what educators do, often seen as an occupation dominated by women with 'care' the main focus (McGillivray, 2008 as cited in Ward 2018). The attempt to professionalise the sector, through government-driven regulations and the requirement for highly qualified staff, are not matched by pay and conditions as received in other education sectors (Ward 2018). One way to increase the pay and conditions for staff resulting in more educators remaining in the sector, is to increase the government subsidies to ensure qualified educators are delivering high-quality education for young children. Lobbying governments, in the form of activism for the sector, may result in more money for services, but often what occurs is an increase in the fees charged to families resulting in ECEC being elitist, only affordable by those who are wealthy. Access to education and care is every child's right (UN 1989) and all children deserve high-quality settings that meet their needs, led by an experienced and skilled workforce.

Theories of early childhood leadership

To better understand ECEC leaders, examining leadership theory can uncover the various models that have served the sector over the decades. ECEC leadership was based on researchers exploring school and business models, but the ECEC sector has its own unique complexity of issues requiring its own unique theory. In other sectors, leadership is separated from management tasks, whereas in ECEC the two often overlap or are enacted by the same person. Many leaders display several leadership styles as they go about their daily work, with different events and issues requiring styles that suit the specific circumstances. For example, if something occurs of a regulatory nature, a leader may need to take an authoritarian style (Jiang, Chen, Sun & Yang 2017) and direct educators to act in a particular way to ensure the safety and wellbeing of children and staff. Whereas, in regular day-to-day dealings, leaders may enact a distributed leadership style and encourage all educators to take part in leadership of the setting (Heikka, Waniganayake & Hujala 2013).

Intentional leadership

'Intentional leadership' builds on the definition of intentional teaching as defined in the EYLF, where educators are 'deliberate, purposeful and thoughtful in their decisions and actions' (DEEWR 2009, p. 45). Intentional leadership is where leaders display courage in their actions and implement responsibilities in 'positive, purposeful ways with respect, care and compassion' (Waniganayake et al. 2017, p. 6).

Ethical leadership

To be an 'ethical leader' is to focus on supporting the team and to ensure that inclusion, equity and justice remain important foci in ECEC settings. Relationships are often seen as the core of an educator's work, whether that be the relationship with children, families, other staff, management or the local community. Being able to navigate those relationships from a leadership position, requires ethical leadership (Kilderry 2013). Intentional leaders, deliberate in their actions, place 'ethics at the core of their work' (Davis et al. 2015, p. 144). Ethical leadership requires 'taking a stand and explaining the reasons that underpin … decisions, based on a consideration of prevailing community values and beliefs about a particular issue' (Waniganayake et al. 2017, p. 18). Understanding personal morals or ethical beliefs can provide awareness of where professional decision-making can stem from. Understanding personal beliefs and then being aware of others' beliefs can assist in creating an inclusive and respectful working environment where decisions can be made that respect everyone's rights and ensure the best outcomes for those involved.

Distributed leadership

'Distributed leadership' is increasingly seen as an effective style in ECEC (Denee & Thornton 2018) and the benefits include staff satisfaction, effective professional learning and positive learning outcomes for all team members (Leithwood, Mascall & Strauss 2009). Described as relying on building relationships by recognising professional expertise and 'creating a culture of learning' (Heikka et al. 2013, p. 39), this style embraces individuals' strengths and shares the leadership load among the team. Leaders encourage and support educators to take responsibility for leading tasks that they have a specific skill or interest in, developing their overall leadership skills. Even though leadership roles and tasks are distributed within the team, the positional leader still has a responsibility for overseeing the enactment of leadership to ensure the goals of the setting are being achieved and that educators receive the professional learning required to undertake their role or task (Denee & Thornton 2018). Denee and Thornton (2018), along with Nolan and Molla (2018) promote the concept of mentoring and coaching as a way to support and strengthen educators' leading abilities and skills.

Pedagogical leadership

Strong leadership is an indicator of quality in ECEC (Davis et al. 2015; Gibbs et al., 2019, p. 174). When looking at the characteristics of strong leadership, Siraj-Blatchford and Manni (2007, p. 13) found that 'a clear vision, especially with regard to pedagogy and curriculum' was highly important. The vision for a setting often falls on the director to develop and ensure the whole team are working towards the same vision, but with the introduction of the 'educational leader' position within the NQS (ACECQA 2020), leading towards a centre's vision is now shared between several people in positional leadership roles (Waniganayake et al. 2017). 'Pedagogical leadership' is often separate from administration and management roles within ECEC leadership, however Heikka and Waniganayake (2011) state the two need to work in tandem rather than be separate and in isolation. These authors stress the importance of pedagogical leadership in not only improving the outcomes for children's learning, but in increasing the professionalisation of the sector and improving the image held by society about the ECEC sector and its role in building community (Heikka & Waniganayake 2011).

Early childhood leaders

The Australian ECEC workforce consists of 91% women and 85% of the workforce holds an ECEC qualification; being degree (24%), diploma (39%) or certificate (39%), with 41% being in their current position for between 1 and 5 years (The Social Research Centre 2016). Leadership is taught in degree programs to a varying extent and newly graduated educators are often thrust into leadership positions without feeling they have the confidence to enact the role (Sims, Forrest, Semann & Slattery 2015). They often 'lack important professional skills and experience' (Gibbs et al. 2019, p. 176). Leadership, while not defined by the NQS (ACECQA 2020), is embedded in many of the elements that underpin quality practice. Frequent changes in legislation and increasing demands on those destined for a leadership role, exacerbate the complexity educators face (Gibbs et al. 2019).

Who are the early childhood leaders?

Leadership is enacted by those in both formal roles and in everyday practice. It is a socially enabled practice, a 'dynamic activity that can be undertaken by anyone and is not limited to those in formal leadership roles' (Gibbs et al. 2019, p. 174). Practising ECTs are now recognising the importance of leadership, and view leadership roles and responsibilities as key elements in their day-to-day practice and in the provision of quality ECEC programs (Hujala 2013). However, Rodd (2013) noted that some ECTs are reluctant to identify with leadership roles, although these are inherent in their positions and responsibilities. There is limited research looking at the understandings of pre-service teachers (PSTs) as they transition into the field, nor is it understood what knowledge and attributes PSTs believe they need as they make this transition. This challenges the tertiary education sector as they consider active and meaningful ways to involve PSTs in developing understandings, skills and attributes of leadership enactment, relevant to the ECEC sector. Hsue (2013) reported leadership learning occurs within ECEC settings. Leadership is often grouped with management tasks, carried out by those in roles of coordinators or directors, and at times undertaken in autocratic, authoritarian and power assertive styles (Rodd 2013; McCrea 2015). Research now points to more cooperative, democratic and consultative approaches to leadership as being better suited to meeting the needs of the ECEC sector.

Acts of leadership occur at every level within an ECEC setting. Every educator leads a child or group of children and at times, will lead other staff. Formal leadership roles include room leaders, educational leaders, directors, student supervisors and mentors. Some settings may include other leadership roles such as sustainability officer, outdoor learning educator, workplace safety officer and professional learning officer, to name a few.

Room leaders

Usually, each room of an ECEC setting will have one educator who is the room leader, for a group of children. Sometimes this is determined by qualification, other times it is a position applied for. The room leader is responsible for what happens within the room and the supervision of other educators. While the team may take on a distributed style of leadership (Waniganayake et al. 2017), one educator will usually have ultimate responsibility for the room.

Educational leaders

It is a national requirement that all ECEC services have a designated educational leader (ACECQA 2020). Unfortunately, the regulations do not 'stipulate minimum qualifications or the number of hours these educational leaders should work' on educational leader duties (Grarock & Morrissey 2013, p. 11). How settings enact the educational leader role is different in each service, but as stated in the National Quality Framework (NQF), the role of an educational leader is to support the team of educators in 'designing an educational program' that delivers 'optimal learning and developmental outcomes for children' (ACECQA 2020, p. 96).

Director

Leadership is addressed under Quality Area 7 – Governance and leadership in the NQS (ACECQA 2020). Settings require a director, or similar role, to lead the service and ensure the regulations, policies and frameworks are being met. The aim of effective setting leadership is to establish 'shared values for the service that reflect the service context and professionalism and set a clear direction for the service's continuous improvement' (ACECQA 2020, p. 278). Under this standard, the management and leadership tasks are divided and can be enacted by one or more individuals.

Community leadership

The NQS encourages educators to build connections with their local community. Some examples of community engagement include taking children to nursing homes, visits to or by emergency services, visiting local services like the post office, town library and supermarket. Beyond the gate is where settings take their children on excursions into the local community (Elliott & Chancellor 2014). This can be as simple as a picnic in a local park, visiting a supermarket to buy recipe ingredients or more organised excursions like visiting a university or local primary school. These excursions build children's life experience resulting in more knowledge for them to draw on, and thus increasing their understanding of the world (Rogoff 1990). These excursions require leadership by an educator or group of educators. Considerations include ensuring regulatory requirements are met, children's (and staff) safety is maintained, and the excursion is a positive learning experience for all.

Student supervisors and mentors

In order to build and strengthen the ECEC workforce, new ECTs need to be mentored and supported to build their skills, experiences and confidence. This is a professional responsibility of qualified ECEC educators (ECA 2016). All ECEC courses require placements or field experience, and this is where PSTs put into place the theories they have been learning, in the practical experiences of an ECEC setting.

Individual leadership

The unique nature of ECEC leadership means that leadership is distributed among all team members who all implement leadership in one way or another on a daily basis. Being the team member with the highest qualifications, ECTs often have to assume more responsibilities and make decisions regarding policies and practice in the setting, as well as leading and supporting other staff members. This positional leadership is inevitably associated with ECT qualifications and can be a major challenge of their job. Some of the leadership responsibilities and challenges for beginning ECTs, and strategies to prepare them to tackle these challenges are discussed here.

From student to ECT

With their knowledge in children's development and learning, ECEC pedagogy and understanding of multisectoral services, ECEC educators play a pivotal role in young children's development and learning, as well as in building families' knowledge and ability in raising their children when required (Rodd 2013; Aubrey 2011). Leaders should have in-depth knowledge of ECEC and their practices underpinned by up-to-date research (Waniganayake et al. 2017). Applying theories to practice can be challenging, especially at the start of a career when there is perhaps no mentor to provide guidance and support (Hobson, Ashby, Malderez & Tomlinson 2009). In Australia, PSTs have the opportunity to learn about the operation of settings, and apply what they learn at university to various settings. PSTs are supervised and mentored by supervising ECTs with at least the qualification they are aspiring to. In other words, PSTs have opportunities to incrementally apply what they have learned at university to their placements with the guidance of their supervisor. This model of apprenticeship requires the supervisor to work within the PST's current 'zone of proximal development' (Vygotsky 1978). This process takes time, reflection and discussion with more experienced others, and the revelation of how practice should be underpinned by research may also take time.

It is found that beginning ECTs focus on day-to-day survival and experience anxiety about their ability to meet the expectations of the setting (Katz 1997, cited in Pavia et al. 2003). They are accountable to families and the community, which can cause added pressure (Correa Gorospe, Martinez-Arbelaiz & Fernandez-Olaskoaga 2017). As part of a comprehensive literature review, Pillen, Beijaard and den Brok (2013) identified beginning ECTs' professional identity tensions, one of them being the change of role from student to ECT. The transition from student to ECT and often leader, can be challenging, and building a sense of belonging in the workplace is important at this early stage. Correa Gorospe, Martinez-Arbelaiz and Fernandez-Olaskoaga (2017) state building professional identity involves professional engagement that is highly contextualised; the role, responsibilities, setting and people in the setting all contribute to the engagement to the setting (or lack thereof) of a new ECT.

Very few educators enter the profession with an aspiration to be a particular leader (Rodd 2013). Instead, many have stumbled into a leadership role with limited planning (Waniganayake 2013), and many without training (Aubrey 2011). Referring to Collins' (2001) ladder of leadership model, Rodd (2013) discusses how educators are observed as *capable individuals* (level 1), *contributing team member* (level 2) and *competent managers* (level 3), with very few aspiring to be *effective leaders* or *executive leaders* (levels 4 and 5 respectively).

Although ECTs play a leadership role both within and outside settings, they often do not regard themselves as leaders. This could be due to the contradictions and tension between their ideas about leaders and their own experience (McDowall Clark 2012). Mistry and Sood (2012) argue that insufficient training is the primary reason ECTs avoid taking up leadership roles. Whereas Rodd (2013, p. 30) asserts that ECTs are not adequately prepared to lead 'contemporary inclusive, integrated, multidisciplinary, multi-agency early childhood services'. Current ECEC teacher-education programs can raise PSTs' awareness of the relevance of leadership in their future career but they are not able to fully prepare PSTs to take up leadership responsibilities in their future workplace. This reflects the contextual and multifaceted nature of ECEC leadership, an important aspect that education programs need to address.

From ECT to leader

Due to a staffing requirement set by the NQS (ACECQA 2020), service providers must employ a full-time ECT when there are between 25 and 59 children attending the service at any one time. From January 2020, a second 'suitably qualified person' should be employed when enrolments exceed 60 children (ACECQA 2019). The demand for qualified ECTs (and those working towards this qualification) is higher than ever (Future Tracks 2019).

Under these circumstances, being the educator with the highest qualification, ECTs often have to take up leadership roles and responsibilities; such as supporting other educators in curriculum development and supervising PSTs, sometimes before being properly mentored by experienced ECTs in the setting. This is more common in rural and regional areas where settings are often smaller and independent and where networking opportunities are limited (Nolan, Morrissey & Dumenden 2013). For example, one such leadership role is the 'educational leader'. As discussed, the role is primarily to collaborate with educators, to support curriculum development and to implement the cycle of planning and enhancing programs and practice (ACECQA 2020). Although the selection criteria of the educational leader are not prescriptive, this role does require certain skills, knowledge and attributes that beginning ECTs are often still developing. Nevertheless, it is not uncommon for early career ECTs to be appointed to such a role if they demonstrate the capability of doing so.

It is widely acknowledged that formal qualifications of teaching staff in the sector makes a difference in the setting provided to children and their families as well as to leadership decisions (ACECQA 2020; Sylva et al. 2004). Paradoxically, it was found that beginning ECTs abandon the theories they learn at university for practice that they acquire in the workplace, often from their mentor, in order to build a sense of educator identity (Allen 2009). Nolan (2017) also suggests that beginning ECTs often lack confidence in their own beliefs and values, as well as a sense of educator identity.

Identity cannot be built overnight. It is learned and internalised over time, and enacted in ways of doing and thinking, through language, membership, other identification and self-identification (Brubaker & Cooper 2000). Beginning ECTs are encouraged to build networks with other educators through professional networks, such as Early Childhood Australia (ECA). ECTs in rural and regional areas are encouraged to explore online networks to keep in touch with professionals in other parts of the country, with funding opportunities to attend professional learning available from the departments of education in each state. Developing a professional network is not only a good source of support, but a way to build professional identity through the use of shared language, exchanging knowledge and building a sense of belonging.

Building professional capacity

Mentoring

It is predicted that the supply of ECTs will not meet the sector demand, with 33% of all preschool settings without an ECT in 2023 (Future Tracks 2019). Services in rural and regional areas will struggle to employ qualified ECTs due to geographical isolation. Given the demand for qualified ECTs and the high attrition of ECTs (AITSL 2016), strategies to retain beginning ECTs should be further explored. There are complex contextual and personal reasons behind beginning ECTs' decision to leave the profession, but heavy workload and lack of support from supervisors are common reasons (AITSL 2016).

Mentoring is an effective way for novice educators to develop their practice (Hobson et al. 2009), build leadership capacity (Thornton 2015) and enhance outcomes for children (Nolan & Beahan 2013). It is an effective way to provide beginning ECTs with emotional and psychological support and boost their confidence, which has significant implications for retention (Hobson et al. 2009). Mentoring is regarded as a leadership strategy that enhances professional development in ECEC (Rodd 2013; Wong & Waniganayake 2013). Nolan (2017) also suggests that professional development should be supported by strategies such as coaching and mentoring.

RESEARCH HIGHLIGHT

How mentoring can support beginning ECTs and their mentors was explored in the first statewide mentoring program for ECTs between 2011 and 2014, in Victoria (Nolan & Beahan 2013). This program offered mentees targeted support in the delivery of their program and provided an opportunity for experienced ECTs to take on leadership roles in mentoring beginning ECTs. To be a mentor, participants needed to have at least 3 years of experience, to have demonstrated the breadth and depth of knowledge in ECEC, as well as having experience in mentoring. Mentees were beginning ECTs who had less than 3 years of experience working in early childhood settings. Mentors were provided with training; both face-to-face workshops and online forums were used to facilitate communication and interactions between mentors and mentees. The study was framed by a socio-cultural perspective which views knowledge as both socially and culturally constructed.

Both mentors and mentees found the relationships that were developed through this program reciprocal and beneficial to their professional development. Nolan (2017) proposed that developing a mentoring program incorporating respectful, responsive, reciprocal and reflective elements can enhance both mentors' and mentees' professional development and professional identity.

A traditional view of mentoring sees it as a hierarchical relationship, where the experienced mentor passes skills and knowledge to the new person (Murphy & Thornton 2015). A contemporary view reconceptualises the relationship as more equitable and reciprocal, 'based on the development of rapport, mutual trust, respect, and openness to learning'

(Rodd 2013, p. 173). It is also regarded as a professional development opportunity for both mentor and mentee (Hudson 2013). In New Zealand, this relationship is framed as 'educative mentoring' in which mentors and mentees learn with and from each other. It is a process of knowledge co-construction; mentors and mentees construct the meaning of leadership, teaching and learning within their context. While a mentor's knowledge and experience are important in supporting a mentee's understanding of their role, a mentee's knowledge and experience are regarded as equally important in knowledge construction (Education Council of Aotearoa New Zealand 2015; Langdon 2011).

Effective mentoring requires open communication, and a personal connection between mentor and mentee in order to define and cultivate the relationship (Yoon & Larkin 2018; Siraj-Blatchford & Manni 2007). A mentor is different from a supervisor or line manager who has the supervisory role to make sure tasks are completed and objectives are met. A mentor provides guidance and support in a non-threatening environment and engages in reflective dialogue with the mentee as a critical friend (Rodd 2013). A mentor could be someone in the same setting, someone within the community or even online. Ideally, a mentor has the same qualification and responsibilities as the ECT because they would be able to share their experiences. More importantly, a mentor is someone the ECT feels connected with, who shares similar views about children, families and pedagogical approach.

Wong and Waniganayake (2013) stress the importance of *adequate fit* between the dimensions of mentoring; dispositions, skills, knowledge, roles and responsibilities. These ideological similarities are crucial in building and maintaining a relationship, as they form the cornerstone for knowledge construction and building of trust. Conversely, ideological differences mean mentors and mentees will spend most of their time and energy settling their differences. Beginning ECTs are encouraged to seize opportunities to take part in mentoring and professional development programs, and be proactive in establishing relationships with more experienced ECTs. Professional relationships could potentially develop into mentoring scenarios.

Professional learning

Leadership requires flexibility, creativity, vision and courage to bring new ideas to the people and the organisation. Leaders have a vision to lead the team and to provide high-quality outcomes for all children and families (Waniganayake et al. 2017). This requires leaders to embrace new thinking and practice, sometimes different from their own, and a commitment to lifelong learning. Ongoing professional learning is core to being a critically reflective educator and integral to leadership roles in ECEC. As the room leader, educational leader or director, ECTs may be directly offering professional learning to team members or organising relevant, externally sourced professional learning, recognising that professional learning approaches are diverse, with no one right way, but targeted to the context and people involved.

Effective leaders should aim to create a culture of learning within the setting, where educators feel safe to share ideas and are supported to learn from each other

(ACECQA 2020). ECTs should be encouraged to look for professional learning opportunities within and outside the setting and share new learnings with fellow educators. An ongoing cycle of review will support a culture of professional inquiry and improve the quality of the education provided at the service. All these reflect the importance of ongoing professional learning to build educators' capacity to handle the ever-changing demands of ECEC in Australia.

Conclusion

ECEC is a complex sector and its leadership can be a challenging space, especially when enacted by a recently graduated ECT. Understanding different styles of leadership can equip educators of all levels with the skills and knowledge required to inform their practice. Professional learning and strong mentoring programs are two ways that can support educators in their leadership role and improve the quality of ECEC for young children.

Similar to other professions, ECEC has its own challenges but it is also rewarding and meaningful. Being an ECEC professional is a choice and a privilege. PSTs often think they are 'just a teacher' and they choose this profession because they 'like children'. The reality is they are also leaders in the setting and the ECEC sector. The opportunities for educators to make a positive difference to the lives of children and families are there. With its contextual and multifaceted nature, early childhood leadership can be challenging, especially for recently graduated ECTs, but also exciting and creative. Understanding different styles of leadership can equip educators of all levels with the skills and knowledge required to inform their practice. Professional learning and strong mentoring programs are two ways that can support educators in their leadership role and improve the quality of ECEC for young children.

RESEARCH INTO PRACTICE

Reflect on your workplace:
- How is leadership shared in your workplace?
- How would you develop the skills and capacity of team members, leading to improved shared leadership?
- How would you create opportunities for professional learning?
- What are the systems or processes that support continuous improvement and learning?
- What is the knowledge and experience of the team? How do you collect and share this collective knowledge?
- How are resources allocated and targeted to support the quality improvement plan (QIP)?
- How do you capture the voice of children, families and communities on various aspects of your service, and how are you going to include them in your evaluation of the quality of your service?

References

Allen, J 2009, 'Valuing practice over theory: how beginning teachers re-orient their practice in the transition from the university to the workplace', *Teaching and Teacher Education*, vol. 25, no. 5, pp. 647–54, doi:10.1016/j.tate.2008.11.011.

Aubrey, C 2011, *Leading and managing in the early years,* 2nd edn, Sage, Thousand Oaks, CA.

Australian Children's Education and Care Quality Authority (ACECQA) 2020, *Guide to the national quality framework,* ACECQA, Sydney. Retrieved from https://www.acecqa.gov.au/sites/default/files/2020-01/Guide-to-the-NQF_2.pdf

Australian Children's Education and Care Quality Authority (ACECQA) 2019, *Educator to child ratios,* Australian Children's Education and Care Quality Authority, Sydney. Retrieved from https://www.acecqa.gov.au/nqf/educator-to-child-ratios

Australian Insititute of Teaching and School Leadership (AITSL) 2016, *Spotlight: what do we know about early career teacher attrition rate in Australia?,* AITSL, Melbourne. Retrieved from https://www.aitsl.edu.au/docs/default-source/research-evidence/spotlight/spotlight---attrition.pdf?sfvrsn=40d1ed3c_0

Brubaker, R & Cooper, F 2000, 'Beyond "identity"', *Theory and Society*, vol. 29, no. 1, pp. 1–47. Retrieved from www.jstor.org/stable/3108478

Collins, J 2001, *Good to great: why some companies make the leap and others don't*, Harper Collins, New York.

Correa Gorospe, JM, Martínez-Arbelaiz, A & Fernández-Olaskoaga, L 2018, 'Professional identity and engagement among newly qualified teachers in times of uncertainty', *European Early Childhood Education Research Journal*, vol. 26, no. 1, pp. 26–36, doi: 10.1080/1350293X.2018.1412013.

Davis, K, Krieg, S & Smith, K 2015, 'Leading otherwise: using a feminist-poststructuralist and postcolonial lens to create alternative spaces for early childhood educational leaders', *International Journal of Leadership in Education*, vol. 18, no. 2, pp. 131–48, doi: 10.1080/13603124.2014.943296.

Denee, R & Thornton, K 2018, 'Distributed leadership in ECE: perceptions and practices', *Early Years*, vol. 36, no. 1, pp. 1–16, doi:10.1080/09575146.2018.1539702.

Department of Education, Employment and Workplace Relations (DEEWR) 2009, *Belonging, being and becoming: the early years learning framework for Australia*, Commonwealth of Australia, Canberra. Retrieved from https://docs.education.gov.au/node/2632

Early Childhood Australia (ECA) 2016, *Code of ethics,* ECA, Canberra. Retrieved from http://www.earlychildhoodaustralia.org.au/our-publications/eca-code-ethics/

Elliott, S & Chancellor, B 2014, 'From forest preschool to bush kinder: an inspirational approach to preschool provision in Australia', *Australasian Journal of Early Childhood*, vol. 39, no. 4, pp. 45–53.

Future Tracks 2019, *Upskilling in early childhood education: opportunities for the current workforce,* The Front Page, Australia. Retrieved from: https://www.futuretracks.org.au/images/downloads/UpskillReport.pdf

Gibbs, L, Press, F & Wong, S 2019, 'Complexity leadership theory: a framework for leading in Australian early childhood education settings', in P Strehmel, J Heikka, E Hujala, J Rodd, M Waniganayake (eds), *Leadership in early education in times of change*, Verlag Barbara Budrich, Opladen. Retrieved from https://researchers.mq.edu.au/en/publications/complexity-leadership-theory-a-framework-for-leading-in-australia

Grarock, M & Morrissey, AM 2013, 'Teachers' perceptions of their abilities to be educational leaders in Victorian childcare settings', *Australasian Journal of Early Childhood*, vol. 38, no. 2, pp. 4–12.

Heikka, J, Waniganayake, M & Hujala, E 2013, 'Contextualizing distributed leadership within early childhood education: current understandings, research evidence and future challenges', *Educational Management Administration and Leadership*, vol. 41, no. 1, pp. 30–44, doi:10.1177/1741143212462700.

Heikka, J & Waniganayake, M 2011, 'Pedagogical leadership from a distributed perspective within the context of early childhood education', *International Journal of Leadership in Education*, vol. 14, no. 4, pp. 499–512, doi:10.1080/13603124.2011.577909.

Hobson, A, Ashby, P, Malderez, A & Tomlinson, PD 2009, 'Mentoring beginning teachers: what we know and what we don't', *Teaching and Teacher Education*, vol. 25, no. 1, pp. 207–16, doi:10.1016/j.tate.2008.09.001.

Hsue, Y 2013, 'Professional training for beginning directors of early childhood education programs in Taiwan', in E Hujala, M Waniganayake & J Rodd (eds), *Researching leadership in early childhood education,* Tampere University Press, Finland, pp. 113–26.

Hudson, P 2013, 'Mentoring as professional development: "growth for both" mentor and mentee', *Professional Development in Education*, vol. 39, no. 5, pp. 771–83, doi:10.1080/19415257.2012.749415.

Hujala, E 2013, 'Contextually defined leadership', in E Hujala, M Waniganayake & J Rodd (eds), *Researching leadership in early childhood education*, Tampere University Press, Finland, pp. 47–60.

Hujala, E, Waniganayake, M & Rodd, J (eds) 2013, *Researching leadership in early childhood education*, Tampere University Press, Finland.

Jiang, H, Chen, Y, Sun, P & Yang, J 2017, 'The relationship between authoritarian leadership and employees' deviant workplace behaviors: the mediating effects of psychological contract violation and organizational cynicism', *Frontiers in Psychology*, vol. 8, p. 732, doi:10.3389/fpsyg.2017.00732.

Kilderry, A 2013, 'Ethical leadership', *Teacher Learning Network Journal*, vol. 20, no. 2, pp. 14–15.

Langdon, F 2011, 'Shifting perception and practice: New Zealand beginning teacher induction and mentoring as a pathway to expertise', *Professional Development in Education*, vol. 37, no. 2, pp. 241–58, doi:10.1080/19415257.2010.509658.

Leithwood, K, Mascall, B & Strauss, T (eds) 2009, *Distributed leadership according to the evidence*, Routledge, New York.

McCrea, NL 2015, *Leading and managing early childhood settings: inspiring people, places and practices*, Cambridge University Press, Melbourne.

McDowall Clark, R 2012, 'I've never thought of myself as a leader but ...: the early years professional and catelytic leadership', *European Early Childhood Education Research Journal*, vol. 20, no. 3, pp. 391–404, doi: 10.1080/1350293X.2012.704762.

Mistry, M & Sood, K 2012, 'Challenges of early years leadership preparation: a comparison between early and experienced early years practitioners in England', *Management in Education*, vol. 26, no. 1, pp. 28–37, doi:10.1177/0892020611427068.

Murphy, C & Thornton, K 2015, *Mentoring in early childhood education: a compilation of thinking, pedagogy and practice*, NZCER, Wellington.

Nolan, A 2017, 'Effective mentoring for the next generation of early childhood teachers in Victoria, mentoring and tutoring', *Partnership in Learning*, vol. 25, no. 3, pp. 272–90, doi: 10.1080/13611267.2017.1364800.

Nolan, A & Beahan, J 2013, *2013 Statewide mentoring program for early childhood teachers*, report, Department of Education and Training, Melbourne.

Nolan, A, Morrissey, AM & Dumenden, I 2013, 'Expectations of mentoring in a time of change: views of new and professionally isolated early childhood teachers in Victoria, Australia', *Early Years*, vol. 33, no. 2, pp. 161–71, doi:10.1080/09575146.2013.781137.

Nolan, A & Molla, T 2018, 'Teacher professional learning in early childhood education: insights from a mentoring program', *Early Years*, vol. 38, no. 3, pp. 258–70, doi:10.1080/09575146.2016.1259212.

Pavia, L, Nissen, H, Hawkins, C, Monroe, ME & Feilimon-Demyen 2003, 'Mentoring early childhood professionals', *Journal of Research in Childhood Education*, vol. 17, no. 2, pp. 250–60, doi:10.1080/02568540309595014.

Pillen, M, Beijaard, D & deb Brok, P 2013, 'Professional identity tensions of beginning teachers', *Teachers and Teaching*, vol. 19, no. 6, pp. 660–78, doi:10.1080/13540602.2013.827455.

Rodd, J 2013, *Leadership in early childhood. The pathway to professionalism*, 4th edn, Open University Press, Sydney.

Rogoff, B 1990, *Apprenticeship in thinking*, Oxford University Press, New York.

Sims, M, Forrest, R, Semann, A & Slattery, C 2015, 'Conceptions of early childhood leadership: driving new professionalism?', *International Journal of Leadership in Education*, vol. 18, no. 2, pp. 149–66, doi:10.1080/13603124.2014.962101.

Silva, K, Melhuish, E, Sammons, P, Siraj-Blatchford, I & Taggart, B 2004, 'The effective provision of pre-school education (EPPE) project: findings from pre-school to end of key stage 1', *Sure start*, University of London, Institute of Education. Retrieved from https://dera.ioe.ac.uk/18189/2/SSU-SF-2004-01.pdf

Siraj-Blatchford, I & Manni, L 2007, *Effective leadership in the early years sector: the ELEYS study*, Institute of Education, University of London.

Teaching New Zealand 2015, *Guidelines for induction and mentoring and mentor teachers*, Education Council of Aotearoa, Auckland. Retrieved from: https://teachingcouncil.nz/sites/default/files/Guidelines%20for%20Induction%202017_0.pdf

The Social Research Centre 2016, *National early childhood education and care workforce census*, Department of Education, Skills and Employment, Canberra. Retrieved from https://docs.education.gov.au/node/45126

Thornton, K 2015, 'The impact of mentoring on leadership capacity and professional learning', in C Murphy & K Thornton (eds), *Mentoring in early childhood education: a compilation of thinking, pedagogy and practice*, NZCER, Wellington, pp. 1–13.

United Nations (UN) 1989, *The convention on the rights of the child*, UNICEF, New York.

Vygotsky, LS 1978, *Mind in society: the development of higher psychological processes*, Harvard University Press, Cambridge, MA.

Waniganayake, M 2013, 'Leadership careers in early childhood: finding your way through chaos and serendipity into strategic planning', in E Hujala, M Waniganayake & J Rodd (eds), *Researching leadership in early childhood education*, Tampere University Press, Finland, pp. 61–78.

Waniganayake, M, Cheeseman, S, Fenech, M, Hadley, F & Shepherd, W 2017, *Leadership contexts and complexities in early childhood education*, 2nd edn, Oxford University Press, Melbourne.

Ward, U 2018, 'How do early childhood practitioners define professionalism in their interactions with parents?' *European Early Childhood Education Research Journal*, vol. 26, no. 2, pp. 1–11, doi:10.1080/1350293X.2018.1442043.

Wong, D & Waniganayake, M 2013, 'Mentoring as a leadership development strategy in early childhood education', in E Hujala, M Waniganayake & J Rodd (eds), *Researching leadership in early childhood education*, Tampere University Press, Finland, pp. 163–80.

Yoon, HS & Larkin, KA 2018, 'When tensions between ideology and practice become personal: unpacking mentorship in early childhood teacher education', *Journal of Early Childhood Teacher Education*, vol. 39, no. 1, pp. 50–72, doi:10.1080/10901027.2017.1404506.

CHAPTER 21

Rethinking research in early childhood: (re)turning the kaleidoscope

Jeanne Marie Iorio[1] and Will Parnell[2]

DOI: https://doi.org/10.37517/978-1-74286-555-3_21
[1] University of Melbourne
[2] Portland State University

Introduction

A kaleidoscope offers a plethora of possibilities to us as viewers. One turn of the kaleidoscope and we have a wholly new view, with delightful and perhaps perplexing surprises we had not noted before.

Davies (2014) shares a concept of (re)turning – returning questions, ideas, prior thoughts – and she offers us the possibility of actively seeking and re-searching for meaning. For us, (re)turning the kaleidoscope is our metaphoric effort to sense-making and a way to enact meaning-making. With each turning and (re)turning of the kaleidoscope, the movements of small objects inside – beads, small pieces of glass, tiny rocks – are disrupted. But with each disruption, something new emerges – possibly more complex – a new collaboration of materials, or a re-thinking of the previous pattern. We see this metaphor of disruption within the kaleidoscope as our own hope for disrupting traditional research – which searches for the right answer – to engaging in research that forefronts meaning-making. This disruption leads towards messy questions and more questions, responsive to the current challenges and issues within our local and global communities (Parnell & Iorio 2016).

Disrupting research attempts to illumine some of the multifaceted issues of revealing ideas and experiences from the early childhood field through story, narration and sharing voices – by unmasking the complex nature of *connecting* with complex human and more-than-human[1] stories rather than just with numbers, facts and figures. We recognise that this unmasking and revealing can only be achieved with new approaches and ways of considering the generating and proliferating of data that requires alternative readings about the lives of young children, their families and the communities in which they live, move and have being. It is only through the metaphoric turning and (re)turning of the kaleidoscope that this can happen.

To advance the work of educators, lecturers and researchers towards practices of meaning-making in early childhood education, we seek to understand research that challenges assumptions and thinking in a variety of different contexts, including research with young children, their families, their communities and in their more-than-human encounters. This sort of work is not a reductionist's way that looks for numbers or to experiment on the life worlds of young children, rather, as Moss (2017, p. xiv) relates, this alternative conception of research 'allows for, indeed desires, wonder and surprise, new thinking and new understandings, research that is suffused with a relational ethos, an ethics of care, encounter and hospitality'. This hospitality offers us notions of reciprocal relationality – a way of thinking with the connective tissues that require movements between our earthly bodies and human bodies – activating the linked realms of living and blurring experiences to expand hospitality in our encounters with one another and the more-than-human. In order to rethink research practices in the field of early childhood, we hope to uncover a few larger issues related to our reconceptualist work in re-searching.

In coming to understand children, families and our related early childhood practices through alternative research methodologies, new perspectives emerge and contribute to making meanings about learning that attach to the heart and the head simultaneously. This becomes an alchemist's point of view. Our intent through this chapter is to offer illustrations of *rethinking research*, inclusive of practices that disrupt the expected research paradigms in order to create spaces for new conversations about early

---

[1] More-than-human includes place, waterways, landforms, multi-species, flora, fauna, and histories and stories of futures, pasts, and present.

childhood education. Within this moving kaleidoscope, we see how the disruption of the multi-coloured objects makes space to construct and re-construct our identities, to ask enduring questions, to make initial attempts at new meanings with existing findings; gathering and interpreting data, as well as discussing and sharing understandings and initiating new lines of inquiry.

The static kaleidoscope: staying the same at every turn

We so often find that research in the early childhood field stands on the shoulders of giants; the same giants, often harking back to *economic benefit* as the justification for early childhood education. 'The story of quality and high returns' is situated as the 'most dominant of dominant discourses today' (Moss 2019, p. 10). As Moss reminds us, 'We live in a world of stories, or discourses, ways of thinking and talking about things … But within the multitude of stories or discourses, certain ones can become particularly influential' (p. 5). This is evident as we consistently hear the same argument and the same studies cited to us over and over again, much like a single-coloured kaleidoscope staying the same at every turn.

> The same 'iconic studies' (NESSE 2009, p. 29), which have been, in Helen Penn's words, 'endlessly recycled in the literature' (NEESE 2011, p. 39). These are the kind of studies that get funded, these are the kind of studies that get included by academic (and political) gatekeepers when asked to review the literature, these are the kind of studies that are used to rationalize increased public spending on early childhood education – spending that is used to impose increasingly powerful technologies in the interests of more tightly governing the child to maximize the extraction of human capital (Moss 2017, p. xiv).

These claims are told far and wide and taken as the single 'truth' about early childhood education, as the World Bank, the United Nations Educational, Scientific and Cultural Organisation (UNESCO), the Organisation for Economic Co-operation and Development (OECD) and the European Union all tout the same story, reiterating dominate paradigms of reductionist, statistical and *hard-sciences* research in place, even in the range of social sciences (*see* Bloch, Swadener & Cannella 2018; Moss 2017).

The reach of this story of quality and high returns, inclusive of the ideas and the imposing technologies to govern children and extract human capital, as described by Moss (2017; 2019), forms a direct line to choices in research. For example, in many countries, research reports informing early childhood policy and decision-making, reference the big three cost-benefit studies: The Perry Preschool Program, Abecedarian Project and the Chicago Longitudinal Study/Child–parent Center program (see NIEER.org for more information). The underlying current within these studies is the need for *intervention* and dosages of quality early childhood education in order to 'fix' the child or 'close the gap', implying the child as deficit and needy in order to be prepared for the future. The constant presence of these studies, under the intent of evidence and proof, imply a need to create new studies with these same intentions. This is limiting what stories and responses are being told to this assumed 'truth'-laden data, which links back to the same languages of evidence and proof with little or no awareness of children and families as capable and contributing citizens of the now (Rinaldi 2006).

What is equally discomforting is how these dominant discourses support the commodification of the early childhood field. As research studies and modelling articulate cost-benefit analysis; assessments, tools and programs emerge as the measurable way to 'inject' quality early childhood education into young children. For example, as adult–child interaction assessments are used to surveil educator behaviour, no matter what the context, training programs emerge as the fix-all for lacking adult–child interaction practices. Both the assessment and training program cost money, and enable many to profit off the *quality agenda* as defined through cost-benefit and quality studies. It is a vicious circle with only certain people positioned to benefit, and where the knowledge production by academics begins and ends within the market. Fraser and Taylor (2016) note how:

> Academics are no longer esteemed for being public intellectuals committed to general public discourse on crucial issues and/or collaborating with community partners. Instead, we are constituted as commercial agents expected to pursue commercially viable projects, sometimes with the help of specially designated intermediaries (Kauppinen 2012, p. 10–11).

And so, in this sense, the kaleidoscope remains static, even when turned.

Turning and (re)turning: thinking *with* and the practice of hope

We believe that thinking *with* socially relevant issues of our times can help create study-worthy endeavours. In the places and spaces of research, where ideas are recycled to include the same endless points, we have to search out where to find the challenges, the new ideas mixed with longstanding sources, and in the cracks and small fissures that have surfaced, new and old knowledges. Hence, turning and (re)turning the colourful kaleidoscope brings with each movement something to consider, the unknown, surprises and more questions. It generates research that acts against the fatalism of market, return-on-investment and cost-benefit analysis. It offers hope and for us, this is the 'practice of hope' (Iorio & Tanabe 2015; 2019). The *practice of hope* is a pedagogy with the intent of working towards and *with* social change and gives us a new discourse that makes visible the stories and complexities in the margins, and engages with the process of meaning-making.

> Built on theories of hope and the intent of being 'wide-awake' (Greene 1995) and acting, the practice of hope includes the way in which we see academics (and ourselves as academics) attempting to work in universities towards social justice. We take inspiration from philosopher Maxine Greene (1997) who reminds us 'to think of things as if they could be otherwise' (p. 1), pointing out that imagination can offer new ways to see the world and our existence as academics. (Iorio & Tanabe 2019, p. 14)

A strong example of what we mean by thinking *with* socially relevant issues through the *practice of hope* is the Out and About project.

RESEARCH HIGHLIGHT

Out and About is a research project lead by Catherine Hamm (La Trobe University) and Jeanne Marie Iorio (the University of Melbourne) in regional and urban Victoria (Iorio, Hamm, Parnell & Quintero 2017). This research project is a response to the current devastating state of the environment (Solomon, Plattner & Knutti 2009) reached by choices made by humans to benefit humans with little or no understanding of the impact on the planet. These choices indicate a lack of relationship between humans and the Earth. Through the Out and About research project, children and educators are supported to build a deep relationship with plants, animals, insects, landforms and waterways in order to make choices that sustain and reshape the environment by acting on climate change. 'Place' is an important part of this work and is understood as not 'culturally or politically neutral' (Mignolo 2003 in Tuck, McKenzie & McCoy 2014, p. 1), instead place is a 'territory that is Indigenous and which has been and continues to be subject to the forces of colonization' (Tuck, McKenzie & McCoy 2015, p. 1). Engaging *with* place in this manner serves as a provocation to think *with* the ethical, historical and political entanglements.

Specifically, Out and About aims to understand the practices educators use as they support children in building a deep relationship with a local place in their community and rethink common futures. This is situated within 'common world' pedagogies (Common Worlds Research Collective 2014; Taylor & Guigini 2012; Taylor & Pacini-Ketchabaw 2015) and focuses on learning in relation with children's and educators' *common worlds*, inclusive of human and more-than-human connections and relationships. Common world pedagogies are the practices that identify how culture and nature are already entangled (Latour 2004). Out and About is geo-historically specific about Australia's colonial past, present and futures and its entanglements with 'other beings, non-living entities, technologies, elements, discourses, forces and landforms' (Common World Research Collective 2014 n.p.).

As a qualitative research project multisensory methods (walking, listening, smelling, talking, touching) (Pink 2008) morph and evolve, making visible the relations between more-than-human, place and people. The 'contact zone' (Haraway 2008) plays a primary part as it frames places to include more-than-human and human entanglements. Children, educators and researchers all participate in 'place-making' (Pink 2008, p. 179) and engage with *place* as a pedagogical contact zone (Hamm & Boucher 2018).

Living in and with documentation as methodology (Giamminuti 2017) contributes to the data collection. As well, the field notes, videography, photography, artefacts, and reflections written by teachers, educators, researchers, children, parents and community participants all play a role in the making of the learning narrations. Documentation in this research draws on the practice originating in the municipal infant–toddler centres and preschools in Reggio Emilia, Italy. In the context of Reggio Emilia, the intention of documentation is to make visible children's ideas and theories so the community – children, families, educators, and community members – contribute to creating learning experiences together (Dahlberg, Moss & Pence 2007; Edwards, Gandini & Forman 1998; Parnell 2011; Rinaldi 2006). It should be noted that this documentation is deeply located in the community where the research takes place. Therefore, the focus of the documentation is on making visible relations with place and more-than-human.

Educators and researchers have been actively evolving their documentation and narration processes and note how this is a living document open to change and revision. Latour's (2005) understandings of *tracing* and *assembling* are used throughout the ongoing data analysis and offer a way for educators and researchers to pay attention to events and connections within the data.

Many ideas and actions have emerged from the Out and About project that work towards the common good and connect educators to the communities where their setting is located. For instance, in one site in regional Victoria, educators supported the children in their idea to bring Out and About beyond their school and across Victoria. The intention of the children, as documented by the educators, was to share *the act* of Out and About to address climate change. That is, the children wanted others to build deep relationships with local places and more-than-human so that their daily actions would include caring for the planet. Co-participating with the educators and researcher, the children created an Out and About manifesto (Out and About 2020) of their work, inclusive of seven propositions for action. They then made their intent public through the creation of a website; challenging schools to go Out and About. Within the manifesto, intentions and actions become visible.

A research project situated *with* socially relevant issues creates teaching pedagogies and, at the same time, engages with the *doing* of action and advocacy. This type of research becomes an example of how teaching and learning can be complex when the purpose is socially relevant. This research disrupts the common purposes of education as a preparation and for economic benefit and forces us to let go of the dependency on

reductionist views of numbers, rankings and measurements. Possibilities are opened up through using this type of research that re-situates children and families as capable and contributing citizens of the now. Through our metaphor of the kaleidoscope, these are the moments of turning and (re)turning where endless opportunities and possibilities continue to emerge.

Turn and (re)turn: (re)imagining literature and sourcing knowledges

While we have spent time teaching and learning with our current and past research students, fellow research colleagues, and co-re-searching participants who journey with us in our questions and findings, we have learned to give more credence to counter-narratives in the bodies of literature and oral traditions, which builds passion in us. A recent example of rethinking citation practices comes from Todd's (2016) work as she describes her fluctuating desire and disappointment in seeing a prominent scholar's talk on climate disregard, to only cite prominent White[2] scholars. 'He did not mention Inuit. Or Anishinaabeg. Or Nehiyawak. Or any Indigenous thinkers at all' (p. 7). As Todd teaches us, colonising perspectives miss very important parts of knowledges; *ways of knowing* that have long been written, explored, researched and examined.

Further, DiAngelo's (2018) major points about 'White supremacy' – the White domination of society enacted as the norm – show how a prevailing culture (blanketed whiteness) governs and takes full advantage without regard or recognition for non-dominant discourses and ways of knowing, doing and being. This colonising power overruns the earth, people and the more-than-human. This is an economic, social, political moving force that requires more than mindfulness on the part of White scholars engaging in

---

2 Words such as White, Black, Asian etc. are capitalised when denoting race.

early childhood research and practices. How we raise our children matters greatly to how we care for our earthly resources, including the more-than-human and us! These notions take us back to Moss' (2017) 'ethics of care, encounter and hospitality' (p. xiv). Where this great care shows up matters a great deal!

Todd (2016) takes scholars to task about mindful notions by reminding us:

> So, I waited. I waited through the whole talk, to hear the Great Latour credit Indigenous thinkers for their millennia of engagement with sentient environments, with cosmologies that enmesh people into complex relationships between themselves and all relations … I waited. I waited, with bated breath, as I do through most of these types of events … It never came (pp. 6–7).

In our estimation, Todd's 'waiting' is less about citation practices themselves, and more about a way of knowing and an acknowledgement of those divergent perspectives from the dominant colonising forces that reify and reinforce the status quo even when attempting to reconceptualise. In fact, even the acts of citing and using written knowledges that are less familiar to the dominant discourses can misappropriate and be inhospitable if enacted through a colonising way.

We have to do better as we reconsider our work with the literature. Literature itself is not the sole way to work on coming to knowing. Martin (2016) offers the practice of 'coming alongside' as a respectful means for non-Indigenous people to engage with Aboriginal and Torres Strait Islander Peoples' worldviews. As Martin suggests, we must find ways to come 'alongside' local knowledges, people and places as a respecter of ways of knowing. *Coming alongside* is really important for learning to both collaborate and push boundaries, entangling ways of knowing and (re)constructing knowledges and engaging in intentional relationships. Place and more-than-human, then, are prominent protagonists. Practice walking *with* land and listening, learning and looking *with* creek, rocks, trees, birds and so on. Ask to practice walking alongside in an attempt to live *with*, rather than live *from*. As we bring this sort of work and meaning to the foreground, we reshape pedagogy, praxis, and practices and this requires more than literature and written contexts of research.

One powerful illustration of such work springs out of our own context as educator-researchers who stay situated within the setting and close with the educational experiences coming forth; even as our professional roles of department heads and professors would ask us to live outside of that rich context. In this example, Will (author 2) witnessed posts from fellow educators and graduate assistants on Facebook that spoke of looking at, watching and observing worms, and bringing worms into the classroom, stored in worm bins. He immediately asked on Facebook if the educators and children wished to look *with* worms instead of *at* them. First, he seemed to be ignored. Yet, he knew this would be an opportunity to redefine the construct of pedagogy. What would it mean to teach and learn simultaneously with children and worms? All of us wondered what looking *with* worms could accomplish.

We began to consider where the worms look and what are they seeing and experiencing. Entering into this journey required some knowledgeable expertise (Taylor & Pacini-Ketchabaw 2015). The graduate assistants quickly organised, with the help of technology, digital atelier spaces, where children dreamt up ways to connect with worms. They learned that the light hurts worms and to touch worms hurt the worms' skin. Leaving worms under the dirt and in the earth was the best course through the experience but how could they investigate looking where worms looked? What did worms see down there? Recreating spaces where they could be under earth and crawling around could happen in a digital landscape. Also, YouTube could be a place to find videos of natural worm habitats, to consider how they lived, what they were eating, and what the land needed from worms in order to stay safe, healthy and alive itself. This work would inspire the principles and practices of our Inventing Remida Portland Project (IRPP) (Parnell, Downs & Cullen 2017).

RESEARCH HIGHLIGHT

The IRPP is a cultural and educational project housed at Portland State University, created to foster intelligent moderation of resources in the next generation. IRPP is inspired by the Remida Creative Recycle Center in Reggio Emilia, Italy, which works with city waste management, schools, educators, city inhabitants and local manufacturers. Remida represents an optimistic approach to our environmental predicament; promoting the idea that waste materials can be resources. Like Remida centres in Italy and around the world, the IRPP collects discarded materials that would otherwise become trash in our landfills and incinerators, and gives these materials new life and purpose within educational contexts.

Further, we knew we had to engage one another divergently from our past colonising practices of looking at worms. This way, new to us, was about older knowledges, more mature than our own in terms of coming to know, and interspecies (what comes up between species), more-than-human entanglements, and relationships. This work required a foregrounding in more than research literature (Hamm 2018). We had to think with the prominence to respectfully centre Indigenous ways of doing, thinking and being.

This sort of labour toils in the soil of how we go about re-searching. We are propelled into contested territories and, as Anzaldua (2012) proposes, borderlands as spaces and places of hybridity born of painful experiences, and fostering people who both contest and accept such places for co-existence. Reconceptualising research in early childhood education is another place for such an apt borderlands metaphor.

Turning and (re)turning: identities and researching

Considering Urietta's (2007) 'figured worlds' where identity production occurs alongside of the social context, co-construction of identities as researchers coming through figured worlds shape our ways of knowing, doing, being and re-searching. As Domingues (2019) informs us, co-constructing social identities in early childhood education both adapts to, and adopts, imprints of identities. These identities then shape our world(s) and our *doing* of research. This effect is mutual, as in we are being shaped and shaping at the same time. Keating (2009, p. 226) tells us, 'Identities are constantly under construction'. Carrying a multiplicity of identities within us as we move through the world informs the ways in which we come to our work, notes Domingues (2019). We believe this affects how we think, act, wonder, question, interact and walk with place, people and the more-than-human, thus also propelling our questions and what we seek to know.

This entanglement with ways of coming to know the multiplicity of identities and figured worlds brings us back to former research as a poignant example. In the 2017 Reconceptualizing Early Childhood Education conference in Toronto, Parnell, Anderson, Molloy-Murphy and Oh (2017) share in their conference paper presentation about how they came to know their most desirous research questions. They framed their work on Deleuze and Guattari's (2003) *concepts of desire*. Parnell, as part of this presentation, describes his research process as a set of experiences and practices,

> I tend to share out my questions as I formulate them. Usually, they feel confusing to me at first and so I try to explain and gather up feedback. Sometimes, I do this with elders or with younger theorists and researchers. They tend to give me alternative points of view and help me grow to better ask my own questions. When I find myself sharing my questions with researchers and teacher educators whom I admire and their response is more than encouraging to me, I know I have met the litmus test of something more deeply held and desirous. Usually a response may sound something like, 'Oh, that is really good! Or, I want to know more about that too!'
>
> Very recently, I have been more deeply involved with the notions of documentation as a way to live life and make deeper meaning, not only about pedagogical stance or narration. I am very interested in this question of documentation as something we learn *with* and live *through*, rather than an extra 'thing' to do or produce about children. We tend to live in the documentation with the children and this place feels unhurried and calm. We use our thinking brains together and feel up a storm about what we see in the documents, which reflect past learning experiences and evoke messages about what we were doing, thinking and feeling. My thoughts on this used to feel less complete, so I asked around and gathered up feedback and other ideas, working with other educators and the more-than-human documents, photos and artifacts at hand. (Parnell, Anderson, Molloy-Murphy and Oh 2017, p. 4)

In this illustration, we find research linked to making connections that forge markers of/in identities. Locating and fostering knowledges in socially significant issues quickens when we consider many figured worlds and look in on former research and findings or the paucity and absence of such study.

Turn and (re)turn: multiplicities of methodologies

Methodology as overarching approaches to re-searching intertwines with questions

Often, in academia, we hear about how questions inform the type of methodology and approaches we use in research. This point of view comes from dominant writings on how to research and reiterates discourse steeped in reductionist ideas of cost-benefit and return-on-investment. In post-approaches, we also find that methodology and the theoretical perspectives that undergird them can attract researchers towards certain types of social issues and problems in practices, and this informs the questions asked. In some cases, the question has come directly out of a desire to use certain methodologies. For example, Anderson (2014) desired to use phenomenology and a/r/tography as a way to understand meaning, so found a purpose, problem and question that made alignments to this sort of research practice.

Holding such tensions about where research begins – in a problem, purpose, methodology, question or someplace else – requires patience and perseverance in winding our way through the spirals of investigation origins. It calls for a commitment of researchers towards meaning-making and a willingness to disrupt traditional methods as the only way to *do* research. Jackson (2017, p. 666) challenges us to engage in 'thinking without method' as:

> Thinking without method relieves qualitative inquiry from the twin forms of epistemological imperatives of knowledge production and a conventional dependency on procedural method. Freedom from this reliance gives us a new starting place: the outside of method. The outside is an important concept in Deleuzian thought and undergirds my argument for thinking without method in qualitative inquiry.
>
> In his book *Foucault*, Deleuze (1988) reads his own concept of the outside through Foucault's theory of power, so ideas about relations, forces and resistances are crucial to constitute the outside of both method and thought. In this section, I take up these intersections in an introductory manner because in qualitative inquiry, method has taken on normalizing forms. Giving prominence to relations that compose the outside is a radical shift that takes qualitative research into the new.

This radical shift that moves qualitative research into the new creates the opportunity to be in the 'middle of relations' (Jackson 2016; 2017) where 'arrangements of activities, gestures, materials, functions, territories, expressions, sounds, odors and all sorts of bodies' and researcher's thinking becomes a 'stranger to itself' (Jackson 2017, p. 672). For example, how might the typical act of the researcher *mining* the data become new as data provokes the researcher. Moving to the 'outside of method' disrupts the power of the researcher manipulating and moving data, to the data as provocation – a provocation that encourages surprising relations, connections, and arrangements, while making thinking strange and open to infinite possibilities.

Manning (2016, p. 53) offers 'research creation' as another way to move against method. Research creation:

> generates new forms of experience; it situates what often seem like disparate practices, giving them a conduit for collective expression; it hesitantly acknowledges that normative modes of inquiry and containment often are incapable of assessing its value; it generates forms of knowledge that are extralinguistic; it creates operative strategies for a mobile positioning that take these new forms of knowledge into account; it proposes concrete assemblages for rethinking the very question of what is at stake in pedagogy, in practice and in collective experimentation.

Within research creation, Manning (2016) refers to Whitehead's (1978, p. 55) concept of 'superject – which emphasises that the occasion of experience is itself what proposes its own knower–known relations, resulting in a subject that is the subject of the experience rather than a subject external to the experience'. In this sense, researchers are repositioned in relation *with* knowledge, pushing the boundaries of power and methods within the research process. In addition, there is a recognition of how the researcher is not outside the research experience, rather they are intertwined and intersecting towards complexity. This is evident in the Out and About and the Studying *with* Worms projects as, in working outside of method, the researchers disrupted the usual set research cycle of time (e.g. enter a setting for eight weeks, collect the data, leave the setting) and chose to be in relation; researchers *in relation* with community. Part of being in relation required a commitment to time; time to be with, think with, question with, wonder with. Time with and relations with furthered purposeful co-participation where going Out and About and Studying *with* Worms enacted teaching with complexity towards social issues and the common good.

Turn and (re)turn: looking and finding with data

Learning how to process data while making and taking methodological twists and turns can seem complicated and frustrate researchers. At the same time, if we think about the development of research projects as spirals where we go forward and rise in our work, we can slow down the frenetic sense of too much data and clogs in flow. Sorting, sifting, making sense and looking with the data to where it points us can open up the data as the agent of the research. This way of looking is a different sort of 'paying attention'. This paying attention happens *with* rather than *to* the data. The data talks and tells us what it sees and wants to show. An example of this can be found in the Out and About project as educators and children walk *with* cliff, positioned on the far side of beach. Listening *with* cliff is paying attention to the movements of rocks, sand and tree roots embedded within. This act of listening *with* informs how educators and child bodies move. With the sounds of rocks moving down cliff to the beach, bodies move away from the bottom of cliff. This is the same with data; when we pay attention *with* data, how do our bodies and minds move? What emerges from these converging relational moments?

Instead, more traditional qualitative research often asks researchers to analyse data – coming up with themes, patterns, designs out of data – moving us away from the data's own agency, potentially reducing its authenticity. More recently, studies in narrative inquiry, phenomenology, a/r/tography and so on have pushed the boundaries of data treatment towards interpretation of data. This orientation towards interpretation opens up the research narratives, interview data, observations and field notes to making deeper meaning through metaphor and subjectivity. This way also asks the researchers and co-researchers to move away from the original narratives and keep adding to the narrative to see more deeply. Seamon (2012) explores such complexifying of data as cross-hatching. Such treatments of metaphor and a/r/tographic representations recreating narrative, re-storying metaphor, regenerating meaning and so on leads to new and inventive knowledges, practices and approaches to educational experiences. While on the one hand these are novel approaches that push the boundaries of classic lines of research analysis out into a place of interpretative agency, we are reminded that there are more ways to be *with* data that keep the data close at hand in its original intentions.

Data analysis and interpretation do not seem to work for all data processing, for the consideration of what is sought and brought to light. There are burgeoning alternative ways to look in on data such as this notion of *looking with* the data; where it points and what it is saying. Further, in post-qualitative approaches; such as in feminist/new materialisms work, Coleman, Page and Palmer (2019, n.p.) suggest, 'First, the energy required to overthrow conventional (abstract, ideal) reasoning in favour of messy mattering of methods is precisely the energy that is required to break down barriers and borders that prevent us from understanding and affirming difference without prejudice'. Coleman, Page and Palmer's notions of unconventional and messy mattering can be followed in Jackson's thinking. Jackson (2017, p. 671) opens us up to the possibilities of surprise, concept creation and the unexpected, where 'What we glean from Deleuzian thought is that critique without creation remains within a dogmatic image of Method.' Jackson asks us to have our eye jump over the wall of tradition and see anew from outside; potentially outside of all that we have known before and further outside of the data's conventions. Perhaps this sort of researching does live in a perpetual state of becoming.

Continuing the ideas...

In continuation, we are compelled to ask: 'What is there that we do not see?' This question becomes a different sort of query that requires Barad's (2007) diffraction and intra-action in space-time-mattering, or event horizons. These places are where space-time-matter collide, offering generative newness rather than conclusions and conventions of summaries, and going back to what was already known and presumed. As we move beyond the dominant discourses in early childhood education, we hope to create research that does more than replicate cost-benefit and market goals. Rather, *rethinking research* in early childhood education offers emerging and surging questions and (in)conclusive becomings that respond *with* the children, families, and communities locally and globally.

Thinking without method, moving against method, creates conditions where socially relevant issues are engaged with and research is situated within the practice of hope as commonplace. This is where, when and how we can turn and (re)turn the kaleidoscope and not get stuck seeing only one view. Instead, we live *with* the perpetual changes and evolutions of the kaleidoscope; discovering new questions, *ways of knowing*, doing and acting. In these relational moments of meaning-making, awe and wonder rise up our anticipation to wholly new ways of living, moving about and having our being as we work beyond market, value-added, return-on-investment and hope towards the common good.

References

Anderson, IM 2014, *Early childhood educators' perception of Oregon's professional development system: a hermeneutic phenomenological study*, unpublished doctoral dissertation, Portland State University, Oregon.

Anzaldúa Gloria 2012, *Borderlands = La frontera: the new mestiza*, Aunt Lute Books, San Francisco.

Barad, K 2007, *Meeting the universe halfway*, Duke University Press, London.

Bloch, MN, Swadener, BB & Cannella, GS (eds) 2018, *Reconceptualizing early childhood education and care – a reader: critical questions, new imaginaries & social activism*, 2nd edn, Childhood studies, v. 7, Peter Lang, New York.

Coleman, R, Page, T & Palmer, H 2019, 'Feminist new materialist practice: the mattering of methods', *Mai: Feminism & Visual Culture*, vol. 4. Retrieved from https://maifeminism.com/feminist-new-materialisms-the-mattering-of-methods-editors-note/

Common Worlds Research Collective 2014. Retrieved from www.commonworlds.net

Dahlberg, G, Moss, P & Pence, A 2007, *Beyond quality in early childhood education and care: a postmodern perspective*, Routledge/Falmer, London.

Davies, B 2014, *Listening to children: being and becoming*, Routledge, London.

Deleuze, G & Guattari, F 2003, *Anti-Oedipus: capitalism and schizophrenia*, Continuum, London.

DiAngelo, R 2018, *White fragility: why it's so hard for white people to talk about racism*, Beacon Press, Boston.

Domingues, MA 2019, *Identifying with Remida: early childhood educators' experiences with reuse materials in Reggio Emilia inspired identity studies*, doctoral dissertation, Portland State University, Oregon. Retrieved from https://pqdtopen.proquest.com/doc/2280703066.html?FMT=ABS

Edwards, C, Gandini, L & Forman, G (eds) 1998, *The hundred languages of children: the Reggio Emilia approach – advanced reflections*, Ablex, Wesport, CT.

Fraser, H & Taylor, N 2016, *Neoliberalization, universities and the public intellectual*, Palgrave, New York.

Giamminuti, S 2017, 'Research as an ethic of welcome and relationship: pedagogical documentation in Reggio Emilia, Italy', in W Parnell and JM Iorio (eds), *Disrupting early childhood education research: imagining new possibilities*, Routledge, New York, pp. 9–25.

Hamm, C 2018, 'Reimagining narratives of place: respectfully centering Aboriginal perspectives in early childhood education', in W Parnell & JM Iorio (eds), *Meaning making in early childhood research: pedagogies and the personal*, Routledge, New York, pp. 107–20.

Hamm, C & Boucher, K 2018, 'Engaging with place: foregrounding Aboriginal perspective in early childhood education', in N Yelland and D Bentley (eds), *Found in translation: connecting reconceptualist early childhood ideas with practice*, Routledge, New York.

Haraway, D 2008, *When species meet*, University of Minnesota Press.

Iorio, JM & Tanabe, CS 2015, 'A modest proposal re-imagined: disrupting and rethinking educational decision-making', *Teachers College Record*, vol. 117. Retrieved from http://www.tcrecord.org, ID Number: 18828

Iorio, JM, Hamm, C, Parnell, W & Quintero, E 2017, 'Place, matters of concern, and pedagogy: making impactful connections with our planet', *Journal of Early Childhood Teacher Education*, vol. 38, no. 2, pp. 121–35.

Iorio, JM & Tanabe, CS 2019, *Higher education and the practice of hope*, Springer, Singapore.

Jackson, AY 2016, 'An ontology of a backflip', *Critical studies – Critical methodologies*, vol. 16, no. 2, pp. 183–92, doi.org/10.1177/1532708616634735.

Jackson, AY 2017, 'Thinking without method', *Qualitative Inquiry*, vol. 23, no. 9, pp. 666–74.

Keating, A (ed.) 2009, *The Gloria Anzaldua reader: Latin American otherwise*, Duke University Press, Durham, NC.

Latour, B 2004, 'How to talk about the body: the normative dimension of science', *Body & Society*, vol. 10, no. 2–3, pp. 205–29.

Latour, B 2005, *Reassembling the social: an introduction to actor-network-theory*, Oxford University Press, New York.

Manning, E 2016, *The minor gesture*, Duke University Press, Durham, NC.

Martin, K 2016, *Voices & visions: Aboriginal early childhood education in Australia*, Pademelon Press, Sydney.

Moss, P 2019, *Alternative narratives in early childhood: an introduction for students and practitioners*, Routledge, New York.

Moss, P 2017, 'Forward', in W Parnell and JM Iorio (eds), *Disrupting early childhood education research: imagining new possibilities*, Routledge, New York, pp. xiii-xvi.

Out and About 2020, *Out and about manifesto*. Retrieved from https://www.goingoutandabout.net/manifesto

Parnell, W 2011, 'Revealing the experience of children and teachers even in their absence: documenting in the early childhood studio', *Journal of Early Childhood Research*, vol. 9, no. 3, pp. 291–309, doi:10.1177/1476718x10397903.

Parnell, W, Anderson, I, Molloy-Murphy, A, Oh, S 2017, 'Quickening early childhood research agency: detangling knotty questions to re-locate "find a home in the world"', paper presented at the international conference of the Reconceptualizing Early Childhood Education, Toronto.

Parnell, W, Downs, C & Cullen, J 2017, 'Fostering intelligent moderation in the next generation: insights from Remida-inspired reuse materials education', *The New Educator*, vol. 13, no. 3, pp. 234–50.

Pink, S 2008, 'An urban tour: the sensory sociality of ethnographic place-making', *Ethnography*, vol. 9, no. 2, pp. 175–96, doi:10.1177/1466138108089467.

Rinaldi, C 2006, *In dialogue with Reggio Emilia: listening, researching and learning*, Routledge, New York.

Seamon, D 2012, *Challenges for qualitative approaches in environment-behavior research: ideology, ethics, and understanding phenomena*, Paper presentation at the annual meeting of the Environmental Design Research Association (EDRA), Seattle.

Solomon, S, Plattner, GK, Knutti, R & Friedlingstein, P 2009, 'Irreversible climate change due to carbon dioxide emissions', *Proceedings of the National Academy of Science*, vol. 106, no. 6, pp. 1704–09, doi:10.1073/pnas.0812721106.

Taylor, A & Guigini, M 2012, 'Common worlds: reconceptualising inclusion in early childhood communities', *Contemporary Issues in Early Childhood*, vol. 13, no. 2, pp. 108–19.

Taylor, A & Pacini-Ketchabaw, V 2015, 'Learning with children, ants, and worms in the anthropocene: towards a common world pedagogy of multispecies vulnerability', *Pedagogy, Culture & Society*, vol. 23, no. 4, pp. 1–21, doi:10.1080/14681366.2015.1039050

Todd, Z 2016, 'An Indigenous feminist's take on the ontological turn: "ontology" is just another word for colonialism', *Journal of Historical Sociology*, vol. 29, no. 1, pp. 4–22, doi:10.1111/johs.12124.

Tuck, E, McKenzie, M & McCoy, M 2014, 'Land education: Indigenous, post-colonial, and decolonizing perspectives on place and environmental education research', *Environmental Education Research*, vol. 20, no. 1, pp. 1–23, doi:10.1080/13504622.2013.877708.

Urrieta, L 2007, 'Identity production in figured worlds: how some Mexican Americans become Chicana/o activist educators', *The Urban Review*, vol. 39, no. 2, pp. 117–44.

Whitehead, AN 1978, *Process and reality*, Free Press, New York.

CHAPTER 22

Learning to surf: embracing change in the early childhood sector

Jen Jackson

DOI: https://doi.org/10.37517/978-1-74286-555-3_22
Victoria University

Introduction

This final chapter has the task of looking forward, to consider how educators can draw on research to survive and thrive in times of change. This is an important task, given the extent of change to the early childhood education and care (ECEC) sector that has occurred in recent decades. These changes can be seen as efforts to bring ECEC into a more cohesive shape, by integrating education and care practices, and consolidating ECEC both as a sector and a profession. Yet it seems too soon to say that ECEC has achieved a stable shared understanding of what its identity as a coherent sector and profession might mean, and turbulence and uncertainty remain in many parts of the sector. The only thing that seems certain about the future is that more change will come.

The prospect of ongoing change may feel discouraging for early childhood educators. Tayler (2016) describes the 'change fatigue' evident in the Australian ECEC sector, after more than a decade of intense policy and regulatory reform (p. 27). Educators may also feel that children and families are arriving at ECEC services with an increasingly complex array of challenges, preferences and needs – including shifting patterns of family formation and work–life balance, and growing socio-economic disparities (OECD 2011). These challenges pose a threat to the retention of capable educators in the ECEC sector, and to the wellbeing of those educators who value the unique rewards of ECEC practice enough to remain.

Resilience to change is a feature of all professional practice. Achieving stability in ECEC, as a sector and profession, does not mean achieving rigidity. ECEC services and professionals must remain flexible enough to bend – without breaking – as future waves of change buffet the sector. They must learn to find a point of balance on unstable ground, and to stay afloat in the turbulent waters. This echoes the 'ocean swimmer' analogy of French philosopher, Gilles Deleuze, which Lines, Roder and Naughton (2018) apply to ECEC practice.

Research is a valuable tool for remaining buoyant and balanced in uncertain times. It can make unexpected changes more comprehensible, and break unsolvable problems into causes and effects, which then point the way to potential solutions. It can inspire, provoke, explain, affirm and even entertain. A professional can use research like a surfer uses their board, to carve a path through the waves of change, instead of feeling that they are being pulled under and drowning. While novice 'surfers' may just aim to stay upright, experienced professionals manoeuvre their 'boards' freely, each displaying their own style and character.

This chapter aims to help early childhood professionals learn to *surf* the waves of the future, by sharing research relevant to the challenges they may face. Previous chapters have already shared research relevant to specific aspects of ECEC practice, so this chapter takes a big-picture view, looking at the sector and profession of ECEC as a whole. To continue the surfing metaphor, this chapter looks at the ocean in which ECEC professionals are swimming, and the waves, tides, currents and eddies (as well as one tsunami!) that they may encounter in their work. By providing an overview of selected research, it aims to inspire ECEC professionals to embark on their own research journeys, and learn to surf in their own individual ways.

The waves of policy reform

In Australia and many other nations, policymakers have generated some of the largest waves of change to wash through the ECEC sector. The suite of policy reforms introduced under the National Quality Framework agenda (NQF) for ECEC aimed to improve the quality and consistency of ECEC service provision, and lift outcomes for all children and families (COAG 2009). They signified a shift towards greater cohesion in how ECEC was framed in policy discourse, which had previously been fragmented:

> In policy terms early childhood education and care has been associated with labour market intervention; providing family support; providing support and intervention for 'children at risk' and children with additional needs; enhancing children's learning and development; preparing children for school; and community capacity building. The lack of coherence between these objectives and consequent regulatory and funding mechanisms creates a complex and unfocused system for services and families. (Press 2007, p. 186)

The reforms sought to *re-vision* the ECEC sector as a key contributor to lifelong learning (Tayler 2011, p. 213), paving the way for increased government investment, and professionalisation of the workforce.

While many ECEC educators may support the intent of the NQF reforms, to improve quality and increase public recognition for the sector, they encounter struggles in translating these policies into practice. The NQF focus on 'practice quality' – including new requirements for educators' qualifications, and a new assessment and rating process for ECEC services – positions it as a *performative* policy, in which 'performance related practices, such as teaching and learning, are expected and regulated through measurable criteria' (Kilderry 2015, p. 634). While Australia has had various forms of performative policy for ECEC services in the past, the new expectations under the NQF appeared more challenging than previous regimes (Jackson 2015).

Research shows that educators can respond to performative policies in a number of ways. These range from vulnerable educators experiencing the 'terrors of performativity' (Ball 2003, p. 216); through to experienced educators exercising various forms of resistance, and reframing quality practice in their own preferred ways (Fenech, Sumsion & Shepherd 2010). Other educators have been found to thrive on the opportunities that performative policies provide, to gain 'satisfaction and rewards' against external measures (Ball 2012, p. 31). The first lesson from research therefore shows that policies are experienced differently by different educators, depending on their knowledge, dispositions and professional status.

Other educators are demonstrating *post-performative* ways of responding to policy; balancing adherence to policy expectations with high levels of professional autonomy (Kilderry 2015, p. 649). These educators recognise their own power in the policy process – in that policy cannot achieve anything alone, but depends on educators to interpret and implement it – and transform the policy into something that will work for them, their philosophy and their practice. In research on teaching in schools, these kinds of educators have been described as 'critical consumers' of policy (Fullan 1994, p. 1). Instead of the waves of policy crashing over them, they are riding these waves to reach their own objectives.

Becoming a *critical consumer* of policy begins with recognising how policy can support your own goals. The language of policy documents may seem confusing or disconnected from professional practice (Kilderry, Nolan & Scott 2017), often because policy discourse results from complex compromises between diverse stakeholders' views (Pohle 2013). Yet the policy goals of the NQF are well aligned with those of educators (Cahir 2010), who also have an interest in improving outcomes for children and families. In grappling with policy language, educators may find it worthwhile to look for the 'theory of change', or how the policymakers expect the policy to solve a particular problem. Recognising the logic of policy, and embracing or critiquing it constructively based on lived experience, is part of being a *reflective professional*.

Starting from this view of common interests helps to avoid the negative effects of policy. For example, the documentation requirements in the NQF – an especially challenging area of policy implementation – were intended to support the *quality of thinking* in pedagogical decision-making, not the *quantity of paperwork* that gets produced. Thoughtful, succinct pedagogical documentation can satisfy policy requirements, while assisting educators to reflect on and support children's learning and development (Jackson & Cloney 2019).

It is difficult to grapple with policy alone. Just as policy documents typically require large groups of diverse stakeholders to create, they require an even larger group of diverse educators to experiment, reflect and interpret how they will look in practice. No one person has responsibility for determining how to implement policy, and all educators have a part to play in solving this puzzle. This includes educators in all types of early childhood services, and with all kinds of qualifications and roles, because it is often in the diverse experiences of educators that the richest reflection occurs. Local networks are especially valuable in providing a 'mediating layer' between policy and practice, translating policy so it works in local contexts (Barber, Chijioke & Mourshed 2010, p. 18). These networks can also generate 'inside-out' accountability, in which educators take responsibility for driving improvement (Thiers 2017, p. 10).

Research from the field of policy studies suggests that policy cannot succeed if it is only *done to* early childhood educators; it must be *done with* them. In complex systems like the ECEC sector, meaningful change can only happen when 'top-down' policies meet 'bottom-up' innovations generated by educators (Chapman & Ainscow 2019, p. 11). This not only requires a 'theory of change', which aims to solve the problem identified by policymakers; but also a 'theory of action', which sets out the possibilities and limitations in what educators are prepared to do within the scope of their values (Patton 2011, p. 250). The current popularity of *co-design* approaches in policymaking indicates that policymakers are increasingly recognising the need to listen and respond to the ideas and experiences of those who will be implementing the policies in practice (Blomkamp 2018).

This thinking is already visible in some areas of Australian ECEC policy. The statement of philosophy that all Australian ECEC services are required to develop under the NQF is a striking example of a *theory of change* (outcomes need to be improved through higher quality practice), combined with a *theory of action* (values that guide practice). Even in the National Quality Standard (NQS) assessment and rating process, in which educators are subjected to the top-down regulatory gaze – one of the perceived tools of performativity (Osgood 2006, p. 5) – there is scope for educators and regulators to negotiate understandings of quality (Jackson 2015). This gives hope that the future relationship between ECEC policy and practice in Australia can be negotiated, rather than prescriptive. Research provides strong evidence for the benefits of this approach.

The tide of economics

The waves of ECEC policy reform in Australia have been generated by the tide of economic growth. Policymaking in Australia, as in other countries, is strongly influenced by economic rationalism, which uses money as the main method of defining value (Pusey 1991). The most successful argument for government investment in ECEC was made by a famous US economist, James Heckman, who used neuroscience to demonstrate that investing early in children's learning delivers greater benefits to the economy than investing later (Heckman 2000). This finding was supported by major US studies, which showed that high-quality support for early learning increased children's earning power when they grew up (through better educational outcomes); and reduced costs to government; such as crime and healthcare. This economistic way of thinking about learning is known as the 'human capital agenda' (Smith, Tesar & Myers 2016).

In Australia, economic rationalism is evident in many arguments for increased investment in ECEC. A major 2018 report for government cites the economic research from the US, adding that 'social and emotional skills are critical to enable children to thrive in the future economy' (Pascoe & Brennan 2017, p. 16). The economic discourse has also been adopted within the ECEC sector, as illustrated in an ECEC advocacy group's recent position paper about the economic benefits of 3-year-old preschool (see ELAA 2018). Another recent Australian report by ECEC advocacy group The Front Project states that every $1 that governments spend on high-quality preschool, delivers $2 of benefits over a child's lifetime (The Front Project 2019).

RESEARCH HIGHLIGHT

Early childhood advocacy group, The Front Project (2019), with economists PricewaterhouseCoopers, produced research that estimated the economic benefits of investing in preschool.

The report used a complex economic model to show how quality preschool increases children's chances of succeeding at school, getting a job, and staying healthy and financially secure in adulthood. The model also counted the economic benefits of preschool in enabling parents to engage in paid work. Economic modelling research is often used to analyse the likely impact of government investment.

While the tide of economic rationalism has brought benefits to ECEC in attracting government investment, all tides have both ebbs and flows. Economistic (i.e. money-focused) approaches to the provision of ECEC can also be seen in views of the ECEC sector as a market, and the resurgence of private for-profit ECEC services in Australia, especially in long day care and family day care. Australian families also tend to base their decisions about ECEC participation on economic considerations; trading off between ECEC fees and paid work (Productivity Commission 2011). Australian policymakers have extended government subsidies to private ECEC providers, in recognition of the contribution that they make in enabling more families to participate in the workforce, thereby maximising their economic contributions (McShane 2016, p. 183).

At the same time, researchers have expressed concerns that the focus on economic benefits in ECEC means that the education and care of children has been 'commodified' (Press, Logan, Woodrow & Mitchell 2018, p. 328). Other research suggests that educators themselves are positioned as commodities (Osgood 2012) whose labour can be purchased as cheaply as possible. While some research has identified for-profit ECEC providers with a commitment to quality (Duhn 2010), the prevailing view in research is that ECEC services that exist to make a profit are less likely to prioritise the interests of educators and children (Fenech 2019; Goodfellow 2005; Kilderry 2006; Meagher & Cortis 2009; Woodrow 2008).

There are benefits for ECEC educators in understanding the ebbs and flows of economic tides, and how they are championed or critiqued in research. Ball (2012, p. 27) argues that being able to 'follow the money' is important for all educators, in understanding their professional contexts. It can assist in more informed democratic decision-making, as political parties tend to use economic arguments to justify their ECEC policies. It can also help in advocacy, and in framing arguments to address economic issues in the ECEC sector, such as educators' wages. The Australian ECEC sector receives a complex mix of public investment from federal and state governments, as well as private investment from families. Recognising the investment logic (i.e. the motivations and constraints) for each contributor can help ECEC advocates gain support from different stakeholders, and drive positive change. Economic thinking is not just for researchers but is practised by everyone in their day-to-day lives; in fact, the word comes from the Greek *oikonomikos*, which means managing the resources of a household (Waring 1999, p. 15).

Of course, ECEC should not only be valued in economic terms. Press et al. (2018, p. 328) argue that ECEC is better understood as a social good, and 'a site for social cohesion and democratic practice'. Other research perspectives criticise the human capital agenda more broadly, for placing too much priority on the economic benefits of learning, and not enough on the social and cultural impact (*see* Smyth 2007). The economic perspective also risks under-valuing the caring aspects of ECEC work, which are central to the professional identities and values of many educators (Vandenbroeck 2014). Because care for children in the home is unpaid, care has not historically been attributed any economic value (Waring 1999).

Research can be valuable in providing alternative perspectives to economic discourse; both empirical and theoretical. Smith et al. (2016, p. 133) suggest 'thinking with theory and policy' to challenge what they describe as 'edu-capitalism' in Australian ECEC policies. Others believe that ideas like fairness and social justice can exist in ECEC policy and practice, alongside the pursuit of economic growth (Smyth 2007). ECEC systems in the Nordic countries are examples of economic rationalism existing alongside a strong commitment to children's rights and family wellbeing (Campbell-Barr & Nygård 2014). Surfing the economic tides that shape the ECEC sector means staying afloat in the ebbs and the flows, and not letting what matters most in ECEC practice get swept away in the riptide of economic thinking.

The currents of social change

Relationships between educators, children and families are the heart of ECEC practice (DEEWR 2009). Many research disciplines are valuable for understanding human relationships, including sociology, psychology, history and philosophy. Each of these disciplines itself has many strands, and new perspectives are constantly emerging, including perspectives from Indigenous and non-Western cultures (Connell 2007). Nuttall and Grieshaber (2018) identify cultural diversity and social change as priority directions for early childhood research in Australia, as educators swim in the cross-currents of shifting demographics and norms.

The currents of social change affect all aspects of ECEC practice, beginning with the families who choose to engage with ECEC settings, and their reasons for doing so. Historical research into ECEC participation in Australia describes the changing relationships between early childhood teachers (ECTs) and the communities that they serve, as preschool evolved from a 'philanthropic activity' aimed at improving the lives of children in working-class families (Brennan 1994, p. 7), to a universal system that middle-class families also accessed to benefit their children (Hunkin 2016). Meanwhile, educators in early child care settings, were positioned as substitutes for parental care, with low expectations of their qualifications and expertise (Brennan 1994). These historical observations of the role of ECEC in Australian society are valuable for understanding the present state of the sector, as well as for imagining what might be next.

Rising social inequality is a prominent feature of the contemporary social context for ECEC in Australia. While many educators are confident in responding inclusively to cultural and linguistic diversity among children and families, research indicates lower levels of awareness of the specific needs of disadvantaged children and families (Nolan & Lamb 2019). Too often, these families remain invisible to educators, as they are the least likely to engage with ECEC services in the years before school (Pascoe & Brennan 2017). Researchers developing the European quality standard for ECEC concluded that ECEC systems cannot be described as *quality* until they take responsibility for actively supporting all children in their communities; not only those whose families seek out ECEC participation themselves (Working Group on ECEC 2014).

Relationships with families are a longstanding strength of ECEC services in Australia (Brennan & O'Donnell 1986). Research on child-rearing and family life is therefore also valuable to ECEC professionals. A wealth of sociological research exists about parenting; such as Smyth's (2017, p. 65) insights into 'parenting for cognitive development' in Australia, or Mayo and Siraj's (2015) comparison of parenting in advantaged and disadvantaged households. As in Reay's (2000) earlier work, Mayo and Siraj (2015) found that families from all backgrounds shared similar aspirations for their children, but differed in their capacity to support them. These kinds of studies can yield valuable insights for educators seeking to strengthen their engagement with families, and to reach those families who might feel least confident and capable in ECEC settings.

RESEARCH HIGHLIGHT

In 2017, Smyth conducted an in-depth qualitative study of 'parenting for cognitive development' (PCD) practices, involving 29 Australian parents whose children were about to start school.

All parents reported reading to their children, although the frequency and importance that they placed on reading varied. Parents with degrees were more likely to engage in PCD, but diversity in income made no difference.

The study also found that parents felt less pressure to engage in PCD at home if they knew that their child was undertaking a lot of learning and creative activities at preschool.

Contemporary ECEC practice also aims to develop inclusive attitudes among children. Research from conflict-affected communities has shown that ECEC services can be powerful sites for fostering tolerance and peace (Fitzpatrick 2007); and recent UK research explores possibilities for counteracting terrorism (Meehan & Meehan 2019). In Australia's individualistic society – in which individuals are primarily expected to take care of themselves and their immediate families (Hofstede Insights n.d.) – educators must balance upholding the rights of children in child-centred programs with instilling a sense of responsibility and respect towards others. Biesta's (2019, p. 2) work on the philosophy of education encourages educators to see their classroom as:

> … not a place where students can be free, but rather a space where students can encounter their freedom and begin to see that freedom is not just a blessing but also a burden.

This may mean prioritising democracy and inclusion over individualistic aims.

Perhaps the most important research on social change takes place within educators' own communities. There are many data tools available to understand demographics and challenges in Australian communities; such as the Australian Early Development Census (AEDC) (for child outcomes at entry to school), and Australia's Health Tracker (for risk factors to children's health) (Australian Health Policy Collaboration 2017). These data sets are becoming simpler to access and analyse and ECEC professionals are beginning to use them to guide their practice (Steel & ECA 2015). There is a large and growing body of research around place-based initiatives, child-friendly communities and the importance of children's agency in exploring local challenges and solutions (Dockett, Kearney & Perry 2012). Knowledge of Country, including local history and language, is also foundational to the inclusion of Indigenous perspectives in ECEC programs (Hamm 2018). The currents of social change are both local and global, and may be explored using research on a large or small scale.

The tsunami of education

Some researchers in the early childhood sector are concerned that the waves of policy reform will culminate in a tsunami that will engulf the ECEC sector, namely the 'schoolification' of ECEC (Press 2007, p. 193). The 'human capital agenda' – in which skills, knowledge, and experience are viewed primarily in terms of their value or cost to the economy – positions ECEC as part of the process of lifelong learning, beginning in early childhood, and continuing through school, to tertiary education, to entry into the workforce. Iorio and Tanabe (2015, n.p.) observe that 'the whole readiness project is based on the process of producing employees', and questions where this leaves other objectives, like 'citizenship, democratic learning and knowledge production'.

If each stage of learning is defined as preparation for the next, then the expectations of the subsequent stage will also place pressure on all prior stages. An example of this can be seen in secondary education in Australia, where university admission processes have caused schools to focus on Australian Tertiary Admissions Rank (ATAR) scores, rather than holistic learning (Pilcher 2018). If ECEC is seen primarily as preparation for primary school, there is a risk that this will distort expectations about ECEC learning and pedagogy. A large body of research demonstrates the benefits of quality ECEC programs through children's subsequent performance on academic tests at school (AIHW 2015). While these studies demonstrate the impact of ECEC, they risk narrowing definitions of its value.

Surfing in a tsunami is not easy, but research can provide some strategies for surviving – and even thriving. The first is to remain curious and adaptive about the possibilities for strengthening the focus on children's learning within play-based ECEC programs. This means understanding what learning looks like in the early years, across a broad range of areas, not only pre-academic skills (like literacy and numeracy). The Victorian Curriculum and Assessment Authority (VCAA) has published research-informed resources to help educators to 'build a bridge' between the holistic learning described in ECEC curriculum frameworks, and the learning sciences (Cloney, Jackson & Mitchell 2019, p. 9). They recognise the important role that ECEC services play in developing general capabilities like executive function, social skills and motor skills – all of which are essential to young children thriving in the 'here and now', as well as laying foundations for later learning.

A second strategy is to push back against the tsunami, and recognise that ECEC has much more to offer schools than simply preparing children to perform well on literacy and numeracy tests. ECEC curriculum, pedagogy and assessment practices may in fact provide answers to many of the challenges that school teachers in Australia are currently facing. The holistic, child-centred Early Years Learning Framework for Australia (EYLF) (DEEWR 2009) defines five Learning Outcomes that are as relevant to students in Australian schools as they are to young children (Jackson & Endekov 2019). As schools aim to support a broader set of outcomes; including skills such as creativity, collaboration, personal growth and wellbeing (Lamb, Maire & Doecke 2017), ECEC educators already have holistic development at the centre of their programs.

There is also scope for early childhood pedagogies to push up into schooling. Educators in the school system are increasingly using inquiry-based or problem-based learning, including approaches that are built around their students' interests and strengths (Leadbeater 2016). Subjects such as science and mathematics, which have traditionally involved rigorously structured curriculum, are now being taught in a way that fosters dispositions; such as investigating and problem-solving (Timms, Moyle, Weldon & Mitchell 2018), which aligns well with early childhood educators' understanding of these disciplines (Simoncini & Lasen 2018). There are even moves to incorporate play as a learning strategy in some secondary schools (Parker & Thomsen 2019). The human capital agenda itself is evolving to recognise the value of these approaches, with skills like problem-solving and creativity being linked to success in the workforce (Lamb et al. 2017).

Awareness of these research developments can help ECEC educators find ways to reconcile a strengthened focus on learning with the uniquely valuable qualities of ECEC practice. It may even help ECEC educators to generate a tsunami of their own! While ECEC has much to gain from its closer association with schooling, as a sector that enjoys relatively high levels of government support and public trust, school education also has much to gain from encounters with educators who can articulate the evidence base for their pedagogies. Rather than the future of ECEC looking more like school education, it may be that the future of schooling (at all levels) will come to look more like ECEC.

The eddies of evidence

The previous sections have described some ways in which research can help early childhood professionals to understand and navigate the complexities of their policy, economic, social and educational contexts. Yet educators may still be left wondering exactly how research is to be used. In school education, there is increasing pressure for teachers to use 'evidence-informed practice', and to draw on research about 'what works' (Gale 2017, p. 172). These ideas are also present in ECEC practice and were discussed in Chapter 1.

'Evidence-informed practice' is a different way of thinking about using research (Higgins 2017, p. 93), which does not expect research to deliver neatly-packaged solutions. It replaces the *positivist* view of research (proving truths) with a *constructivist* view (providing perspectives). Constructivist views recognise that all human knowledge is constructed, not fixed and that truths may be interpreted in multiple ways. Cannella and Grieshaber (2001, p. 175) challenge educators to resist the positivist, perfectionist drive to 'learn exactly all the right actions and methods', and instead embrace research as fluid and contestable:

> Research as a construct should be questioned, and, if used (perhaps because of political contexts or circumstance), at least reconceptualized to include

multiple voices, flexibility, and a continued challenge to the imposition of research on others as truth. (Cannella & Grieshaber 2001, p. 179)

Evidence-informed practice therefore involves early childhood professionals taking ideas from research and interpreting them according to their own perspectives, rather than looking for authoritative proof. Cannella (2005) especially argues for recognition of knowledge traditions outside of the Western mainstream, and is critical of those who support their own claims of expertise by excluding the perspectives of others.

Engaging with research in this way is a form of critical reflection. Educators encountering a piece of research can question whether it is useful to their practice, either in providing new strategies, or in helping them to understand the children and families with whom they work. A wide variety of research may be useful for these purposes, from large-scale research that describes data trends across the early childhood sector (Jackson 2016); through to small-scale qualitative studies that examine practice in detail. The *International handbook of early childhood education* (Fleer & van Oers 2018) describes a diverse range of methods used in contemporary ECEC research, including narratives, cultural-historical approaches, quantitative studies, policy analysis and co-research with children. Learning how to read different kinds of research and appraise their value, is a valuable skill in its own right. Reading research may not always lead directly to action, but may simply inform how educators think about their practice (Cannella 2005).

Educators can also become researchers within their own services. 'Practitioner inquiry' (Fleet, De Gioia & Patterson 2016) or action research (MacNaughton & Hughes 2008) in ECEC refers to educators applying the tools of research in their own practice. Educators can become researchers through any systematic investigation of the questions that arise in their work; as part of the cycle of planning, doing and reflecting that characterises ECEC practice (Department of Education and Training 2016). As educating young children is both art and science (Marzano 2007), engagement in research can be both a scientific way of approaching practice (Higgins, 2017), and an artistic expression of wondering and exploring (Pinedo-Burns & Bentley 2018, p. 31).

Surfing the eddies of evidence also requires early childhood professionals to get comfortable with ambiguity. Research often raises more questions than it answers, and research itself is an ongoing conversation with many voices. MacNaughton (2004, p. 93) describes this way of thinking as an ongoing process of 'becoming', in which nothing is certain, but 'there are only shifting and multiple truths and effects to be found'. This acceptance of ambiguity is visible in the 'social-ecological theoretical underpinnings' that inform the EYLF, which emphasise that perspectives on learning are constructed within social and historical contexts (McShane 2016, p. 186). Collaborative critical reflection with colleagues can be a valuable way to test and critique the multiple truths and perspectives that research may reveal and conceal, and develop evidence-informed practices that align with early childhood professionals' own capabilities, interests and philosophies (Macfarlane, Noble, Kilderry & Nolan 2006).

Conclusion

Like the ocean, the contexts in which early childhood professionals live and work will never stay still. This chapter has outlined some of the waves, tides and currents that swirl around educators in contemporary Australia, and which push and pull at ECEC practice in potentially destabilising ways. Alongside the major ebbs and flows outlined in this chapter, new ripples or whirlpools will spring up from time to time, bringing fresh complexities to the ECEC sector and profession. As reflective professionals, educators must remain true to their values in the face of change, while remaining adaptive and agile in their practices.

This book was motivated by a belief that research is valuable to all educators, in navigating complexity in their practice. It recognises that the use of research in practice is a 'rather messy social learning process', in which expert knowledge is interpreted through educator experience (Chapman & Ainscow 2019, p. 16). The metaphor of surfing is intended to show that research should not be expected to provide certainty or stability, but instead provides a way to soar – and to play – as the waves come crashing around. Educators are adept at engaging children in playful exploration and wondering about the problems and conundrums that emerge in their day-to-day lives. Using research in practice can be similarly playful and exploratory, testing ideas, sharing with colleagues and continually posing the next interesting question.

Like surfing, using research in this way takes time and practice. ECTs in Australia come from mixed educational and social backgrounds (Jackson 2016), and some may feel that research is too difficult and complex to offer any benefit. Educational leaders have a valuable role to play in opening up research to their colleagues, encouraging them to deepen and extend what they know. This involves recognising the many ways in which knowledge is created and maintained; including realising that valuable knowledge may be stored in educators' bodies (those actions they can do without thinking) not only their brains (Ord & Nuttall 2016). Just as research itself is a conversation in which knowledge may be demonstrated in various ways, so too are professional conversations about research in ECEC practice.

This chapter is also a kind of conversation, which draws on numerous other researchers' valuable work. At the same time, it is a personal view, compiled from the perspective of a single author – 'This is my surfboard, with which I can carve my own pathway through the waves'. It is hoped that this book enables all readers to design and deploy their own evidence-informed *surfboards*, using whichever parts of the research conversation spark their interest and inspiration. Hang in there and enjoy the ride.

RESEARCH INTO PRACTICE

This book has explored many different kinds of research, on many different topics.

How can you:

- develop your curiosity about what research can tell you – not just about educating and caring for young children, but about the wider social context in which education and care occurs?
- find quality research on topics that interest you, in a library or online academic search?
- discuss research with your colleagues, and share your interpretations of what you have found?
- stay open to challenging or contradictory ideas, and find your own way through ambiguity?
- become an 'educator-researcher', and systematically investigate questions in your practice?

References

Australian Health Policy Collaboration 2017, *Australia's health tracker*, Australian Health Policy Collaboration, Melbourne. Retrieved from http://www.atlasesaustralia.com.au/ahpc/aust-health-tracker-area.html

Australian Institute of Health and Welfare 2015, *Literature review of the impact of early childhood education and care on learning and development: working paper*, Australian Institute of Health and Welfare, Canberra. Retrieved from www.aihw.gov.au/getmedia/321201fc-ca0c-4c20-9582-7c3dc5c9d1b9/19438.pdf.aspx?inline=true

Ball, SJ 2012, 'Show me the money! Neoliberalism at work in education', *FORUM*, vol. 54, pp. 23–28, doi:10.2304/forum.2012.54.1.23.

Ball, SJ 2003, 'The teacher's soul and the terrors of performativity', *Journal of Education Policy*, vol. 18, no. 2, pp. 215–28.

Ball, SJ 2012, *Global education inc: new policy networks and the neo-liberal imaginary*, Routledge, London.

Barber, M, Chijioke, C & Mourshed, M 2010, *How the world's most improved school systems keep getting better*, McKinsey & Company, Sydney. Retrieved from https://www.mckinsey.com/industries/social-sector/our-insights/how-the-worlds-most-improved-school-systems-keep-getting-better

Biesta, G 2019, *Obstinate education: reconnecting school and society*, Klim, Aahus.

Blomkamp, E 2018, 'The Promise of co-design for public policy', *Australian Journal of Public Administration*, vol. 77, no. 4, pp. 729–43, doi:10.1111/1467-8500.12310.

Brennan, D 1994, *The politics of Australian child care: from philanthropy to feminism*, Cambridge University Press, Cambridge, England.

Brennan, D & O'Donnell, C 1986, *Caring for Australia's children: political and industrial issues in child care*, Allen & Unwin, Sydney.

Cahir, P 2010, 'The national quality standard – translating this win for children into practice', *Every Child*, vol. 4, no. 1, pp. 4–5.

Campbell-Barr, V & Nygård, M 2014, 'Losing sight of the child? Human capital theory and its role for early childhood education and care policies in Finland and England since the mid-1990s', *Contemporary Issues in Early Childhood*, vol. 15, no. 4, pp. 346–59.

Cannella, GS 2005, 'Reconceptualizing the field (of early care and education)', in N Yelland (ed.), *Critical Issues in Early Childhood Education*, Open University Press, Berkshire, pp. 17–39.

Cannella, GS & Grieshaber, S 2001, 'Identities and possibilities', in S Grieshaber & GS Cannella (eds), *Embracing Identities in Early Childhood Education*, Teachers College Press, New York, pp. 173–80.

Chapman, C & Ainscow, M 2019, 'Using research to promote equity within education systems: possibilities and barriers', *British Educational Research Journal*, vol. 45, no. 5, pp. 899–917, doi:10.1002/berj.3544.

Cloney, D, Jackson, J & Mitchell, P 2019, *Assessment of children as confident and involved learners in early childhood education and care: literature review*, ACER, Melbourne. Retrieved from https://research.acer.edu.au/early_childhood_misc/11/

Connell, R 2007, *Southern theory: the global dynamics of knowledge in the social sciences*, Allen & Unwin, Sydney.

Council of Australian Governments (COAG) 2009, *National partnership agreement on the national quality agenda for early childhood education and care*, Commonwealth of Australia, Canberra.

Department of Education and Training (DET) 2016, *Victorian early years learning and development framework*, DET, Melbourne.

Department of Education, Employment and Workplace Relations (DEEWR) 2009, *Belonging, being and becoming: the early years learning framework for Australia*, Commonwealth of Australia, Canberra. Retrieved from https://docs.education.gov.au/node/2632

Dockett, S, Kearney, E & Perry, B 2012, 'Recognising young children's understandings and experiences of community', *International Journal of Early Childhood*, vol. 44, no. 3, pp. 287–305, doi:10.1007/s13158-012-0073-y.

Duhn, I 2010, 'The centre is my business: neo-liberal politics, privatisation and discourses of professionalism in New Zealand', *Contemporary Issues in Early Childhood*, vol. 11, no. 1, pp. 49–60.

Early Learning Association Australia (ELAA) 2018, *A fair and smart Australia: the case for three-year-old preschool*, ELAA, Melbourne. Retrieved from https://elaa.org.au/wp-content/uploads/2018/07/18053_ELAA-Position-Paper-Apr18_DD04.pdf

Fenech, M 2019, 'Pursuing a social justice agenda for early childhood education and care: interrogating marketisation hegemony in the academy', in K Freebody, S Goodwin & H Proctor, *Higher education, pedagogy and social justice: politics and practice*, Macmillan, Cham, pp. 81–96.

Fenech, M, Sumsion, J & Shepherd, W 2010, 'Promoting early childhood teacher professionalism in the Australian context: the place of resistance', *Contemporary Issues in Early Childhood*, vol. 11, no. 1, pp. 89–105.

Fitzpatrick, S 2007, 'Developing a culture of respecting difference in early childhood centers in Northern Ireland', *Young Children*, vol. 62, no. 6, pp. 14–17.

Fleer, M & van Oers, B 2018, *International handbook of early childhood education*, Springer, Singapore. Retrieved from https://www.springer.com/gp/book/9789402409253

Fleet, A, Gioia, KD & Patterson, C 2016, *Engaging with educational change: voices of practitioner inquiry*, Bloomsbury Academic, London.

Fullan, M 1994, *Teachers as critical consumers of research, education research and reform*, OECD, Paris.

Gale, T 2017, 'What's not to like about RCTs in education?', in A Childs & I Menter (eds), *Mobilising teacher researchers: challenging educational inequality*, Routledge, Oxon, pp. 172–84.

Goodfellow, J 2005, Market childcare: Preliminary considerations of a "property view" of the child. *Contemporary Issues in Early Childhood*, 6(1), 54–65.

Hamm, C 2018, 'Reimagining narratives of place: respectfully centring Aboriginal perspectives in early childhood education', in JM Iorio & W Parnell (eds), *Meaning making in early childhood research: pedagogies and the personal*, Routledge, New York, pp. 85–95.

Heckman, JJ 2000, 'Policies to foster human capital', *Research in Economics*, vol. 54, no. 1, pp. 3–56.

Higgins, S 2017, 'Room in the toolbox? The place of randomised controlled trials in educational research', in A Childs & I Menter (eds), *Mobilising teacher researchers: challenging educational inequality*, Routledge, New York, pp. 92–103.

Hofstede Insights n.d., *Country comparison: Australia*, Hoftstese Insights, Helsinki. Retrieved from www.hofstede-insights.com/country-comparison/australia/

Hunkin, E 2016, *Problematising quality reform policy in Australian early childhood education and care*, unpublished doctoral dissertation, Deakin University, Melbourne.

Iorio, JM & Tanabe, CS 2015, 'Early childhood finally pushed up: the incredible ridiculousness of the readiness chain', *Teachers College Record*, vol. 13, ID no. 18264. Retrieved from http://www.tcrecord.org

Jackson, J 2015, 'Embracing multiple ways of knowing in regulatory assessments of quality in Australian early childhood education and care', *Australian Educational Researcher*, vol. 42, no. 4, pp. 515–26.

Jackson, J 2016, 'The view from the helicopter: examining the Australian early childhood workforce using the national census of population and housing', *Australasian Journal of Early Childhood*, vol. 41, no. 4, pp. 72–79.

Jackson, J & Cloney, D 2019, *Assessment of children as confident and involved learners*, presented at the VCAA Twilight Seminar, Victoria Curriculum & Assessment Authority, Melbourne.

Jackson, J & Endekov, Z 2019, *Achieving our educational goals: a declaration for system transformation*, Mitchell Institute, Victoria University, Melbourne. Retrieved from http://www.mitchellinstitute.org.au/wp-content/uploads/2019/08/A-Declaration-for-System-Transformation.pdf

Kilderry, A 2006, 'Early childhood education and care as a community service or big business?', *Contemporary Issues in Early Childhood*, vol. 7, no. 1, pp. 80–83.

Kilderry, A 2015, 'The intensification of performativity in early childhood education', *Journal of Curriculum Studies*, vol. 47, no. 5, pp. 633–52.

Kilderry, A, Nolan, A & Scott, C 2017, 'Out of the loop: early childhood educators gaining confidence with unfamiliar policy discourse', *Early Years: An International Journal of Research and Developmen*, vol. 37, no. 4, pp. 341–34, doi:10.1080/09575146.2016.1183595.

Lamb, S, Maire, Q & Doecke, E 2017, *Key skills for the 21st century: an evidence-based review*, NSW Department of Education, Sydney.

Leadbeater, C 2016, *The problem solvers: the teachers, the students and the radically disruptive nuns who are leading a global learning movement*, Pearson, London.

Lines, D, Roder, J & Naughton, C 2018, 'Ocean swimmers: re-imagining relationality in MAPS, an early childhood arts research project', in JM Iorio & W Parnell (eds.), *Meaning making in early childhood research: pedagogies and the personal*, Routledge, New York, pp. 99–100.

Macfarlane, K, Noble, K, Kilderry, A & Nolan, A 2006, 'Developing skills of thinking otherwise and critical reflection', in K Noble, K Macfarlane & J Cartmel (eds), *Circles of change: challenging orthodoxy in practitioner supervision*, Pearson Education, Frenchs Forest, pp. 11–20.

MacNaughton, G 2004, 'The politics of logic in early childhood research: a case of the brain, hard facts, trees and rhizomes', *Australian Educational Researcher*, vol. 31, no. 3, pp. 87–104.

MacNaughton, G & Hughes, P 2008, *Doing action research in early childhood studies: a step by step guide*, McGrawHill Education, Melbourne.

Marzano, RJ 2007, *The art and science of teaching: a comprehensive framework for effective instruction*, Association for Supervision and Curriculum Development, Alexandria, VA.

Mayo, A & Siraj, I 2015, 'Parenting practices and children's academic success in low-SES families', *Oxford Review of Education*, vol. 41, no. 1, pp. 47–63, doi:10.1080/03054985.2014.995160.

McShane, I 2016, '"Educare" in Australia: analysing policy mobility and transformation', *Educational Research*, vol. 58, no. 2, pp. 179–94.

Meagher, G & Cortis, N 2009, 'The political economy of for-profit paid care: theory and evidence', in D King & G Meagher (eds), *Paid care in Australia: politics, profits, practices*, Sydney University Press, pp. 13–42.

Meehan, C & Meehan, P 2019, 'Exploring the role of 'RE' in early childhood education and care as a response to the PREVENT agenda in England', *Early Child Development and Care*, vol. 189, no. 7, pp. 1174–88, doi:10.1080/03004430.2017.1369978.

Nolan, A & Lamb, S 2019, 'Exploring the social justice work of early childhood educators', *Policy Futures in Education*, vol. 17, no. 5, pp. 618–33.

Nuttall, J & Grieshaber, S 2018, 'The historical emergence of early childhood education research in Australia', in M Fleer & B van Oers (eds), *International handbook of early childhood education*, Springer, Singapore, pp. 511–29.

Ord, K & Nuttall, J 2016, 'Bodies of knowledge: the concept of embodiment as an alternative to theory/practice debates in the preparation of teachers', *Teaching and Teacher Education*, vol. 60, pp. 355–62, doi:10.1016/j.tate.2016.05.019.

Organisation for Economic Co-operation and Development (OECD) 2011, *Doing better for families*. Retrieved from https://www.oecd.org/els/soc/47701118.pdf

Osgood, J 2006, 'Deconstructing professionalism in early childhood education: resisting the regulatory gaze', *Contemporary Issues in Early Childhood*, vol. 7, no. 1, pp. 5–14.

Osgood, J 2012, *Narratives from the nursery: negotiating professional identities in early childhood*, Routledge, Oxon.

Parker, R & Thomsen, BS 2019, *Learning through play at school*, The Lego Foundation, Billund. Retrieved from https://research.acer.edu.au/cgi/viewcontent.cgi?article=1023&context=learning_processes

Pascoe, S & Brennan, D 2017, *Lifting our game: report of the review to achieve educational excellence in Australian schools through early childhood interventions*, Victorian Government, Melbourne.

Patton, MQ 2011, *Developmental evaluation: applying complexity concepts to enhance innovation and use*, Guilford Press, New York.

Pilcher, S 2018, *Crunching the number: exploring the use and usefulness of the Australian Tertiary Admission Rank (ATAR)*, The Mitchell Institute, Victoria University, Melbourne. Retrieved from http://www.mitchellinstitute.org.au/papers/crunching-the-number/

Pinedo-Burns, HJ & Bentley, DF 2018, 'I have a voice. I have a story. The artistic practice of practitioner research', in JM Iorio & W Parnell (eds), *Meaning making in early childhood research: pedagogies and the personal*, Routledge, New York, pp. 31–55.

Pohle, J 2013, *Opening the black box of policy change: analysing policy discourse 'in the making'*, paper presented at the ECPR General Conference, Bordeaux, France. Retrieved from https://ecpr.eu/Filestore/PaperProposal/a92a4a9e-4433-49f4-93f9-0b87d23ef413.pdf

Press, F 2007, 'Public investment, fragmentation and quality early education and care – existing challenges and future options', in B Pocock & A Elliott (Eds), *Kids count: better early childhood education and care in Australia*, Sydney University Press, pp. 181–98.

Press, F, Logan, H, Woodrow, C & Mitchell, L 2018, 'Can we belong in a neo-liberal world? Neo-liberalism in early childhood education and care policy in Australia and New Zealand', *Contemporary Issues in Early Childhood*, vol. 19, no. 4, pp. 328–39, doi:10.1177/1463949118781909.

Productivity Commission 2011, *Early childhood development workforce: research report*, Productivity Commission, Melbourne.

Pusey, M 1991, *Economic rationalism in Canberra: a nation-building state changes its mind*, Cambridge University Press, Melbourne.

Reay, D 2000, 'A useful extension of Bourdieu's conceptual framework?: emotional capital as a way of understanding mothers' involvement in their children's education?', *The Sociological Review*, vol. 48, no. 4, pp. 568–85, doi:10.1111/1467-954X.00233.

Simoncini, K & Lasen, M 2018, 'Ideas about STEM Among Australian early childhood professionals: how important is STEM in early childhood education?', *International Journal of Early Childhood*, vol. 50, no. 3, pp. 353–69.

Smith, K, Tesar, M & Myers, CY 2016, 'Edu-capitalism and the governing of early childhood education and care in Australia, New Zealand and the United States', *Global Studies of Childhood*, vol. 6, no. 1, pp. 123–35, doi:10.1177/2043610615625165.

Smyth, C 2017, 'Maximising advantage in the preschool years: parents' resources and strategies', *Australasian Journal of Early Childhood*, vol. 42, no. 3, pp. 65–72.

Smyth, P 2007, *Social investment in human capital: revisioning Australian social policy*, social policy working paper no. 8, Brotherhood of St Laurence, Melbourne. Retrieved from http://library.bsl.org.au/jspui/bitstream/1/910/1/Smyth_social_investment_1.pdf

Steel & Early Childhood Australia (ECA) 2015, *Are you using the AEDC data to inform your QIP?* The Spoke, ECA's blog, ECA, Canberra. Retrieved from http://thespoke.earlychildhoodaustralia.org.au/are-you-using-the-aedc-data-to-inform-your-qip/

Tayler, C 2011, 'Changing policy, changing culture: steps toward early learning quality improvement in Australia', *International Journal of Early Childhood*, vol. 43, no. 3, pp. 211–25.

Tayler, C 2016, 'Reforming Australian early childhood education and care provision (2009–2015)', *Australasian Journal of Early Childhood*, vol. 41, no. 2, pp. 27–31.

Thiers, N 2017, 'Making progress possible: a conversation with Michael Fullan', *Educational Leadership*, vol. 74, no. 9, pp. 8–14.

Timms, M, Moyle, K, Weldon, P & Mitchell, P 2018, *Challenges in STEM learning in Australian schools*, ACER, Melbourne. Retrieved from https://research.acer.edu.au/cgi/viewcontent.cgi?article=1028&context=policy_analysis_misc

Vandenbroeck, M 2014, 'The brainification of early childhood education and other challenges to academic rigour', *European Early Childhood Education Research Journal*, vol. 22, no. 1, pp. 1–3, doi:10.1080/1350293X.2013.868206.

Waring, M 1999, *Counting for nothing: what men value and what women are worth*, 2nd edn, University of Toronto.

Woodrow, C 2008, 'Discourses of professional identity in early childhood: movements in Australia', *European Early Childhood Education Research Journal*, vol. 16, no. 2, pp. 269–80.

Working Group on Early Childhood Education and Care 2014, *Proposal for key principles of a quality framework for early childhood education and care*, European Commission, Brussels. Retrieved from https://ec.europa.eu/assets/eac/education/policy/strategic-framework/archive/documents/ecec-quality-framework_en.pdf

Glossary

ACECQA – the Australian Children's Education and Care Quality Authority works with all Australian governments to provide guidance, resources and services to support the sector to improve outcomes for children.

AEDC – the Australian Early Development Census measures five important areas of early childhood development: physical health and wellbeing, social competence, emotional maturity, language and cognitive skills (school-based), and communication skills and general knowledge. With data collected every three years since 2009, the AEDC provides national data to inform policy, planning and action for health, education and community support.

APST – Australian Professional Standards for Teachers; these standards articulate what educators are expected to know and be able to do at four career stages – Graduate, Proficient, Highly Accomplished and Lead.

biophilic design – this is a concept usually used within the building industry to increase occupant connectivity to the natural environment through the use of direct nature, indirect nature, and space and place conditions.

CLASS – the Classroom Assessment Scoring System is a tool for analysing the quality of educator–child interactions.

COAG – the Council of Australian Governments was the peak intergovernmental forum in Australia. In June 2020, COAG was replaced by the National Federation Reform Council (NFRC).

EAL – English as an Additional Language.

early childhood – this is defined as the period from birth to 8 years of age. It is a time of remarkable growth with brain development at its peak. During this period, children are highly influenced by the environment and the people that surround them.

early childhood educator – in Australia, this is a person who is qualified to work with young children and their families – birth to 5 years old – in early childhood settings.

early childhood settings – long day care, occasional care, family day care, multi-purpose Aboriginal Children's Services, preschools and kindergartens, playgroups, creches, early intervention settings and similar services'.

ECA – Early Childhood Australia has been a voice for young children since 1938. ECA is the peak early childhood advocacy organisation, acting in the interests of young children, their families and those in the early childhood field. ECA advocates to ensure quality, social justice and equity in all issues relating to the education and care of children from birth to 8 years.

Glossary

ECEC – Early Childhood Education and Care is defined internationally as more than preparation for primary school. It aims at the holistic development of a child's social, emotional, cognitive and physical needs in order to build a solid and broad foundation for lifelong learning and wellbeing.

equity – equity is the quality of being fair and impartial, which will require unequal treatment of individuals to ensure fairness.

EYLF – the Early Years Learning Framework for Australia is the nationally approved learning framework. It describes the principles, practice and outcomes essential to support and enhance young children's learning from birth to 5 years of age, as well as their transition to school.

formative assessment – the goal to monitor children's learning to provide ongoing feedback that can be used by educators to improve their interactions with young children and to improve learning. More specifically, formative assessments help educators to identify children's strengths and weaknesses and target areas that need attention.

HLE – the Home Learning Environment is a reflection of the home environment and interactions in and around the home with family members.

intentional teaching – this involves educators being thoughtful, purposeful and deliberate in their decisions and actions. Intentional teaching is an active process and a way of relating to the children that embraces and builds on their strengths.

learning stories – these are a form of observation that tells a story about what an educator sees, hears, knows and interprets about a child and their learning. They may include contributions from the child, the child's family and other stakeholders.

LDC – long day care is a centre-based education and care setting provided by professional staff where babies, toddlers and children attend, up to school-starting age.

nature-deficit disorder – is the idea that human beings, especially children, are spending less time outdoors, and not enough time in nature.

NQF – the National Quality Framework provides a national approach to regulation, assessment and quality improvement for ECEC and school-age care services across Australia.

NQS – the National Quality Standard sets a high national benchmark for ECEC and school-age care services in Australia. The NQS includes seven Quality Areas that are important outcomes for all children and their families.

pedagogical documentation – is dialogue about teaching and learning that takes place in ECEC. Documentation in this sense is embedded in the learning process of educators and children as it not only documents the learning but becomes a part of the learning.

preschool – is defined as the two years before a child begins formal schooling.

QIP – a quality improvement plan helps settings self-assess their performance in delivering quality education and care, and to plan future improvements. Every setting must ensure a QIP is in place.

Reggio Emilia approach – an approach to early childhood education that stems from northern Italy and views young children as individuals who are capable and curious about their world and have a powerful potential to learn from all that surrounds them.

schoolification – can drive ECEC settings to adopt practices that are usually more related to primary school; such as higher staff–pupil ratios, longer hours away from home, more teacher-directed pedagogies, greater attention to academic content and less playtime.

SEL – social and emotional learning.

SES – socio-economic status is the social standing or class of an individual or group. It is often measured as a combination of education, income and occupation.

SNAICC – the Secretariat of National Aboriginal and Islander Child Care is the national peak body representing the interests of Aboriginal and Torres Strait Islander children and families.

SOLD – Supporting Oral Language Development; a series of professional learning sessions for educators, related to fostering young children's oral language.

STEM – stands for science, technology, engineering and mathematics, and is an interdisciplinary approach for teaching and learning.

summative assessment – refers to the assessment of children where the focus is on the outcome of an activity. This contrasts with formative assessment, which summarises the children's development at a particular time.

UNICEF – the United Nations International Children's Emergency Fund works in over 190 countries and territories to save children's lives, to defend their rights, and to help them fulfil their potential, from early childhood through to adolescence.

universal access – ensures that a quality preschool program is available for all children in the year before full-time school.

Index

21st Century skills 186, 238
Aboriginal and Torres Strait Islander
    children 8, 46, 62–63, 99
    Closing the Gap report 8
    cultural capital 289
    culture 46, 149
    Elders 46
    families 8, 287–89
    knowledge 2, 332
    On Country Learning 46
    worldviews 317
    Yarning 46
abstract ideas 222, 225, 229, 322
abuse, *see* child abuse
access
    to ECEC programs 12–13, 18
    equity and 2, 19, 31, 276
    universal access 5, 21
accountability 6, 20, 27, 31, 297, 328
advocacy 30–33, 54, 315, 329, 330
affordance 56–59, 146, 181
agency 124–33, 237–47, 258, 271, 332
aggression 99, 110, 118
anxiety
    children's 95, 99, 109, 142
    teacher 303
arts 220–33
artistic expression 221, 335
aspirations 4, 8, 276, 292, 331
assessment
    as learning 258
    authentic 252
    for learning 251, 255
    formative 21, 255
    of learning 258
    quality 252, 253
    rating and 327, 328
    summative 258, 260
    unbiased 253
assimilation 39, 41, 42, 44, 45
attachment 98, 106, 111–13
    difficulties 106
    insecure 111
    style 98
    theory 112, 113
Australian Children's Education and Care Quality Authority (ACECQA) 33
Australian Early Development Census (AEDC) 162, 332
Australian Institute for Teaching and School Leadership (AITSL) 32, 33
Australian Institute of Family Studies 283
Australian Professional Standards for Teachers (APST) 32, 33
autonomy
    development 96
    emerging 82, 127, 132, 146
    professional 327
    sense of 224
    workforce 27

babies, *see* infants
behaviour
    anti-social 111
    disengaged 106
    management 14, 96, 114
    positive 47
    problems 110, 118
    prosocial 110, 113, 118
    sedentary 76, 78, 84, 85
    social 110, 116
behavioural
    challenges 111–19
    indicators 102, 103, 107
    outcomes 12
    professional 101
biodiversity 65, 70–73, 148
biophilic design 63–74
Bourdieu, P. 284, 285, 286
brain
    architecture 98, 181
    damage 96
    development 93, 104, 286, 287
    maturation 104
    structures 116
Bronfenbrenner, U. 15, 111, 114, 271, 282, 284, 285
bush kindy 46

Canning River Kids project 46
capability
    children's 187, 205
    leadership and 6, 304
change fatigue 325
child abuse 93–107
    emotional 94, 97–98, 104
    mental 94
    physical 94, 96
    protection 93–102
    psychological 98
    safety 93–106
    sexual 94–104
    verbal 97
Child-initiated Pretend Play Assessment (ChIPPA) 163–64
child neglect
    abuse and 93–104
    medical 98
    protection 93–102
    safety 93–106
    supervisory 98
    victims of 94
children's rights 8, 30, 93–106, 127–31, 223, 254, 270, 275, 330–32

Index

child safe
- frameworks 102
- legislation 99
- organisations 100
- principles 93, 101
- Standards 100–02

chronosystem 272, 284

Classroom Assessment Scoring System (CLASS) 14, 17–19, 21

cognition 22, 140, 227

cognitive
- capacity 106
- development 12–17, 72, 78, 114, 199, 201, 331–32
- functioning 64, 99, 111
- skills 14, 110–11, 162–63

collaborative learners 235

common world pedagogies 314

Common World Research Collective 314, 315

community
- building 282–95
- local 15, 16, 293, 299, 302
- partnerships 284, 287

compassion 104, 299

Conceptual PlayLab 189

Conceptual PlayWorld 190

Council of Australian Governments (COAG) 3, 6, 99

creative
- practice 239
- thinking 140, 157

creativity
- developing creativity 139
- fantasy 222
- imagination and 144, 145, 149, 186, 222
- knowledge and 139
- learning and 145, 153
- social contexts and 145

critical
- reflection 32, 35, 45, 101, 133, 204, 251, 261–64, 292, 335
- thinking 186, 187, 223

cultural
- capital 284–89
- competency 8
- contexts 144, 260, 270–72
- diversity 149, 331

Curious Young Minds STEM Literacy Program 189, 191

curriculum
- Australian National 4, 186, 241
- decisions 283
- diverse expectations 34
- emergent curriculum 188, 192
- preschool 117

decision-making
- children 128, 133, 140, 152, 251
- family 15, 285
- opportunities 129
- participative 28

- professional 299
- responsible 115, 118
- shared 28, 129, 64, 133

Deleuze, G. 319, 320, 322, 326

democratic professionalism 27, 28

Department of Education, Employment and Workplace Relations (DEEWR) 4

depression 95, 99, 111, 142

design principles 63–74

development
- artistic/creative 132, 145, 231
- brain 93, 104, 286, 287
- cognitive 12–17, 72, 78, 120, 199, 201, 331, 332
- concept development 14
- early childhood 23, 63
- emotional 102–23, 140, 144, 158
- healthy 93, 96, 142
- holistic 333
- language 156–69, 175, 178, 199, 244
- literacy 170–84
- mathematical 204–19
- motor 78, 84, 179
- outcomes 3, 15, 19, 285, 301
- physical 77
- social 144, 145, 160, 280
- STEM 202
- trajectories 11
- workforce 2, 27

Dewey, J. 221, 229, 260, 261

digital
- age 234
- disconnect 237
- play 240
- technologies 181, 186, 192, 235–38

dignity 39, 40, 41, 43–45, 47

disability 18, 40, 42, 94

disadvantage/d
- areas of 5
- background 11, 19
- communities 12
- cycle of 5
- socio-economic 111, 163

disclosure
- accidental 104
- clear 104
- purposeful 103

dispositions, learning 151–54, 189, 205–06, 223, 258, 262, 334

dissociation 105

divergent thinking 140

diversity
- breadth of 41
- children 43, 298
- cultural 149, 331
- family 282, 291
- forms of 41
- human 39, 40, 43, 45
- linguistic 331
- place of 30

documentation
    analysing 260
    anecdotal records 255
    assessment 251–62
    diary records 255
    digital documentation 258, 261, 291
    learning stories 255, 258
    narrative and running records 255–58
    observation 252
    pedagogical 239–46, 252–63, 327
    photographic records 255–56
    reflective practice 261
    summative records 260
dominant and non-dominant discourses 312–17, 323
duty of care 94–102
dysconsciousness 45

E4Kids study 11–25
Early Childhood Australia (ECA) 97, 101, 297, 304
Early Childhood Development Census (ECDC) 162, 332
early intervention 99, 118–19
Early Learning STEM Australia (ELSA) 189
Early Years Learning Framework (EYLF) 2, 38, 110, 125, 138, 171, 190, 206, 222, 235, 25, 269, 283, 297, 333
ecological framework *see* social ecological framework
economic discourse 329, 330
Educational Leader 300–06
Effective Provision of Pre-School Education (EPPE) study 290
emotional
    abuse 94, 97
    challenges 115, 167
    competence 110, 115, 117, 119
    outbursts 106
    regulation 104, 110
    responsiveness 3
    skills 13, 21–22, 115–20, 154, 329
engineering 186–87, 197, 198
environment, physical 13, 138–43, 146–48, 182, 293
environmental print 178
Epstein's model 284–85
equity
    access and 2, 5, 31, 276
    E4Kids Study 19–20
    justice and 299
    social equity 286
ethics
    Code of Ethics 97, 101, 297
    early childhood educator practice and 31
    ethics of care 311, 317
    leadership 299
evidence-informed 6
exclusion, macro and micro 40, 41
exosystem 272, 284
family
    circumstances 94
    community and 5, 33, 282–92
    educator relationships 287, 288
    experiencing vulnerability 5, 162–63
    literacy practices 172
    rights 30, 254
    school partnerships 289
    violence 98, 99, 111
    wellbeing 330
family day care 4, 274, 297, 329
figured worlds 319, 320
Foucault, M. 320

gender 13, 29–30, 60, 94, 100, 287

Heckman Curve 12
holistic
    approach 60
    development 333
    learning 188, 251, 260, 264, 333
    play 140
home learning environment (HLE) 15, 16, 290
hypervigilance 105

identity
    changes 271, 274
    children's 9, 46, 67, 110, 253, 261
    educator 30, 304
    entrepreneurial 31
    home 272
    professional 33, 303, 305, 325
    school 271, 272
imagination, *see* creativity
inclusion 39–47
inclusive
    attitudes 43
    communities 38–49
    education 38–49
    play 154
Indigenous, *see also* Aboriginal and Torres Strait Islander
infants/babies
    nutrition 78–81, 86
    physical activity 77–78
inquiry-based learning 188–90, 194–95
integration 40–42
intentional
    leadership 299
    practices 115–16, 119, 125, 129
    teaching 146, 151, 182, 191, 230–32, 240, 262–64, 299
intervention
    early 99, 118–19
    effective 20
    mathematics 206
    models 21
    oral language 161
    Response to Intervention Framework 115
    SEL (social and emotional learning) 117–19
Inventing Remida Portland Project 318

kinaesthetic
    aural 224–26, 235, 238

Index

development 231
learning 227
physical 224–26
representations 235
visual 224–26

language
body 105, 106, 164
delays 106
descriptive 161, 189
expressive 158–66
oral 15, 157–68, 178, 212
printed 175
receptive 15, 158, 163
unbiased 253
verbal and non-verbal 157–58, 229
written 172, 175, 178
leadership 296–307
capacity 305
community 302
distributed 299
ethical 299
formal 300–01
individual 302–04
intentional 299
pedagogical 300
styles 28, 299, 301, 307
learning
deep 46, 235–47, 255
practice guide 21, 22, 128
stories 255, 258
learning environment
digital 189
home 15, 16, 290
physical 115, 146–48
resources and 148–50
Let's Count Program 189–90
Lifting our Game report 5–6
literacy
development 171–82
early reading 160–61, 175
early writing 175–81
Little Scientists Program 189, 190
loose parts 54, 58–61, 68, 149

macrosystem 272, 284
Malaguzzi, L. 141, 153, 224, 229
maternalism 29
mathematics
concepts 186, 217, 218
data 207, 214–16
measurement 186, 198, 207–14
number and counting 207–12
pattern and structure 207–11
problem-solving 198, 221
representation 214, 215
spatial sense 186, 197, 207–09
STEM and 185–87, 197, 198
meaning-making 140, 144, 145, 193, 220–31, 235–44, 311–23
mental health 7, 83, 96, 99, 111–18, 142, 153, 284

mentoring 300, 305–07
mesosystem 271, 284, 285
microsystem 271, 284
modalities 14, 226–46
more-than-human 311–19
morphology 159
motor development 58, 77–84, 176–79, 333
multiliteracies 244, 245
multimodal
the arts and 225–29
learning 235–47
meaning-making 140, 145
representations 228, 235, 241–47
multi-tiered approach to social and emotional learning 115
musical play 226–28
My Time, Our Place: Framework for School Age Care in Australia 269

National Early Childhood Development Strategy 3, 11
National Partnership Agreement 11
National Principles for Child Safe Organisations 100–01
National Quality Framework (NQF) 3, 88, 139, 301, 326
National Quality Standard (NQS) 2, 11, 31, 53, 77, 125, 148, 240, 251, 266, 269, 296, 328
nature-deficit-disorder 142
needs
basic 97
diverse 100, 287
emotional 93
physical 83, 93
neglect, *see* child neglect
neuroscience 140, 328
new learning 139, 177, 189, 234–47
new learning ecologies 235–39
notification process 94–103
numeracy 22, 162, 241, 333
nutrition
baby-led weaning 82
bottle feeding 80
breastfeeding 78–82
formula 78, 79–80
fussy eating 82, 87, 88
healthy eating 78–82, 85–89
infant feeding guidelines 80–81
meal planning 85–86, 88
responsive feeding 78–79, 86
solid foods 78–82

observation, *see* documentation
observation, informal 252
oral language
components 157–60
low levels 162–63
skills 157, 160–65
Organisation for Economic Co-operation and Development (OECD) 5, 33, 34, 287, 312
Out and About project 314–22

Index

outdoor play
    biophilic design, *see* biophilic design principles
    environments 54, 63, 73
    risky play 83, 89, 143
    space affordances 58
    spaces 53–74, 153
    trees 58, 65–67, 72–73

play
    active 82, 88, 143
    arts-based 226
    child-led 120
    creative 142, 144
    dramatic/dance 222–28
    drawing 222–30
    free 83, 141, 239
    high-energy 82, 83
    imaginative 53–72, 150, 190
    learning and 139–53, 186, 189, 222–32
    musical 226–28
    new technologies 237
    playfulness 68, 74, 140–53
    pretend 66, 150, 164, 217
    program(s), play-based 171–74, 218, 240, 333
    risky 83, 89, 143
    rough and tumble 83, 143
    sociodramatic 60, 61, 68
    unstructured 83, 142–53
policy reform 326–33
problem-solving
    the arts and 221–31
    maths and 205
    play and 146–53
    STEM and 186–98
    social and emotional learning and 116–17
professional
    development 26, 103, 130, 190, 275–77, 305–06
    identity 29–33, 303 05, 330
    networks 277, 304
    practice 8, 29–35, 95, 102, 279, 297, 325, 327
professionalisation 6, 27, 326
professionalism 6, 26–30
prosocial 110–19
protective factors 111
psychological
    harm 98, 153
    neglect 98

qualifications
    early childhood teacher 302
    high-quality interactions and 6, 14, 18, 26
    National Quality Framework and 327
    types of 34, 304
quality
    contested 4
    education and care 2–6
    NQS areas 9
    practice 12, 252, 261, 300, 327, 328
    provision 3, 235, 297, 307
    relationships 98, 113–18, 286
    services 3, 6, 8, 28, 276, 296
Quality Improvement Plan (QIP) 9, 307

readiness, school 274–75, 279
reading comprehension 160, 161
records, *see* documentation
Reggio Emilia Approach 141, 229, 245, 263, 315, 318
relationships
    family and community 282–93
    leadership and 299, 305–06
    positive 98, 110, 154, 278, 283
reporting
    mandatory 99–107
    obligations 102–03, 107
    pathways 100, 103
representations, *see* multimodal
research
    creation 321
    disrupting 311
    rethinking 310–24
resilience
    to change (professional) 325–26
    children's 116, 127, 143, 152–53
Response-to-Intervention (RTI) 115
rights, *see* children's rights
risk
    aversion 70
    benefit analysis 70
    factors (child abuse and neglect) 99–111
    management 56, 59, 83, 143
risky play, *see* play
Rousseau, J. 222
running record, *see* documentation

scaffold (learning) 114, 164, 192, 202, 223, 230, 244, 262
school-age care 269–79
'schoolification' 333
science
    concepts 186, 193
    exploration 72, 227
    Little Scientists program 189, 190
Science, Technology, Engineering and Mathematics (STEM)
    Curious Young Minds STEM Literacy program 189, 191
    Habits of Mind program 189, 190
    learning 185–202
    literacy 189–92
    phenomena 197, 198
screen time 78, 84, 105, 108, 237–38
Secretariat of National Aboriginal and Islander Child Care (SNAICC) 8
sedentary behaviour 76, 78, 84–85
self-esteem 95–201
self-regulation 7, 59, 87, 110–17
semantics 158–65

Index

semiotic
    literacy development and 172
    meaning-making 224
sensory
    experience 72, 140, 147
    explorations 221
    memories 65
    variability 70–74
sexual abuse, *see* child abuse
Shonkoff, J. 7, 93, 98, 104, 111
sleep disturbance 106
social
    capital 240, 284–90, 333
    competence 110, 119, 144, 162
    contexts 116, 144–46, 157–60, 270–77, 319–37
    ecology 236, 284
    functioning 98, 104
    justice 5, 31, 275, 291, 314, 330
    media 93, 254, 291
    process 15
    skills 13, 21–22, 68, 84, 114–19, 161–63, 329, 333
    support 94, 112
    social-cognitive learning 116
social and emotional learning (SEL) 110–20
Social Ecological Framework/Model 111, 112, 284
socio-economic
    disadvantage 111, 162, 163
    factors 16, 20
    position 288
    status (SES) 13, 163, 287
spatial sense 186, 207, 209
state of flow 141, 152
STEM, *see* Science, Engineering, Mathematics and Technology
strengths-based approach 273, 290–92
Studying *with* Worms project 321
substance abuse 94, 99, 111
Supporting Oral Language Development (SOLD) 156–69
survival response 104
symbolic domains 224
syntax 158–65

Teaching Through Interactions (TTI) Framework 114
technology 32, 185–98, 236–47, 318
toddlers
    assessment 251, 253
    early literacy 173–78
    nutrition 82–88
    outdoor play 56, 83
    physical activity 82–85
    sedentary behaviours 84, 85
transitions
    effective 269–78
    horizontal transitions 272
    programs 270–77
    to school 188, 269–77
    school-aged care and 269–79
    vertical transitions 272
Transition to School: Position Statement 275
transmediate 228
trauma-informed practice 103–06
trees, *see* outdoor play

United Nations Convention on the Rights of the Child (UNCRC) 93–101, 223, 254
United Nations Educational and Scientific and Cultural Organisation (UNESCO) 312
universal access 5, 21

verbal ability 14–20
violence, *see* child abuse
vocalisms 225, 229
Vygotsky, L. 139–45, 172, 230, 262

ways of knowing
    children's 254
    hundred 229
    Indigenous 316, 317
    kinaesthetic 224
    non-dominant 316–23
wellbeing
    biophilic design and 63
    connection to place and 54
    health and 78–84
    play and 142
    physical 98
    safety and 100
    social and emotional 109–19, 143, 153, 229, 262
workforce
    autonomy 27
    conditions 6
    development 2, 27
    diversity 6, 30, 34
    gender 29–30

zone of proximal development 230, 262, 303

www.ingramcontent.com/pod-product-compliance
Lightning Source LLC
Chambersburg PA
CBHW061123070526
44584CB00033B/4205